MACROECONOMICS
1978

READINGS ON
CONTEMPORARY
ISSUES

EDITED BY
PETER D. McCLELLAND

CORNELL UNIVERSITY PRESS ITHACA AND LONDON

First published 1978 by Cornell University Press.
Published in the United Kingdom by Cornell University Press Ltd.,
2-4 Brook Street, London W1Y 1AA.

International Standard Book Number 0-8014-9867-8
Library of Congress Catalog Card Number 77-6193
Printed in the United States of America

FOREWORD

To the student

When you signed up for a course entitled Macroeconomics you probably had two expectations. The first was that you were about to study many of those problems featured in the national news media. Inflation, unemployment, prospective energy shortages, the inadequacies of our present welfare system—these are but a few of the macroeconomic issues encountered almost daily as you read the newspaper or watch the evening news on television. Probably your second expectation, fostered by the same sources, was that your studies would help you to understand why economists have sharply differing opinions on how these problems should be attacked. If your course reading were confined to a textbook—any textbook—you would be in for a disappointment. These books invariably include little about contemporary problems, and even less about the national debate on how to solve them. The reasons are rather simple. Each author has his own opinion on the ideal solutions, and his text, not surprisingly, tends to emphasize that point of view. As for contemporary issues, no textbook that appears today (never mind last year) can possibly deal with them, because the lag between finished manuscript and appearance in the bookstore is usually twelve to eighteen months, sometimes longer.

This reader's main objective is to remedy these two defects. Assembled in late May of 1978, it attempts to give empirical flesh to those theoretical skeletons that you will be learning about in lectures and from the textbook. It also emphasizes, wherever possible, different points of view on how to solve some of our most pressing macroeconomic problems. It cannot promise you a definitive resolution of those problems. But it should give you a sense of why they matter, and why macroeconomic theory is relevant in attempting to solve them. The ultimate hope is that you will emerge from this reader and your course with a sense of how crucial these issues are to the future well-being of our nation and its citizens.

To the instructor

Teaching macroeconomics to undergraduates is a demanding assignment. The lecturer who strives to integrate textbook theory with national problems is constantly bedeviled by the speed with which the leading contemporary issues change—from inflation to unemployment to energy and back to inflation again, to mention but one of several recent sequences. Also in a constant state of flux are the mechanisms that dominate current analysis of these problems. The unabashed Keynesian approach tempered by a belief in the Philips Curve has given way to such disparate topics as Okun's Law, rational expectations, and the merits of monetary targets. In the popular press, there is no shortage of commentary on both problems and associated causal mechanisms. The difficulty is that several dozen articles from different sources cannot be incorporated easily (or at all) into the reading list of a course in which enrollment may run to hundreds. At least not without creating pandemonium in the library. This book attempts to solve this impasse. Readings were culled from a range of material in May, assembled in early June, and with the aid of photo offset made available in bound form by mid-August. The result is viewed by both the editor and Cornell University Press as merely a first step. Our intention is to modify this volume annually, in terms of both topics covered and articles included. We hope that you will help us with that modification. If you have any suggestions, I would appreciate hearing from you (Economics Department, Cornell University, Ithaca, N.Y. 14853). Such ongoing interaction with those who study and teach the subject will be a crucial ingredient if the annual readers are to satisfy the instructor while achieving that most important of objectives: fostering the student's interest in, and understanding of, contemporary American macroeconomic issues.

Peter D. McClelland

Ithaca, New York

3

CONTENTS ————————————————————————————————

Foreword   **3**

I INFLATION AND UNEMPLOYMENT

1. A Surge in Prices, and More to Come. (U.S. News & World Report, March 13, 1978.) Inflation is returning to center stage as a macroeconomic problem. U.S. News & World Report lists some of the causes and notes some of the likely effects on individual prices by 1983 if the inflation rates of the past do not slow down in the future.   **10**

2. Edward Meadows, Our Flawed Inflation Indexes. (Fortune, April 24, 1978.) How is the rate of inflation measured, and what are the major defects of these measures as indicators of changes in the aggregate price level? Edward Meadows reviews the three main inflation indexes: the Consumer Price Index, the Wholesale Price Index, and the GNP deflator.   **12**

3. Sharon P. Smith, An Examination of Employment and Unemployment Rates. (Federal Reserve Bank of New York Quarterly Review, Autumn, 1977.) How are employment and unemployment rates calculated, and why is one measure more reliable than the other? An economist with the Federal Reserve Bank of New York examines these two key measures of economic activity and suggests some of the reasons why measured unemployment has been so high in recent years.   **17**

4. The Explosive Issue of Youth Unemployment. (Business Week, October 10, 1977.) Even those economists who agree on the causes of high unemployment frequently disagree about the appropriate policies to reduce it. In back of those disagreements are often contrasting views on how serious the problem really is.   **22**

5. David M. Lilly, The Threat of Inflation. (Federal Reserve Bank of Dallas Review, December, 1977.) A member of the Board of Governors of the Federal Reserve System outlines the dangers of continued inflation and suggests some of the ways that it can be brought under control.   **24**

6. Living with Inflation: Consider the Alternative. (Dollars & Sense, May—June, 1978.) In contrast to the previous article, Dollars & Sense argues that living with inflation may be preferable to the consequences of policies designed to slow inflation.   **28**

7. The Tough Talk Won't Be about Wages This Time. (U.S. News & World Report, December 26, 1977/January 2, 1978.) What are the forces for "cost-push inflation" that are likely to originate as a result of contracts negotiated by major labor organizations in 1978? U.S. News & World Report outlines the principal contracts to be negotiated and the probable bones of contention.   **31**

8. Now It's Government Itself Pushing Prices Higher and Higher. (U.S. News & World Report, December 19, 1977.) Traditional macroeconomic theory—either Keynesian or monetarist—emphasizes monetary and fiscal policy as the main policy tools whereby the government may contribute to inflationary pressures. This article notes some of the other kinds of federal activity that can also create upward pressures on prices.   **33**

II MONETARY AND FISCAL POLICY

9. How the Money Supply Has Behaved under Carter and His Predecessors. (Business Week, November 21, 1977.) Expansion of the money supply in nominal and real terms is charted from Harry Truman to Jimmy Carter.   **35**

10. In a Dozen Years, One Balanced Budget. (U.S. News & World Report, January 30, 1978.) A chart of the government budget for the past twelve years emphasizes the dominance of deficit financing in recent years.   **35**

11. Federal Debt: Fast Approaching a Trillion. (U.S. News & World Report, January 30, 1978.) Repeated large deficits have resulted in a rapid increase in the federal debt. U.S. News & World Report graphs the results.   **36**

12. Carter's Anti-Inflation Pitch. (Wall Street Journal, April 12, 1978.) An outline of the President's new anti-inflation program.   **37**

13. Robert W. Hartman, The Budget and the Economy. (Condensed from Chapter 2 of The Brookings Institution, *Setting National Priorities: The 1979 Budget.*) An economist with The Brookings Institution presents a detailed review of budget proposals made by President Carter in January of 1978.   **38**

14. Milton Friedman, Tax Shenanigans. (Newsweek, December 19, 1977.) A right-of-center critique of Carter's budget proposals.   **50**

15. What's in The Budget, and Who Pays the Bill? (Dollars & Sense, March, 1978.) A left-of-center critique of Carter's proposed budget.   51

16. Peter D. McClelland, A Layman's Guide to the Keynesian-Monetarist Dispute. Articles in the first section illustrate one of the dilemmas of current macroeconomics. Economists have widely different views on how inflation and unemployment should be attacked, and those differences show no signs of being resolved. There are two main reasons for this disagreement. One stems from a difference in values. Some economists, for example, emphasize equity considerations; others, the preservation of certain freedoms. The second major reason for disagreement is differing views on how the economy works. This article attempts to summarize the main arguments in the theoretical dispute between the two dominant schools of thought in contemporary macroeconomics.   54

17. John Kenneth Galbraith, The Trouble with Economists. (The New Republic, January 14, 1978.) A leading critic of the economics profession traces the rise to dominance of Keynesian thought and suggests why a Keynesian approach to inflation and unemployment is no longer satisfactory.   57

18. Milton Friedman, Inflationary Recession. (Newsweek, April 24, 1978.) Does a rapid increase in the money supply cause inflation, and do inflationary pressures subsequently cause recession? A leading monetarist argues that for both questions the answer is yes.   64

19. Heading 'Em Off at the GNP Gap. (Citibank Monthly Economic Letter, March, 1978.) From a monetarist's perspective, Citibank reviews and criticizes the 1978 Economic Report of the President.   65

20. Walter W. Heller, The Right Tax Cut Mix. (Wall Street Journal, May 1, 1978.) A former Chairman of the Council of Economic Advisors summarizes the case for a tax cut.   70

21. Allan T. Demaree, Why the Tax Cut Looks So Dangerous. (Fortune, May 22, 1978.) The case against the tax cut is outlined by Demaree.   71

22. Arthur M. Okun, The Great Stagflation Swamp. (The Brookings Bulletin, Fall, 1977.) Out of a growing sense of the limited capacity of fiscal and monetary policy alone to curb inflation have come a number of proposals for regulating wages and prices. A leading exponent of this approach outlines his proposal for a tax-based incomes policy.   73

23. Henry C. Wallich, Testimony to the Joint Economic Committee. (Federal Reserve Bulletin, February, 1978.) Another exponent of a tax-based incomes policy explains how his proposal would work and why it should be adopted by the government.   80

24. Nancy Ammon Jianakoplos, A Tax-Based Incomes Policy (TIP): What's It All About? (Federal Reserve Bank of St. Louis Review, February, 1978.) A tax-based incomes policy is based upon a set of premises acceptable to most Keynesians. They are not acceptable to most monetarists. This article clarifies the key premises and explains why monetarists oppose this approach to combating inflation.   84

25. Dennis Roth, Full Employment and Balanced Growth Act of 1978. (Congressional Research Service, March 31, 1978.) One focus of present policy debates is the Humphrey-Hawkins Bill. This article provides a concise summary of its history, including recent amendments.   89

26. Charles C. Killingsworth, Will Full Employment Cause Inflation? (Social Policy, January/February, 1977.) A vigorous exponent of the Humphrey-Hawkins Bill argues the case for even stronger measures than those incorporated into the 1978 version of this Act.   91

27. Yale Brozen, What Humphrey-Hawkins Won't Do. (National Review, April 28, 1978.) An opponent of the 1978 Humphrey-Hawkins Bill argues that its main provisions are misguided or dangerous—or both.   97

28. Christopher Jencks, The Minimum Wage Controversy. (Working Papers, March–April, 1978.) Tax-based incomes policies, the Humphrey-Hawkins approach to full employment, and a minimum wage bill: these are at the storm center of popular debate over macroeconomic policy. The present article examines the employment and welfare implications of a minimum wage of $2.65 an hour.   99

29. Richard G. Davis, Monetary Objectives and Monetary Policy. (Federal Reserve Bank of New York Quarterly Review, Spring, 1977.) In 1975 the Federal Reserve changed its strategy in implementing monetary policy to one of emphasizing growth ranges for several measures of the money supply. A senior economic adviser of the Federal Reserve Bank of New York describes why the change was made and some of the problems encountered in the attempt to implement this new approach to monetary policy.   102

30. Carl M. Gambs, Money—A Changing Concept in a Changing World. (Federal Reserve Bank of Kansas City Monthly Review, January, 1977.) Recent institutional changes in credit markets have blurred what is meant by "money" and complicated the task of monetary authorities. Gambs describes the main institutional changes and how they have made progressively more difficult a descriptive task that, on the face of it, seems simple enough: What should be counted as part of the money supply?   108

31. Anne Marie Laporte, Behavior of the Income Velocity of Money. (Federal Reserve Bank of Chicago, Economic Perspectives, September/October, 1977.) The institutional changes described in Gambs's article have had a marked effect on the velocity of money. Laporte charts the recent upward trend in velocity and explains how this movement is caused by changes in the practices of financial institutions.   118

III ENERGY AND GROWTH

32. Jimmy Carter, The President's Address on Energy Problems. (Vital Speeches of the Day, December 1, 1977.) Since taking office, President Carter has urged the Congress to adopt his energy program. In a speech to the nation, he outlines what that program is and why he views its adoption as so important for the national welfare.   **121**

33. Jai-Hoon Yang, The Nature and Origins of the U.S. Energy Crisis. (Federal Reserve Bank of St. Louis Review, July, 1977.) Two contrasting views of the energy crisis are spelled out by an economist. He explains why he thinks that the "lump-of-energy" view is wrong and why the economist's market-oriented view is right.   **124**

34. Steven Rattner, Energy: Where Did the Crisis Go? (New York Times, April 16, 1978.) The previous two articles assume that an energy crisis exists. Rattner asks whether it has disappeared, and if so, why. Much of the explanation is again market-oriented, focusing on the impact of higher prices on supply and demand.   **135**

35. H. M. Douty, The Slowdown in Real Wages: A Postwar Perspective. (Monthly Labor Review, August, 1977.) The trend in real wages is affected by the rate of inflation and the growth of real productivity. A former Assistant Commissioner for Wages and Industrial Relations with the Bureau of Labor Statistics examines the historical trends in both variables, the linkages between the two, and likely future developments.   **137**

36. How Tax Policy Dampens Economic Growth. (Business Week, April 24, 1978.) One basic determinant of economic growth is capital formation, which in turn is affected by tax policies. Business Week outlines some of the prevailing theories about how these economic variables interact, and some of the policy implications of those interactions.   **143**

37. Long Swings II—Kuznets Explains History. (Citibank Monthly Economic Letter, February, 1978.) Is the American economy subject to "supercycles," several decades in duration? The evidence suggests that in the past it was, with much of the explanation focusing on the impact of changing population growth on population-sensitive activities.   **145**

38. Americans Change: How Drastic Shifts in Demographics Affect the Economy. (Business Week, February 20, 1978.) The previous article outlined some of the linkages in the past between population growth and economic activity. The structure of the American population is presently undergoing some radical changes that will have both economic and social effects in the decades ahead. Business Week outlines these structural shifts and speculates about their likely impact between now and the year 2000.   **150**

39. Daniel Bell, Mediating Growth Tensions. (Society, January/February, 1978.) A leading sociologist attempts to clarify why economic growth is a popular issue and some of the more common confusions about the merits and demerits of growth.   **155**

IV POVERTY, WELFARE, AND INCOME DISTRIBUTION

40. Martin Rein and Lee Rainwater, How Large Is the Welfare Class? (Challenge, September/October, 1977.) Data from a ten-year survey reveal the structure of the welfare class and suggest which kinds of welfare reforms are likely to be successful.   **160**

41. Food Stamps: Who Gets Them and What Do They Accomplish? (Focus: Institute for Research on Poverty Newsletter, Winter, 1977–1978.) Food stamps constitute America's only universal minimum income program. This article examines the origins of the program, its present successes and failures, and why replacing it with a cash grant system encounters widespread opposition.   **164**

42. Taming a 148-Billion-Dollar Federal Giant: Will Anything Work? (U.S. News & World Report, May 16, 1977.) At the heart of the President's welfare proposals are objectives that would require reorganization of a massive federal bureaucracy. U.S. News & World Report sketches the history of HEW, outlines its present size and programs, and speculates about the chances for major reform.   **168**

43. One More Plan to End Fraud in Welfare: Interview with Joseph A. Califano, Jr. (U.S. News & World Report, January 9, 1978.) The Secretary of Health, Education and Welfare outlines the administration's approach to a range of welfare problems.   **173**

44. Joseph A. Califano, Jr., National Health Care Planning. (Vital Speeches of the Day, December 1, 1977.) The Administration's approach to national health care is outlined by the Secretary of Health, Education and Welfare.   **177**

45. Leonard Robins, Retreat from National Health. (The Nation, February 11, 1978.) Has the President changed his stance on the need for a strong national health insurance program? The evidence suggests that perhaps he has.   **180**

46. Saul Hoffman, Black/White Income Differences, 1967–1974. (Economic Outlook USA, Spring, 1977.) What are the causes of black/white income differences, and have these differences changed in recent years? Hoffman surveys the evidence and suggests that the answer is far from uniform across all age categories.   **183**

47. Young Blacks out of Work: Time Bomb for U.S. (U.S. News & World Report, December 5, 1977.) One of the most pressing social problems of the nation has, to date, been little affected by government policies. This article outlines the major policies and indicates why they have had so little success.   **185**

48. James N. Morgan, Myth, Reality, Equity and the Social Security System. (Economic Outlook USA, Autumn, 1977.) Popular misconceptions concerning the structure and functioning of the social security system are outlined by Morgan, including why the "trust fund" concept is false.   **189**

49. Pro and Con: A Tax Credit for College Tuition? (U.S. News & World Report, April 3, 1978.) Two members of Congress reach opposite conclusions about the need for this particular revision in the tax laws.   **192**

V AGRICULTURE AND FEDERAL FARM POLICIES

50. What Is Parity? (Dollars & Sense, February, 1978.) Much of the present farm unrest focuses on a single variable: parity. This article outlines the origins of the measure, how it is calculated, and why it is central to the current dispute over agricultural policy.   **194**

51. Catherine Lerza, Farmers on the March. (The Progressive, June, 1978.) Lerza discusses present farm problems, and the government response to them, from the perspective of the farmer.   **195**

52. Farmers Gain Little, Consumers Lose More. (Citibank Monthly Economic Letter, May, 1978.) Citibank offers an economist's appraisal of the farm problem, emphasizing the costs to consumers of higher prices and more taxes.   **199**

53. Marvin Duncan and C. Edward Harshbarger, A Primer on Agricultural Policy. (Federal Reserve Bank of Kansas City Monthly Review, September–October, 1977.) All of the previous articles assume that the federal government will continue to intervene in the market for agricultural produce. The present article outlines the major forms of intervention in the past.   **202**

VI INTERNATIONAL

54. Economic Penalties of Propping the Dollar. (Business Week, April 3, 1978.) An M.I.T. economist outlines the arguments for letting the U.S. dollar fluctuate freely on foreign exchange markets.   **210**

55. Henry C. Wallich, Reflections on the U.S. Balance of Payments. (Challenge, March/April, 1978.) A member of the Board of Governors of the Federal Reserve System suggests why government intervention in foreign exchange markets may be desirable. He also diagnoses the present balance of payments problems.   **211**

56. Is the Dollar Skidding on an Oil Slick? (Citibank Monthly Economic Letter, December, 1977.) The present article emphasizes what the previous article ignored: the monetarist explanation for current balance of payments difficulties.   **215**

57. Sidney Lens, The Sinking Dollar and the Gathering Storm. (The Progressive, May, 1978.) Lens offers a left-of-center perspective on a range of international trade problems, including the dollar's decline and the rise of LDC indebtedness.   **219**

58. Hold That Line. (Newsweek, January 2, 1978.) The linkages between higher oil prices and American balance of payments problems have been explored in previous articles. The present article outlines the political infighting and conditions of supply and demand which resulted—for the moment—in no further increase in OPEC prices.   **222**

MACROECONOMICS

1

A Surge in Prices, and More to Come

Latest burst of inflation is only the start. What economists see ahead now—

Inflation, after easing a bit in the second half of 1977, is flaring up again and causing new worry over the health of the economy.

In January, consumer prices rose at an annual rate of 10 percent. Some economists predict similar increases through March.

Behind the sudden surge are higher prices for meats and fresh produce, climbing interest rates, and added labor costs, a result of both the latest boost in the minimum wage and heavier Social Security taxes.

Evidence of soaring prices shows up almost everywhere.

The prices farmers get are on the rise after a long, steep decline. The Department of Agriculture estimated this increase at 3 percent for February alone. Cattle in feeder lots in Oklahoma City command more than $51 per 100 pounds, up from $40.75 a year ago.

A new survey by the National Federation of Independent Business, which includes more than a half million firms, found that this year companies expect the largest price increases since 1974, when inflation hit 14 percent. Almost half of the firms that responded to the survey plan to boost prices during the first quarter.

"Little alternative." Those results don't surprise Purdue University economist William C. Dunkelberg, who notes that small firms are particularly hard hit by the 15 percent rise in the minimum wage that took effect January 1. "These firms have little alternative but to pass the increase on to consumers," he says.

Executives who do the buying for major corporations are bracing for price hikes of 7 to 13 percent this year in major supplies, including metals, plastics and chemicals. Most blame rising labor costs and excessive government spending.

The declining value of the dollar in world markets is making imports more costly. That's one reason Americans will soon pay more for imported cars. Chrysler Corporation, for example, plans an average boost of 1.6 percent on four models it imports from Japan—the third increase since September.

Federal efforts to shore up the dollar by tightening credit have put upward pressure on interest rates. On February 28, the maximum interest allowed on government-backed mortgages was raised from 8.5 to 8.75 percent. That means an additional $6.23 a month on a new 30-year, $35,000 mortgage.

Despite the bleak news, many economists are reluctant to predict a long period of double-digit inflation. Says James Pate, chief economist for Pennzoil: "There's been entirely too much wolf-crying, although I am very concerned about the weakening of the dollar and the size of federal deficits."

The deficit will be about 60 billion dollars in the current fiscal year and may approach 80 billion in the fiscal year beginning next October 1.

A positive view. Ben Laden, the chief economist for T. Rowe Price Associates, Inc., Baltimore-based investment counselors, contends that consumers are in relatively good shape to deal with the price surge. Real disposable income—buying power—was 5.7 percent greater in the fourth quarter than it was a year earlier, he says.

Laden is predicting that consumer prices, after rising at a seasonally adjusted rate of 8 percent in the first quarter, will slow to a 5.5 percent rate by the second half of the year. By that time, he thinks, meats, especially pork, and some other foods will become somewhat cheaper.

Federal economists still maintain that the basic inflation rate is about 6 percent a year. In the last five years, the average was 7.9 percent.

The Pictogram on these pages shows what another five years of increases on par with those of the last five will do to the prices of many items. A cartload of groceries that now costs $50 will cost $77. A man's topcoat that costs $125 now will go to $149. And the cost of sending a youngster to a private college will rise to an average of more than $7,700 a year, up from $5,200 now.

The Pictogram also shows how much of an increase in income a four-person family will need in order to avoid a loss of purchasing power and a lower standard of living. Today's $30,200 income will have to go to $48,100.

Thus, rapidly rising living costs lead to demands for higher pay which, in turn, leads to heavier labor costs and higher prices. ☐

PICTOGRAM®

If There's No Letup In Inflation—

What you would

if prices keep soaring as

Shopping Cart of Food

Now	$50
1983	$77

Up 54%

Day in a Hospital

Now	$100
1983	$179

Up 79%

To maintain your buying power after paying federal taxes—

(married couple with two children)

you earned this much in 1973—	...you would have to earn this much today—	...and this much in 1983 if prices keep climbing at the speed of the last five years—
5,000	$ 7,011	$ 11,108
10,000	$ 14,601	$ 22,530
15,000	$ 22,452	$ 35,280
20,000	$ 30,195	$ 48,056
25,000	$ 38,211	$ 61,744
50,000	$ 79,463	$124,038
75,000	$116,149	$177,304
100,000	$152,455	$230,020

Note: Figures assume that 1978 price increases average 6.5 percent, and that taxpayers take itemized deductions equal to 17 percent of income or the zero-bracket amount if it is higher.

...pay for major needs in 5 years

...they have since 1973—

New House

Now $55,000
1983 $89,600
Up 63%

New Car

Now $5,000
1983 $6,875
Up 38%

Clothes Washer

Now $200
1983 $268
Up 34%

Electric Bill

Now $100
1983 $158
Up 58%

Man's Topcoat

Now $125
1983 $149
Up 19%

Woman's Dress

Now $60
1983 $71
Up 18%

1 Year in College
(tuition, room and board in private four-year college)

Now $5,200
1983 $7,740
Up 49%

Tank of Gasoline
(20 gallons, regular grade)

Now $13.28
1983 $24.16
Up 82%

Source: U.S. Depts. of Labor, Commerce, and Health, Education and Welfare; USN&WR Economic Unit

2

The gross national product, the various inflation indexes, and the employment statistics were once tucked away in the daily financial section, where they could be pondered by businessmen and economists and ignored by the general public. Now these same numbers are the stuff of which front-page headlines and televised congressional hearings are made. A blip in an important index may create strong public pressure for remedial action—and the pressure may persist after the blip has been erased by a revision in the data. Communities stand to gain or lose millions in federal aid from a change in the local unemployment rate, and an uptick in inflation triggers multimillion-dollar adjustments in wages and pensions.

In this three-part series, FORTUNE takes a look at how the principal economic indicators are compiled, how accurate they are, why they are being endlessly revised, and how they might be made better. The subsequent articles will deal with the unemployment rate and the G.N.P.

Verena Brunner, an attractive blonde field economist for the Labor Department, begins her day at a small, scruffy supermarket in New York City's Spanish Harlem. The *ambiente* is cordial there, and staccato Spanish punctuates the air as Miss Brunner quietly goes about her business, moving past bins of melons and mangos, searching for a predetermined list of groceries that make up part of the consumer price index. Miss Brunner isn't buying; rather, she's on a "quality assurance" mission for the Bureau of Labor Statistics. She has replaced the regular data collector for the day to make sure the "regular" hasn't been doing sloppy work or "curbstoning" (the BLS term for faking it, while sitting, presumably, upon a curbstone).

As Miss Brunner travels from the ghetto grocery store far uptown to a department store on the fashionable East Side and a half dozen more establishments throughout midtown Manhattan, store clerks recognize her by the dark blue notebook she carries under her arm. Emblazoned with the legend, "Consumer Price Index," it's

Research associate: Patricia Hough

the trademark of the 500 BLS data collectors across the country who visit stores selected by computers in Washington and note the prices of various items also picked by the computers in accord with sophisticated statistical techniques.

The grand result is our chief indicator of inflation, and possibly the single most important statistic produced by the government. The consumer price index, designed to measure the price change of a fixed mar-

ket basket of goods and services over tim[e] influences consumers' confidence and i[n]vestors' plans. A change of 1 percent in t[he] index can trigger a billion dollars' worth [of] income transfers, affecting about half t[he] population. All 31 million Social Securi[ty] recipients have their payments tied to t[he] C.P.I. by a cost-of-living escalator, as do 2[.?] million retired members of the civil-se[r]vice and the military.

Changes in the index also directly affe[ct]

Our Flawed Inflation Indexes

by EDWARD MEADOWS

Illustration by James Flora

The consumer price index and other
official measures of prices aren't
as accurate as they should be, and they
have a persistent upward bias.

he food-stamp allotments for 20 million recipients, the subsidies for the 25 million children who are served food under the National School Lunch Act and the Child Nutrition Act, and benefits for millions more who partake of health and welfare programs with "poverty level" eligibility requirements tied to the C.P.I. Then, too, there is the growing number of private contracts governed by a C.P.I. escalator. The contracts cover such various matters as rent, child-support payments, and, most notably, the wages of nine million unionized workers whose cost-of-living escalators are tied to the C.P.I.

Those union workers loom large in the life of the C.P.I., for the index was born a child of labor's needs, being first used by the government to adjust the wages of shipbuilders during the World War I inflation. Every change in the C.P.I.'s methodology since then has been suspiciously watched by the unions, out of fear that the index may suppress wages by underreporting inflation. In fact, most economists agree that the problem is just the opposite: because of sundry inherent biases, the index has been exaggerating inflation for decades.

The quality problem

No one seriously denies that the biases exist; the debate is over their magnitude. Yale economist Richard Ruggles offers one of the larger estimates. He suggests that if the C.P.I. had taken improvements in the quality of products into account, prices would be seen to have fallen steadily from

1949 to 1966, whereas the C.P.I. had them rising 36 percent in that period. (Ruggles concedes that prices *have* been going up since 1966, though less than the index indicates.) The C.P.I. simply fails to adjust adequately when the higher price of, say, a color TV set reflects only the higher costs of building improved circuitry. The consumer may be paying more, but he's getting more too. And while the BLS continues to price that particular model, the consumer is free to switch to a cheaper one.

The BLS does attempt to allow for some of the changes in quality by subtracting the cost of a new feature from the increased price. But this works only when the improvement is apparent and easy to value. It ignores improvements that don't raise costs, or that actually lower them.

In many cases, of course, quality is subjective, and attempts to measure it can be contentious. A case in point, famous in BLS folklore, arose in 1971 when automobiles acquired antipollution equipment. The BLS decided that the anti-smog gear represented a price increase without a quality increase, since performance wasn't improved and maintenance became more expensive. But an interagency committee set up by the Office of Management and Budget overruled the bureau, arguing that society as a whole would benefit from cleaner air. The cost of the equipment was kept out of the C.P.I., and the decision still rankles at the BLS. Says John Layng, the assistant commissioner in charge of price statistics: "That was one of the big ones we lost."

A pervasive source of upward bias is

found in the market basket itself, which remains fixed for far too long. The brand-new index, released for the first time in February, is in fact based on a consumer-expenditure survey conducted in 1972-73, when the Census Bureau interviewed 20,000 families to see how they disposed of their money. Obviously the survey shows how Americans spent their incomes *before* the quadrupling of oil prices and before the dramatic food price increases of the mid-1970's. But economists know that, if one effect of price increases is to lower people's real income, the other effect is to cause switching from higher-priced goods to lower-priced substitutes. This "substitution effect" grows stronger over time, as alternative products evolve.

Shiskin's improvements

The commissioner of the Bureau of Labor Statistics, Julius Shiskin, admits the obsolescence of the C.P.I.'s "new" market basket. He and other economists acknowledge that the problem lies in the practice of conducting consumer-expenditure surveys only once every ten or more years. That was okay in former, more stable periods of price behavior. But in the volatile 1970's, more frequent studies are needed.

And, indeed, the bureau now has money in its budget to begin an ongoing survey. According to Commissioner Layng, the data collection will start next year, and information from the continuous expenditure survey will be incorporated into the index by the mid-1980's. (The BLS has also embarked on a continuing point-of-pur-

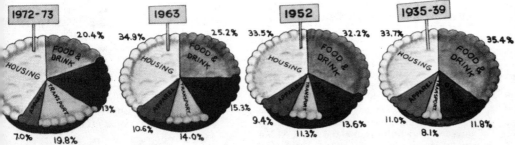

Once a month the Bureau of Labor Statistics computes the price of the "market basket" of consumer goods and services that make up the consumer price index. Family budgets have changed a lot over the years, with food accounting for a shrinking percentage of total purchases and housing and transportation for a growing share. But the market basket is revised only once every ten years or so, and the "new" C.P.I., based on a consumer-expenditure survey taken in 1972-73, is already out of date.

Wholesale Prices Run a Wayward Course

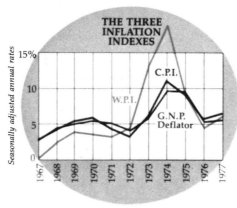

chase survey to ensure that its data collectors are checking retail outlets typical of the ones where most consumers shop.)

Oddly enough, the issue generating the most heat on the BLS these days is relatively unimportant. From its inception, the C.P.I. has measured the price experiences not of everyman but of two specific groups —urban wage earners and clerical workers, who between them make up only about 40 percent of the population. As part of the recent overhaul of the C.P.I., the BLS began publishing a second index, covering the entire urban and suburban civilian population. The broader index is obviously a good idea, but organized labor is up in arms, suspecting some long-range plot to phase out the older index and perhaps understate the effect of inflation on the working man. It is too soon to know how closely the two indexes will track each other, but in the first two months they moved in close tandem—that is to say, upward more than they would have had the biases been stripped out.

Part of the spiral?

There is no way to ascertain how strong that upward bias might be, though there is a fair amount of support for Professor Ruggles's estimate, which on the basis of quality changes alone works out to better than 2 percent a year. Even more problematic is what role the C.P.I. may have in *causing* inflation by triggering excessive increases as a result of those escalator clauses, which feed the wage-price spiral. Wages are hard-fought matters, and it is at least conceivable that the unions would be getting increases of the same size even if there were no C.P.I. at all. Still, given the importance now attached to these numbers, they should be as good as the taxpayers' money, in reasonable quantities, can buy. Continual revision of the market basket will help, and a number of economists, including Northwestern University's Robert J. Gordon, argue that there are mathematical techniques that the BLS could use to isolate the price effect of quality improvements from other price changes. "These days," he notes, "computer time

The wholesale price index is frequently used by journalists as an indicator of what will be happening to consumer prices later on. The top two charts measure the soothsaying ability of two different versions of the W.P.I.—the "finished goods" and "all commodities" indexes —by comparing them with the consumer price index, which is lagged here by one quarter. The "finished goods" index, which counts only goods ready for sale to distributors, does a better job than the "all commodities" W.P.I., which contains a grab-bag of raw materials, intermediate goods, and finished goods. Neither, however, is awfully close to the mark. At bottom is an unlagged comparison of the three major price indexes—the C.P.I., the all-commodities W.P.I., and the G.N.P. deflator. It's obvious that the W.P.I. runs a wayward course.

is cheap and the technique could be adopted for a few important product categories with little additional expense." It might be just as well, all the same, to keep George Meany in the dark until the bugs are worked out.

The broadest measure

Journalists and Wall Streeters may chart the flight path of the C.P.I., but economists have traditionally preferred the "implicit price deflator of the Gross National Product." That mouthful refers to the price index that results when statisticians in the Commerce Department's Bureau of Economic Analysis "deflate" current-dollar G.N.P. to a constant-dollar amount. They begin by dividing the various subcategories of current-dollar G.N.P. by the relevant price indexes. For instance, the C.P.I. indexes are used to deflate various classes of consumer outlays; the wholesale price indexes are used for some classifications of capital goods; special indexes, such as the telephone-equipment index provided by A.T.&T., are used to deflate special categories. Then the "deflated" sums are added, to arrive at a single figure for *real* G.N.P. When this figure is divided into current-dollar G.N.P., what falls out is the deflator.

The virtue of the G.N.P. deflator is its breadth of coverage, which also, however, encompasses some rather broad categories of error. The deflator picks up errors from the C.P.I. and the wholesale price index, and it adds a few of its own. Services loom large, since they account for almost half the G.N.P., and there is no good way to measure changes in the quality of services. So far, the BEA hasn't really tried; it simply attributes all increases in the cost of haircuts or government to inflation.

The G.N.P. deflator also suffers from a chronic tardiness that makes it less useful for short-term analysis. It is first released with the early G.N.P. estimates, about twenty days after the end of the quarter. These estimates involve much guesswork, and users must wait for the third or fourth revision before the figures begin to settle down. That's because many of the private and governmental sales data the BEA rees on to compute G.N.P. just aren't available in time for the initial quarterly estimates and some not for a considerable time afterward. In the meantime, BEA statisticians make estimates based on recent trends. Their early estimates aren't necessarily any better than those made by private forecasters, but because of the official auspices, they carry a lot more weight.

Adding to the deflator's short-term unreliability is the distorting effect of the frequent shifts in U.S. spending patterns. If housing, where prices have gone up much faster than the overall average during the last few years, falls on its face for a quarter, the deflator will be held down because that higher-priced item is less important in the total G.N.P. These problems are corrected for in two specialized BEA indexes—which do not, however, make the newspaper front pages.

The least reliable measure

If the C.P.I. and the deflator have their problems, they are paragons of statistical science compared with the other main inflation indicator, the wholesale price index. The W.P.I. is put to many important uses —as a "materials escalator," for example, in at least $100 billion worth of long-term contracts, and to revalue corporate assets at replacement cost, as required by the Securities and Exchange Commission. The Justice Department pores over breakdowns of the W.P.I., looking for evidence of monopolistic practices. And of course the news media see the W.P.I. as a forecaster of consumer prices. Yet Yale's Professor Ruggles, who recently completed a major study of the W.P.I. for the Council on Wage and Price Stability, concluded that the index "fulfills its functions so badly that a major effort should be made to replace it."

How does the wholesale price index err? Let us count the ways. Even its name is misleading, for the W.P.I. doesn't measure wholesalers' prices. Instead, it gauges prices from producers in mining, manufacturing, and agriculture. To measure those price changes, the BLS sends out forms each month to about 3,000 firms that have volunteered to report their prices on about 10,000 items. The quotations are used to construct separate price indexes for 2,800 commodities. These are then combined into averages, weighted by the quantity of goods shipped back in 1972.

However, the BLS adequately prices only 27 percent of the products made by the 550 major U.S. industries, and many of the price changes listed in the W.P.I. are based on reports from only one or two firms. Worse than that, the selection of the items to be priced is arbitrary and frequently out of date. Professor Gordon points this out as a major source of upward bias in the W.P.I. The index for office machinery, he notes, has shown increasing prices just during those years when electronic computing equipment offered dramatic reductions in price per computation. Whereas in 1952 it cost $1.26 to do 100,000 multiplications, now they can be done for less than a penny. Yet the W.P.I. has missed the price drop, because most types of modern office equipment, including computers, aren't even priced by the BLS.

A candid admission

"The W.P.I. is based on very thin data," admits Commissioner Layng. "We have pushed the data base too far, basing 2,800 price series on 10,000 quotes." And if the price quotes are too few in number, their quality is highly suspect, for many companies habitually report only their list prices. These may equal transactions prices when demand is strong. But in the doldrums of recession, producers shave prices through cash discounts, or by offering free shipment to the buyer's warehouse, or by any number of other devices. Thus, industrial prices rise and fall more sharply with fluctuating demand than the W.P.I. indicates.

"Businessmen are too secretive about their prices," complains Layng. "We think we're getting good price quotes, but it's hard to tell. Price is a sensitive topic to most businessmen." He concedes that the BLS doesn't always get to the bottom of the matter. "For instance, in the steel industry there are firms that have large sales forces with some pricing latitude. Now, we go into the accounting department for detailed prices, but it may not be aware of the discounts used by salesmen."

Double and triple counting

Layng has pointed out that the W.P.I. is biased because it gets its reports mostly from the bigger firms, leaving out smaller and perhaps more competitive ones. Upward bias creeps in because the W.P.I., like the C.P.I., isn't properly adjusted for quality improvements. Professor Gordon finds this bias especially strong when it comes to durable goods such as electric appliances, which, he notes, have grown increasingly energy efficient and reliable.

The W.P.I.'s biggest distortion of all comes from double, triple, and even more redundant counting of price changes. If the price of cotton rises, and the price hike is passed on to yarn producers, and by them to cotton-fabric producers, and by them to finished-cotton-fabric makers, and finally to shirtmakers, the price increase will have been counted five times in the W.P.I.

The problem led Layng's predecessor, Joel Popkin, to upgrade three supplementary series—for raw goods, intermediate goods (those sold from one producer to another for further processing), and finished goods ready for sale to distributors. Late last year the BLS officially recognized the deficiency of the original "all commodities" W.P.I. by announcing that it was switching emphasis from this measure to one of Popkin's improved indexes, the finished-goods series. And in belated recognition that W.P.I. was something of a misnomer, the BLS this month is changing the name of its three-way tabulation to the Producer Price Indexes.

Guided by Ruggles's report, Layng and his technicians at the BLS have outlined a program of major overhaul for the W.P.I. They want to cover many more industries, gather larger samples of prices, use scientific sampling techniques to replace the judgmental procedures now in force, attempt better reporting of transaction prices, and further eliminate multiple counting. Unfortunately, the reform plan is a piecemeal affair, dependent on future funding by Congress. The best the BLS can do with present funds is to enact the easiest revisions, and even those wouldn't come to fruition till the mid-1980's.

Time for repairs

So it's evident that our price indexes are imprecise guides at best, and highly flawed ones by any reckoning. Their manifold errors could seriously mislead the policymakers. Yet, because they are now so much used by prognosticators, contract negotiators, and Presidents, they can't just be left to the statisticians either.

If these figures are to bear the heavy informational burdens thrust upon them, they'd better be as good as they can be. It's clear that they can be improved by some relatively simple expedients, and this does seem to be one place where Congress can spend to good advantage by amply financing complete and competent upgrading of all the price indexes. Meanwhile, it's wise to take abrupt gyrations in the numbers with a skeptical and stoic calm.

3

An examination of employment and unemployment rates

The persistence of high rates of unemployment after more than two years of economic recovery has increased the controversy over what the best measure of labor market conditions is. The usefulness of the unemployment rate, the traditional measure, has been called into question; the employment ratio is the most frequently recommended alternative. Too frequently, the debate has implied that an absolute choice must be made between the two statistics. Such a view is mistaken, for no single measure can hope to provide a complete assessment of labor market conditions.

At the outset, it must be recognized that each measure suffers from some shortcomings. The unemployment rate has the most deficiencies, and because of them that rate has become an increasingly imperfect measure of labor market conditions. Analysts are therefore regarding the unemployment rate with increasing reservations, and some have suggested that the employment ratio be given more emphasis in the analysis of the labor market as it reflects demand pressures in the economy as a whole.

The two measures defined

The unemployment rate refers to the percentage of the civilian labor force that is seeking work but does not have a job.[1] This widely used statistic is not the only unemployment rate that the Bureau of Labor Statistics (BLS) regularly reports. A number of other unemployment rates, such as the percentage of household heads in the labor force who are unemployed, the percentage of teenagers in the labor force who are unemployed, and the percentage of the labor force out of work for fifteen weeks or longer are also available for evaluating labor market conditions. No matter whether the total or a segmental unemployment rate is ex-

amined, all these rates are intended to represent the proportion of labor force participants that offer labor for sale but are unable to find employment at the current level of wages. Thus, each measures the unutilized or excess supply of labor in the market at existing wages.

The employment ratio, in contrast, is defined as the proportion of the noninstitutionalized *population* in the working ages—16 years of age and older—that is employed, and it thus measures the extent of utilization of potential labor resources.[2] Employment ratios analogous to many of the published unemployment series may be constructed. These ratios measure the proportion of labor resources whose services have been purchased in the labor market.

A rate of unemployment supposedly indicates the extent of utilization of available rather than potential labor resources. The unemployment rate is also used to help assess the hardship experienced by workers who are willing to work and are available for work but are unable to find jobs. But whether the unemployment rate indicates hardship or need as precisely as one would like has come to be questioned. Its accuracy is impaired in several ways. The measured rate can be considered too low because it fails to include "discouraged workers", that is, the people who do not seek work if they do not believe they are likely to obtain jobs and thus leave the labor force temporarily or remain outside it. Similarly, the rate fails to include those who want to work full time but are forced to work part time because of economic conditions. In-

[1] The civilian labor force refers to all noninstitutionalized individuals 16 years of age and over who are employed or are without a job and seeking work.

[2] If the employment ratio were defined as the proportion of civilian labor force that is employed, it would simply be the mirror image of the unemployment rate. In that case, it could be obtained by subtracting the unemployment rate from 100. But then, any statistical or institutional factors that caused defects in the unemployment rate would cause the same defects in an employment ratio based on the civilian labor force. That is why the employment ratio uses the relevant population rather than the labor force in the denominator.

Reprinted from Federal Reserve Bank of New York *Quarterly Review*, Autumn, 1977.

stead, all part-time workers with jobs are treated as employed whether or not they would prefer full-time work.[3] The measured rate can be considered too high because of the expansion in the coverage of such programs as unemployment insurance as well as the rise in benefit levels. Applicants must remain in the labor force to receive these benefits even though they may not be seriously looking for jobs. Such behavior imparts an upward thrust to the unemployment rate. And the increases in these programs have also served to weaken the tie between the unemployment rate and "hardship".

Changing participation rates and their impact

The employment ratio avoids to a greater degree than the unemployment rate a statistical problem that is caused by changing labor force participation rates, *i.e.,* the proportion of the population 16 years of age and over who are at work or are looking for work. Changes in these participation rates have altered the composition of the labor force in recent years. The changes suggest that a basic structural alteration in the pattern of choice among work in the market, work at home, and the amount of leisure desired is under way, particularly in certain demographic groups. As a result of these changes, a larger proportion of the labor force now consists of women and teenagers. Indeed, the secular increase in labor force participation rates (see top panel, Chart 1) is attributable largely to this change in behavior by women and teenagers. And these groups in the labor force are among those that traditionally have experienced higher than average rates of unemployment. It is now recognized that for this reason alone a given rate of aggregate demand will be associated with a higher level of unemployment than in the past.[4]

Experience shows that rates of labor force participation respond to a host of influences. In the short term, the rate of business activity may have the most effect. On the one hand, the rate of participation in the labor force typically increases during upswings in economic activity because individuals perceive increased job opportunities. If, as sometimes happens, the growth of the labor force is faster than that of employment, the resultant increase in the unemployment rate should

not be construed as a sign of weakening economic conditions. On the other hand, if during an economic decline workers become discouraged and leave the labor force, the resulting tendency toward a lower unemployment rate should not be construed as a sign of improving economic conditions.

Changes in the long-term trend of labor force participation rates also affect the interpretation of the two measures. Should the rate of participation in the labor force and the age-sex composition of the population

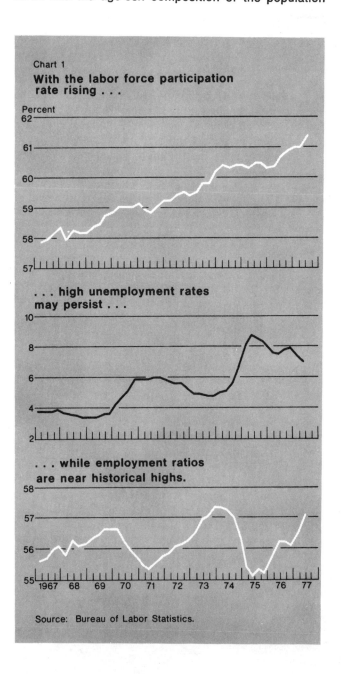

Chart 1
With the labor force participation rate rising . . .

. . . high unemployment rates may persist . . .

. . . while employment ratios are near historical highs.

Source: Bureau of Labor Statistics.

---

[3] It should be noted that this treatment of part-time workers impairs both the unemployment rate and the employment ratio, and also creates difficulties of interpretation with respect to both.

[4] While it can be shown that an increasing proportion of the unemployment rate stems from the changing composition of the labor force, this by no means is the only or even the principal explanation for today's high unemployment rates. For further discussion of this point, see "The Changing Composition of the Labor Force" by Sharon P. Smith in this Bank's *Quarterly Review* (Winter 1976), pages 24-30.

remain constant for a considerable period, the unemployment rate and the employment ratio would suggest similar assessments of labor market conditions. However, if the labor force participation rate changes, the unemployment rate and the employment ratio can yield different assessments. Among all the possible scenarios, here are two. If the labor force participation rate is rising, then the employment ratio may suggest stable labor market conditions although the unemployment rate would be increasing. If the labor force participation rate is falling, the unemployment rate may suggest a strengthening of labor market conditions although the employment ratio would be declining. It thus seems clear that when changes in labor force participation rates occur, whether for cyclical or secular reasons, *both* the unemployment rate and employment ratio ought to be looked at to obtain more accurate appraisals of labor market conditions.

The relationships being discussed are highlighted in Chart 1, which shows quarterly data for the labor force participation rate, the civilian unemployment rate, and the employment ratio. During periods when labor force participation rates are more or less constant, as they were during most of 1970-72, a rise in the unemployment rate and a decline in the employment ratio suggest worsening labor market conditions. In fact, whenever these statistics move in opposite directions and participation rates are roughly the same, both statistics yield similar labor market appraisals. In recent years, however, it has been more typical for the labor force participation rate to rise—it went up strongly from 59.8 percent at the end of 1973 to 62.3 percent in September of this year. Consequently, the present employment ratio of 57.3 percent is associated with an unemployment rate of 6.9 percent; in 1973, the same employment ratio was accompanied by an unemployment rate of only 4.8 percent.

Characteristics of the two measures

The employment ratio is in general less subject to error than the unemployment rate. Because the impact of measurement error on the unemployment rate appears to be increasing, the unemployment rate is becoming the less reliable measure with which to assess labor market conditions.

Unemployment data are collected in a survey of households, and one individual usually responds for all members of the household. As a result, the recorded employment rate is affected by the accuracy of replies by the individuals who report on the labor force status of all members of the household. It has been observed that reports given by most households show higher unemployment when they have recently been added to the survey sample than in later interviews.

This is documented in a study by Robert E. Hall.[5]

Because of the difficulty of determining whether individuals actually are looking for and are available for work, a count of the employed is likely to be much more accurate than a count of the unemployed.[6] Moreover, because the employment figure is much larger than the unemployment figure, sampling errors that are to be expected in either statistic introduce a smaller possibility of error into the employment ratio than the unemployment rate. Seasonal fluctuations also are much smaller in employment than they are in unemployment.

In addition to these statistical problems, the unemployment rate is affected by institutional influences. Among the most publicized are those that occur as a consequence of unemployment compensation and of work registration requirements in certain welfare programs. To be eligible to receive benefits under the above programs, individuals are required to register as unemployed with the United States Employment Service or to register for manpower training.[7] These individuals are defined by the BLS to be unemployed, since registration with a public employment service is viewed as a means of actively seeking employment. However, these programs, like any income-maintenance plan, also create disincentives to seek employment in a more active fashion than by merely registering for employment to obtain benefits. As a result, it is likely that some recipients of benefits under these plans are voluntarily unemployed—that is, they basically choose not to work—and so would not be counted in a more precise measure of unemployment.

A number of analysts have attributed much of the present high rate of unemployment to Government benefits programs. Ehrenberg and Oaxaca, as well as Feldstein,[8] have suggested that a large portion of un-

[5] "Why is the Unemployment Rate So High at Full Employment?" *Brookings Papers on Economic Activity* (3, 1970), page 375.

[6] The BLS defines the employed as those who, during the survey week, worked either as paid employees or in their own profession or business, worked without pay for fifteen hours or more on a farm or a family-operated business, and those with jobs but not at work because of a labor-management dispute, illness, vacation, etc. The unemployed are defined as those who did not have a job during the survey week but were available for work and (according to the survey respondent) actively looked for a job at some time during the four-week period immediately prior to the survey.

[7] Some welfare recipients are exempt from these work registration requirements. These include certain categories such as the ill or incapacitated (with medical verification) and mothers or other members of the household charged with the care of children under age 18.

[8] See Ronald Ehrenberg and Ronald L. Oaxaca, "Do Benefits Cause Unemployed to Hold Out for Better Jobs?" and Martin Feldstein, "Unemployment Compensation: Its Effect on Unemployment", both in the *Monthly Labor Review* (March 1976).

employment is voluntary, because the high levels of unemployment compensation enable unemployed workers to engage in a longer period of search before taking another job or simply to enjoy leisure-time activities. Moreover, Feldstein believes that the present system of unemployment compensation costs some employers less in contributions to unemployment programs than the benefits that are paid to the employees they lay off. He concludes that this system thereby encourages employers to organize production so as to exaggerate seasonal and cyclical variations in unemployment and to create more temporary jobs than would otherwise exist.

Clarkson and Meiners maintain that the single most important factor contributing to the high level of unemployment is the change in certain welfare eligibility requirements.[9] They argue that the current overall unemployment rate has been inflated by as much as 2.1 percentage points because of the work registration eligibility requirements that were introduced in 1971 into the Aid to Families with Dependent Children (AFDC) program and into the food stamp program. In their view, these registrants represent a group of individuals who either are largely unemployable or have no need or desire to work but are counted as unemployed because they have to register to obtain benefits.

Clarkson and Meiners estimate a "corrected" unemployment rate by omitting from both the unemployment and the civilian labor force figures all those work registrants who have been required to register to be eligible for AFDC or food stamp benefits. This is undoubtedly an overadjustment since many welfare recipients actually do want a job. Indeed, nearly a fourth of all the AFDC recipients who register for work with the public employment service are exempt from registering. Moreover, a study of AFDC recipients indicates that nearly half of them have had recent labor market experience.[10] These facts cast doubt on the assumption that none of the welfare recipients are employable or seeking a job. In sum, while it appears that the work registration requirements of the welfare programs inflate the unemployment rate, the extent of overstatement is likely to be considerably less than the 2.1 percentage points suggested by Clarkson and Meiners.

An increasing awareness of the foregoing sorts of problems is reflected in the new unemployment insurance benefits bill signed into law on April 12, 1977.

[9] Kenneth W. Clarkson and Roger E. Meiners, "Government Statistics as a Guide to Economic Policy: Food Stamps and the Spurious Increase in the Unemployment Rates", *Policy Review* (Summer 1977).

[10] Robert George Williams, *Public Assistance and Work Effort* (Research Report Series No. 119, Industrial Relations Section, Princeton University, Princeton, N.J., 1975).

Under this legislation, individuals may be denied unemployment compensation if they do not actively seek work, do not apply for suitable work to which they are referred, or do not accept an offer of suitable work. Contrary to past practice, under the new law individuals may be required to accept positions that are significantly different in tasks and pay from their past jobs if the position is within the individual's "capabilities", if the individual is offered either the Federal minimum wage or more than the unemployment benefit, if the job does not entail unreasonable travel, and if it does not endanger the individual's "morals, health, or safety". It is too early to ascertain the extent to which the law may affect labor market statistics.

The need for further study

All in all, the unemployment rate tends to be inaccurate for both statistical and institutional—including legislative—reasons. In addition, the possible size of any error seems greater than for any associated with the employment ratio. In large part, this is because it is simply easier to identify clearly those who are working than to identify clearly those who want to work and are seeking work, since it is difficult to determine how many of the latter are in fact available for work. Further study of labor supply behavior under various income maintenance programs is necessary to formulate techniques that will eliminate from the unemployment numbers those who are really voluntarily unemployed.

Although at present the unemployment rate is a less accurate measurement than the employment ratio, this does not imply that the unemployment rate should be abandoned as a means of assessing labor market conditions. Instead, it calls for action to correct the shortcomings in all statistics relating to the labor market. For this reason, the Emergency Jobs Programs Extension Act of 1976 (Public Law 94-444) established a new National Commission on Employment and Unemployment Statistics. (The last major evaluation of employment and unemployment statistics was made fourteen years ago.) The new commission is charged with the responsibility of evaluating the present statistics as well as with making recommendations for their improvement.

In seeking the proper statistics to assess labor market conditions, the measure chosen should depend on the question being posed. For example, the Employment Act of 1946 calls for the Federal Government to take all feasible action to encourage the "conditions under which there will be afforded useful employment opportunities, including self-employment for those able, willing, and seeking to work, and to promote maximum employment, production, and purchasing power". To find out whether maximum—or full—

Chart 2

Relationship between the Consumer Price Index and the Employment Ratio

Percentage change in prices*

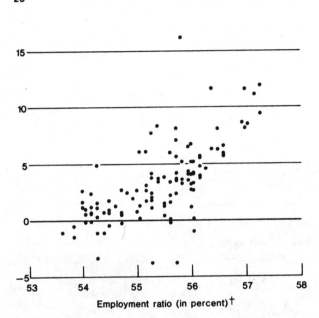

Employment ratio (in percent)†

*Change from previous quarter (at annual rate), 1948-77.

†By quarters, 1948-77.

Source: Computations based on data from the Bureau of Labor Statistics.

Chart 3

Relationship between the Consumer Price Index and the Unemployment Rate

Percentage change in prices*

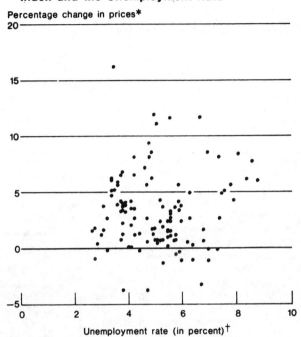

Unemployment rate (in percent)†

*Change from previous quarter (at annual rate), 1948-77.

†By quarters, 1948-77.

Source: Computations based on data from the Bureau of Labor Statistics.

employment has been achieved, the unemployment rate is conceptually the more appropriate measure, although its inaccuracies seriously compromise its relevance at the present time.

If, however, the primary interest is the relation between wage changes or inflation and the condition of the labor market, the employment ratio may be the better statistic to use because increasing inaccuracy of the unemployment rate has weakened the relationship between that statistic and excess demand. This has been pointed out by Geoffrey Moore[11] and is illustrated in Charts 2 and 3, which show a much stronger association between the percentage change in the consumer price index and the employment ratio than between the percentage change in the consumer price index

[11] "Employment, Unemployment, and the Inflation-Recession Dilemma", *AEI Studies on Contemporary Economic Problems* (1976).

and the unemployment rate. Of course, the observation of correlation between these statistical series does not prove the existence of any causal relationship between them.

If the unemployment rate included only the involuntarily unemployed, the rate could be interpreted as an indirect measure of the inflationary pressures resulting from excess demand. This, in fact, is the interpretation that underlies the Phillips curve relation. In that relation, wages are expected to rise when there is excess demand—which is taken to be indicated by a low unemployment rate—and the rate of wage increase is expected to be the faster the greater the excess demand. However, if the unemployment rate is increasingly affected by the inclusion of the voluntarily unemployed, this relationship becomes blurred and the employment ratio may provide a better indication of demand pressures.

Sharon P. Smith

4

The explosive issue of youth unemployment

A sharp division of views on its seriousness and strategies to combat it

By any statistical measure, youth unemployment remains a significant and seemingly intractable problem on the national economic scene. Despite the fact that the recovery is 2½ years old, the overall teenage unemployment rate ticked up to 17.5% last month—not far below the 20.8% high it hit in July, 1975. For black teenagers, the rate hovered above an astounding 40% for the second month in a row. Numerous youths of varying economic and racial backgrounds continue to report difficulty in finding jobs. And nearly half of the 6.9 million Americans currently counted as unemployed are under 25.

All of this has combined to make youth unemployment a controversial and politically explosive issue. Only a month or so ago, Congress voted approval of a multifaceted youth employment bill that will pour some $1.5 billion in the next year into a variety of programs to provide job and training opportunities for 250,000 young people. Under pressure from disgruntled congressmen, particularly the Black Caucus, President Carter has promised to accelerate such spending.

Unease. Yet despite the sense of crisis, many economists are uneasy about the Administration's new policy initiatives. Robert Taggart, who heads the Labor Dept.'s new Office of Youth Programs, worries that the new youth bill is "a patchwork of inflated expectations, untested ideas, and unrealistic timetables." And many experts remain sharply divided on both the seriousness of teenage unemployment and the best strategy to reduce it.

Though the causes of the problem are complex, several major factors stand out:

■ The depth of the recent recession and the lagging pace of the recovery. Last year when the teenage jobless rate stood at 19%, the Congressional Budget Office estimated that five to six percentage points of that rate came from the generally lackluster state of the economy.
■ A big jump in the teenage population as a result of the postwar baby boom. From 1955 to 1974, the 16- to 19-year-old group doubled to more than 16 million. Moreover, the group's rate of participation in the labor force—the percentage either employed or seeking

work—has been rising sharply for more than a decade.
■ The winding-down of the Vietnam war and the ending of the draft. The number of young men in the armed forces fell more than 1 million from 1968 to 1974, adding new pressures to a labor market in which increasing numbers of women were already competing for the entry-level and part-time jobs sought by teenagers. Also, some economists contend, progressive hikes in the minimum wage have reduced the number of jobs available to the young (BW—Sept. 19).

A general problem. While economists tend to agree about what has caused the surge in teenage joblessness, many remain uncertain as to how much hardship this unemployment really entails, whether the problem will diminish in the years ahead, whether its effects are long-lasting, and to what extent its high levels are more statistical artifacts than reflections of urgent need.

Michael J. Piore of the Massachusetts Institute of Technology, for one, insists that "the current problem is not youth unemployment at all, but unemployment generally." He says that teenage unemployment has always been high—hanging in at more than 12% even in 1968 and 1969 when the overall jobless rate was 3.5% and 3.6%. Moreover, he stresses, the largest relative increase in joblessness has been among prime-age adults. The unemployment rate for males 35 to 44 jumped from 1.5% in 1969 to 4.1% in 1976—a rise of 173%, compared with a 56% rise in the teenage rate.

"Unemployment for adults is far more serious than for youths," contends Piore. "What could be more discouraging to a youngster than seeing his father unemployed?"

Urban Institute economist Ralph E. Smith questions this assessment. "You have to look at employment as well as

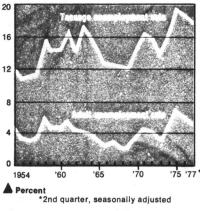

Teenage unemployment far outstrips the adult rate

Teenage unemployment rate

▲ Percent
*2nd quarter, seasonally adjusted

1954   '60   '65   '70   '75 '77*

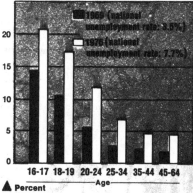

And it stays that way in good and bad years

■ 1969 (national unemployment rate: 3.5%)
□ 1976 (national unemployment rate: 7.7%)

16-17 18-19 20-24 25-34 35-44 45-64
—Age—
▲ Percent

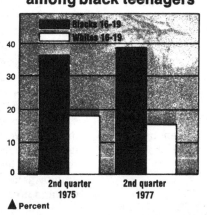

Joblessness grows worse among black teenagers

■ Blacks 16-19
□ Whites 16-19

2nd quarter 1975   2nd quarter 1977
▲ Percent

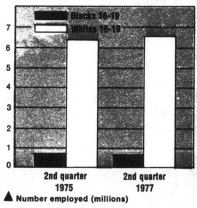

And jobs for black teenagers have declined

■ Blacks 16-19
□ Whites 16-19

2nd quarter 1975   2nd quarter 1977
▲ Number employed (millions)

Data: Bureau of Labor Statistics

Robert McAuley—BW

MIT's Piore: The problem is not youth unemployment but overall unemployment.

Harvard's Feldstein: Many jobless are students looking only for part-time work.

unemployment statistics," he says, noting that teenage employment dropped 420,000 between the end of 1973 and the end of 1975, while adult employment increased. Further, Smith estimates that another 700,000 teenagers either left the labor force or were discouraged from entering it, so the loss in teenage jobs was actually more than 1 million. "The recovery has helped teenagers somewhat," he says, "but adults a lot more."

Lasting effects? Smith believes that the current level of teen joblessness could have lasting negative effects, but others are uncertain. Experts note that one of the most striking characteristics of labor markets in both expansionary and reces-

sionary years is that unemployment rates decline sharply with age. "Whatever their job problems as teenagers, experience has shown that most people eventually find jobs," says Rand Corp. analyst Sue Berryman Bobrow. Adds Harvard's Richard Freeman: "Teenage unemployment may be mainly a transitional problem without long-term consequences. We just don't know."

One reason for the uncertainty, besides the striking drop in joblessness at the older age levels, is the special character of teenage unemployment. Teenagers tend to remain unemployed for shorter periods than adults and to change jobs far more frequently. Many remain dependent on their families and are not even seeking permanent or fulltime employment. Others are really engaged in a process of testing jobs for suitability before they settle down.

"Unemployed teenagers are a highly diverse group," says Freeman, "and their individual problems are of different magnitudes. A youngster who is looking for a part-time job to earn enough to buy a stereo may be upset if he can't find work readily, and he certainly adds to the unemployment statistics. But he is hardly going to suffer long-term damage."

An adjunct to school. Martin Feldstein, also a Harvard professor and president of the National Bureau of Economic

Teenage unemployment has been high even in good years, says Piore

Research, points to another factor that has been pushing the jobless rate up: the rise in school enrollments and the laborforce activity of students. Some 45% to 50% of 18- and 19-year-olds now attend school, and more than 40% of them participate in the job market. Most of these move in and out of the labor force frequently, seeking part-time work during the school year or full-time work during vacations. Thus they may end up being counted as unemployed several times a year. And because students generally represent the more "employable" elements of the teen population, says Feldstein, their temporarily high turnover during schooling tends to raise the figure for teen joblessness.

Experts note that while unemployment is a serious problem for some students who depend on their earnings to support them in school, it is less significant for many others. Moreover, because students usually accept work unrelated to their ultimate career choices, their job woes are different from those of young people seeking permanent, full-time positions.

Big gainers tomorrow. While they may differ regarding the seriousness of current youth/labor problems, economists such as Piore and Smith tend to

agree that macroeconomic policies are the best approach to bringing the present high jobless rate down to more traditional levels. "Teenagers suffered disproportionately in the recession," says Smith, "and they will make substantial gains when the economy begins to grow more rapidly." Moreover, he notes, the teenage population is now declining, both absolutely and as a percentage of the working population, and it will drop sharply by 1990.

From this viewpoint, much of the teen labor problem may prove to be temporary. And if today's teen "crisis" stems mainly from cyclical and demographic factors that are likely to improve, the real question, says Sue Bobrow, is whom

A question of who is really hurt and who is only inconvenienced

the nation should worry about. "For which kids will this period of heightened joblessness intersect with their ability to get skills?" she asks. "Personally, I'm not too worried about middle-class white kids; they aren't happy, but they'll survive O.K. But black and disadvantaged teenagers are far more at risk."

Economist Bernard Anderson of the University of Pennsylvania's Wharton School concurs. "There's no question," he says, "that black teenage unemployment is the single most serious problem in the American labor market today." He notes that the unemployment rate for black teenagers has been above 25% for a decade and has soared to 40% in recent years.

A hard core of losers. Moreover, Anderson says that while white teenage employment has risen nearly 10% since the recovery began, jobs for black youths have actually dropped 6½%. "When you consider the fact that the labor-force participation by black kids has been dropping at the same time that their numbers are still growing," says Anderson, "you can see the dimensions of the problem."

The recession exacerbated the situation, especially in the inner cities, where surveys indicate that up to 75% of black teenagers are either unemployed or outside the work force. "The slowdown has not only reduced the number of available jobs," says Anderson, "but has also left a pool of menial jobs that youngsters are reluctant to accept since they involve no chance of advancement."

As economists see it, the problem is to find ways to bridge the gap between school and meaningful work for lowskilled young people. Anderson is hopeful that the new youth employment act will provide some answers. But no one thinks the problem will go away any time soon.   ∎

5

The Threat of Inflation

Remarks by

David M. Lilly
Member of the Board of Governors
Federal Reserve System

before a

Business Conference
Sponsored by Federal Reserve Bank of Dallas
Dallas, Texas

November 10, 1977

It is a pleasure for me to be here in the Eleventh District and to appear before so distinguished a group of banking and business leaders. Since I joined the Board of Governors last year, and even before that time, I have focused particular attention on the need to improve our economic education and understanding—an improvement that is sorely needed in our society and should be actively advanced.

Because your positions place you in the forefront of economic education in your communities, I would like to discuss with you today an issue that, while perhaps the greatest threat to our economic society as we know it, has not yet received the public attention that it deserves. That issue is inflation. It's a disease that could change the entire fabric of our life unless it is brought under control. And I must say to you in all frankness that we at the Federal Reserve feel very lonely when the Government institutions that worry about inflation are asked to stand up and be counted. We live in almost virtual isolation, a condition that I hope will change, and change dramatically, as time goes on.

The seriousness of inflation cannot be overestimated. Except for a brief period after World War II, prices in this country in recent years have been rising faster than in any other peacetime period in our history. Most recently, there has been some respite from double-digit inflation, but a resurgence of inflation could jeopardize the future of our country, if past experience is any guide. No country in history has been able to maintain widespread economic prosperity, once inflation got out of hand. And

the unhappy consequences are not just of an economic nature. Inflation inevitably causes disillusionment and discontent. It robs millions of people who have set aside funds for education or retirement, and it hits the poor and the elderly especially hard.

Inflation has also been a contributing factor to the fall of governments. Even in this country, the distortions and injustices created by inflation have contributed to a distrust of government officials and governmental policies. History teaches us that the discontent bred by inflation can provoke disturbing social and political change. The ultimate consequences of inflation could well be a significant decline of economic and political freedom.

To appreciate the threat of inflation fully, one must understand how it has infected our economy. There is in our society a built-in inflationary bias that has grown more intense over the last decade. Our long-range problem of inflation has its roots in the structure of our economic institutions and in the financial policies of our Government. This basic fact is all too frequently obscured by outside events that increase the rate of inflation noticeably, such as a crop failure or action to raise oil prices. The plain truth is, however, that the United States—and many other countries throughout the world—has developed an underlying bias toward inflation that has only been magnified by these special influences.

Where does this leave our traditional tools of policy? Fiscal and monetary policies still have important roles to play in our fight against inflation, but they can no longer do the entire job. Removal—or even a reduction—of structural barriers will help us squeeze the inflationary bias from the economy and remove the distortions that we, ourselves, have made a part of our system.

One indication of these distortions is the constant penchant of our society to run budget deficits. I have no desire to delve deeply into the pros and cons of budget deficits—nor to criticize what is our very commendable national willingness to provide for the less fortunate members of our society. The record shows, however, that since 1950, deficits have outrun surpluses by 23 to 5. That is a runaway score in anybody's language, and it has tended to put the Government's stamp on inflation.

Reprinted from Federal Reserve Bank of Dallas *Review*, December, 1977.

But let me give you some examples of how the Government has contributed *indirectly* to the inflationary bias in our economy. Let me explain, first, some of the structural problems we have created and the structural reforms that must be made to supplement traditional monetary and fiscal policies as the best hope of unwinding inflation.

For many years, the Federal Government has regulated various forms of transportation—trucks, railroads, airlines, and ships. A certain amount of regulation is undoubtedly good, but analysts estimate that regulation of transportation in this country has raised costs anywhere from 10 to 30 percent.

Tariffs, together with import barriers, are another factor in this bias. Granted tariffs and import barriers have benefited certain industries and groups of Americans. But they have also served to increase prices of some commodities or to prevent a drop for others.

The list of examples is legion—restrictive building codes, agricultural price supports, the market power of business and unions, pollution controls, safety regulations, pension costs, mandatory retirement, and the minimum wage laws. Taken together or individually, they increase the economy's bias for inflation.

Let me give you a current example. It is our estimate that the rate of inflation for next year will be 1 percent more because of the new payroll taxes (social security and unemployment insurance), the new minimum wages, and the proposed energy taxes.

I am not making a moral judgment on these programs. I am only suggesting that Congress may well have offset them by other deflationary actions.

Let me take a moment to explain one bias that is particularly troublesome to me. That is the innovation that has crept into our economic thinking in recent years of indexing price increases. Since the economy experienced double-digit inflation several years ago, there has been more and more emphasis on indexing. The "cost-of-living adjustment" has frequently been called an engine of inflation by government economists. Nevertheless, more and more labor contracts now include the same type of provisions.

There are some economists who believe a cost-of-living escalator—or indexing—is a perfectly rational approach to the nagging problem of inflation. As costs go up, incomes also go up by the same amount and the effects of inflation are nullified, or so the argument goes. But indexing also has one destructive feature that makes it an unacceptable approach to inflation. It serves to take away the incentive of people to fight the inflation itself. It is an admission of defeat. It is, literally, throwing in the towel, and that is one thing I and my colleagues at the Federal Reserve will never do.

While I am on this point, let me say that I have been particularly distressed of late by business' tacit acceptance of these new sorts of escalators and arrangements—almost as a matter of course now—and by their effects on the structure of the labor market. For one reason or another—fear of strikes or delays perhaps—management is simply not pressing as hard as it should be or as it once did to hold down labor costs. This is also a form of giving up the fight; I don't think there is another area in which structural inflation so clearly has a life of its own, or in which we have acquiesced so easily to *expectations* of continuing inflation. We need now to examine much more diligently the structure of the labor market—to look closely at the fact that we have permitted high unemployment to exist while concurrently granting high wage increases. We need to look at other such distortions that have been allowed to occur. These practices are inimical to our goals of full employment and stable prices.

What we as a people have done, in summary, has been to subject our available resources to increasing intense demands. At the same time, we have sought to ensure that incomes do not get eroded when excessive pressures generate inflation. This amounts to creating upward pressures on costs and prices, and then arranging to perpetuate them. It is an awesome combination and one which we at the Federal Reserve must cope with.

I become very disappointed when I see the Federal Reserve alone in its struggle against inflation. Too often, our perseverance is attributed to callousness about the answer to the following question: Won't the unemployment picture worsen if we try to reduce inflation? But the answer to that question happens to be an emphatic NO. There is no longer a meaningful trade-off between unemployment and inflation. Inflation is one of the major causes of unemployment in the current environment. It leads to hesitation and a sluggish buying. Today's high unemployment rate is, fundamentally, the legacy of an inflation that surely could have been avoided if proper steps had been taken in time.

I hope you have not become discouraged by my remarks thus far. Now that I have painted a rather gloomy picture of inflation, let me offer some measures designed to bring it under control. And I must emphasize that inflation *can* be brought under control if we work together. Only a few years ago, we had double-digit inflation. The present rate of inflation is half what it once was, but we must do better and we can.

Conventional thinking about the economy, however, is out of date. Ways must be found to reduce unemployment while at the same time avoiding a new wave of inflation. The areas that must be explored are many and difficult, but we must open our minds if we are to have any chance of ridding our economy of its inflationary bias.

The first step in an anti-inflationary program is prudent monetary and fiscal policy. This is essential. Any heightening of inflationary expectations will erode business and consumer confidence and impair the economic expansion now underway. Thus, any attempt to make a "quick fix" of our major economic problems by a heavy dose of economic stimulation may be counter-productive. Only a steady, moderate policy will provide the foundation for both a lessening of inflation and a return to full use of our labor force and productive capacity.

But prudent monetary and fiscal policy is not all that is required. Inflation is more than an evil of the business cycle. As I have emphasized, it is a structural phenomenon as well. We must improve the efficiency and flexibility of our markets. Structural changes in our economy will be hard to come by. But we must make the effort if we are to have any success in our struggle.

For example, steps must be taken to improve competition among businesses through increased emphasis on antitrust policy, changes in regulatory procedures, and an easing of barriers to international trade. Local building codes that do not reflect modern construction techniques should be reexamined and changed where necessary. We should begin to substitute economic incentives for the morass of costly and inefficient safety and environmental regulations we have imposed on certain industries.

As I mentioned, I have a special interest in our labor market policies. Our job training programs should be strengthened to increase productiveness of workers, particularly minorities and teenagers. These programs should provide a better match between worker skills and business requirements. We also need expanded job bank programs. The Federal minimum wage law is pricing many teenagers out of the job market. It has been estimated that a 25-percent rise in the minimum wage is associated with an average of a 3- to 6-percent reduction in teenage employment When the minimum is raised, employers tend to

ignore the less skilled worker and seek the more productive employee. Employers may also attempt to get along with fewer employees. Some Federal laws—such as the Davis-Bacon Act, which requires the payment of "prevailing wages" on government construction contracts—continue to escalate costs. As I indicated, we must find alternatives to automatic cost-of-living adjustments that have the same effect. There is also a belief that the unemployment compensation laws provide such generous benefits that incentives to work are reduced. Reform of the welfare system to increase work incentives, a rethinking of mandatory retirement policies—these are also needed. I could go on, but I think you get the picture.

A restructuring of our economic system—along the lines I have outlined—would improve the efficiency and effectiveness of our conventional tools. During periods of excessive demand, for example, less restraint would be required to bring inflation under control. Consequently, I am convinced that structural reforms deserve more attention from Congress and, yes, from the general public than they have been receiving. Too many people have tended to concentrate on overall fiscal and monetary policies. These traditional tools are, of course, useful and essential; but once inflationary expectations have become widespread, the tools must be used with great care and moderation. We must work to remove the inflationary bias of our economy.

On our part, we at the Federal Reserve will continue to provide money and credit sufficient to accommodate a continuation of the orderly economic expansion. We will strive to avoid excessive growth in money and credit that would stimulate further inflationary pressures. The Federal Reserve System, moreover, is committed to a gradual reduction over the longer run as one of the conditions that must be achieved in order to bring about an end to the inflation. As I have tried to emphasize, however, other conditions are also necessary to reach this happy end, including progress in reducing the structural distortions that have added to our economy's inflationary bias.

But these policies require public support and understanding. People must understand that this problem of inflation is a serious long-term threat to our social and economic system. People must understand that government programs, no matter how worthy, are likely to have inflationary consequences unless they are accompanied by an appropriate means of financing. Even programs that are superficially costless may still impede the efficient workings of markets and the flexible adjustment of prices. Such programs may impose very heavy burdens of their own.

The Federal Reserve, in this struggle against inflation, has a unique role to play. Congress has enabled the Federal Reserve System to operate independently of day-to-day political pressures. Considerable scope for independent judgment has been permitted by providing for the appointment of members of the Federal Reserve Board for long, staggered terms. Moreover, Congress has placed the Federal Reserve System outside the usual appropriations process.

This provides us with a unique environment especially conducive to adopting a longer-run point of view. And it is this longer-run perspective that leads us to our great concern about the problem of inflation. We hope to convince others that this concern is warranted and that this struggle against inflation is worthy of their support.

Let me offer one idea that might have appeal for Americans who are worried about inflation. Many people who have been worried about the destruction of our environment succeeded in pushing through requirements for "environmental impact statements" for many types of development. Although many businesses have complained about the "red tape" produced by these statements, they have served a purpose in helping to protect our environment. In some cases, projects have been canceled or modified because of their impact on the environment. We should, perhaps, borrow a page from this book and require "inflation impact statements" to be filed by the Government in connection with changes in the minimum wage, import restrictions, and other regulations that give our economy an inflationary bias. True, this would add another layer of red tape to already cumbersome procedures, but it would awaken the public to the cost that must be borne when new legislation is adopted and new procedures are instituted. Some Federal agencies have already mandated such an approach.

Somehow, inflationary pressures have to be uprooted. But that cannot be done without changing a number of ideas and attitudes that have been popular for a generation or more. Consequently, we should have no illusions about finding a quick and easy solution. It will take years of prudent and vigorous public policies and restraint on the part of consumers, workers, and business firms alike. Even so, I am confident that with the imagination you and other business leaders across the country are displaying, we can work to put an end to inflation and restore the conditions essential to a stable prosperity.

LIVING WITH INFLATION: CONSIDER THE ALTERNATIVE

It's springtime, and Jimmy Carter is falling in love with one of Jerry Ford's old sweethearts: the dream of controlling inflation. He's quite shy about the whole affair, and has rejected the suggestion from some of his advisors that he launch a dramatic, all-out public campaign against rising prices. Still, he did take to the airwaves in mid-April to announce the following anti-inflation schemes:

• Federal white-collar employees will be limited to a 5.5% pay increase, less than had been budgeted for them this year. Top Carter appointees will have salaries frozen for a year.

• Carter's ceiling on total federal spending will be strictly enforced, with vetoes if necessary.

• Logging on federal lands will be increased, to ease lumber shortages.

• Businesses and unions will be urged to hold price and wage hikes below the average rate of increase for the last two years.

• Finally, Congress will be urged to pass a hospital cost-control bill and other Administration proposals.

This is great news if you're buying lumber, unless you also happen to be a federal white-collar employee. But for most of us, the impact of Carter's new romance with "fiscal responsibility" is less clear. Will the new policies be enacted? If so, will they really cure inflation? And will the cure be better or worse than the disease?

Asleep at the Wheel?

It's easy, at this point, to be skeptical about any new Carter plans. Our president has made it perfectly clear that his policy pronouncements should be taken with a grain of indecision. From the on-again, off-again tax cut, to the no-surprises 1979 Budget, to the indifference about the falling dollar and the ho-hum urban policy (see *Capitol Contacts,* p. 9), Carter's approach has been to promise them anything but give them about what they got last year.

This is no mere character defect, but rather a result of the fundamental indecision in U.S. ruling circles today: there is no clear consensus among business and government policymakers about how to solve the economy's problems. In the absence of such a consensus, economic policy is dominated by the conflicting pressures of myriad interest groups, some of which are likely to block almost any significant change.

In this environment, a presidential promise is an attempt at verbal pacification, a measure of what seems popular to say, as often as it is an indication of what will be done. So perhaps the news from the White House should be rephrased. Jimmy Carter has announced that it now seems popular to emphasize fighting inflation — a change from last year, when fighting unemployment was still more fashionable.

There are some real changes in the economy that lie behind this change in attitude. The official unemployment rate has inched downward from 9% three years ago to "only" about 6% today. That's still a recession by 1960's standards, but apparently it's what now passes for prosperity. Meanwhile, inflation, which had slowed down to less than a 3% annual rate of increase in early 1976, has recently speeded up to around 7%.

But the simple fact of more inflation and less unemployment doesn't mean that everyone *should* be worrying about inflation. The widely-held belief that poor and working people suffer the most from inflation is at best a half-truth. On the one hand, it is true that the rich have more savings to fall back on, and probably more ability to increase their incomes to compensate for inflation.

On the other hand, the things that poor and middle-income people buy have not, on average, been going up in price any faster than the things rich people buy. Moreover, inflation has often been associated with times of rising employment, while anti-inflationary policies usually throw more people out of work.

Something for Everyone

It is often taken for granted on the left and among liberals that prices have been going up faster on necessities than on luxuries, and that inflation is therefore a particularly severe problem for the poor. To test this idea, *Dollars & Sense* examined the impact of inflation on the budgets of households at three different income levels (see box, next page). From 1967 to January 1978, there was an 84.7% increase in the average price of the items in a low-income

Dollars & Sense magazine, 324 Somerville Ave., Somerville, MA 02143 (monthly, $7.50/yr.).

household's budget, 85.5% for median-income households, and 86.0% for the rich.

In short, there is no significant difference in the rate of price increase experienced by people at different income levels. Inflation, in recent years, has included something for everyone. Therefore, inflation should have little impact on the distribution of income — which is consistent with the fact that there

has been almost no change in the distribution of income during the recent years of rapid inflation (see *D&S #29*).

While inflation itself may hit rich and poor budgets equally hard, the causes of inflation are often particularly good for the poor: the same forces which cause inflation often cause an expansion in employment opportunities. Inflation occurs when demand exceeds supply; that is,

when the total amount that businesses, government and workers are trying to buy is greater than the amount of goods and services being produced.

Increased spending by business often (though not always) means that employers are creating more jobs; increased deficit spending by government will also generally lead to growth in employment. And increases in the number of people working — as well as the higher wage levels that workers are able to win when unemployment rates are low — lead to more consumption spending by working people.

Thus inflation is frequently (certainly not always) associated with low unemployment. Conversely, the government's favorite remedy for inflation, reducing total spending, reduces employment as well. When the government spends less (or raises taxes, which reduces private spending), fewer goods and services are bought, leading business to cut back on production and employment. With lower employment, workers as a whole spend less, further reducing the demand for goods and services. Eventually this lowers demand enough to slow the increase in prices.

Some observers claim that this mechanism, the "tradeoff" between inflation and unemployment, no longer works since both inflation *and* unemployment have been high in recent years. But in the last major attempt to use it, the "tradeoff" did work: President Ford traded millions of workers' jobs, in the 1974-76 recession, for a reduction in the rate of price increase from over 13% annually in the first quarter of 1974 to under 3% annually in the first quarter of 1976. While failing to permanently "Whip Inflation Now," Ford did demonstrate that by causing the greatest economic slump since the 1930's it was possible to temporarily whip inflation two years later.

CALCULATING INFLATION'S IMPACT

To examine the impact of inflation, we used the budgets for different income groups from the U.S. Bureau of Labor Statistics 1972-74 survey of consumer expenditures, the latest such data available. We looked at three income levels: $5,000 to $6,000; $10,000 to $12,000; and $25,000 and over. (Median household income in 1973 was $10,530.)

The technique we used can best be explained by an example. Suppose that the poor spend 2/3 of their income on food and 1/3 on clothing. Then the average price rise for the poor would be 2/3 of the food price increase plus 1/3 of the clothing increase. Suppose that the rich spend 1/2 their income on food and 1/2 on clothing; then their average price rise would be 1/2 the food increase plus 1/2 the clothing increase. If food goes up faster in price than clothing, then prices are rising faster for the poor, since they spend more of their incomes on food.

Actually, we used three income levels and 13 expenditure categories: food at home, food away from home, alcohol, tobacco, rent, homeownership, utilities, housekeeping and house furnishings, transportation, health care, clothing, personal care, and recreation. The result was that from 1967 to January 1978 prices rose 84.7% for the lower-income group, 85.5% for the middle group, and 86.0% for the rich. Looking only at January 1975 to January 1978, there is even less difference in the three rates.

The reason for these near-identical results is that some of the things going up fastest in price make up a larger share of rich people's budgets (such as homeownership and food away from home), while others make up a larger share for the poor (such as utilities and health care). A similar pattern holds for the items with the slowest price increases.

We also looked more closely at food eaten at home. Dividing it into 15 smaller categories, and carrying out the same kind of calculation, we found that from 1967 to 1977 food prices increased 92.9% for the lower-income group, 92.8% for the middle group, and 90.4% for the rich. (The rich are more heavily into beef, which has had slower-than-average price increases, accounting for the small difference here.)

These calculations should be interpreted with caution. It is particularly unfortunate, but unavoidable, that they are based on surveys done before the big food and fuel price increase of the mid-1970's, and that they do not include information on how budget patterns have actually changed in response to inflation: they reflect only how inflation has affected average 1973 budgets.

Sources: *Bureau of Labor Statistics*, Bulletin 1959, Report 455-4, press releases.

The terms of the inflation-unemployment tradeoff seem to be growing worse — it takes more unemployment than it used to in order to achieve the same amount of reduction in inflation. This is caused by the growing dependence of the economy on international trade, which introduces some inflation that is beyond U.S. control, and by the steady increase in monopoly power of large corporations, which makes them able to resist price decreases in recessions.

Why Not the Best?

Given the choice between inflation and unemployment, why not always choose inflation? People are better off with jobs and rising prices, after all, than with no jobs and constant prices; if those are the choices, it should always be politically popular to favor full employment and accept inflation as an unfortunate side effect. One drawback to this approach is that many people are on

At today's levels of unemployment, a "wage squeeze" on profits is not likely to occur. A second problem with a permanent-inflation economy is more serious. As international trade has become more important to U.S. business, rapid inflation here puts U.S. goods at a competitive disadvantage. Capitalists need to control inflation in order to win the foreign trade wars just as they need periodic bouts of unemployment to discipline labor and prevent a wage squeeze on profits; for both these reasons, a permanent inflation/full employment economy is unacceptable to them.

But as any used-car salesman knows, you can't always sell the naked truth. Imagine Jimmy Carter going on TV to tell us that three million people are going to be laid off in order to keep up profits and productivity and to out-compete the Germans. Capitalism not only needs to throw people out of work periodically; it also needs a way to mobilize

fixed-income programs can be changed to include cost-of-living adjustments.

There is no evidence, on the other hand, that the government can control peacetime inflation by any means except a recession — which leaves almost all workers, employed and unemployed, worse off. Other anti-inflation measures frequently mentioned include "jawboning," a form of public prayer for self-restraint by businesses which has no measurable effect on the world; and wage-price controls, which have worked only when the U.S. was fighting World War II and the Korean War, but which fell apart within a year or two when attempted in the early 1970's.

So despite the obvious hardships caused by inflation, most workers are better off living with it, fighting for wage increases to keep up with it, and fighting *against* the usual anti-labor form of anti-inflation policies.

Meanwhile, back in the White House, what of Jimmy Carter's new-found love for controlling inflation? Shy and indecisive as he is, he doesn't seem ready to do anything about it yet; he just wanted us all to know that it's on his mind. If inflation, or the balance of trade, continue to get worse, he may decide to make a more serious proposal. But if we're lucky, his springtime romance may turn into nothing more than a midsummer night's dream.

While inflation itself may hit rich and poor budgets equally hard, the causes of inflation are often particularly good for the poor: the same forces which cause inflation often cause an increase in employment.

---

fixed incomes. Before the introduction of cost-of-living increases for Social Security benefits in 1972, this was probably a politically decisive number of people.

Concern for retired people, or for workers whose wages haven't been keeping up with inflation, however, is hardly the most important obstacle to a permanent full-employment-with-inflation economy. There are two major reasons why capitalism won't work that way for long. First, a prolonged period of low unemployment increases the bargaining power of labor, and allows workers to make gains in wages and working conditions at the expense of profits; this occurred most recently in the late 1960's, when total profits, corrected for inflation, began dropping after 1966, while total wages continued to climb.

mass popular support for doing so. And so far, a great national campaign against inflation has been the most successful technique anyone in Washington has found.

The View from Below

Anti-inflation politics do strike a responsive chord in many people. For those on fixed incomes, and for those whose wages don't, or just barely do, keep up with inflation, the hope that the government will control price increases is always appealing. Yet it is almost always a false hope. There is some evidence that workers, by fighting hard, can make wages keep up with inflation. On average, wages have been going up as fast as prices over the last decade or so. And the important case of Social Security shows that

7

The Tough Talk Won't Be About Wages This Time

Fewer big strikes, less emphasis on outsize pay boosts— but a push for job security, broad labor-law changes. Those will be key elements in unions' demands in 1978.

By all the rules, 1978 should be a relatively quiet year on the labor-relations front. The calendar of contracts up for renewal is the lightest in at least three years, limiting the prospects for crippling strikes.

But observers already can see the potential for trouble in several key industries. And apart from employer-worker bargaining, labor legislation in Congress is almost certain to cause tensions between labor, management and the Carter Administration.

Few experts see much danger of a militant push by unions for bigger pay hikes than have been negotiated in the last two years. Instead, the emphasis most likely will be on job security—and in industries such as construction, job security sometimes means acceptance of smaller rather than larger wage hikes.

"I don't really see a lot of trouble in 1978," is the way Labor Secretary Ray Marshall sums up the outlook.

"Collective bargaining and wage determination in the U.S. will move forward on automatic pilot during the year ahead," predicts Arnold Weber, an economist at Carnegie-Mellon University in Pittsburgh.

Adds Wayne L. Horvitz, director of the Federal Mediation and Conciliation Service: "There will be no trend setters in 1978. The heavy hitters came up in 1976—freight trucking and autos in particular—and their contracts don't expire until 1979."

Even so, some degree of conflict is assured in several key industries:

• Barring an unforeseen breakthrough in bargaining, 1978 will begin with 170,000 coal miners still on strike.

• The nation's railroads and the largest rail union are on collision course over the size of freight-train crews; this dispute could boil over before midyear.

• If employment in construction picks up suddenly, building-trades unions might adopt a tougher bargaining stance.

• Contracts expire for some 150,000 workers in retail food stores, and wage demands have been higher in this sector lately than in most other industries.

• Agreements between the Postal Service and its 600,000 workers expire, too, and the deficit-ridden agency, struggling to remain independent of direct congressional control, will be reluctant to agree to sizable wage boosts.

"We're going to be busy," says Horvitz, the Government's chief mediator. "When you add together the Postal Service, the shipyards, aerospace, maritime trades and the New York City hospitals, you come up with a full agenda."

In all, 1.7 million workers will be directly affected by major contract talks— those covering 1,000 or more persons. This compares with 4.7 million in 1977 and 4.2 million in 1976. Besides the approximately 650 major contracts coming up for renegotiation, the Mediation Service estimates that 60,000 other contracts involving fewer than 1,000 workers will expire.

A drop in pressure. There is little likelihood that bargaining in 1978 will result in big increases in the size of settlements, compared with 1977. In addition to other wage increases they receive, about two thirds of all union members now get cost-of-living raises that typically allow them to recover 75 to 80 per cent of the loss of buying power caused by consumer-price increases. This means less pressure on union negotiators to "catch up" with inflation at the next round of bargaining.

As the chart on this page notes, pay and benefit increases resulting from settlements in 1977 for bargaining groups of 5,000 or more workers averaged 9.6 per cent in the first year of contracts, compared with 8.5 per cent for big contracts negotiated in 1976.

But first-year wage and fringe-benefit increases fell in size this year for bargaining units of 1,000 or more workers, according to the Labor Department, from 8.4 per cent in 1976 to 7.8 per cent in 1977—a trend toward less-expensive settlements in smaller industries.

Economists for the United California

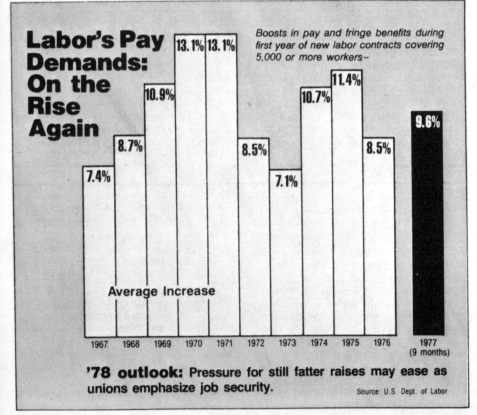

Labor's Pay Demands: On the Rise Again

Boosts in pay and fringe benefits during first year of new labor contracts covering 5,000 or more workers—

1967	1968	1969	1970	1971	1972	1973	1974	1975	1976	1977 (9 months)
7.4%	8.7%	10.9%	13.1%	13.1%	8.5%	7.1%	10.7%	11.4%	8.5%	9.6%

Average Increase

'78 outlook: Pressure for still fatter raises may ease as unions emphasize job security.

Source: U.S. Dept. of Labor

Bank expect a slight dip in the size of 1978 settlements, to the lowest level since 1973. Labor and management experts who were questioned by the Conference Board, a private business-research organization, look for an increase, though not a big one. Weber, of Carnegie-Mellon University, predicts that settlements in 1978 will remain at about the 1977 levels.

Almost everyone agrees that unions will continue to emphasize job security in bargaining. The United Auto Workers in 1976 negotiated seven additional holidays a year as a way of maintaining employment levels. The United Steelworkers in 1977 strengthened its plan to provide extra jobless benefits to members during layoffs. More recently, East and Gulf Coast longshoremen expanded their concept of a guaranteed number of hours of work annually. This trend is expected to continue, observers say, so long as unemployment remains high.

"Hard times tend to focus union interest on income and job protection," says William W. Winpisinger, president of the International Association of Machinists, many of whose members in the aerospace industry have been hurt by job cutbacks.

Noting the "profound impact" of high unemployment on union members and their leaders, Weber adds: "Their concern over job security wouldn't be dissipated if unemployment dropped to 4 per cent tomorrow."

Crew sizes. Railroad talks may attract the most public attention in 1978. Railroads are seeking to reduce the size of the standard freight-train crew from four persons to three by eliminating a brakeman's job. This would leave the engineer, conductor and one remaining brakeman on freight trains. At stake: 50,000 jobs costing the companies about 750 million dollars a year.

Early in 1977, the United Transportation Union, which bargains for brakemen, and two railroads in the South attempted to negotiate locally a solution to the crew-size dispute, and thus pave the way for a settlement on other railroads. The bargaining broke down, however, and the railroads then demanded that crew size be negotiated nationally at the same time as wage increases.

This the UTU has refused to do, citing a federal court decision in 1967 that classified crew sizes as an issue to be discussed on a local rather than national basis. Railroad negotiators claim that this decision does not apply to the present round of negotiations.

While the wage agreement in railroading has a December 31 expiration date, provisions of the Railway Labor Act will postpone a strike threat, if it occurs, until March or April at the earliest. Even then, President Carter can forestall a strike for an additional 60 days by naming a special committee to examine the dispute and recommend settlement terms.

Some railroad and UTU sources say the railroads could tie up negotiations indefinitely if they go into court to seek a reversal of the 1967 decision. By so doing, the railroads might entice the other 12 unions involved in the negotiations to settle immediately, thus increasing pressure on the UTU to bargain nationally over crew sizes.

Wage talks involving employes of the Postal Service also are expected to cause problems. Burdened by a heavy deficit, the Postal Service may seek to remove the present no-layoff clause in its contracts with the four big postal unions. That same deficit also could make the service resist more than a moderate wage boost. By law, postal strikes are forbidden, and unresolved issues must be settled by arbitration.

Aside from collective bargaining, labor and management will be clashing head on early in 1978 over legislation that is pending in the Senate to revise the National Labor Relations Act. Already passed by the House of Representatives, the bill would stiffen penalties against companies that commit unfair labor practices, particularly during union organizing drives, and would speed up the process of allowing workers to decide whether to be represented by a union.

Considered "must" legislation by labor, the bill faces either a filibuster or an attempt by opponents to weaken its provisions with amendments when it comes to the Senate floor for debate, probably in February. The AFL-CIO is planning to flood the offices of Senators with more than 1 million letters and postcards urging passage of the legislation.

Spotlight on imports. Labor and business may be less divided if the AFL-CIO makes good its threat to push for passage of legislation in 1978 to stem the tide of imports into this country. Because hundreds of thousands of jobs have been lost to foreign competition, unions are preparing to fight back through political rather than economic means, by seeking a broad system of quotas and tariffs on imported goods.

Some businesses hard hit by imports may line up beside labor on such legislation. The main opposition, in that event, could be the Carter Administration, which has preferred to negotiate voluntary reductions of some imports rather than impose higher tariffs.

So despite the slender bargaining schedule, there still is little assurance that 1978 will be a calm year for either labor or management.

When Strikes Could Flare in '78

Major labor agreements that expire in the coming year—

JAN. Metal-trades council—Ingalls Shipbuilding (13,000 workers)
Retail Clerks—Philadelphia grocery stores (14,000)

FEB. Graphic Arts—New York printing companies (4,750)

MARCH Insurance Workers—Metropolitan Life (6,500)

APRIL Diesel Workers Union—Cummins Engine (6,000)
Retail Clerks—N.Y., N.J. supermarkets (11,200)

MAY Machinists—McDonnell Douglas (11,30
Electrical Workers—Niagara Mohawk Power (7,150)
Hotel and Restaurant Employes—Seatt restaurants, hotels (5,000)

JUNE Retail, Wholesale employes—N.Y. voluntary hospitals (40,000)
Maritime unions—East Coast tankers, freighters (51,700)
Peninsula Shipbuilders Association—Newport News Shipbuilding (16,900)
State, County, Municipal Employes—Pennsylvania State government agencies (14,800)

JULY Retail Clerks—California food stores (53,850)
Hotel and Restaurant Employes—Chicago restaurants (5,000)
Longshoremen, Warehousemen—Pacifi Maritime Association (11,000)
Postal unions—U.S. Postal Service (600,000)

AUG. Electrical Workers—Alabama Power (7,200)
Machinists—Beech Aircraft (6,050)
Marine, Shipbuilding Workers—Bethlehem Steel Shipbuilding (5,300)
Electrical Workers—General Telephone of Florida (8,100)

SEPT. Hotel and Restaurant Employes—Washington, D.C., hotels (8,000)
United Retail Workers—Jewel Companies Chicago supermarkets (14,000)

OCT. Clothing and Textile Workers—children apparel (7,000)
Teamsters—United Parcel, California (4,
Typographical Union—New York-area printing companies (4,000)

NOV. Television, Radio Artists—radio, TV commercials (58,000)
Screen Actors—commercials (32,000)
Machinists—TWA, United Airlines grour service (28,800)
Clothing and Textile Workers—N.Y., N.J., Conn., Mass. laundries (15,000)

DEC. Machinists—Eastern Air Lines ground service (11,000)

8

Now It's Government Itself Pushing Prices Higher and Higher

A wave of federal actions is pounding the economy, boosting costs, keeping cheaper goods off the market—and undermining Carter's hopes for cooling inflation.

Despite all the talk in Washington about curbing inflation, one of the prime factors pushing prices higher and higher is turning out to be the U.S. Government itself.

Jimmy Carter therefore is finding out just how difficult it will be to come even close to his goal of reducing the inflation rate to 4 per cent or less by the end of his first term in office.

Although consumer prices rose only 3.7 per cent in the past three months at a seasonally adjusted annual rate, most economists see a quick return to a rate of 6 to 6½ per cent in 1978.

A major reason: the wave of inflationary pressure caused by Government actions that will hit the economy early next year, atop a series of inflation-fueling steps in recent weeks and months.

The Carter plan to aid the steel industry, announced by the White House on December 6, is the latest price-boosting action. It will, in effect, bar foreign-made steel priced below the costs of the most-efficient overseas producers. Exclusion of the low-priced metal, mostly from Western Europe and Japan, could add to the tabs of thousands of items that are made with steel, from automobiles to refrigerators.

You get details of the President's plan on page 67.

What's ahead. Coming up are increases in Social Security taxes and the minimum wage that will push up costs of doing business for virtually every company in America. The increases, in turn, will be passed along to consumers in the form of higher prices.

In prospect, too, are measures to discourage oil consumption and encourage development of new sources, largely by steps that raise fuel costs for utilities and consumers.

The specifics:

• Increases in Social Security taxes next year will add 6.8 billion dollars to employers' payroll costs under present law—with billions to be added in future years under legislation now pending.

• Starting January 1, the minimum wage will be boosted to $2.65 an hour, compared with the present $2.30. As the floor is lifted, other wages will be bumped up, raising production costs. What's more, the minimum wage will be upped in stages to $3.35 by Jan. 1, 1981.

• Unemployment-insurance taxes paid by business will be hiked by 3 billion dollars in 1978, as a result of congressional action last year. These costs also will be passed along to the public.

Another program moving toward enactment in Congress—the energy package—will have a strong effect on the economy. Solving the energy problem is an overriding federal goal, but it will mean higher fuel prices for everyone, with a ripple effect that will push up costs of items ranging from automobiles to petrochemicals.

Difficult choice. Few in the Administration or Congress want higher prices. But the desire to avoid fueling inflation conflicts with political commitments and realities.

The Government, for instance, has promised to help farmers, who have been selling their products at prices that, on the average, have trended down since 1974. So moves designed to calm farmers' anger are under way, at the expense of consumers.

For example, the minimum price for much of the milk that is sold to the dairies in this country is set by the Agriculture Department. Last spring that price was hiked. The result was an increase of about 6 cents a gallon in the retail price of milk.

Newly ordered cuts in sugar imports

Ways Washington Is Fueling Inflation

Steel
Action
Low-priced imports to be blocked.

Impact
Boost in cost of making many products from autos to refrigerators to new buildings.

Social Security
Action
Employers' taxes to climb 6.8 billion dollars in 1978 under present law.

Impact
Higher business costs that will be passed along to consumers.

Red Tape
Action
Mounting federal paper work and regulations.

Impact
More than 65 billion dollars a year in costs to business and taxpayers.

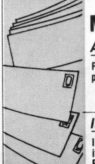

Mail
Action
Proposed increases in postage rates.

Impact
Increase in prices for items delivered by Postal Service.

and increased sugar tariffs are designed to protect U.S. growers. But they also are expected to boost the retail price of sugar about 15 per cent. Sam I. Nakagama, chief economist of the brokerage firm of Kidder, Peabody & Company, estimates that the sugar tariff by itself will add one half a percentage point to the annual inflation rate for food.

Acreage cuts that will restrict the supply of grains, and higher price supports for wheat, corn and other major crops will shore up the price of a broad range of foods. That will help farmers—although not as much as they want. But it will also inflate supermarket prices.

Even though prices at the farm have dipped since '74, retail price tags have climbed, primarily because labor costs of getting the food from the farm to the consumer have jumped 30 per cent during that period.

Import restrictions. Government actions to assist American manufacturers who are hurt by imports also force consumers to pay more.

The Carter Administration has negotiated agreements with foreign producers to reduce exports of shoes and television sets to the U.S. According to Barry Bosworth, director of the Council on Wage and Price Stability, that means fewer low-priced items in the stores, leaving no choice for the consumer but higher-priced goods.

Besides such new Government actions, federal regulations—especially those that call for antipollution equipment—already are making steel, energy, automobiles and other products more expensive.

A study by economist Robert DeFina, of Washington University in St. Louis, puts the 1976 cost to business of complying with federal energy and environmental regulations at 7.8 billion dollars.

The same study claims that Government rules on consumer health and safety add 5 billion dollars to business costs; on-job safety and working conditions, 4 billion. Regulations that cover financial transactions cost business another 1.1 billion. That is in addition to the Government's 3.2-billion-dollar burden of administering the regulations—an amount that must be covered by tax payments.

The total cost of just the major categories of regulations studied amounted to 65.5 billion dollars.

In another study, the U.S. Commission on Federal Paper Work found that Government-generated paper work costs industry and individuals between 34.5 and 41.5 billion dollars.

Vicious cycle. Carter has pledged to make regulations simpler and more predictable, but the evidence so far indicates that there will be more, not less, cost-boosting regulation.

The Coast Guard, for example, is seeking new tanker-safety rules that the oil industry contends would add 1 billion dollars a year to fuel costs. Regulations to implement a tougher mine-safety act passed by Congress will raise coal costs.

All this is in addition to price increases by Government-owned "businesses" that are themselves at the mercy of inflation-spawned costs.

The U.S. Postal Service wants to raise first-class mail rates again, to 16 cents for business letters. Amtrak, the Government-owned rail-passenger system, has upped fares 5 per cent this year.

Finally, there is the massive federal debt, now more than 700 billion dollars, and growing an estimated 80 billion dollars this year. This ocean of red ink puts more and more money into circulation, thus adding to inflationary pressures by making a larger amount of dollars available to chase after today's supply of goods.

President Carter, determined to keep the recovery going, will press for tax cuts in 1978, even if the cuts increase the budget deficit for the year. With more money in consumers' pockets as a result of the tax reduction, businessmen will find it somewhat easier to push up prices to cover increased costs.

It all adds up to a Government that operates like an engine of inflation, and knows it, but seems unable to stop or even slow down.

Minimum Wage

Action

Increase to $2.65 an hour on January 1, from $2.30; more hikes later.

Impact

Wage rates bumped up at all levels.

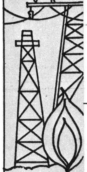

Energy

Action

Expected from Congress: higher taxes, higher price ceilings, other steps to discourage fuel use.

Impact

Extra costs for utilities, industry, consumers.

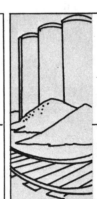

Grain

Action

Price supports raised, acreage farmers may plant reduced.

Impact

Expected increase in prices farmers get and prices in stores.

Red Ink

Action

Increase of 80 billion dollars in public debt in year ending September 30.

Impact

Boost in amount of money in circulation, weakening buying power of dollar.

Sugar

Action

Cuts in imports, increases in tariff.

Impact

15 per cent increase in retail sugar price.

Unemployment Insurance

Action

3-billion-dollar increase in taxes paid by companies in 1978.

Impact

Additional costs passed to consumer as higher prices.

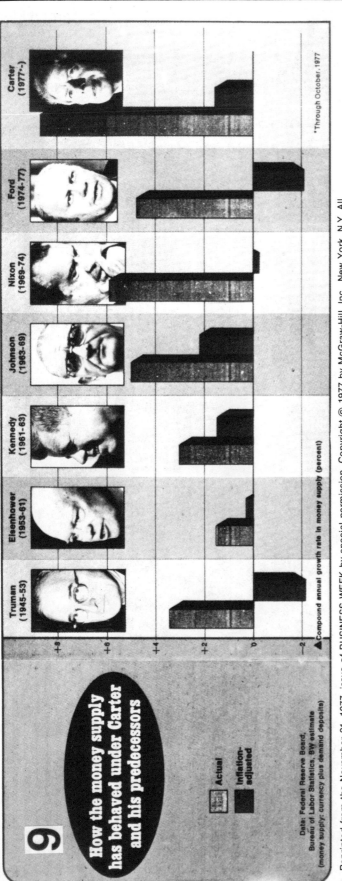

9

How the money supply has behaved under Carter and his predecessors

Truman (1945-53)　Eisenhower (1953-61)　Kennedy (1961-63)　Johnson (1963-69)　Nixon (1969-74)　Ford (1974-77)　Carter (1977-~)

Actual
Inflation-adjusted

▲Compound annual growth rate in money supply (percent)

*Through October, 1977

Data: Federal Reserve Board;
Bureau of Labor Statistics, BW estimate
(money supply: currency plus demand deposits)

Robert McAuley—BW

Reprinted from the November 21, 1977, issue of BUSINESS WEEK by special permission. Copyright © 1977 by McGraw-Hill, Inc., New York, N.Y. All rights reserved.

10

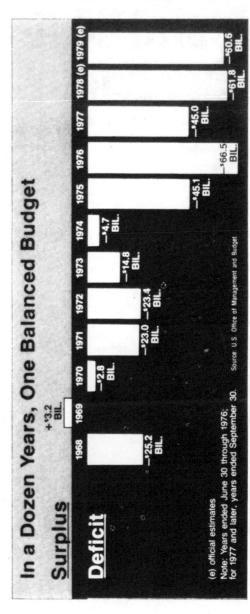

In a Dozen Years, One Balanced Budget

Surplus

Deficit

1968	1969	1970	1971	1972	1973	1974	1975	1976	1977	1978 (e)	1979 (e)
—$25.2 BIL.	+$3.2 BIL.	—$2.8 BIL.	—$23.0 BIL.	—$23.4 BIL.	—$14.8 BIL.	—$4.7 BIL.	—$45.1 BIL.	—$66.5 BIL.	—$45.0 BIL.	—$61.8 BIL.	—$60.6 BIL.

Source: U.S. Office of Management and Budget

(e) official estimates
Note: Years ended June 30 through 1976;
for 1977 and later, years ended September 30.

U.S. NEWS & WORLD REPORT, Jan. 30, 1978

Reprinted from "U.S. News & World Report."
Copyright 1978 U.S. News & World Report, Inc.

35

Federal Debt: Fast Approaching a Trillion

Sometime in the next few months, the mountainous debt owed by the Federal Government will soar past the three-quarter-trillion-dollar mark, well on the way to totaling 1 trillion by the early 1980s.

That path is clearly marked, assuming present trends in spending and borrowing continue—and all signs suggest they will.

As the Pictogram shows, the debt has skyrocketed in recent years.

It took 167 years, from 1776 to 1943, for the Government to go into debt for as much as 100 billion dollars. World War II caused a 47 per cent increase of the debt in just 12 months, in 1943-44.

Nineteen years elapsed before the debt climbed to 300 billion dollars. Since then, the pace has accelerated. The half-trillion point was reached in 1975, and on Nov. 17, 1977, the total hit 700 billion dollars.

The projected deficit of 61.8 billions in the Government's operations for the fiscal year that started October 1 will contribute to the debt. So will borrowing for agencies such as the Postal Service and the Rural Electrification Administration, whose operations are outside the regular budget.

All this is proving increasingly costly for U.S. taxpayers—individuals and corporations alike. Interest alone now amounts to 48.6 billions annually.

Today's federal obligations come to $3,291 for every man, woman and child in the nation, an increase of 8.7 per cent just in the past year. By 1982, if the debt continues on its present course, the burden for every individual will be $4,400.

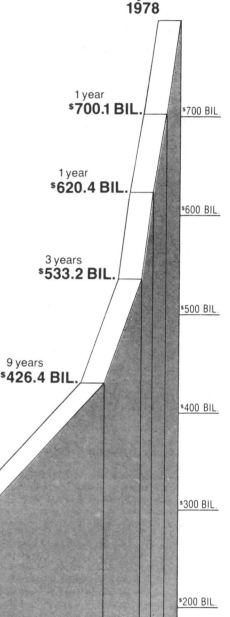

Debt will near or top **$800 BIL.** by end of 1978

1 year **$700.1 BIL.**

1 year **$620.4 BIL.**

3 years **$533.2 BIL.**

9 years **$426.4 BIL.**

19 years **$302.7 BIL.**

PICTOGRAM®

It took 167 years for the debt to top $100 billion...

...Now, it takes only about 1 year to reach each additional $100 billion

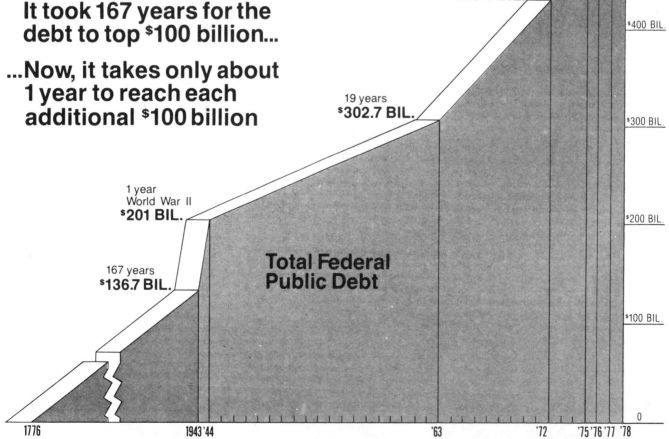

1 year
World War II
$201 BIL.

167 years
$136.7 BIL.

Total Federal Public Debt

1776   1943 '44   '63   '72   '75 '76 '77 '78

Note: Debt totals are as of June 30, except for 1977, which is as of November 17.

Source U S Dept of the Treasury

Carter's Anti-Inflation Pitch

Federal Plan to Restrain Wage-Price Rise Includes 5.5% Cap On Salary Boosts of Some U.S. Employes

By Robert S. Greenberger

WASHINGTON—President Carter committed his personal prestige to the battle against inflation in a strong pitch for broad public cooperation to restrain the rise of prices and wages.

As expected, yesterday's widely publicized speech focused sharply on steps the government itself will take to harness inflation, including a 5.5% cap on pay raises for white-collar federal employes this year and a freeze on the salaries of Executive Branch appointees and senior White House staff members. Carter administration officials view these actions both as the showcase of their anti-inflationary program and so a means of increasing their credibility as they appeal to the private sector for voluntary aid in the war against inflation.

But the President didn't set the 5.5% pay-raise standard as a guideline for the private sector. While answering questions from editors following his speech before the American Society of Newspaper Editors, Mr. Carter reiterated "The level I have set for the private sector—and it's a voluntary-compliance provision—is to take the increases for the last two years and have the 1978 increases be less than that two-year average. And that would apply to both prices and wages."

Excludes Mandatory Controls

The President stressed once again that he has ruled out mandatory wage and price controls as a remedy for curing inflation. "I think, even if inflation should continue to escalate and reach a very high level, that wage and price controls—mandatory wage and price controls—would be ill-advised and also counterproductive," he responded to a questioner. "I don't think they would work. The only instance in which I can think wage and price controls might be applied would be a case of national emergency like an all-out war or some tragedy of that kind where normal economic processes would not be at work."

The only surprise came when the President announced that Robert Strauss, his special trade representative, would assume additional responsibility as "a special counselor on inflation." Mr. Strauss, a skilled negotiator, will coordinate the deceleration efforts of the private sector and "he will have specific authority to speak for me in the public interest," Mr. Carter said.

Mr. Carter also made it clear that he won't hesitate to engage in presidential "jawboning" in an effort to hold down inflation.

"Let me be blunt about this point," he declared. "I am asking American workers to follow the example of federal workers and accept a lower rate of wage increase. In return they have a right to expect a comparable restraint in price increases for the goods and services they buy. Our national interest simply cannot withstand unreasonable increases in prices and wages. It is my responsibility to speak out firmly and clearly when the welfare of our people is at stake."

Acknowledging the intractable nature of the current inflation problem, the President refrained from promising any quick results. "Reducing the inflation rate will not be easy and it will not come overnight," he said.

Pledges U.S. Deficit Restraint

Although the President promised to keep the budget deficit in fiscal 1979, which begins next Oct. 1, "at or below the limits I have proposed," he didn't call for any specific program cuts. Instead, he said he would oppose any new programs that would expand the deficit beyond the projected $59.6 billion. Mr. Carter said actions currently being considered by Congress, including tuition tax credits, highway and urban transit programs, postal service financing, additional defense spending and farm legislation, would add $9 billion to $13 billion to spending next year.

Mr. Carter said "I will work closely with the Congress, and, if necessary, will exercise my veto authority to keep the 1979 budget deficit" at its current projection. He added, "I will veto any farm legislation, beyond what I have already recommended, that would lead to higher food prices or budget expenditures."

When asked if he would veto tuition tax-credit legislation, the President said, "My present intention would be to veto any bill that was costly and was unconstitutional." He said he didn't favor such measures because regardless how limited the initial proposals were, they would "inevitably rapidly grow with each succeeding budget and, the first thing that you know, tuition tax credits would be the major federal expenditure for all education in the United States."

He also said he opposes a rollback this year in Social Security taxes, an idea that is gathering momentum on Capitol Hill. But he added, "I can't say unequivocally that I would veto any such measure that came to my desk."

Reduce Some Purchases

Among other steps the government will take to fight inflation, the President said "all Executive Branch agencies will avoid or reduce the purchase of goods or services whose prices are rising rapidly, unless by so doing he would seriously jeopardize our national security or create serious unemployment."

In addition, he reiterated his theme of cutting "inflationary costs which private industry bears as a result of government regulations." He said he would work to eliminate "unnecessary regulations" and to ensure that future regulations don't impose "unnecessary costs on the American economy." He cited progress made in lowering airline fares and said "the airline regulatory reform legislation must be enacted this year."

The President said he supports "sunset" legislation, which would "ensure that we review these regulatory programs every few years and eliminate or change those that have become outdated." He also called on congressional budget committees to "report regularly to the Congress on the inflationary effect of pending legislation."

Noting that housing and construction costs have soared recently, Mr. Carter, as expected, said he planned to explore ways to expand timber harvests from government and private lands "and other means of increasing lumber yields in ways that would be environmentally acceptable, economically efficient and consistent with sound budget policy." He said he would receive a report on this within 30 days from the Agriculture Department, Interior Department and Council on Environmental Quality.

Urges Hospital-Cost Legislation

The President exhorted Congress to pass legislation to contain hospital costs "as the most effective step we can take toward reasonable hospital prices." He said that this and the airline-deregulation bill are two of the "most important measures the Congress can pass to prevent inflation."

Initial reaction on Capitol Hill to the President's address ranged from comments by some Democrats that Mr. Carter sounded serious to Republican assertions that the speech was empty rhetoric. The House will begin considering today the expensive farm bill passed last week by the Senate, and there were indications that the House would reject the measure. However, even if the bill clears the House, there aren't sufficient votes in Congress to override the President's expected veto.

Some of the bills mentioned by the President, dealing with hospital costs and airline deregulation, currently are bogged down in congressional committees and face uncertain prospects for this year. On the major controversial energy legislation that Congress has wrestled with for a year, the President said, "If Congress does not act, then oil imports will have to be limited by administrative action under present law, which is not the most desirable solution."

Mr. Carter's statement was consistent with what several of his top advisers have been saying for weeks. But the President himself stopped short of specifically saying he would impose import duties in the absence of congressional action, a step Federal Reserve Board Chairman William Miller and others have urged him to take.

Program "Hits at the Roots"

Nevertheless, Mr. Miller said in a statement that the President's program "hits at the roots of the problem; the upward pressure on prices caused by rising costs and a declining dollar, and the growing dependence on imported petroleum."

Mr. Carter said that a Cabinet level task force headed by the Commerce Department will be developing measures to increase U.S. exports and would report to him within 60 days.

13

The Budget and the Economy

ROBERT W. HARTMAN

THE DECISIONS underlying President Carter's proposed budget for 1979 were dominated by considerations of its effect on the economy. The economy was slowly recovering from the 1975 recession and no breakthrough for decelerating inflation was in sight. The budget and economic plan try to maintain economic recovery without boosting the economy so much that inflation is accelerated. This is to be accomplished primarily by stimulating the private sector through tax reduction and by curbing inflation through a voluntary response to federal guidance.

The programmatic emphases in the administration's 1979 budget proposals can best be described as a holding action. In 1977, the new administration was very active, proposing substantial revisions in President Ford's 1978 budget, most of which were accepted, and legislation for a major revision of social security, a new energy program, and welfare reform to take effect in 1981–82. But aside from a few small initiatives, the 1979 budget mainly continues the 1978 programs. There is no evidence that the administration plans to reset national priorities.

■ ■ ■

Federal Policy and Nonfederal Demand

One way of looking at the relation of nonfederal sources of demand to the federal sector is to think of the national economy as a huge plumbing system in which the flow of national product is reduced by drains from the system and enlarged by injections into the system. The nonfederal drains discussed in this chapter can be summarized as:

—personal saving and the surplus of social insurance trust funds of state and local governments;[9]
—business saving, mainly the retained earnings and depreciation allowances of firms;
—operating surpluses of state-local governments; and
—imports.

These drains are shown in table 2-7 for selected full-employment years and for 1977.

9. These have been grouped together because they play a similar role in the economy. When a person is employed in the private sector, surpluses that accumulate in a company-sponsored pension program are counted as "personal saving" in the national income accounts. When, however, the person is employed—say, as a teacher—by a state or local government that participates in a public pension program, any surpluses in those funds are counted as a component of the state-local sector's surplus. With the state-local government work force growing more rapidly than that in the private sector for the last twenty years (state-local employees accounted for 9.3 percent of employees on nonfarm payrolls in 1955 and 15.2 percent in 1977), a spurious reduction in the personal saving rate will appear in the national income accounts. Adding together personal savings and state-local social insurance surplus removes this bias.

Cross references are to material not included in this excerpted version.

The principal nonfederal injections into the flow of national production are domestic investment and exports. At any level of economic activity the federal budget deficit (surplus) must offset any excess (inadequacy) of drains in relation to injections. Thus, in the peak years of 1955–56, a federal surplus was needed at high employment to offset the excess of nonfederal injections over drains. In the 1960s, the prosperity period showed a balance between drains and injections allowing the federal budget to show a balance at full employment. By 1972–73, the nonfederal sectors were saving more than they were investing at full employment, leading to a small federal deficit at full employment.[10]

A major problem for the administration, therefore, was to determine what the balance of drains and injections will be as the economy moves closer to full employment over the next few years. Although there is reason to believe that the drain from personal saving will rise in proportion to GNP from the low levels of 1977, state-local operating surpluses and imports were atypically high in 1977; a small

Table 2-7. Drains from and Injections into the National Economy as a Percentage of GNP, Selected Calendar Years, 1955–77[a]

Item	1955–56	1965–66	1972–73	1977
Drains				
Personal saving plus state-local social insurance fund surplus	4.55	4.91	5.49	4.37
Business saving[b]	11.95	12.48	11.13	12.03
State and local other funds surplus[c]	−0.61	−0.48	0.40	0.72
Imports[d]	5.17	5.30	7.43	10.34
Total	21.06	22.20	24.48	27.48
Injections				
Domestic investment[e]	17.00	16.41	16.46	15.55
Exports[f]	5.34	5.71	7.02	9.29
Federal deficit	−1.28	0.08	1.00	2.64
Total	21.06	22.20	24.48	27.48

Sources: *Economic Report of the President, January 1978*, pp. 257, 266–67, 343; Bureau of Economic Analysis, *The National Income and Product Accounts of the United States, 1929–74 Statistical Tables* (GPO, 1977), pp. 108–09; *Survey of Current Business*, vol. 57 (July 1977), p. 32; *Survey of Current Business*, vol. 58 (February 1978), pp. 2, 6–7. Figures are rounded.
a. Average of percentages for each year.
b. Gross retained earnings plus statistical discrepancy.
c. State-local surplus in the national income and product accounts, excluding surplus of social insurance funds.
d. Imports of goods and services plus net transfers and interest paid to foreigners.
e. Residential construction, business fixed investment, and inventory investment.
f. Includes net capital grants of $0.7 billion received by the United States in 1972.

reduction in these drains, relative to GNP, could be expected in 1978 and 1979. On balance, then, the unusually high ratio of drains to GNP of 1977 were forecast to remain about the same for the next few years.

The outlook for nonfederal injections relative to GNP was not very optimistic. Residential construction, already at a peak level in 1977, would do well to maintain its share of GNP. Exports, which depend heavily on real economic growth among U.S. trading partners, seemed to have little near-term potential for injecting demand into the economy. Business investment, though showing signs of life, gave little evidence of a dramatic upturn.

10. There is reason to believe that fiscal (and monetary) policy was too stimulative in 1972–73, resulting in excessive demand for goods and services.

It thus seemed unwise to allow the historically high federal deficit of 1977—about 2.6 percent of GNP—to fall.[11] If this deficit, which seemed necessary to maintain real national product growth at 5 percent in 1977, were to be reduced without any offsetting increases in domestic investment or exports, the rate of output growth would be reduced, making the ascent to full employment that much longer and less certain.

. . .

Fiscal Policy in the President's Budget

The fiscal policy implied by the Carter administration's 1979 budget is designed with two apparent goals in mind: first, to offset the tendency toward growing fiscal restraint under existing tax and spending programs; and second, to begin a long-term program of reducing the relative size of the federal budget.

The Fiscal Policy Proposals

In discussing the impact of fiscal policy on the economy, attention is often paid to the budget deficit or surplus. However, the budget deficit incorporates two quite different aspects of federal fiscal activities: first, the automatic response of the budget (especially receipts) to swings in economic activity, and second, discretionary actions undertaken to affect the economy. To focus on the second of these, economists often rely on a measure called the full-employment surplus, which is the difference between receipts and expenditures of the federal government measured at full-employment GNP.[15] Changes in the full-employment surplus can measure the federal budget's effects on the economy undistorted by the budget's response to the economy. An increase in the full-employment surplus indicates that the federal budget is becoming more restrictive; a decline in the full-employment surplus (or a larger full-employment deficit) signifies increasing stimulation of the economy by the federal government. An unchanged full-employment surplus means that fiscal policy is, in effect, neutral—it is neither adding to nor restraining the rate of growth implicit in the nonfederal sector.

Historically, the full-employment surplus was positive (receipts exceeded outlays at full employment) in the 1950s and early 1960s. But since 1965, the full-employment budget has been in surplus in only two years (1969 and 1974), and the full-employment deficit averaged about $7 billion (0.7 percent of full-employment GNP) in the decade 1966–75.[16] In relation to 1978 estimates of full-employment GNP, this average would translate into a full-employment deficit of about $15 billion.

Table 2-9 summarizes the course of the full-employment surplus over the six half-years that make up fiscal years 1977–79. The first

11. Naturally, if exports or domestic investment were to rise, there would be an automatic reduction in the federal deficit as higher incomes drove up federal receipts. The presentation of the federal deficit as an offset to nonfederal drains in table 2-7 does not distinguish between such a passive adjustment in the deficit and a deliberate attempt to use the deficit to maintain or enlarge aggregate demand. This distinction is made in the discussion of fiscal policy later in this chapter.

15. The concept of full-employment GNP is the same as potential GNP (see table 2-1). In 1977–79, this corresponds to the GNP that would be produced if the unemployment rate were 4.9 percent.

16. The full-employment budget data on which this discussion is based are from *Economic Report of the President, January 1978*, p. 55, and unpublished data from the Council of Economic Advisers.

thing to note is that the federal budget swung sharply toward stimulus between the first half of fiscal 1977 and the first half of 1978. This

Table 2-9. Full-Employment Surplus under Current Law and as Proposed by the Administration, Fiscal Years 1977–79[a]

Billions of dollars

| | Fiscal year[b] | | | | | |
Item	1977:I	1977:II	1978:I	1978:II	1979:I	1979:II
Full-employment surplus under current law[c]	−9.1	−19.1	−27.2	−15.4	−3.4	12.5
Effect of administration proposals[d]	...	...	−1.6	−5.5	−31.0	−33.4
Spending initiatives	...	...	...	−2.6	−5.0	−5.2
Energy proposals	...	...	−0.2	−0.2	−1.5	−0.4
Tax simplification and reform	...	...	−1.4	−2.7	−22.5	−25.5
Excise tax and unemployment tax changes	...	...	0.0	0.0	−2.0	−2.3
Full-employment surplus as proposed	−9.1	−19.1	−28.8	−20.9	−34.4	−20.9

Sources: Unpublished quarterly data from the Council of Economic Advisers; *Survey of Current Business*, vol. 58 (February 1978), pp. 25–27; and author's estimates.

a. National income accounts basis; semiannually at seasonally adjusted annual rates.

b. The Roman numerals after the year designate the first and second halves of the year; for example, 1977:I stands for the first six months of fiscal 1977, or October 1, 1976, to March 31, 1977.

c. The full-employment surplus is the difference between full-employment receipts and expenditures. Full-employment receipts under current law means receipts that would accrue at full employment, under the tax laws existing on January 1, 1978, with temporary provisions extended. Full-employment expenditures are equivalent to those that would prevail at full employment under the Office of Management and Budget's concept of a current services budget.

d. Estimated for actual gross national product.

$18 billion swing was attributable to rapid expenditure growth and a small income tax cut in calendar 1977 that more than offset growing income taxes and a payroll tax increase in early 1978.[17]

Under current tax and spending laws, however, this fiscal position of the government would more than reverse itself between 1978:I and 1979:II. The underlying fiscal policy would move from a $27 billion full-employment deficit in 1978:I to a $13 billion full-employment surplus eighteen months later. The reason for this growing "fiscal drag" is that even at a continuous full-employment level (that is, trend real economic growth of 3.5 percent) tax receipts rise proportionately much more than expenditures under current law; receipts rise fast generally because income tax rates on increments to income are greater than the tax rate on previous dollars of income and, in this case, because payroll taxes are scheduled to rise much faster than income beginning in 1979.

The administration's long-term fiscal plan may be readily discerned by looking at the changes in current law it proposes and their effect on the full-employment surplus. The salient fact is that the proposed full-employment deficit for the last half of fiscal 1979 ($21 billion) is almost the same as the full-employment deficit two years earlier ($19 billion in 1977:II). In effect, the administration's fiscal plan for the 1977–79 period as a whole can best be characterized as one of neither restraint nor stimulus compared to policies whose effect was being felt at the time the budget was being drawn up. The idea, in other words, is to end the period with a fiscal policy no more stimu-

17. This discussion does not take into account revisions in the budget for a spending "shortfall." See the final section of this chapter and appendix A.

lative than at the start, making it possible to shift toward restraint as full employment is reached in the near future. This broad fiscal prescription is a passive one, designed to offset only the federal government's own tendency to slow the economy and to leave economic growth to the forces in the nonfederal sectors of the economy.

The proposed fiscal policy is slightly more stimulative than that of the past decade. The full-employment deficit for 1978 and 1979 averages about 1.1 percent of full-employment GNP. The administration's justification for this is twofold. First, the unemployment rate is well above the average for the past decade. Second, nonfederal drains on the economy—especially the international trade deficit and state-local government surpluses—are high, necessitating an unusually high injection of demand by the federal government until these drains are reversed or private investment picks up steam.

For 1978 and 1979, the administration's fiscal policy mostly reflects a transition from the 1977 stimulus program to its new proposals. In the first half of 1978, spending from the stimulus program enacted in 1977 peaks. For the second half of 1978, the administration seems willing to allow a slight tightening of fiscal policy. In the first half of fiscal 1979, there is a sharp increase in the full-employment deficit as the proposed tax cuts go into effect.[18] By the second half of 1979, the underlying fiscal drag restores fiscal policy to where it was two years earlier. Thus, the essence of the administration's short-run plan is the expectation that nonfederal demand will strengthen somewhat over the course of 1978 so that it will supplant the slight reduction in fiscal stimulus. For fiscal 1979, the administration's bet is that real growth can be maintained at the previous year's level by adopting a policy of neutralizing the built-in fiscal drag.

Composition of the Fiscal Program

The decision to aim for an offset to fiscal drag in fiscal 1979 meant that the administration had to choose among alternative tax cuts or spending initiatives amounting to about $30 billion.[19]

Table 2-10 shows that the administration proposed most of the offsetting on the tax side—about three-quarters of the total new fiscal action consists of tax cuts. Spending programs were boosted less than 2 percent above the current services level of fiscal 1979.

Why tax cuts to offset fiscal drag? There seem to be several reasons. One of these is President Carter's promise to limit the size of the federal government. This has led to an emphasis in the long-range fiscal plan on the goal of limiting outlays to 21 percent of GNP by fiscal 1981. In 1977, outlays were 21.9 percent of GNP. With the sharp increases in President Carter's stimulus program (and significant inherited growth in national defense spending), the ratio in 1978 rises to 22.6 percent. By limiting spending increases in 1979, the administration is able to project federal spending of 22.0 percent of

18. Not too much should be made of semiannual swings in fiscal policy because it takes time for the nonfederal sector to adjust. For example, although the full effect of the cut in tax liabilities is shown in the first half of 1979, it will probably influence spending before that and the full effect on spenders will not be complete for some time beyond 1979:I.

19. Yet another alternative would have been a planned easing of monetary policy, accompanied by less fiscal stimulus. Whatever might have been the merits of such an approach, it had an insuperable shortcoming. The weakness of the U.S. balance-of-payments position made it incautious to lower interest rates—such an action drives funds out of the United States and its international accounts suffer.

Table 2-10. Outlays and Receipts in the Administration's Proposed Budget,
Fiscal Years 1977–79[a]

Billions of dollars

Item	1977	1978	1979 Current services	Proposed	Difference
Outlays	401.9	462.2	492.4	500.2	7.8
Receipts	356.9	400.4	463.8[b]	439.6	−24.3
Deficit	45.0	61.8	28.6[b]	60.6	32.0

Source: *The Budget of the United States Government, Fiscal Year 1979*, p. 11; *Special Analyses, Budget of the United States Government, Fiscal Year 1979*, p. 19. Figures are rounded.

a. This table and subsequent ones in this chapter are on a unified budget basis. This differs from the national income and product accounts basis used in previous tables primarily by including financial transactions in the outlay estimates and by estimating receipts on a cash, rather than a liability, basis. See *Special Analyses, Budget of the United States Government, Fiscal Year 1979*, pp. 45–68, for a description of these differences.

b. These are the receipts and deficit that would accrue if the economy were to reach the levels forecast by the administration and if tax laws of 1978, including temporary provisions, were extended.

GNP in 1979, which is a step in the intended direction.[20]

Also discouraging the use of federal spending to offset drag is the apparent political difficulty of instituting truly temporary spending programs. The administration's economic stimulus program of 1977, for example, featured a sharp rise in the number of public service employment slots. This was defended both within the government and publicly as a temporary measure that would phase down as the economy recovered. In the 1979 budget, proposed for a period in which unemployment is expected to be about 1.5 percentage points below its level at the time temporary public service employment was first boosted, the administration has proposed no phasing down at all.[21] This lesson must have sunk in: most spending programs, regardless of their special nature at inception, are hard to pare. This implies that, although a case could be made for additional temporary spending in fiscal 1979, acceptance of the case by the administration would mean removing spending items from its long-run agenda because the temporary programs would persist. As pointed out in chapter 10, the agenda for spending programs is already quite full (especially if 21 percent of GNP in fiscal 1981 is regarded as a rigid commitment), and the administration would be squeezing out preferred spending programs if it accepted "permanent temporary" ones.

A third argument for emphasizing tax cuts is that they can be carried out quickly. As indicated in table 2-9, fiscal drag begins during the second half of fiscal 1978 and then becomes sharply restrictive in the first half of fiscal 1979 (in large part because of an increase in payroll taxes on January 1, 1979). Most spending stimulus programs could not be put into effect quickly enough to offset forces of such magnitude. The local public works program, as an example of federally assisted stimulus, would not peak until about a year and a half after federal allocations were made, which would be about one year too late.[22] A tax cut, on the other hand, can be put into effect quickly. During the administration's deliberations over tax cuts, the newspapers reported that it would seek an effective date of July 1, 1978, for its program. However, the congressional budget process would have made such an early start difficult, so the effective date for

20. See chapter 10 for whether the 1981 goal is likely to be reached.

21. New proposals under the Comprehensive Employment and Training Act would bring the level down in later years. See chapter 3.

22. The public service employment program, however, was carried out quite rapidly, as promised. See chapter 3.

individual income tax cuts was pushed ahead to October 1.[23] The administration clearly hopes that enactment of its tax legislation in the summer of 1978 will begin to affect spending right away, even if the effective date is October. While that hope may be ambitious, it is almost certain that tax changes will affect spending before any feasible expenditure program could.

Finally, and probably most important for calculating the politics of any fiscal proposal, were the facts that a combination of factors has been raising personal taxes and that members of Congress, many up for reelection in 1978, have been receiving complaints from constituents about the need for tax relief. The most visible tax change, of course, is the sharp rise in the social security tax slated for 1979. Fashioning an income tax cut that is progressive and at the same time offsets the social security tax increase for most workers necessitates a personal tax cut on the order of the $18 billion reduction proposed by President Carter.[24]

Although there is economic sense in trying to offset fiscal drag in general, there is little economic sense in offsetting the increase in one tax by a decrease in another tax. People's real incomes are also affected by many things besides the payroll tax hike, such as inflation (which raises taxes disproportionately), expanding federal grant programs (some of the grants-in-aid to state governments are resulting in tax cuts by states), growing transfer programs (the large increase in student aid discussed in chapter 4 is initially the equivalent of reduced tuition for a large segment of the population), new excise taxes (such as those proposed for energy), and so on. However, from a political point of view, there is obvious appeal in emphasizing direct comparisons showing that income tax gains offset payroll tax losses.

TAX CHANGES. The tax cuts proposed by the administration amount to about 5 percent of total federal taxes (table 2-11). The program has three principal components.

Individual incomes taxes are reduced by about 9 percent in fiscal 1979 by means of a cut of about 11 percent in tax rates and a revenue gain of about 2 percent from a reform package. The cuts are the result of replacing personal exemptions with a tax credit of $240 per person and a reduction in the marginal tax rate for each income bracket from 14–70 percent to 12–68 percent. Most of the revenue increases in the reform package derive from the elimination of the deductibility of state sales taxes and gasoline taxes and a tightening of the rules for deducting medical and casualty expenses.

As noted in chapter 5, where the tax changes are discussed in greater detail, these tax reductions are heavily tilted toward taxpayers with incomes under $30,000. Since these consumers are normally ones who spend a large fraction of the income they receive, they might be expected to consume more after the tax reduction.

Corporation income taxes are cut by 7.4 percent. (But because the proposed changes are phased in, this fraction rises to 9 percent in 1980.) The largest reduction by far is accomplished through a cut in the corporation tax rate from 48 percent to 45 percent (with

23. Under the congressional budget process the second concurrent resolution for fiscal 1978 set a floor on tax receipts of $397 billion. Any tax legislation that would reduce receipts below that level in 1978 requires passage of a third concurrent resolution, just as President Carter's 1977 stimulus package did. Members of Congress seem reluctant to consider third concurrent resolutions every year.

24. See chapter 5 for a full discussion of the incidence of recent tax changes.

Table 2-11. The Administration's Tax Reduction Program, Fiscal Years 1978–79
Amounts in billions of dollars

| Tax | 1978 | 1979 | | Difference between 1979 proposal and current services | |
		Current services	Proposed[a]	Amount[a]	Percent
Individual income	178.8	214.0	195.7	−18.3	−8.6
Corporation income	58.9	68.8	63.7	−5.1	−7.4
Excise	20.2	18.7	17.6	−1.1	−5.9
Social insurance	124.1	142.5	141.9	−0.6	−0.4
Other	18.3	19.8	19.7	−0.2	−1.0
Total	400.4	463.8	438.6	−25.3	−5.5
Addenda					
Tax reduction[b]					
Individual				−22.5	−10.5
Corporation				−6.3	−9.2
Tax reform[b]					
Individual				4.2	2.0
Corporation				1.1	1.6

Sources: *The Budget of the United States Government, Fiscal Year 1979*, p. 49; *Special Analyses, Budget of the United States Government, Fiscal Year 1979*, pp. 11, 19; Congressional Budget Office, *An Analysis of the President's Budgetary Proposals for Fiscal Year 1979* (CBO, 1978), p. 12. Figures are rounded.
a. Excludes energy tax proposals, which would lower individual income taxes by $5.6 billion and corporation income taxes by $1.2 billion, and raise excise taxes by $7.9 billion, for a net tax increase of $1.1 billion.
b. Excludes energy tax, excise tax, and social insurance tax proposals.

corresponding reductions in the rates on profits of less than $50,000) effective in October 1978. Furthermore, the 10 percent investment tax credit would be extended to cover new structures, and the maximum credit available to a corporation would be increased so that it could offset up to 90 percent of the tax liability otherwise owed. These reductions are partly offset by proposed business tax reforms (table 2-11). The most important of these are limitations on the deductibility of corporate yachts, business meals, and other entertainment expenses and a phasing out of the deferral of tax on export earnings and on profits from abroad. While the extension of the investment tax credit to structures should strengthen this particularly weak component of investment, the corporate rate cut is probably not as effective an investment stimulant as other business tax changes (mainly those allowing more liberal treatment of depreciation).

The administration proposes a small reduction in two other taxes. Repealing the telephone excise tax and reducing the payroll tax on unemployment insurance is a token gesture toward reducing government taxes that feed directly into private sector costs. As the combined revenue loss is $1.6 billion in a $2 trillion economy, such a measure is a droplet in a sea of other changes.

SPENDING CHANGES. The proposed overall spending increase for fiscal 1979 over 1978 amounts to about $40 billion. Only $7.8 billion of this represents an increase from the 1979 level of current services. Most of the increase in spending, in other words, results from more or less automatic increases in entitlement payments (such as social security, federal employee retirement, Medicare, and Medicaid), in interest on the federal debt, in annual pay raises for federal workers, and in military procurement spending as a result of past increases in the defense budget (see table 2-12).

The $7.8 billion increase above current services represents only about 1.5 percent of the budget. When the budget was introduced, there were only three domestic initiatives listed that involved substantial expenditures in fiscal 1979.

First, the President's energy proposal contained two large spending items. One was the accelerated development of a strategic petroleum reserve, scheduled to reach 1 billion barrels by 1985. The other was

Table 2-12. Composition of Changes in Outlays from Fiscal Year 1978 to Fiscal Year 1979

Billions of dollars

Item	Amount
Outlays, fiscal year 1978	462.2
Increases mandated under current law	**30.2**
Social security	10.6
Medicare and Medicaid	5.5
Pay and retirement for federal employees	5.6
Defense (excluding pay and retirement)	5.9
Net interest	4.4
Farm price supports	−3.7
All other	1.9
Current services outlays, fiscal year 1979	**492.4**
Initiatives of the President	**7.8**
Energy programs	3.4
Education, training, employment, and social services	1.0
Defense	1.0
Allowance for contingencies	1.7
All other increases	2.5
Hospital cost increase limitations	−0.7
Social security changes	−0.6
All other reductions	−0.5
Outlays proposed by the President, fiscal year 1979	**500.2**

Sources: *The Budget of the United States Government, Fiscal Year 1979*, pp. 456–69; *Special Analyses, Budget of the United States Government, Fiscal Year 1979*, pp. 17, 20, 33–34.

a variety of rebates to offset the administration's proposed taxes on crude oil and on "gas guzzler" automobiles.[25]

Second, the administration proposed a number of initiatives in education and training. The most significant increases in outlays are for a private sector manpower program ($250 million) and for youth employment programs ($273 million). Less significant in 1979, but presaging large spending increases in future years, are the administration's education proposals. Substantial increases were announced in the budget for aid to disadvantaged children (title I of the Elementary and Secondary Education Act) and other elementary and secondary education programs (training and education programs are discussed in chapters 3 and 4).

The other major "initiative" was carried in the budget as a $1.7 billion "allowance for contingencies" (table 2-12). By early spring, the contingencies had arrived. First, in an attempt to head off a tuition tax credit plan gaining momentum in Congress, the administration proposed a student grant and loan alternative, with estimated outlays of $200 million in 1979 (see chapter 4 for details). Second, in March the President announced his national urban policy, which implied additional spending in 1979 of $742 million spread among a variety of programs. (Tax reductions of $1.7 billion were also proposed; see

25. These are discussed in Joseph A. Pechman, ed., *Setting National Priorities: The 1978 Budget* (Brookings Institution, 1977), chap. 10.

chapter 6.)

Beyond these initiatives, the administration supported small increases above current service levels in hundreds of different programs, but there are few cutbacks from current service levels. The most significant of these are listed in table 2-12: a repeat of the administration's request for legislation to control hospital costs and some previously tendered proposals to curb social security benefits. A modest effort to reduce impact aid for education and to reduce pay increases for federal blue-collar employees are also part of the President's program.

．．．

Evaluation of the Economic Program

One of the perils faced by every administration's economic plan is that the assumptions on which it is based will be overturned by events that are difficult to forecast. Since the President's budget has to make assumptions about the economy as much as two years in advance, such unanticipated events are guaranteed to occur. But even by the spring of 1978, there were an uncommon number of surprises. Among these were (1) an abnormally cold, wet winter that reduced production and sales in the first two months of 1978; (2) a sharp lowering of the exchange value of the dollar in the early months of 1978, which led to an increase in short-term interest rates; (3) a prolonged coal strike, which was settled in late March only after wage concessions that by any measure are inflationary were granted; (4) a revision of unemployment statistics by the Department of Labor showing that unemployment had declined substantially throughout 1977 instead of being stuck at a fixed rate after April as the earlier data had showed (the revised series showed an unemployment rate in February 1978 of 6.1 percent, *below* the administration's goal of 6.2 percent for the end of 1978); and (5) in March 1978, the Office of Management and Budget lowered its estimates of federal spending in fiscal 1978 by about $9 billion on the basis of actual spending in the first few months of that year, which showed another "shortfall" developing (see appendix A).

Even without these postbudget events, the administration's inflation forecast was dubious. It predicted consumer price increases in 1978 and 1979 at a 6 percent rate, despite the several special factors —payroll tax increases, minimum wage increases, dollar devaluation —that were known to be putting upward pressure on prices. This forecast could be correct only with a substantial deceleration of food prices, a very modest rise in energy prices, and some success with the voluntary wage-price program.[32] All of these seem overoptimistic.

As indicated in chapter 7, food prices are likely to rise faster than the administration assumed. Moreover, by early spring Congress was considering farm legislation that would raise prices further. (President Carter indicated he would veto such a measure.)

Energy prices may be affected by the decline in the exchange rate of the dollar. The OPEC cartel sets prices in dollars and the portfolios of the major OPEC holders of surpluses are primarily in dollar form. The deterioration of the buying power of oil-production income caused by the decline in the dollar's value gives OPEC an "excuse"

32. See *Economic Report of the President, January 1978*, pp. 80–81.

for another round of price increases. These would presumably be tempered by OPEC's assessment of the demand for oil and the consequences of a price raise.

Equally in doubt is the contribution of the voluntary anti-inflation program. For such a program to have any chance of moderating wage and price increases, an administration would have to demonstrate by word and deed that it was serious about making deceleration of inflation a high-priority goal for government actions, and it would have to take steps to ensure that the private sector modified its behavior. Although the April anti-inflation message started the ball rolling on government actions, the response of the private sector is the key to the voluntary anti-inflation strategy. It is too early to tell what that response will be.

The postbudget news that unemployment is closer to the full-employment range than previously believed and that the cost of imports will rise even more as a result of further devaluation leads to the conclusion that inflation for 1978 is likely to be higher than the forecast rate. By April, some private forecasting services were predicting a rise of nearly 7 percent in consumer prices for 1978. For 1979 and the years beyond, the chances of a decelerating inflation rest on whether the administration's anti-inflation program succeeds.

The administration's forecast of real economic growth of about 4.75 percent for both 1978 and 1979 seems to be consistent with the fiscal policy it advanced, which would raise expenditures and cut taxes just about enough to offset what otherwise would be a restrictive change in the federal budget. Thus the administration's forecast of real growth depends primarily on the expectation that accelerated growth in business fixed investment and net exports will offset a somewhat slower growth in consumption and a leveling off of housing expenditures. Although the forecast was at the optimistic end of the range of private forecasts, it was not considered seriously out of line.

Postbudget events do not significantly change this evaluation. The budget shortfall in 1978 does raise some doubts about growth in the second half of 1978, but these may be offset if production makes up for winter delays and the coal strike and if stronger net exports result from the decline in the exchange value of the dollar.

The inflation-raising consequences of early developments in 1978 may, however, affect real growth in 1978 and 1979 by changing monetary policy or expectations. If inflation accelerates, and especially if it is accompanied by only a gradual improvement in the U.S. balance of trade, there will be strong pressure on the Federal Reserve to "do something." If the Fed responds by slowing monetary growth and allowing interest rates to rise, the administration's real growth forecast will prove too high. Business investment and construction will fall short of the forecast growth. And even if the Federal Reserve were to maintain credit flows, an acceleration of inflation might discourage investment if corporate leaders regarded it as worsening the long-term economic outlook. In all, the real growth forecast seems more fragile than when the budget was formulated.

But the improved unemployment picture may make the administration accept some slowing in its forecast growth.

The President's budget is by no means the last word on fiscal policy. Congress must pass on all the proposed changes in the budget, and it may well differ on both the overall fiscal plan and the details. Indeed, for the budget to emerge from Congress in an election year with the modest spending increases proposed by the President would be quite unusual. All the evidence, moreover, indicates that most of the administration's proposed tax reforms are unpopular. These factors point to a more stimulative budget. Nonetheless, it is hard to imagine that Congress will show an even larger deficit than the President proposed at a time when inflation is quickening. This problem may be solved in 1978 by projecting spending shortfalls into the 1979 budget, which would allow Congress to increase spending for some programs more than the President proposed without taking the unpopular action of raising the deficit. But as the economy moves closer to full employment, some politically unpopular budget choiccs will have to be made.

By Milton Friedman

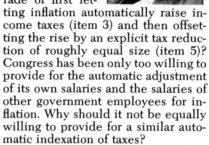

Tax Shenanigans

The President has recommended and Congress is likely to approve:

1. A whopping increase in the social-security tax on wages.

2. Heavy new taxes and substantial increases in existing taxes as part of the so-called energy bill.

In addition:

3. Inflation will automatically raise income-tax rates by pushing individuals into higher brackets, reducing the real value of exemptions and deductions stated in dollars, and artificially overstating income subject to tax through paper capital gains and inadequate depreciation allowances.

4. Accelerating inflation will automatically raise the hidden tax that has been imposed on holders of government-issued money and long-term debt—you would not be wrong to regard the green pieces of paper you carry in your pocket as receipts for taxes paid.

5. President Carter has said he will recommend cuts in individual and corporate income taxes to offset the increases under items 1 and 2. The rumored size of the cuts would, as it happens, just about equal the automatic increase under item 3.

PUZZLES

Query: Why increase taxes on wages (item 1) and then propose to offset the increase by reducing taxes on income (item 5)?

Answer: In order to continue deceiving voters about the true character of social security and thereby increase the fraction of their income they are willing to have the government take in taxes.

Social security is *not* a system under which "nine out of ten working people in the United States are now building protection for themselves and their families" (as HEW misleadingly describes it). Social security *is a* system under which nine out of ten working people pay taxes to finance payments to persons not working. There is little connection between the taxes an individual pays and the amount he is entitled to receive.

Promises *have* outrun resources. The social-security system *is* in trouble. But it would be far preferable to bring into the open the welfare component of the system by drawing on general revenues than to raise still higher the wage tax—in my opinion, one of the worst taxes on the books.

Query: Why go through the charade of first letting inflation automatically raise income taxes (item 3) and then offsetting the rise by an explicit tax reduction of roughly equal size (item 5)? Congress has been only too willing to provide for the automatic adjustment of its own salaries and the salaries of other government employees for inflation. Why should it not be equally willing to provide for a similar automatic indexation of taxes?

Answer: If you were a congressman, would you want to give up a system that provides more tax revenue for you to spend, yet at the same time lets you vote for tax reduction? In addition, this system has facilitated an increase in the effective graduation of the income tax, thereby continuing the process of imposing heavier taxes on the productive members of society and granting larger subsidies to the unproductive.

Query: Why impose heavy taxes on energy and then propose either to rebate them to consumers or to offset them by other tax reductions?

Answer: The *ostensible* reason is to promote energy conservation. But that objective would be better served by setting energy prices free and letting the market allocate energy. The real reasons are to transfer control of energy from the market to a government bureaucracy (i.e., to socialize energy), and to redistribute income from some groups to others.

THE BOTTOM LINE

These measures have little to do with the total tax burden on the American people. That burden is measured by the amount that government spends, not by the receipts that are labeled "taxes." If government spends more than it receives in the form of "taxes," you pay the difference—in concealed form.

Neither the President nor the Democratic leadership in Congress has proposed to reduce the fraction of your income spent by government. Hence, the bottom line is that *President Carter and the Congressional leadership are proposing to raise, not lower, the total tax burden on the American people.* The disputes about taxes are important both as a smoke screen and because they *will* affect who bears the burden.

WHAT'S IN THE BUDGET, AND WHO PAYS THE BILL?

D&S spent much of Boston's blizzard-induced state of emergency last month poring over Jimmy Carter's fiscal 1979 federal budget. The budget turned out to be a lot like the man himself: the closer you look, the less you see.

Covering the twelve months beginning October 1978, this budget is the first prepared entirely by Carter's administration. The people who promised to shake up the capital have produced a tax and spending plan that's a masterpiece of business-as-usual. It's designed to avoid offending any strong interest groups too much, to promote confidence among corporate executives, and to change as little as possible about government policy.

It's hardly shocking to discover that the chief executive is not about to keep a number of his campaign promises. What politician ever does? But it's worth looking at Candidate Carter's contradictory picture of the future in order to see how far short President Carter inevitably had to fall. His promises included:

• Less big government — specifically, a smaller share of the nation's Gross National Product being spent by federal agencies. Along with this was supposed to come "zero-base budgeting," a system requiring all departments to justify their entire funding requests from scratch, as if all programs were new.

• A job for every American willing and able to work;

• A $5 to $7 billion cut in military spending;

• A completely revamped tax code closing the loopholes for the rich;

• Major new programs to reform the welfare system, aid the cities, and provide national health insurance.

• A balanced budget by 1980.

There were two unspoken messages in this hodgepodge of conflicting plans. To business, Carter was projecting himself as a "fiscally responsible" Democrat; to organized labor, liberals, and minority groups, he was the man who would end the Nixon-Ford hard times, loosen the purse strings, and provide jobs and services.

The Frugal Half-a-Trillion

As Carter turned to the business of preparing a real-world budget, his advisers insisted that continued stimulation of the economy was necessary to keep business profits and production recovering and to keep the unemployment rate moving downwards toward a (still high) level of 6% by the end of 1978. But he still needed to demonstrate that he was not a free spender, and he had to keep a few promises. Enter

the main features of the budget and tax plan he unveiled late in January:

• A budget deficit (more being spent than comes in from taxes) projected at $61 billion, the same as fiscal 1978. When the government spends more than it collects, there's more money around to buy products, bolster profits, and pay workers. Budget deficits have been the mechanism by which all administrations since World War II have jolted the economy out of its tendency toward recession.

• Total spending of $500.2 billion. Although this half-a-trillion-dollar budget is, as usual, a record high, it represents an increase of only 2% over what the expected 6% inflation rate would add to the 1978 spending level. That's a real increase just big enough to ensure that few programs would have to be cut, but just small enough to nudge the government's share of the Gross National Product down from 22½% to 22% (at least according to the Administration economists' projections of a healthy, growing GNP).

• A tax cut (contributing to the deficit) of $23.5 billion for individuals and $8.4 billion for corporations. The cut is coupled with a scattershot collection of "reform" proposals which would eventually deprive corporations of about $2 billion worth of loopholes and would arrange the effect of the individual cuts so that any family of four would save about $300, whether their income was $10,000 or $100,000.

We'll take the two sides of the budget in turn. First the spending, then the taxes.

Zero-Base Xeroxing

Only whoever pushed all the preliminary paper can tell us wheth-

Dollars & Sense magazine, 324 Somerville Ave., Somerville, MA 02143 (monthly, $7.50/yr.).

er this document was truly concocted through zero-base budgeting. But *xerox*-base budgeting seems much more likely. Agency by agency, line by line, it shows spending increases just slightly larger than necessary to maintain the current level of services.

Alan Greenspan, chairman of the Council of Economic Advisers under Gerald Ford, commented, "If Carter's economic and budget messages did not have his name on them, I would not know which Administration had issued them."

Welfare payments, Medicaid, food stamps, public housing, and rent supplements, for example, account for 5.3% of Carter's proposed budget; in the fiscal 1976 proposal, Ford's first, they accounted for 5.0%. Ford wanted to turn around the trend of spending a declining share of the budget on the military, which had been going on since protests at home and defeat abroad ended the Vietnam escalation in 1968. So does Carter.

The major difference is that Carter might get what he wants. Congress wouldn't go along with Ford's hawkish plans for the Bicentennial budget, and the military share has continued to drop slightly — from 26.2% in 1975 to an estimated 23.3% in 1978. But Carter might be able to sell his proposed $10 billion military increase to his fellow Democrats and hold the line for the Pentagon at 23.5%. (This figure for the military share of the budget does not include either military aid or costs of past wars which the government is required to keep paying, such as veterans benefits and interest.)

Carter, unlike Ford, serves some butter along with the guns. Not much, mind you, but enough to demonstrate some concern for public services. Examples are some extra Title I education money (for low-income areas, remedial reading, etc.), some extra community clinic money, and a slight change in funding formulas which will allow localities to shift more highway construction aid to mass transit projects.

Of course, there are some cuts. There's more money for clinics, but less for Public Health Service hospitals. There's more access to mass transit money, but highways still get nearly three times as much and Amtrak will have to drop routes and raise fares because its subsidy is frozen at the 1978 level. And hard-pressed family farmers may be surprised to learn that the administration hopes to spend $3 billion less on price supports and disaster aid.

"If Carter's economic and budget messages did not have his name on them, I would not know which Administration had issued them."
—Ford Advisor Alan Greenspan

But most important is not what's in the budget, but what's missing. Though government figures show more than six million active job-seekers unemployed, there is no new jobs program in the budget. The 725,000 temporary CETA positions are continued for another year, urban public works will get only the $2 billion left over from the fiscal 1978 appropriation, and $0.4 billion is budgeted for a "major effort" to involve business in planning training programs "to benefit large numbers of minority youth."

There's no plan for building decent housing or putting the millions of unemployed urban teenagers to work improving their communities. There's an addition of $5.5 billion for the Medicaid and Medicare systems to meet their spiralling hospital and doctors' bills, but no alternative way of delivering medical care, or even insurance. The budget contains, as the *Wall Street Journal* commented in its headline, "Nothing Bold, Little New."

"I like the conservative approach," AT&T Chairman John D. deButts told the *Journal.* "I like the fact that there are not a bunch of fancy programs in it, that he sticks to the middle of the road."

Plug the Holes and Open the Gates

Carter started talking about tax reform back in the second week of his general election campaign, when he told a Birmingham shopping center audience that the U.S. tax system is "a disgrace to the human race." A week later, in St. Louis, he insisted, "We will shift the burden of taxes to where the Republicans have always protected — on the rich, the big corporations, and the special interest groups — and you can depend on that if I am elected."

Yet the "tax reform" which Carter has been preparing for over a year does almost nothing to significantly shift the tax burden. It attacks specific loopholes and inconsistencies, but the net effect is small. And the small reforms will be further watered down by the Congress, as usual.

Corporate income taxes will make up 14% of total taxes taken in, which is slightly less than they accounted for in 1977 and 1978. Carter proposes to gradually phase out two loopholes available to multinational corporations — the Domestic International Sales Corporation and the deferral of taxes on foreign subsidiaries — which he attacked by name in the campaign. The former allows companies to escape half their taxes on some export earnings; the latter exempts foreign profits from taxation if they are re-invested abroad.

Beginning to phase out these provisions would save the Treasury $0.6 billion next year; the full value, achieved in three years, would be about $2 billion.

But Carter's plan also calls for giving these revenues back with interest, through an immediate hike in the corporate investment tax credit worth $2 billion and a cut in the corporate tax rate worth $4 billion.

The investment tax credit has been the favorite corporate tax break in recent years, allowing companies to deduct from their taxes 10% of the value of new investments in machinery. This is supposed to encourage them to expand production, but there's no evidence that it does anything other than reward them for their regular activities. Two-thirds of the benefits of this credit go to the top one-tenth of one percent of U.S. corporations — that is, the same giant multinationals whose more visible loopholes Carter wants to phase out.

Specifically, Carter's plans would allow companies to write off as much as *90%* of their taxes this way (the old limit was 50%) and would allow them to deduct the cost of building new factories (even if they close old ones and move away) as well as buying new machines.

On top of all this, the corporate income tax rate itself has been whittled down over the years from 52% in 1954 to 48% (on income over $50,000) today. Carter wants to drop it to 45% next year and 44% in

fiscal 1980. (This official rate is far above what companies really pay, thanks to all the breaks which they get. A Congressional study of 1974 taxes estimated the real "effective" rate at an average of 22%.)

Individual Taxes Intact

Individual income taxes, under Carter's plan, would make up 43% of tax revenue; social security and similar taxes would bring in another 32%. Both of these figures simply continue recent trends. Equally important, the burden of the income taxes has not been shifted to richer taxpayers.

The $23.5 billion cut (largely offset by higher social security taxes) comes from slicing 2% off the income tax rate, across the board. In other words, taxpayers will save 2% of their taxable income no matter what bracket they are in; thus higher-income people will gain more from the cut.

This effect is to be countered somewhat by substituting a tax credit for dependents (that is, an amount actually subtracted from the taxes owed) in place of the current tax exemption (an amount deducted from taxable income). This arithmetic works out to save people in lower brackets, for the first time, the same amount per dependent as people in higher brackets. Carter's plan also calls for eliminating some of the write-offs available to the (mostly higher-income) people who itemize deductions on their returns.

Though Carter proposes banning deduction of yachts and hunting lodges as "business expenses" and even dares to go so far as to suggest cutting the business-lunch deduction in half, he leaves the capital gains loophole untouched. Attacked by tax reformers as the biggest giveaway to rich individuals, this provision taxes income from selling real estate, stocks, and bonds at only half the rate of income from working a job. Though a recent Brookings Institution study estimated that only 8% of the population is able to make use of this special treatment, the Carter Administration dropped any intention of reforming it months ago.

All in all, the combined effect of the individual tax cut and "reforms" would cut just $278 from the average tax bill of four-person families making $10,000 to $20,000. It would save families in the $20,000-$50,000 range an average of about $325, and families in the $50,000 to $100,000 range about $250. Some reform.

The message of Jimmy Carter's first budget, then, adds up to what both he and Jerry Ford kept saying in their own ways during the 1976 campaign: The solution to the problems facing ordinary Americans are not going to come out of the White House.

Sources: Federal budget documents; *NY Times* 9/14/76, 9/26/76, 1/22/78; *Wall St. Journal* 1/24, 1/25; *People & Taxes* 10/77, 12/77. For the economic context which shapes Carter's (or whoever's) budget decisions, see "Presidential Platforms and Economic Prospects," *D&S* #15 and "Truman Vs. Truman," *D&S #20.*

16

A Layman's Guide to the Keynesian-Monetarist Dispute

Peter D. McClelland

How curious it is that as the United States economy recovers from the worst recession since World War II, one famous economist advocates a lowering of taxes[1] while another equally famous economist favors a reduction in government spending.[2] And why should the economics profession be so sharply divided on the merits of renewed efforts to regulate wages and prices?[3] The answer must surely lie in sharply differing views about the causal processes of our economy. Regrettably, the key areas of disagreement are almost impossible to detect in either the popular literature or the textbooks written by these men. The following brief survey attempts to remedy this defect.

The best place to begin is where Milton Friedman and other monetarists usually begin: with the quantity equation of exchange, or

$$MV \equiv PQ ,$$

where M is the quantity of money in a society, V is its velocity of circulation (or the average number of times money changes hands in a year), Q is the quantity of real goods and services created and sold during that year,[4] and P is the average price of those goods. Every transaction in the marketplace is a two-way swap: the seller turns over goods or services valued at a price, and the buyer surrenders cash equal to that price. It must therefore *always* be true that the total value of cash turned over by buyers equals the value of goods and services received. That value, in turn, is nothing more than the sum of each commodity multiplied by its market price. This is why between the symbols MV and PQ one finds not an equals sign, but an equals sign plus a third line to indicate an identity. The relationship $MV \equiv PQ$ always holds.

A word of explanation concerning velocity. Economics has a long-standing tradition of illustrating complex mechanisms with oversimplified examples. Following in those footsteps, let us consider a medieval community in which the total sales in the village during a single year are as follows:

  4,000 pairs of shoes at $10 per pair = $40,000
  60,000 bushels of wheat at $1 per bushel = $60,000.

The value of PQ is thus $100,000, or ($10 × 4,000) + ($1 × 60,000). Suppose that the total money supply in this community consists of 20,000 one-dollar bills. This is then the value of M. The implied velocity[5] is

$$V = \frac{PQ}{M} = \frac{\$100,000}{\$20,000} = 5 .$$

Notice that V is calculated as a residual. We do not observe it directly in our medieval community (or anywhere else) but infer it from other data. If total transactions were $100,000 and the money supply was only 20,000 one-dollar bills, then on the average each dollar bill *must* have changed hands five times in the course of a year. All perfectly straightforward, one might think. Except that it is not. Lurking in this simple mathematics is a complicated problem that will become more apparent later on.

With the above equation in hand we can easily summarize the basic tenet of the monetarists. They make two assertions and one obvious inference. The assertions are (1) that V is "stable," and (2) that Q is not affected—or not affected very much—by M. (In more technical language this second point might be rephrased to read that Q is determined exogenously.) If these two assertions are granted, one can hardly deny what monetarists continually assert: that the main determinant of changes in the price level are previous changes in the stock of money. In the equation $MV = PQ$, if V is stable and Q is unaffected by M, then P will tend to vary with M. Our problem is therefore to understand what is meant by the two assertions noted. If we can also understand why Keynesians challenge those assertions, we shall be well on our way to understanding the Keynesian-monetarist dispute.

What is meant by the statement "Velocity is stable"? This variable could change for several reasons. The most obvious relate to improvements in the financial institutions of a community. The development of the telegraph, clearinghouses, or commercial banks can accelerate the rate at which the stock of money changes hands. Monetarists readily concede this point—they could hardly deny it—but emphasize that the evolution of financial institutions takes time. No *sudden and large* change in velocity should result from this development if the institutions themselves do not change suddenly.

The main threat to the monetarists' position lies elsewhere. Consider again the example of the medieval village. Suppose that half of those 20,000 dollar bills were actually hidden away in mattresses as a means of storing wealth. In that case, while total velocity was 5, the actual velocity of active money (i.e., the money that is not in mattresses but out in the marketplace) would be ($100,000 ÷ $10,000), or 10. No problems arise for monetarists as long as roughly half of the money supply is held idle in mattresses. But suppose for some reason that 40 percent of this idle money, or $4,000, suddenly becomes active *and* takes on the velocity of other active dollars. Then 14,000 dollar bills would change hands on the average of 10 times a year and the value of PQ would rise to ($14,000 × 10) or $140,000. *Total* velocity (that is, the V in $MV = PQ$), as noted previously, is calculated as a residual. Since the total money supply (M) is unchanged but the value of PQ has risen from $100,000 to $140,000, total velocity now becomes

$$V = \frac{PQ}{M} = \frac{\$140,000}{\$20,000} = 7 .$$

How is this possible? In simplified terms, one can think of any community as having two "piles" of money, one idle and the other active. If some of the heretofore idle dollars are moved over into the active pile, then the supply of dollars bidding for goods and services increases, and the value of goods and services sold must also increase. In our example we achieved the seemingly odd result of an increase in total velocity (from 5 to 7) *not* because of an increase in the rate at which active dollar bills changed hands (that remained constant at 10), but rather because the proportion of the total money supply in active circulation increased[6] from 50 percent ($10,000 ÷ $20,000) to 70 percent ($14,000 ÷ $20,000).

The monetarists now have a problem. If large quantities of dollar bills jump back and forth between active and inactive piles, then clearly velocity will not be "stable." (In our example, when $4,000 moved over, V rose from 5 to 7.) Similarly, if the money supply were doubled *and* all of that extra money were added to the inactive pile, then prices would not tend to increase as the monetarists claim they should. The solution, as one might expect, is to argue that this does not happen. Monetarists usually make this point by claiming that the proportion of cash balances that people desire to hold is very stable.[7] This guarantees that the kind of jumping back and forth illustrated in the above example will not take place. It also means that when the money supply is dramatically increased, almost none of that new money will be held idle. If it is not held idle, it must be spent; if it is spent, it must increase the value of PQ; and if Q is relatively unaffected by changes in M, then the main impact must be to increase *P*. By this one assertion, then, the monetarists retrieve their central notion that changes in prices are largely determined by changes in the money supply.

Since the Keynesians challenge this conclusion, they must disagree with some of the premises in the above argument. One of the main premises in dispute is that the amount of money people want to hold idle cannot change significantly in the short run. Recall the speculative motive and the liquidity preference schedule of standard Keynesian analysis. The basic idea is that if the interest rate rises, the demand for idle cash by speculators will fall; if the interest rate falls, the demand for idle cash will rise.[8] In terms of the example used previously, this is equivalent to asserting that the movement of dollar bills between the two piles of active and inactive money is very sensitive—or at least quite sensitive—to changes in the rate of interest.

We have now clarified at least one major point of disagreement concerning how the economy actually works. The monetarists claim that the desire to hold idle cash is insensitive to interest rate changes (and to other factors as well); the Keynesians claim that the desire to hold idle cash is quite sensitive to interest rate changes. Notice two features. First, at the core of the debate is a question of fact concerning the responsiveness of certain decision makers: When interest rates fall, will the demand for idle cash balances increase by a lot or by a little? Second, when economists write about this dispute, the language chosen will usually include the phrase "the stability of velocity." What is seldom realized when the point is phrased this way is that the substantive issue is whether or not, over a short time period, large quantities of cash are moved between active and inactive balances in response to such changing economic variables as the rate of interest.

The second major puzzle is this: what is meant by the assertion that in the equation $MV = PQ$, Q is independent (or largely independent) of M; or to put the point in different words, that Q is determined exogenously? According to the monetarists, total real output (Q) in the long run is primarily determined by available technology and the supply of factors of production (usually lumped by economists into the four categories of land, labor, capital, and enterprise). Of negligible influence, they argue, is the supply of money. It follows that a large increase in the money supply—if it cannot affect Q, and if V is "stable"—must bring in its wake severe inflation.[9]

The Keynesians believe otherwise. The originator of this school of thought was puzzled by the existence of large-scale and sustained unemployment. Keynes knew only too well that according to classical price theory, if the supply of workers exceeds demand, then the price of workers—the wage rate—should fall until all those who want jobs at the prevailing wage rate can get them. Exit unemployment, one would think, except that it refused to exit in the 1930s. The most obvious answer to this puzzle became a central assumption of all Keynesian models. If wages are inflexible on the down side—if such economic forces as labor contracts and large unions prevent wages from being reduced—then whenever the demand for workers falls, the main effect will be rising unemployment rather than falling wages. How obvious the point appears in retrospect! In terms of elementary supply-and-demand analysis, if the demand curve falls and the adjustment cannot occur on the price (or wage) axis, then it must occur on the quantity (or employment) axis. The solution for unemployment is therefore to stimulate demand. An expansionary monetary policy can accomplish this through the conventional Keynesian mechanisms: an increase in the money supply should lower the interest rate; this lower interest rate should stimulate investment; the increased investment (through the multiplier) will stimulate income and consumption; and thus demand will be increased and unemployment reduced.

The monetarists refuse to accept the above as an adequate description of how our economy actually works. Leave the unemployment alone, they argue, and natural market forces will remove it.[10] If the demand for automobiles falls and workers are laid off in Detroit, the situation will be rectified by the forces of supply and demand. Some unemployed workers will find alternative jobs. Automobile producers will tend to cut prices or develop alternative devices to stimulate demand. If this unemployment is instead fought by an expansion of the money supply, the only result will be more inflation. Recall the point emphasized

earlier: that newly created dollars, according to the monetarists, are like hot potatoes—no one is willing to hold them very long. If they are not held, they must be spent. An expansionary monetary policy is therefore viewed as setting in motion successive rounds of spending and respending that are sure to drive prices up even if, in the process, the demand for cars is stimulated and unemployment in Detroit falls. Finally, that reduction in unemployment would have occurred *sooner or later* through the forces of supply and demand. To put it harshly, the monetarists might say, why bother to feed the horses in order to feed the sparrows when the sparrows will be fed anyway?

The key phrase is "sooner or later." The Keynesian rebuttal is that existing market forces will remove unemployment, at best, very slowly. Equally important, they assert that the main impact of spending and respending dollars should be the bidding for resources that are currently idle rather than for those that are already employed. This in turn implies that the principal impact of injecting new dollars into the spending stream should be a reduction in unemployment rather than a bidding up of the price level.

We have now arrived at the second main bone of contention between these two competing schools. Once again the central issue is a question of fact: How rapidly do labor markets adjust when unemployment occurs? The monetarists reply, "Very rapidly"; the Keynesians, "Very slowly." Here too the language usually used by economists tends to obscure the substantive point. Few would guess that the question "In the equation $MV = PQ$, is Q determined exogenously?" boils down to a dispute over speeds of adjustment in labor markets.

In review, and on close inspection, the main points of disagreement are remarkably uncomplicated. When extra money is created, the monetarists argue that almost all of it is sure to be spent. The Keynesians claim that it is far from clear how much will be spent and how much will be held idle. During a recession, whenever new money is created—and however much of it is spent and respent—the Keynesians believe, the main impact will be the bidding for otherwise idle resources. The monetarists believe that the main impact will be the bidding up of prices.[11] If these are the arguments, why can they not be resolved? The answer is what one might expect: because we lack the tools to prove conclusively which view more accurately portrays how our economy actually works.

If we cannot resolve the debate, we can at least understand two further implications of these conflicting positions. The first concerns the question of whether or not inflation and unemployment are inversely related. When one goes down must the other necessarily go up? The monetarists answer no. Since they argue that changes in the money supply mainly affect prices and not output, it follows that efforts to control inflation by controlling the money supply should not affect total output or, by implication, total employment. The Keynesians believe otherwise. Why they believe that stable prices and full employment are conflicting goals is not always clear. Some concede that when aggregate demand is stimulated, at least some of the spending and respending will bid for employed resources rather than unemployed resources, thereby creating upward pressure on prices. Others suggest that (1) prices are determined partly by wage costs and (2) wage demands tend to be more moderate in periods of high unemployment.

The second implication of the above arguments concerns the effectiveness of fiscal policy as a countercyclical tool. The Keynesian position is so familiar as hardly to bear repeating. If unemployment is caused by inflexible wages and falling demand, the solution is to increase demand. This the federal government can accomplish either by spending more itself or by cutting taxes, thereby giving the public more to spend. In either case the resulting government deficit will have a multiplied effect upon consumption (and possibly a stimulating effect upon investment), causing demand to increase and unemployment to fall.

The monetarists' position is more subtle. They begin by noting that any increase in deficit spending must be financed.[12] That is, before the government can spend more dollars it must first acquire those dollars from somewhere. If it acquires them by expanding the money supply—if the dollars to be spent are newly created dollars—then the anticipated impact will be that outlined above: rising prices and little change in total output and employment. If instead the government finances its deficit by borrowing dollars from the public, the anticipated effects are that (1) increased borrowing will drive up interest rates, (2) the rise in interest rates (perhaps reinforced by rising prices) will cause a cutback in consumption and investment, and (3) this cutback in spending by the private sector *will exactly match* the increase in spending by the government. Fiscal policy therefore has no effect upon the size of the pie, only upon its division between the public and private sectors. But suppose that deficit is financed instead by the printing of new money, as noted above. The same answer applies, argue the monetarists. Total output will remain virtually unchanged but prices will rise as the government uses newly created dollars to bid away goods and services from the private sector. The resulting inflation will be a disguised form of taxation. The public must surrender part of the pie to the government, not because income taxes or sales taxes have increased, but because higher prices force them to relinquish part of the share they heretofore had.

The reader by now should be able to anticipate the Keynesian counterattack. In a world of inflexible wages and economic recession, they argue, the size of the pie can be expanded by an expansion of demand. If government deficits are financed by borrowing procedures that raise interest rates, there is no reason why the resulting cutback in public demand should *exactly* equal the increase in government spending. More to the point, in a recession the appropriate monetary policy is to expand the money supply and *lower* interest rates. But why, one might ask, do Keynesians expect that the spending and respending generated by an expansionary monetary and fiscal policy will have its main impact upon unemployment rather than upon prices? And why do monetarists expect exactly the opposite? The answer is no more complicated than referring to a point made previously. *The substantive issue mainly concerns the speed of adjustment in labor markets.* The Keynesians believe that without government stimulation of demand, unemployment can remain a serious problem for a long time; with that stimulation, it can be alleviated. The monetarists take the opposite view. Disequilibriums in product and factor markets, they argue, should be treated in the same manner as the sheep of Little Bo Peep: leave them alone. The implicit belief is that, if left alone, imbalances will correct themselves; if meddled with, they may become worse.

Notes

1. Walter W. Heller, "The Right Tax Cut Mix," *Wall Street Journal,* May 1, 1978, p. 16. (In this book.)

2. Milton Friedman, "Inflationary Recession," *Newsweek,* April 24, 1978, p. 81. (In this book.)

3. See for example the articles in this section by Arthur M. Okun, Henry C. Wallich, and Nancy A. Jianakoplos.

4. The following analysis focuses exclusively on income velocity and ignores transactions velocity.

5. This assumes that all transactions involve an exchange of dollars and rules out the possibility of bartering with goods only.

6. Expressed in mathematical form, total velocity is the weighted average

$$V = \frac{MA(VA) + MI(VI)}{MA + MI},$$

where MA is active money, VA is the velocity of active money, MI is inactive money, and VI is the velocity of inactive money. Note that $MA + MI = M$ and $VI = 0$.

7. More correctly, what is assumed to be stable is the demand for real cash balances, or nominal cash balances adjusted for changes in the price level.

8. To review the behavioral premise, Keynesians assume that when interest rates are low (i.e., bond prices are high) many speculators will expect bond prices to fall and will therefore delay buying bonds, holding cash in the interim.

9. The key word here is "large." In the equation $MV = PQ,$ if Q—or Gross National Product—increases gradually over time and P is to remain relatively stable, then the money supply should also increase at *roughly* the same rate as Q ("roughly" because gradual changes may also occur in V). This is why monetarists argue for a gradual expansion in $M,$ rather than for a rigidly fixed money supply.

10. "Normal" unemployment, according to the monetarists, is determined by such factors as the interchangeability of job skills, the cost of labor market information, and the extent to which laws and organizations (such as unions) impede the free functioning of the labor market.

11. Notice the implied contrasting expectations concerning interest rate trends. If prices rise, interest rates should also rise to allow for expected inflation in the future. (A lender who normally receives 6 percent and now expects 10 percent annual inflation will demand 16 percent to compensate for being repaid in depreciated dollars.) Thus, if the main impact of an expansionary policy is on prices, interest rates will tend to go up as prices rise. If the main effect is lowered unemployed, then this kind of upward pressure on future interest rates should not occur, or at least not occur in any severe form.

12. Subsequent discussion focuses only upon deficits arising from increased spending. The arguments apply with equal force if that deficit is created by tax cuts.

17

The sociology of professional contentment.

The Trouble With Economists

by John Kenneth Galbraith

By the time of the Great Depression of the 1930s economics had become a subject of respected instruction, research and public guidance in the United States and was an academic discipline of no slight prestige. Harvard, Columbia, Yale, Chicago, Princeton, California and Wisconsin were major centers of such effort. The great names in the field—F.W. Taussig, the noted Harvard teacher, tariff-maker and wartime price-fixer; Joseph Schumpeter who arrived in these years at Harvard; Fred R. Fairchild at Yale whose textbook with Furniss and Buck depressed several undergraduate generations; Edwin W. Kemmerer and Frank A. Fetter at Princeton; Wesley C. Mitchell at Columbia; F.H. Knight at Chicago; John R. Commons at Wisconsin—all had reputations of national reach. Many others in universities and colleges around the country enjoyed only somewhat less esteem.

The Great Depression, beginning in the autumn of 1929 and continuing for 10 years until washed out by military expenditure in 1940-41, is rivaled only by the Civil War as a traumatic event in the American experience. It lingers more strongly than any other in the social memory. When the economic prospect is uncertain, men and women still ask in fear, "Will it be another Depression?" In those years output—Gross National Product—fell by a third. Farmers, still numerous and vocal, went bankrupt and were dispossessed by the tens of thousands. By the mid-1930s the farm debt exceeded the assets, at current values, of all farms. American agriculture was, literally, insol-

John Kenneth Galbraith's most recent book is _The Age of Uncertainty_ (G. K. Hall).

vent. Unemployment rose to around a quarter of the labor force. There was no unemployment insurance until 1933, no effort to increase job opportunities and until then no organized assistance to the impoverished. As now, in relation to the urban crisis, men of high reputation took their stand on principle: far better the suffering and despair than any impairment of the rule of local responsibility for local problems. By the end of March 1933, 9000 banks and around 100,000 other commercial and industrial enterprises had failed. By the mid-1930s bankruptcy was no longer the misfortune of the weak and the small; numerous of the large banks, utilities and railroads were in receivership or in peril. The president of the New York Federal Reserve Bank had observed that while the effects of the failure of the small local banks "could be isolated," danger to the big New York banks had to be taken seriously.

The great economists, with a few exceptions, reacted to these misfortunes with professional detachment and calm. Called on for advice, as they were, most warned of the dangers of "untried experiment," experiment usually being of such character. Or they stressed the danger of inflation. The United States had had a serious inflation in World War I and following; prices had approximately doubled. In Germany and Austria and elsewhere in Central Europe, purchasing power of currencies had totally collapsed, with maximum impact on a generation of scholars who later migrated _en masse_ to the United States. In the manner made famous by generals, the great economists showed a marked affinity for fighting their past wars and did so through a deflation that, between 1929 and 1933, brought the wholesale price index down by more than a third. There was also notable stress on the importance of patience as a therapy—a treatment that is believed to be easier with academic tenure on a regular income. The warnings from Joseph Schumpeter of Harvard and Lionel Robbins of the London School of Economics were especially powerful. They affirmed that depressions end only when they have corrected the maladjustments and extruded the poisons by which they were caused.

On occasion there was organized effort to resist action or to support inaction. In the autumn of 1933, many of the more prestigious members of the profession banded together under Edwin W. Kemmerer of Princeton to oppose monetary and fiscal experiment. A year or so later several Harvard economists collaborated in an astringent attack on the economic experimentalism of the New Deal. This was especially notable, for the effort involved not only the older professors but also younger members of the faculty who were still actively pursuing tenure. The most common mood, however, was one of judicious scholarly contentment. Professors remained concerned with accustomed teaching, research and writing in economic theory, money and banking, statistics and economic history. At the great universities there were no tense seminars on the cause of the depression or its cure. Little such discussion is reflected in the professional journals. Some time in 1934 or 1935, President Roosevelt returned to Harvard to dine with his sons and their friends at the Fly Club. He was greeted by students along Mount Auburn Street (where I was) with shouts of "Fire Tugwell!"—this reflecting the dominant lesson of their practical economic instruction. Among the economists in the administration, Rexford Tugwell was the most notable activist.

There were exceptions to this mood—the professional eccentrics and deviants. Many universities housed one or two—men or the occasional woman who kept asking what might be done nationally, locally or on specific matters to alleviate the suffering. Agricultural and labor economists, living close to their clientele, had a special tendency to be involved, and at considerable cost to their scholarly reputations. Academically, they always were second-class citizens. At the University of Wisconsin, under John R. Commons, there was a widely remarked concern with such issues as unemployment insurance, utility rate regulation and taxation. Wisconsin was thought by many, a peculiar place.

Elsewhere two men were outspoken in advocating their prepared remedies for the depression. One of these was Irving Fisher of Yale; the other was John Maynard Keynes. Fisher urged deliberate expansion of the money supply by reducing the gold content of the dollar. Keynes urged energetic expenditure by governments from borrowed funds. Both men were regarded with deep distaste by the economists of established reputation. *The New York Times* in 1933

thought it "should hardly be necessary to say" that the ideas of Fisher and Keynes "have long been before the public, and that both have been rejected by the large consensus of economic and financial judgment." Keynes and Fisher, with Commons, are among the few economists from the time who are not forgotten. And the veil of forgetfulness is kind, for, with the passing years, those who continued to sit stolidly on their prestige paid heavily for their contentment. Their comfortable negativism, so far as it is remembered, is treated with amused contempt in the intellectual history of those years.

I recur to this history because detachment and contentment are again the tendency of economists in our time. As in some earlier cases they join, paradoxically, with a reputation for earlier activism. Politicians and the public, and not least economists themselves, should know that it is a normal cyclical phenomenon in our profession. What is understood may not be more easily forgiven, but there is a chance that it will be more promptly remedied.

The contentment of the early depression years was followed in the late thirties, in the war years and thereafter, including through the Eisenhower years, by a period of excitement and active innovation in economic policy. This was overwhelmingly in reaction to the increasingly apparent ineptitude of the great men of the past. The polar figure was, of course, Keynes; the unifying idea was the belief that something could be done and had to be done by government to lift and sustain the level of output and employment in the modern capitalist economy. There was much here to discuss. And the discussion was further sustained by the myriad of new economic tasks occasioned by the war and by the development and use during these years of the national accounts—the incorporation into professional thought of National Income, Gross National Product and aggregates of consumer and business spending and saving. Almost simultaneously there were breakthroughs in ideas as to what should be done about unemployment and depression, and in the measurement thereof. Again, however, the great men of the profession—with rare exceptions such as the late Alvin Hansen—continued aloof. Men of lesser reputation—with less reputation to lose—made the Keynesian Revolution.

There was reason for caution by the tactically careful and self-regarding. Those actively associated with the new policies in government were subject to severe criticism. The general complaint was from business, and that was that economists were impairing or destroying confidence. Some reactions were very specific. When the Employment Act of 1946 was under consideration, the National Association of Manufacturers and Donaldson Brown of General Motors filed a brief warning that this measure would enhance government control, destroy private enterprise, unduly increase the powers of the federal executive, legalize federal spending and pump-priming, bring socialism, be unworkable and impractical and promise too much and have other defects. No careful scholar wished to be associated with such destructive activity.

But the heaviest charge was the general effect on confidence. The American business psyche is an acutely vulnerable thing; it associates all change with perverse ideological intent. No large group of similar size and fortune in history has ever been so insecure as the American business executives. The only forms of reassurance that serve are lower taxes and general inaction, and these are required and expected no matter who wins elections. However, in the 1930s and 1940s and continuing in the 1950s and into the 1960s, the results of inaction seemed to be intolerable, and not least for business itself. So the onslaught was faced. Economists accepted their controversial role. And, in time, the more secure and mentally accessible executives came to accept the Keynesian rescue.

With the innovative and combative mood of economists came nearly a quarter century of economic success. At the end of 1968, the President's Council of Economic Advisers congratulated itself on its accomplishments. The language, which then did not seem remarkable, is now rather wonderful to recall:

> The Nation is now in its 95th month of continuous economic advance. Both in strength and length, this prosperity is without parallel in our history. We have steered clear of the business-cycle recessions which for generations derailed us repeatedly from the path of growth and progress. . . . No longer do we view our economic life as a relentless tide of ups and downs. No longer do we fear that automation and technical progress will rob workers of jobs rather than help us to achieve greater abundance. No longer do we consider poverty and unemployment permanent landmarks on our economic scene.
>
> . . . .
>
> Ever since the historic passage of the Employment Act in 1946, economic policies have responded to the fire alarm of recession and boom. In the 1960's, we have adopted a new strategy aimed at fire prevention—sustaining prosperity and heading off recession or serious inflation before they could take hold.
>
> Meanwhile, a solid foundation has been built for continued growth in the years ahead.

These words suggest what all should have feared—that economists had once again settled into a mood of self-congratulation and associated contentment. Erstwhile innovators had become passive conservatives. And this was happening just as the Keynesian measures, once so wonderful, were showing by the clearest of all possible evidence that they produced not merely inflation, not merely unemployment, but an unyielding combination of the two. The evidence was in the plain history of the

next 10 years. The only relief from this combination would be for a brief period preceding the presidential election in 1972, a breathing spell which reputable economists have dismissed as the purchase of an election at the price of far worse troubles to come. Not again would economists speak of strategies for "sustaining prosperity and heading off recession or serious inflation before they could take hold." Or say that poverty and unemployment were not "permanent landmarks on our economic scene." The November 1977 figures show an unemployment rate of 6.9 percent of the labor force. For blacks it was 13.8 percent; for young whites 14.5 percent; for black teenagers 39 percent. If one is young and black and in a central city, he should not, as a matter of statistical expectation, suppose that he can find a job. This is all the more remarkable, for such a person belongs to a politically decisive group. It was from the urban poor and the minorities that the present administration received the solidly affirmative votes that brought it to office.

Meanwhile inflation, like unemployment, is at a highly unsatisfactory level. And, as with unemployment, it becomes much worse when one goes beyond the aggregates. Through the first 11 months of 1977, the wholesale price index rose by just under nine points—from 188.1 to 197.0 (1967 = 100). But industrial prices rose by nearly eleven points (from 188.4 to 199.2) and farm prices *fell* by an even eight points. The fiscal and monetary restraints on which the comfortable Keynesian policy depends do not work on the hard administered prices and negotiated wages of the industrial sector. They do work very well (down to government support levels) on soft competitive markets such as those for farm products. But this is an anti-inflation therapy that does not appeal to farmers. It causes them to drive their tractors into town, experiment with strikes and react adversely to President Carter. They would like the policy even less if they understood their contribution better. If unemployment recedes, wages and industrial prices will rise. Farm prices will also recover, and inflation will get much worse.

In the Cabinet or holding Cabinet rank in the present administration there are no fewer than five economists of the highest professional qualification. At long last a PhD in economics has replaced a law degree as the basic license for practicing the science and art of public administration. This all must applaud. But clearly these talented men and women have come to office at a particularly dismal moment in the history of economics. They are caught in, if not part of, another of the great downswings which, as in the past, have rendered the profession innocuous or worse. In the universities and research institutes the mood is not all bland. There is an active academic discussion of tax incentives and penalties for holding the line on prices and wages, a policy that would require the government to proclaim and, in effect, enforce standards for permissible increases. This discussion leads, inevitably, to consideration of alternatives, including guidelines and controls. A technical journal devoted to this discussion—*The Journal of Post Keynesian Economics*—will make its appearance later this year. Numerous younger economists and some older ones are not in doubt as to the futility of the accepted macroeconomics. But the established response remains overwhelmingly passive. The small tasks of more pleasant times and their refinement still command major attention. Perhaps the accepted design for monetary and fiscal policy does not work. But it can still be taught and avowed in Washington—for, after all, it once served. It is essential that economists and noneconomists alike understand the reasons for this recurrent mood. They are deeply ingrained in the sociology of our profession.

This sociology begins with the instinct of economists, by no means exceptional to our profession, for applause—and with the companion wish to avoid rude controversy. These attitudes must then be set against the deeply inconvenient fact that whatever is good for economic performance will always—I speak with caution—be deeply controversial. And what is most acclaimed for sustaining business confidence will invariably be bad for economic performance. All have heard of contradictions in modern capitalism; all should know that the major immediate contradiction is here. In its great moments economics has understood and resisted the contradiction. At the low points in its cycle, as now, it has not.

In the great creative years during and following World War II, it was taken for granted in Washington that to be effective was to arouse business hostility. Likewise in the universities. Robert Hutchins, president of the University of Chicago, once noted that economics appointments were the most perilous with which he had to deal. (It may be added that he and his followers made selections that were well designed to minimize the risk.) When economists avoid controversy and reach for applause, their advice becomes worse than worthless; it becomes actively damaging. It follows that unless this is clearly understood by economists in responsible positions, their services also will be actively damaging.

Observation of these truths—laws, I am prepared to call them—must, some will say, be motivated by a deep antipathy to business. It is not so. In contrast with many of my liberal friends, I long ago came to terms with the American business system. Liberals, many of them, would break up the large corporations that now, in the number of a thousand or two, account for more than half of all the private product of the United States. I would not. Conservative economists would move similarly against the unions. These, like the large corporations, I accept as part of the broad irreversible current of history. I not only wish to see the system

survive but so deep is my conservative commitment that I want it to have the first essential for survival which, of course, is that it work. I am persuaded that, as the experience so well shows, economists have a remarkably plain choice. They can be popular and applauded in the short run and be failures in the long run. Or they can be controversial in the short run and a success in the long run. (I pass over a third possibility, which is to be innocuous in both the short and the long run. That requires no special instruction.)

Controversy is inevitable regarding both effective policy to expand the economy and effective action to restrain inflation. All policy to expand the economy will be more successful the more successfully it provides income to those who need it most. Expenditure is then prompt and complete. Such policy also usefully reduces social tension: although much effort has been devoted to showing the opposite, income is a remarkably useful antidote to poverty and its associated discomfort. But the policy that professional business spokesmen and the affluent in general will always most approve, the policy that is best for business confidence, will always be the policy that gives these more fortunate groups the most after-tax income.

The situation is similar where inflation is involved. Any policy that restricts or restrains the freedom to set prices and incomes will be heavily attacked, be held bad for business confidence. But in a world of large corporations and strong unions no policy that contends successfully with inflation can avoid some restraint on the freedom of business action—on prices charged, wages paid or received. So a successful anti-inflation policy must also be sharply controversial—and again bad for confidence or what is so described. And the capacity to articulate alarm and to be heard is strongly correlated with business position and income. These voices are wonderfully audible; those of the poor are not. A powerful tendency in modern political economy is for the voice of the affluent, and that of the business spokesman in particular, to be mistaken for the voice of the masses.

A slightly exaggerated example will illustrate my point. Nothing today would be held so good for business confidence (or, again, what is so described) as a large horizontal cut in the progressive income tax accompanied by an equally substantial reduction in the corporate tax and a compensatory slash in welfare expenditures. Such action would be warmly praised by businessmen for its motivating effect. *The Wall Street Journal* recently put the prospective business response with perfect clarity:

> A general tax cut is well worth trying . . . provided it is not shaped by perverse theories. The key is to let producers keep more of what they produce, and the biggest effect will come from cutting rates where they are the highest. If the tax cuts reduce rather than improve rewards for the economy's most gifted,

talented and skilled producers, they will be worse than nothing at all.

Mr. Alan Greenspan, though he can hardly look upon the effect of his economic advice on the career plans of Gerald Ford with complete satisfaction, even more recently held that a tax cut wholly confined to corporate income would be the very best for business confidence.

All economists proposing any tax cut are assured of applause. This applause is the one assuredly positive consequence. Tax cuts do not have any motivating effect on the modern organization man—the significant business figure in our time. He is required by all the weight of the organization ethic to give his best to the business. That he should bung off because he believes he should have a tax cut is inconceivable. And such a tax reduction has little immediate effect on either consumer spending or business investment. If profit prospects are good, a corporate tax cut is not needed to encourage investment. If they are bad, no tax cut will make them good. As practical experience with the last tax cut showed (duly reported by the Council of Economic Advisers), the initial effect of a cut in personal taxes is overwhelmingly to increase savings. Income so saved does not buy goods, and modern business investment, some special pleading to the contrary, proceeds independently of the supply of savings. And a tax cut as now proposed would come at a time when banks are awash with money they wish to lend to good borrowers. Only good economic performance—good employment and demand—will encourage borrowing of these funds. The reduced welfare spending that would be so much applauded would, of course, reduce demand.

In contrast, an energetic jobs program to train and employ the poor, black and young or, in the absence of jobs, to provide the income which, with whatever damage to the soul, does do something for the body, would have a deeply adverse effect on business confidence. So, likewise, expenditures to help make life in the large cities become, if not pleasant, at least safe and tolerable and to reduce the dependence of these cities on regressive taxes. So, in particular, building and rehabilitation work in the central slums. The expansive effect of action along these lines is optimal; money so distributed is put immediately into circulation by people who (unlike the affluent) immediately recirculate—spend—100 cents of every dollar that comes in. The effect on the performance of a lagging economy is total—nothing is lost to savings.

There is another advantage in such action. As noted, modern unemployment is highly structured. Shortages of labor in numerous areas and occupations are combined with disastrous surpluses among the minorities, those without work experience, among women and those in the urban ghettos away from job opportunities. The measures just described are by far the best for reaching those most in needs of jobs. Tax reductions, even if widely distributed among income groups, add to pressure on labor markets that are already strong. Measures that are directed specifically at the unemployed—targeted, in the offensive current jargon—have their initial effect on labor markets that are weak. They are, in consequence, much less inflationary than action that rewards the affluent.

There is a further inverse correlation between what serves business confidence and what best serves the future of capitalism. None surely can doubt that the long-run future of capitalism will be more secure if the poor and the black and the young have the stake in the system that a steady income provides. There is much talk these days of a taxpayers' revolt. It will not, in the higher-income brackets, be the kind of revolution that involves much raw violence. Men like David Rockefeller, Walter Wriston and Gabriel Hauge can, if necessary, be contained. With residents of the South Bronx it might one day be different.

Effective measures for expanding the economy are adverse to business confidence. The contradiction operates even more intransigently where inflation is concerned. There are, we now know, only two basic designs for controlling inflation. One is to have enough slack in plant capacity and enough unemployment so that industrial prices and wages are subject to restraint. And all experience tells us that the unemployment so required is considerable. Or there can be some form of direct intervention on incomes and administered prices. This last is not a total strategy for reconciling high employment with reasonably stable prices. Monetary and fiscal policy—the balancing of total demand for goods and services and their supply—are as necessary as ever. But some form of direct restraint is inescapably a part of any strategy that does not rely on unemployment. And here again, in redoubled amount, comes the controversy that reputable economists so deplore, so struggle to evade—the conflict with the confidence syndrome. Such action, however unpleasant the alternatives, proves wicked bureaucratic intent and is possibly a design for socialism.

It is not easy to be overtly in favor of either inflation or unemployment. The first is the symbol of loose public management, and there is ample evidence that people so regard it and much dislike it. Unemployment has a few more open supporters. The defense of a "natural level" of joblessness unites a group of young economists at MIT with the editors of *Fortune*. And Robert Lekachman has shown that quite a few people believe, correctly, that a little fear makes a labor force more productive and acquiescent. But unemployment also must be deplored by anyone in untenured public office. Given the need to be against inflation and unemployment but to avoid the controversy and adverse business reaction inherent in all effective remedial action, economists have only one choice. That is some talented form of evasion. This means, in practice, the simulation of action as a substitute for action.

In the universities evasion is relatively easy. As in the 1930s, one remains with accustomed preoccupations and ignores unemployment and inflation as irrelevant to one's particular specialization. A posture of scientific preoccupation can even be adduced to support such attitudes. In public life the escape involves more varied techniques ranging from banality to sophisticated fraud. On all the known forms, it should be noted, time is running out.

The most forthright recent effort to simulate action in the absence of action, of course, was President Ford's invention and distribution of the WIN button. This was not highly regarded by economists. Better regarded, in the past, has been the effort to convey the impression that some as yet uninvoked form of monetary or fiscal magic would reconcile stable prices with low unemployment. This was the peculiar belief of the economists currently in office. Few can now suppose that if there is such magic, it would have remained unused for so long.

When economists were summoned by President Ford to meet on the inflation problem in 1974, it was all but

unanimously resolved that diminution of unnecessary regulation would contribute to price stability. This would not have reduced the price index by as much as half of one percent in half a century. This too is coming to be recognized.

Liberals, when devoid of thought, have anciently urged the enforcement of the antitrust laws. This is now widely, if not yet universally, identified as the last wavering gasp of the bankrupt mind.

Bringing representatives of capital and labor together for agreement on price and wage policies in some smoke-filled Washington room is a more recent design for simulating action. Such consultations will have to be part of any general effort at restraint. But as an isolated, unstructured effort, not backed by serious government purpose, they exploit only the constitutional right to free speech. And this too can no longer be disguised. The most transparently fraudulent recent effort to simulate action is the Council on Wage and Price Stability—a toothless body established to contemplate the wage-price spiral, which, while considering the need for action, is legally excluded from action. When steel prices recently rose in the face of a deeply depressed market, the spokesman for the Council first called the increase "awfully big," then, having too vigorously simulated action, said it was "in line with inflation." The Council on Wage and Price Stability is a special insult to the public intelligence. No self-respecting economist or public servant should be associated with it except for the pay.

There is also now only a diminishing future for the use of prediction as a substitute for action—for saying each month, as the inflation and unemployment figures are released, that everything will be better in the third quarter hence. But the press does remain very tolerant of this evasion and duly reports it as though true.

For a substantial group of economists the tax reduction hitherto mentioned is the approved simulation of action. It is held to be effective in expanding the economy. The distortion of priorities and the needs of the poor are ignored, and so is the effect on inflation. The business applause is taken as proof of prospective accomplishment. Mr. Carter, like Mr. Ford before him, is disastrously the victim of this simulation.

There are elements of simulation in the Humphrey-Hawkins bill. Its focus on unemployment is highly useful, and this will be much enhanced by the objections of conservatives who will not distinguish between promise and content. But the Humphrey-Hawkins bill elides the inflation problem. At a four-percent unemployment rate there would have to be strong direct restraints on wages and administered prices to prevent inflation. Still, the best way to get them could be to pass Humphrey-Hawkins, press for its promise of lowered unemployment and let the need for a companion incomes policy become obvious.

One sees the glum position in which the economists of the Carter administration find themselves. The stark, blunt fact is that orthodox monetary and fiscal policies give us not a choice between an unacceptable rate of inflation and an unacceptable level of unemployment, but an unacceptable combination of the two. (It is, perhaps, proof either of progress or of the detachment to which the academic community can rise that the Ford Foundation has announced a series of grants for the study of this problem. One of the studies is expected to last for five years.) Only the uniquely brave or reckless, whether liberal or conservative, can say that the combination of inflation and unemployment is something the system can suffer and survive. All must promise improvement. And, as I've said, all the techniques of evasion are running out. There remains only, as moral support, the ability of all in our profession, when in power, to believe that because the fates have been so wise as to place them there, the fates are obligated also to rescue and provide. Conservative economists, if sufficiently archaic, have some justification for this theology: the full employment equilibrium is basic to the conservative creed; inaction is the way to realize that equilibrium. Liberal economists must believe that they were the chosen—that, as I've said before, God is a Keynesian Democrat.

There is no reassurance to be gained from other countries. There is now no industrial country in the world (the dubious model of Italy possibly apart) which does not have some system of income restraint—either direct action on wages or prices or indirectly through industry-wide collective bargaining. In Switzerland and Germany, the extreme exemplars of the free market (as also in Austria and the Scandinavian countries), this restraint operates through industry-wide trade-union bargaining which accepts that the wages so established bear strongly on prices. Price restraint is achieved either by direct or tacit understanding or by the need to keep products and services competitive in world markets. Britain has a still fragile but much more formal system into which tax policy and agricultural policy have been integrated. *Plan Barre* in France has a similar, if more informal, design. Canada has a frail system of restraints. No country has yet achieved full success. But in all, including Canada and Britain, there can be no doubt: without the effort, inflation and unemployment would be much worse.

That is because all modern industrial countries are subject to the same tyrannical circumstance. In all, the large corporations, unions and numerous individuals have escaped the discipline of the market and gained power over their incomes. The exercise of this power drives up prices. When orthodox monetary and fiscal policy are used to arrest this upward spiral, it is production, not price, that is curbed. And with the curtailment of production goes curtailment of employment. And when employment is curtailed, as Coolidge once affirmed in slightly different words, you get unemployment. Until that unemployment is very great, perhaps up in the recession range of ten percent

or more of the labor force, unemployment and inflation coexist. It's an ungrateful world. Just as economists come into public office in unprecedented numbers, we discover that the economist's life was not meant to be a happy one. Anciently it has been said that ours is a subject that deals with choice. Now we discover that this is true even of public careers. We can be peaceful, fraudulent and afraid. Or we can be innovative, successful and abused.

Certainly no President should be in doubt. If his economists are winning applause, inspiring confidence, he should be deeply alarmed. The effects will spill over him with politically fatal results. I am not reaching for paradox or exaggeration; the historical affirmation is complete. Three Presidents in the last half century have enjoyed supreme business confidence—Herbert Hoover, Richard Nixon and Gerald Ford. Under Hoover and Ford we had the worst depressions of those 50 years, and under Nixon and Ford we had the worst peacetime inflation in our entire history. Hoover and Ford were the only two Presidents in this century who failed of reelection. None of President Carter's economists can hope to be so successful in inspiring business confidence as William Simon and Alan Greenspan. They exuded reassurance beyond anything for which my friends can have any hope. And William Simon, exuding yet more reassurance, even went on to snatch a nearly impossible defeat for the candidate he guided in the recent New Jersey election over a man running on a platform advocating the introduction of a state income tax. Simon and Greenspan have been rewarded with better-paying posts, in accordance with our system of upward failure. But this system may not last indefinitely—not if to be an economist is to be thought a failure.

But more is at stake (obvious issues of social well-being apart) than personal careers. Unless economists understand that our subject is intrinsically contentious—that what is good for the poorest of our people is best for economic performance but worst for gaining applause—our economic policy will be a failure. We will have, as seems now the prospect, more tax cuts that bypass the terrible needs of our cities, that lodge themselves heavily into savings; that, when spent, affect most those markets where labor is already tight; and that thus make the greatest possible contribution to inflation. Unless economists proceed with the greatly contentious task of working out a system of income and price restraint over those who have gained some control of their prices and incomes—a task that must combine patient consultation with use of the powers of the state—inflation will either be uncontrolled or controlled imperfectly, as now, by unemployment. And people, especially the poor, will come to wonder if having economists instead of lawyers in office is all that good.

18

By Milton Friedman

Inflationary Recession

Nearly a dozen years ago, I warned of an inflationary recession (NEWS-WEEK, Oct. 17, 1966). We have since then had three inflationary recessions and a fourth is almost surely on the way.

During the first, the brief mini-recession of 1967, consumer prices rose 2.4 per cent per year; during the longer and more severe recession from December 1969 to November 1970, prices rose 5.3 per cent per year; during the still longer and even more severe recession from November 1973 to March 1975, prices rose 10.8 per cent per year; during the coming recession, prices are likely to rise at least 7 per cent per year.

Each scenario has been the same: rapid growth in the quantity of money followed by economic expansion and then, much later, by rising inflation; a public outcry against inflation, leading the authorities to reduce monetary growth sharply; some months later, an inflationary recession; a public outcry against unemployment, leading authorities to increase monetary growth sharply; some months later, the beginning of expansion, along with a decline in inflation. Back to the starting point.

A WRONG INTERPRETATION

The simultaneous decline in unemployment and inflation produced orgies of self-congratulation by the powers that be. However, this happy state proved short-lived as inflation once again started to accelerate. Needless to say, the political Establishment tried to prolong the happy glow by attributing the acceleration of inflation to special events—bad weather, food shortages, labor-union intransigence, corporate greed, the OPEC cartel, or any straw at which they could grasp. Never any sign of *mea culpa*.

We have now almost completed a fourth repetition of the same scenario, as the accompanying table makes clear.

Consider the rates of monetary growth. The first entry shows the high growth after the 1969-70 recession; the next, the sharply lower growth that responded to galloping inflation and produced the 1973-75 recession; the third, the swing back to high growth, and the final entry, the recent slowdown in response to accelerating inflation. This slowdown has already lasted long enough to assure at least a mini-recession of the 1967 variety.

Consider now the consequences for inflation. Although a change in monetary growth initially affects output and employment, its ultimate effects are primarily on inflation. More than a century ago,

a famous English economist, W. Stanley Jevons, examined the relation between monetary growth and inflation. In 1863, he wrote: "An expansion of the currency occurs one or two years prior to a rise of prices." His finding has held ever since for both the U.K. and the U.S.—of course not precisely, but on the average.

Accordingly, the second half of the table gives the rate of inflation, as measured by consumer prices, for a period two years later than the period of monetary growth in the first half of the table. The correspondence between the rates of growth of M_2 and CPI is striking. Similar comparisons for a much longer period yield the same results. In general, the rate of inflation tends to run something like 0 to 3 percentage points lower than the rate of M_2 growth two years earlier. On this basis, we can predict that

HOW MONEY MATTERS

MONETARY GROWTH			INFLATION	
Period	Per cent per year		Period	Per cent per year
	M_1	M_2		CPI
Dec. 1971 to Jan. 1973	9.3	11.4	Dec. 1973 to Jan. 1975	11.7
Jan. 1973 to Feb. 1975	4.6	7.7	Jan. 1975 to Feb. 1977	6.2
Feb. 1975 to Oct. 1977	6.5	10.1	Feb. 1977 to Oct. 1979	7 to 10*
Oct. 1977 to Mar. 1978	3.9	6.1		

M_1 = Currency plus adjusted demand deposits; M_2 = M_1 plus commercial-bank time deposits other than large CD's; CPI = Consumer Price Index.

*Projections

Leckner Design Associates

inflation from February 1977 to October 1979 will average something like 7 to 10 per cent (it has averaged 6.6 per cent from February 1976 to February 1977 and is still rising). We can also predict that no sustained reduction in inflation can be expected before mid- or late 1979.

If my analysis is correct, what role is played by the many factors other than money that politicians, economists and journalists write about? Three roles: first, they may affect monetary growth—pressures from Congress and the Administration to finance rising government spending and to keep interest rates low are a major reason for high monetary growth; second, they account for the 0 to 3 percentage-point variation in the margin between monetary growth and inflation; third, they affect the shorter-run ups and downs in the inflation rate.

Monetary growth is determined by the Federal Reserve System. The able and public-spirited men who run the system did not permit or produce the wild swings in monetary growth out of malice aforethought. Why then have these swings oc-

curred through the whole of the more than 60 years of the Fed's existence? In my opinion, for two basic reasons: first, because of pressures on the Fed from the President, Congress and the public; second, because of the unwillingness of the Fed to reform obsolete operating procedures, developed when it conceived its mission to be to control credit conditions rather than monetary growth.

THE RIGHT PRESCRIPTION

What is the right policy now? That is easy to say, hard to do. We need a long-term program dedicated to eliminating inflation. The Fed should announce that it proposes to increase M_2 at the annual rate of, say, 8 per cent during 1978, 7 per cent during 1979, 6 per cent during 1980, 5 per cent during 1981; and 4 per cent during 1982 and all subsequent years. To relieve the fiscal pressures on the Fed, such a monetary policy should be accompanied by a budget policy of reducing Federal spending as a fraction of national income—also gradually but steadily.

Such a monetary and fiscal program would eliminate inflation by 1983—for good. Such a gradual program would avoid economic disruption. Indeed, the confidence it engendered might well foster a vigorous and healthy expansion in investment and economic activity—and even a stock-market boom.

The difficulty with this prescription is to make it credible. Promises are one thing. Performance, as we have learned, is something else again. The program is technically feasible. But is it politically feasible not only to announce it but to stick to it? I doubt that it currently is. I hope I am wrong. But, just in case I am not, hold on to your hats as the inflation roller coaster goes on its not-so-merry way.

19

Heading 'em off at the GNP gap

A hard look at the 1978 *Economic Report of the President,* in the following series of pieces, indicates that it's built around a highly risky strategy that ignores many problems on the current scene.

Bibliophiles who began collecting the *Economic Report of the President* when it was first issued in January 1947 now find that their treasures occupy more than two running feet of shelf space. And for the conscientious souls who have dipped into every one of those 31 volumes — read beyond the brief summaries signed by the President and into *The Annual Report of the Council of Economic Advisers* —

it has been a mixed experience. Some made keen, even lively reading while others were about as informative and memorable as a collection of canceled checks. This latest one, alas, falls on the disappointing side of the spectrum.

The failure can't be ascribed to lack of technical competence. Chairman Charles Schultze and his fellow council members, Messrs. Gramley and Nordhaus, all command the high respect of their fellow economists—a profession not noted for generous praise. The problem — one that previous councils encountered — is rooted in a conflict between political goals and the current state of the art of economic analysis.

The Carter Administration — albeit to a lesser degree than its Democratic predecessors in the 1960s—is committed to policies of economic activism. There are, to be sure, vocal critics of heavy-handed federal regulation within the White House circle. But on the large issues of unemployment, government spending, the level of interest rates and the control of inflation, it carries a decidedly interventionist bias. More broadly stated, there's an assumption or presupposition — one that's hardly the exclusive property of the incumbent political party — that economies organized around the private ownership of property are inherently unstable and must be constantly balanced by the policies of a prescient federal establishment.

But the catch is that the very visible hand of government — whenever it does its work anywhere in the world — is more likely to be the very cause of the evils it seeks to banish: uncertainty and instability.

It's a lesson that hasn't been lost to economists. The simple Keynesianism that pervaded college textbooks in the 1950s and early 1960s — and misled a generation of presently influential citizens — is now quite dead. So, too, is the notion that there is a comfortable and stable trade-off between inflation and unemployment — a neat choice between one or the other. Instead, economists are now grappling with the problems of a world badly shaken by inflation — or more specifically, with how the public's perceptions of government policies shape its expectations.

But there's precious little note of this intellectual change in the current *Economic Report* because emphasizing it would clearly conflict with the politics of activism. What the *Report* in effect does is ignore the changes and pursue a demand-management strategy that was essentially fashioned to cope with the problems of the early 1960s rather than those of the late 1970s.

Back in 1962, the "new economists" of the Kennedy Administration were confronted with the need to stimulate demand in an economy that for nearly a decade had been blessed with stable or nearly stable prices.

And in that climate of price stability, they were successful in persuading a reluctant Congress — and a balky Treasury — that taxes could be cut and the budget deliberately unbalanced without risking a wave of inflation.

The present council is operating in a far less congenial environment, and yet it is committed to essentially the same policy. "At the present time," the council writes, "there are still ample supplies of idle labor and capital resources available. In the period immediately ahead, growth in real output can therefore proceed at a rate above its long-term trend without risking a resurgence of demand-induced inflation." But that judgment involves a very long gamble. It assumes not only that the cushion of idle resources is there, but that it is fat enough to prevent an acceleration in prices in a climate that's shot through with high-inflation expectations. And it further compounds the risk of error by downplaying the role of domestic monetary policy and urging other countries — notably Germany and Japan — to pursue more stimulative policies.

Measuring potential

The centerpieces of the council's strategy are its estimates of the GNP gap as shown in the top panel of the chart (page 10). All the numbers are quite precise, but there are nagging questions about the meaning of the gap.

It's really a simple operation to estimate the gap as the difference between "potential" and actual GNP. What's enormously difficult is coming up with a plausible measure of the potential. Among the factors that are involved are the number of hours people are willing to work at varying levels of real income; the quantity of capital invested in productive enterprise; the technology — or new knowledge — embodied in the design of plant and equipment; and finally, the impact of government policy on the willingness of people to work and savers to invest.

In view of these complexities, it's small wonder that estimates of the GNP gap vary as widely as individual judgments. For 1977, George Perry of the Brookings Institution put the gap at $99 billion. The St. Louis Federal

Potential GNP
Which gap do you believe?

billions of 1972 dollars

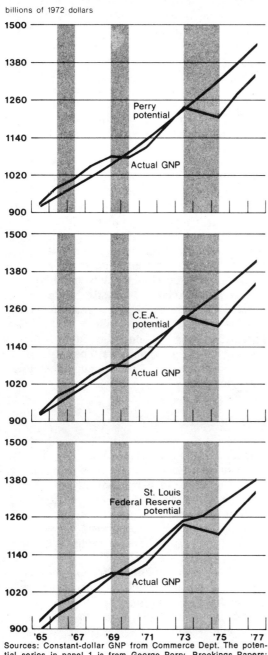

Sources: Constant-dollar GNP from Commerce Dept. The potential series in panel 1 is from George Perry, Brookings Papers; panel 2, from Peter K. Clark, "A New Estimate of Potential GNP;" and panel 3, Robert Rasche and John Tatom, "Potential Output and Its Growth Rate."

Reserve Bank came in with a low $43.2 billion and the council splits the difference by pegging the gap at $74.4 billion. And the clear danger is that an overestimate will lull the authorities into pursuing an expansionary monetary and fiscal policy that will quickly trigger another round of inflation.

To be more specific, reaching the policy goals of both a significantly lower unemployment rate and a balanced budget by 1981 depends on the assumption that the economy will achieve the calculated potential level and so generate the necessary increase in jobs and tax revenues. To reach those goals, real growth would have to be in the 4½-5% range all during 1978-81. But that assumes that the economy is now so far below its potential that such rapid real GNP growth, at such a late stage of the cyclical expansion, would not create strong inflation pressures — a pretty hazardous assumption.

Another shortcoming of the CEA's GNP gap analysis is that it is silent on the relationships between inflation and the rate of unemployment. The Administration's target unemployment rate of 5% for 1981 is based on the unemployment rate of 4.9% that's assumed in calculating potential GNP for that year. And in fact, the size of the tax cut recommended by the Administration depends on the estimate of the gap. But recent research suggests that the "natural unemployment" rate — that which is consistent with a steady rate of inflation — may be above 5½%, and thus attempts to drive the actual unemployment rate below 5% may result in accelerating inflation. So if the monetary authorities tie their policies to unattainable employment goals, another cycle of go-and-stop — of expansion followed by harsh restraint followed by recession — is inevitable.

Even if the concept of the GNP gap were unambiguous and could be measured without substantial error, it's still not clear how much influence a gap of a particular size would have on the rate of inflation. The pervasiveness and intensity of expectations preclude any simple relationship between the size of the gap and the inflation rate.

Easing on down toward controls

Prudent trapeze artists string up safety nets. And an Administration bent on risking an acceleration of inflation must have a fallback plan for controlling prices.

What's spelt out in the *Economic Report* and elaborated on in a press briefing by Chairman Schultze is a series of tripartite labor, management and government conclaves in which "the business community and American workers" agree to "decelerate the rate of price and wage increase." It's a plan that's based on the "initial presumption that prices and wages in each industry should rise significantly less in 1978 than they did on average during the past two years" and it focuses directly on controlling profit margins. Where margins are "squeezed" or wages are "lagging seriously," deceleration in 1978 "would be less than for other firms or groups of workers." But "firms or groups that have done exceptionally well in the recent past may be expected to do more."

Doesn't this really come to a revival of the Kennedy-Johnson price-wage "guidelines" with the 3.2% cap on increases? The report says not, but the answer is hedged. The "program," it says, "does not establish a uniform set of numerical standards" since past inflation has been so distorting as to make it neither possible nor desirable. Yet the next sentence reads, "But it does establish standards of behavior for each industry . . . "

Now there is a distinction between decreeing that profit margins are on average to be smaller, and saying precisely how much smaller. But in the Washington context it's a subtle difference that does nothing to dispel the belief that, despite denials, the Administration — if it continues its presently stimulative economic policies — will eventually move to the compulsion of formal controls.

No one can say with much certitude just when that time will come. But in any case, there should be no wishful thinking about the benignancy of "voluntary" restraints. Jawboning — and more menacing forms of exhortation — mete out harsh punishment to large and conspicuous enterprises while letting others off the hook. And the resulting distortions — the "shortages" created by the failure to raise prices to market-clearing levels — can be just as pernicious as those created by a full-blown system of formal or statutory price controls.

Chopping away at the money tree

Monetary policy is the linchpin of any overall economic strategy because the rate at which the money stock — currency and bank deposits — grows largely determines the public's demand for goods and services, which is called nominal GNP. So even if policymakers avoid error in estimating the GNP gap, they can still come a cropper by creating too much monetary demand — that is, by causing the demand for goods and services, the nominal GNP, to grow faster than the supply, which is the real GNP.

Such an excess of demand causes prices to rise, and the disruptive impact of inflation, in addition to pressures on productive capacity, slows real growth. But long before such an inflationary boom goes very far, public opinion, alarmed by the accelerating inflation, cries out for action — and gets monetary restraint. And the ensuing, typically sharp slowdown in the growth of the money stock soon plunges the economy into recession.

Monetary policy errors most frequently occur when the authorities subordinate the control of the money stock to achieving other, almost always unattainable goals such as unrealistically low levels of unemployment or low interest rates in the face of rapid inflation. And it's into just such error that the current *Economic Report* is liable to lead the Carter Administration.

Each year, the Council of Economic Advisers comments on U.S. monetary policy. In the

1950s and early 1960s, their remarks usually credited monetary policy with the direct ability to influence interest rates and thus indirectly affect business investment spending and home-building. But by 1970, the treatment broadened, and monetary policy was given a somewhat more general and powerful responsibility though a less precisely defined one — that of influencing spending and employment.

This was in line with the growing awareness among economists, both in the United States and abroad, that changes in money-stock growth tend to have large and fairly prompt effects on consumer outlays for autos, home goods and clothing, that the channels through which money influences economic activity may go well beyond the traditional interest-rate routes, and that monetary policy may be more important and more predictable than fiscal policy in its effects on the overall economy. The 1974 *Report* went so far as to advocate a growth in broadly defined money (M_2) equal to the desired rate of growth in GNP.

And during the past three years, a number of central banks, including the U.S. Federal Reserve System, adopted specific targets for growth of either the monetary base (bank reserves plus currency held by the public) or the money stock. This attachment to monetary targets is especially close in Germany, Canada and Britain. To some it has seemed that, on a global basis, monetarism is supplanting or substantially modifying Keynesianism.

Against this background, the latest *Economic Report* is at least ambivalent and may even be read as an attempt to revive the old orthodoxy. Monetary policy gets rather short shrift compared with the extensive discussions of fiscal policy. In part, this is inevitable, since the council participates in shaping and justifying the Administration's fiscal-policy means and goals, while neither the President nor the council has any direct responsibility for monetary policy. But the superficial treatment of monetary policy also seems to reflect some doubts about the efficacy of reaching GNP targets by regulating growth in the monetary aggregates.

Moreover, the discussion of monetary policy that does appear is couched exclusively in terms of credit market conditions — primarily the behavior of long-term interest rates. This reflects the traditional Keynesian view that monetary policy operates solely through interest rates. According to this view, by varying the money supply the monetary authorities can prevent a rise in long-term rates and encourage the increased rate of investment needed to maintain the pace of the recovery. Furthermore, this investment will provide the capacity to head off bottlenecks and shortages, which could lead to a rekindling of the fires of inflation. The behavior of monetary aggregates is seen as important only in so far as it aids the achievement of the interest-rate targets.

This approach is potentially very dangerous since it is likely to produce a rapid expansion of the money stock in a futile attempt to keep market rates from rising, as inflation accelerates and credit demands increase. So the monetary expansion will cause the very inflation that the increased investment was intended to prevent. And when the monetary authorities subsequently try to slow the inflation by sharply reducing monetary growth, the economy will be pushed into recession.

The Right Tax Cut Mix

By WALTER W. HELLER

Given the political headwinds Mr. Carter's $25 billion tax cut is encountering, one is moved to reexamine the economic case for it. That case was strong and widely accepted in January. Has it been weakened by economic developments since then?

Let's remind ourselves of that persuasive, not to say airtight, case as it appeared in January:

—Built-in tax hikes: Without a cut, the economy would by 1979 be moving against a tide of at least $30 billion of new payroll and "inflation tax" liabilities.

—Growth prospects: Some weakening of our economic advance seemed to be in the cards for late 1978 and 1979 unless this tax overburden was removed.

—Inflation outlook: No breakout of inflation (beyond its stubborn 6% basic rate of the past 3 years) was in sight. Besides, U.S. inflation was clearly of the cost-push variety, and $25 billion of tax cut in a $2 trillion-plus economy would not push it into excess-demand terrain.

—Budget impacts: Mr. Carter's $500 billion budget for fiscal 1979 represented only a 1.6% rise in real terms in an economy growing at over 4% a year. The combined tax and budget impacts added up to only a mild fiscal stimulus for the economy.

—Investment incentives: To help pep up the sluggish private investment sector, not only stronger markets but stronger business tax incentives were badly needed.

Let's examine each of these in turn.

Built-in tax hikes: They are still built in. Even if no crude oil taxes are enacted, $14 billion of payroll tax add-ons are going into effect in 1978-'79 (plus another $15 billion or so in 1980). And as inflation pushes our income into higher brackets, the federal tax bite increases another $8 billion a year (over and above the normal rise in tax collections generated by economic recovery and expansion). Without the offset of a hefty tax cut, this undercutting of purchasing power would unduly retard expansion in 1979.

Growth prospects: The outlook for GNP growth is weaker today than it was when the tax cut was launched in January. Even with an expected rebound of GNP at an 8% rate in the current quarter, the prospective rise in real GNP, fourth quarter 1977 to fourth quarter 1978, has slipped from January's 4.8% to perhaps 4.0%, while the year-over-year growth prospect is down from 4.6% to 3.9%. The economic launching pad for 1979 is correspondingly weaker, thus bolstering the case for the tax cut.

Still a Lot of Slack

True, unemployment has behaved better than expected. But there is still a lot of slack in the economy. Operating rates in manufacturing are still poking along at 82.9% of capacity, a bit less than last summer. The Labor Department's broader unemployment measure, which takes discouraged and part-time workers into account, is still running at 8.5%. And after a welcome downswing, the "official" unemployment rate is likely to hover near 6%, or at best a trifle below, for the rest of 1978. If the rate were to drop sharply below 6%, second thoughts on the size and timing of the tax cut would be in order.

Inflation Outlook: The fear of flying into a higher inflation orbit on the wings of a tax cut plays a major role in the rising doubts about the Carter tax program. Is inflation getting worse? Will dropping the tax cut make it better?

Compared with the January outlook, inflation is worse, but not much. Appearances have outrun facts. In the sensitive area of food, especially meat, an estimated 8%-10% price rise this year has replaced earlier projections of about 6%. But non-food commodities in the CPI have been on an essentially even keel for many months. And large stocks of grains and soybeans, plus the rains that came to California, will moderate the food price upswing later in the year.

Import prices are up, but a steadying dollar will limit the rise while a strengthening dollar would reverse the uptrend.

Board of Contributors

The case for a tax cut remains strong. It does not follow that the Carter formula is sacrosanct.

More worrisome for longer-pull inflation prospects is the rise in average hourly earnings at roughly an 8% clip today against 7% a year ago.

The upshot? Against a rise of 6.8% in consumer prices during 1977, the 1978 rise might be a little over 7%. And the "underlying rate" of inflation, stuck at about 6% for the past three years, may be nudging up to 6.5% or so. Far too high, but hardly a panic-button breakout.

In relating the recent spate of price increases to the tax cut, one should note not only that, as in 1977, their pace is likely to ease later in the year, but also that the price increases are coming from the cost side: food, imports, and wages, not bottlenecks, shortages, and excess demand.

Even so, say the critics, dropping the tax cut would sharply improve prospects for reducing inflation. Not so in an economy still running well below its potential. Using the midpoint of "all the statistical estimates I know," Arthur Okun told the Ways and Means Committee Monday that dropping the tax cut would cost $40 billion a year of real output by 1980 while saving only two-tenths of a point on the price level. By any economic or social criterion I know, that's a poor tradeoff.

To fight cost-push inflation, one has to get at the forces that have relentlessly pushed costs up in the face of weak demand. After letting too many horses out of the barn, the Carter program seeks to do just that, partly by setting a Spartan example on federal pay raises, partly by policing its own costly regulations, and partly by unleashing Robert Strauss. A powerful program? No. But it is aimed at the right target and, diligently pursued, offers greater promise of curbing inflation than would a jettisoning of the tax cut.

Budget impacts: Budget revisions since January suggest smaller, not larger, deficits. For fiscal 1978, spending underruns have cut the prospective deficit from $62 billion to $53 billion. Further spending shortfalls in fiscal 1979 are likely to offset, or more than offset, budget increases for agricultural, defense, and other programs.

Spending is likely to end up at or below Mr. Carter's $500 billion.

A more relevant question: How strong a stimulus will the combined budget and tax actions provide? Adjusted estimates of the high-employment budget show that, even if the full Carter program were adopted, the net fiscal stimulus would be less than $10 billion in 1979. Without the tax cut, the built-in tax increases would clearly be a net drag on the economy.

Investment incentives: Even though business investment is hardly drying up, who would argue that it is robust enough to play its full part in sustaining 1978-'79 expansion, boosting productivity, and expanding capacity? The answer is clear: Business tax incentives are fully as much in order today as they were in January.

So the case for a tax cut remains strong. It does not follow that the Carter formula is sacrosanct.

A Basis for Compromise

Bearing in mind both the economic goal of sustaining expansion with a minimum of inflation and the political goal of producing a tax cut that will not only *be* right but *seem* right, I would urge Mr. Carter and the Congress to consider the following basis for compromise.

First, combine an economic good with a political need by substituting perhaps $8 billion of payroll tax cutback for an equal amount of individual income tax cuts. The $25 billion tax cut would then consist of about $8 billion of business and excise tax cuts; $9 billion of individual income tax cuts; and $8 billion of payroll tax cutbacks (in the form of shifting one-third of the cost of Medicare hospital insurance to general revenue financing, the other two-thirds to be shifted in two more $8 billion installments in, say, 1980 and 1981). This would soften the political blow of scheduled payroll tax increases and deliver the happy economic result of combining a rise in purchasing power with a fall in business costs. What better tax medicine can one prescribe for a high-inflation, slow-growth economy?

Second, split the $25 billion tax reduction into two stages, somewhat akin to the 1964-65 tax cut. Illustratively, $15 billion might go into effect Oct. 1, 1978, and another $10 billion the following July 1. If economic events call for a change before the tax bill emerges from Congress late next summer, adjust the staging accordingly. Under this flexible two-stage approach, the economy would have the assurance of the sustaining stimulus of the tax cut, yet the deficit impact would be softened and congressional concerns about doing too much at once would be accommodated.

In short, a $25 billion tax cut still makes good economic sense. But its economic impact could be improved by making room for a sizable payroll tax cut. And its adaptation to political reality—and conceivably also to economic circumstances—would be improved by adopting the two-stage approach.

Mr. Heller is Regents' Professor of Economics at the University of Minnesota, former chairman of the Council of Economic Advisers under Presidents Kennedy and Johnson and a member of the Journal's Board of Contributors.

Why the Tax Cut Looks So Dangerous
by ALLAN T. DEMAREE

s in the case of the ill-fated tax rebate, President's economic policy has again n overtaken by events. The $25-billion cut has lost the allure it had only a few nths ago and is coming under intensi- ng fire. Unemployment has been drop- g fast, productivity is lagging, forecast- are raising their inflation estimates, and may be reaching the limits of our pro- ctive capacity sooner than most people ected. Under the circumstances, a tax as big as Carter wants would heat up in- ion and increase the risk that the econ- y might stumble into recession's maw. t's really a question of how far we can sh our supply of labor and plant capac- . For a long time, it was assumed that un- ployment could come down to 4 percent fore conditions in the labor market in- ced employers to bid up wages. But in re- nt years, women and young people have en entering the job market in greater mbers, and their much higher unem- byment rates have skewed the calcula- n. It is now generally conceded that the por market starts getting tight enough to celerate wage increases when the over- unemployment rate falls below 6 per- nt. Judged by the old standards, the rrent level of 6.2 percent gives an im- ession of slack, but employers know that be illusory. Recently, in fact, non-union ages have climbed faster than union ages, a sure sign that the slack has been sappearing.

Only the growth of productivity can off- t higher wages, and the news on that ont has been pretty dismal. In the past n years, productivity increases have slowed to an annual average of only 1.6 percent, and the rate probably won't go up even that much in the year ahead. With employee compensation expected to rise close to 10 percent this year, unit labor costs will be heading for a rather fright- ening increase of 9 percent (see Business Roundup, page 9).

Into the danger zone

G. William Miller, chairman of the Fed- eral Reserve, fears that we may be in trou- ble on plant capacity too. The Fed's own statistics show operating rates to be a re- assuring four points below the 87 percent level that marked the last crunch in 1973. The St. Louis Fed argues, however, that price increases could pick up sharply when plant usage hits 84 percent of capacity, as it will very soon. Miller's own view is em- pirical—based on "my experience and talk- ing with business people," he says—and he worries that overstimulated demand will push us into an inflationary danger zone where a lot of obsolete, high-cost fa- cilities come into use, and unpredictable bottlenecks begin to show up.

By taking labor, productivity, and other factors into consideration, economists are constantly trying to determine how high the G.N.P. growth rate can be pushed with- out speeding up inflation. Michael Wachter of the University of Pennsylvania has con- cluded that, as of the end of last year, our actual output was at most $35 billion (or 2.6 percent) below the limit of our poten- tial. Wachter believes a $25-billion tax cut could throw us through the ceiling.

Otto Eckstein, a member of the Council of Economic Advisers in the Johnson years, is one of many economists who are alarmed by the budgetary implications of the tax cut. He fears the Carter package would increase the full-employment def- icit precisely when the economy is ap- proaching its limits. He likes Chairman Miller's proposal to delay the effective date of the cut, which would lessen stimulus in the coming fiscal year by $8.6 billion, but he would also reduce the cut itself by an ad- ditional $5 billion. Having had a chance to examine Eckstein's analysis, Miller told FORTUNE, "I think there's a good deal of merit in it. I'm willing to skinny."

Miller is mindful of another risk, which involves him quite directly. By having to finance so big a deficit late in the recovery, when private credit demands are strong, the Administration may force the Fed into a predicament. If the Fed accommodates the deficit by increasing the money sup- ply beyond sensible limits (say, the max- imum 9 percent growth it has set for M- 2), it will be sowing the seeds of future inflation. But if the Fed sticks hard to its targets, tight money may choke off the expansion.

The Fed's actions in the past two weeks have considerably tightened credit. The stream of funds into thrift institutions, which finance housing, has been slowing markedly. With interest rates on compet- itive investments already a full percentage point above average yields on passbook savings, money will flow out of the thrifts if rates go much higher. The resulting set- back to mortgage availability would knock the pins out from under homebuilders, who have been a source of strength in this recovery. Indirectly, it would also tend to crimp consumer spending. Alan Greenspan, chairman of the Council of Economic Advisers in the Ford Administration, points out that homeowners monetized capital gains of $65 billion last year by refinancing or selling their homes. They used much of the proceeds to pay for big-ticket consumer items. That flow of funds into spending will be stanched if high interest rates diminish the attractiveness of refinancing and slow the turnover of houses.

Hearty appetites on a diet

Prospects for corporate borrowers also look worse now than in the days when former Treasury Secretary William Simon was inveighing against "crowding out." Simon was worried about crowding out at a time when the economy was in recession and private demands on the money markets were slight. Last year, corporate borrowing rose to $77 billion (versus only $27 billion in the recession year of 1975), and appetites for financing promise to remain hearty.

But higher interest rates have already restrained some corporate borrowers, and the futures market is guessing that they will keep climbing; futures on ninety-day Treasury bills are selling at prices that imply rates of more than 7.5 percent next year. If T-bills do hit that level, Arthur Okun, the Brookings Institution economist, says, he will bet all comers $10 that a downturn will follow within twelve months. With economic conditions as they are today, Otto Eckstein believes, every $1 billion

added to the federal deficit will crowd out $300 million to $400 million in private borrowing, mainly for corporate investment.

Chairman Miller generally agrees with Eckstein's formulation, and he clearly wants more room to steer between the reefs of too-rapid monetary growth and the shoals of a credit crunch. In its current form, the Carter tax package would require the government to raise around $6 billion in the fourth quarter of this year. Simply delaying it until January 1, as Miller has urged, would relax the strains on financial markets in the fourth quarter, and would hold off the extra stimulus until it could be partly offset by scheduled increases in Social Security taxes.

More fundamentally, in his first two months on the job Miller has been trying to get across some basic points about long-term economic policy. For many years, he believes, we have wrongly concentrated on stimulating demand rather than supply, consumption rather than fixed business investment, which is the engine that powers *anti-inflationary* growth.

"We have the highest percent of the adult population employed that we've ever had," he says. "We have a certain problem with teenagers, with minorities, with blacks. It's very serious. But a lot of that now is structural, and we need to target our structural programs rather than try to use consumption demand to pull up that employment. Macroeconomic policies probably won't do it, and we'll loose the inflation that will destroy jobs. Inflation will wipe out jobs.

"You know, somebody said to me if you push that tax cut back three months, then

that's 150,000 jobs lost. [One person p[ur]suing this line of argument has been Tr[ea]sury Secretary Michael Blumenthal.[I] don't believe that. If you got the busin[ess] investment going, you'd pick up 150,0[00] jobs over the long run, and they'd be s[ound] jobs. I believe that is what's going to ha[p]pen when you show discipline in atta[ck]ing inflation and making room for so[me] measured and continued growth—inste[ad] of letting the thing run until we have a [se]rious recession, which would scare bu[si]ness and stop investment."

Keeping up with reality

Miller is optimistic that Congress w[ill] not let the tax cut get out of hand: "I thi[nk] the evidence is there's going to be so[me] shaving." The imperatives of governme[n]tal procedure dictated that the Admini[s]tration present its tax proposals ear[ly,] acting on views of the economy form[ed] late last year when there was a lot of an[x]iety about the expansion petering out. T[he] lively rebound from the downturn in t[he] first quarter makes that kind of worry se[em] pretty remote these days. Congress is wis[e]ly listening to people like Miller, who a[re] neither saddled with that old forecast n[or] reluctant to change their minds to keep [up] with evolving realities.

The U.S. tax burden is too heavy for t[he] long-run health of the economy. A $25-b[il]lion reduction would be very helpful—[if] government spending were reduced a[c]cordingly. Since, unhappily, there does[n't] seem much chance of that happening th[is] year, the full Carter tax cut looks more a[nd] more like a dangerous proposition.

22

The Great Stagflation Swamp

Arthur M. Okun

Speaking before the Economic Club of Chicago in October 1977, Arthur Okun warned his listeners that the following address would not send them home happy. While in his judgment the economic expansion still has a good deal of vigor and a substantial life expectancy, Okun doubted that the current strategy of economic policy will lead to a happy ending. Contending that we should not rely on more of that same strategy, Okun proposed some remedies for our economic ills, describing his message as a call for action rather than a forecast of gloom.

IN 1977, the United States will record a higher unemployment rate and a higher inflation rate than was experienced in any year between 1952 and 1972. We have not licked either of these two major problems; indeed, they have become intertwined and combined in a way that is historically unprecedented and, by the verdict of many economic textbooks, theoretically impossible. This nation has had serious inflation problems before; it has had prolonged periods of excess capacity and idle manpower before; but it has never previously faced a serious inflation problem after a prolonged period of slack.

The coexistence of stagnation and inflation or, as it has been dubbed, "stagflation," is a new problem. Yet we are dealing with it with old policies that are unlikely to solve it. The Carter administration—in this respect, like the Ford administration—is trying through traditional fiscal and monetary measures to attain both a sustained gradual recovery to full prosperity and a sustained gradual slowdown of inflation.

Arthur M. Okun is a senior fellow in the Brookings Economic Studies program and the author of Equality and Efficiency: The Big Tradeoff *(Brookings, 1975).*

That strategy is not succeeding. The modest recovery targets have been attained reasonably well over the past two-and-a-half years; the economic expansion has been a rather typical, standard-sized advance. But because the recession that preceded it was double sized, it has brought us only halfway back to prosperity. Thus we have paid heavily to keep our recovery moderate, and we have had no relief from inflation during the expansion to show for these efforts.

The basic inflation rate has been stuck at 6 percent since the spring of 1975. Nor is there any basis for confidence that relief is forthcoming. Indeed, in my judgment the inflation rate is more likely to accelerate than decelerate between now and 1979, even with a continuation of a slowly recovering economy. And once it becomes undeniable that the gradualist anti-inflation strategy has failed, I fear that monetary and fiscal policy will be tightened anew to restrain the growth of the economy, thereby courting the next recession.

In my view, a serious effort to deal with inflation and slack simultaneously must go beyond traditional fiscal-monetary policies. It must invoke specific measures to hold down prices and costs in both the private and public sectors. It must break the wage-price spiral that has so firmly and stubbornly gripped the system. I believe that a number of techniques in pursuit of those objectives deserve serious consideration. Let me state emphatically that the worthy candidates do not include a return to price-wage controls, such as the Nixon administration conducted in 1971–73.

Getting Stuck in the Swamp

As an autobiographical obligation, I must record that the most recent unhappy era of our economic history began late in 1965, while I served as an adviser to President Johnson. That is when the critical decisions were

---

made to finance the Vietnam military buildup in an inappropriate inflationary manner. But the historical record will not support any "original sin" explanation of inflation that would attribute our ills of a dozen years to that mistake. Every wartime period in American history has been marked by a severe inflation; indeed, the Vietnam episode was the least severe. But the end of every previous war was marked by the end of inflation.

The unique experience of the seventies is that the end of the war was associated with an intensification of inflation. The double-digit inflation of 1973–74 was the product of many new mistakes and misfortunes: excessive monetary and fiscal stimulus in 1972, the devaluation of the dollar, the mismanagement of U.S. grain supplies, and the OPEC shock to energy prices.

Responding to that rip-roaring inflation, the makers of monetary and fiscal policy adopted extremely restrictive measures that brought on the most severe recession since the late thirties. That recession promptly cut the inflation rate to about 6 percent by the middle of 1975. But there we have been ever since, despite massive excess supplies of idle people, machines, and plants. If our economic institutions responded currently to a slump as they did in 1922 or 1938 or 1949, the recession and prolonged slack would not only have stopped inflation in its tracks but created a wave of falling prices.

In fact, the nature of price- and wage-making has been transformed in the modern era. We live in a world dominated by cost-oriented prices and equity-oriented wages. The standard textbook view of prices adjusting promptly to equate supply and demand applies only to that small sector of the U.S. economy in which products are traded in organized auction markets. And there it works beautifully; the prices of sensitive industrial raw materials *fell* by 15 percent between May 1974 and March 1975.

Elsewhere, however, prices are set by sellers whose principal concern is to maintain customers and market share for the long run. The pricing policies designed to treat customers reasonably and maintain their loyalty in good times and bad times rely heavily on marking up some standard measure of costs. For most products, prices do not rise faster than standard costs during booms nor do they rise less rapidly than costs during slumps.

Similarly, the long-term interest of skilled workers and employers in maintaining their relationships is the key to wage decisions in both union and nonunion situations. The U.S. labor market does not resemble the Marxist model in which employers point to a long line of applicants—"the reserve army of unemployed"—and tell their current workers to take a wage cut or find themselves replaced. Employers have investments in a trained, reliable, and loyal work force. They know that if they curbed wages stringently in a slump, they would pay heavily for that strategy with swollen quit rates during the next period of prosperity. In a few areas, where jobs have a high turnover and thus employers and employees have little stake in lasting relationships, wages do respond sensitively to the level of unemployment. But in most areas, personnel policies are sensibly geared to the long run. Workers seek and generally obtain equitable treatment, and the basic test of equity is that their pay is raised in line with the pay increases of other workers in similar situations. Such a strategy introduces inertia in the rate of wage increase, creating a pattern of wages following wages.

The customer and career relationships that desensitize prices and wages from the short-run pressure of excess supplies and demands have a genuine social function. They are not creations of evil monopolies but rather adaptations to a complex, interdependent economy in which customers and suppliers, workers and employers benefit greatly from continuing relationships. In general, the persistence of inflation is not a tale of villainy. By any standard, and by comparison with other industrial countries, American unions have been remarkably self-restrained in recent years. Business, meanwhile, has kept its markups below levels that would be justified by the current cost of capital.

In combination, business and labor have been raising prices about 6 percent a year and increasing hourly compensation (wages, private fringe benefits, and employers' payroll tax costs) by about 8 percent a year. The 8-and-6 combination allows a typical margin of real wage gains in line with the normal trend of productivity. Precisely for that reason, it becomes self-perpetuating. New wage decisions are made against the background of 8 percent advances in other wages and 6 percent increases in prices. And so they tend to center on 8 percent. Then, with hourly labor costs rising by 8 percent, businesses find their labor costs per unit of output up about 6 percent, and so their prices continue to rise by 6 percent.

There is no handle on either the wage side or the price side by which we can pull ourselves out of this stagflation swamp. Nor can any single industry or union provide a handle, except by making an unreasonable sacrifice of its own self-interest. It must do what everybody else is doing in order to protect itself. Analogously, if all the spectators at a parade are standing on tiptoe in an effort to get a better view, no individual can afford to get off his uncomfortable tiptoe stance. Ending the discomfort requires a collective decision.

Production and Jobs

Because prices and wages respond only a little to changes in total spending, production and employment respond a lot. And that is the fundamental limitation of fiscal and monetary restraints as a means of curbing inflation. Those policies clearly can put the lid on total spending for goods and services. The holddown in total spending is then split between a cutback in production and a slowing of inflation. But that "split" is the result of price and wage determination; it is not controlled by Washington. We learned—or should have learned—in the past three years that the split is extremely unfavorable. The reaction to weaker markets is loaded with layoffs, no-help-wanted signs, cutbacks of production schedules, and slashes in capital budgets. At most, it is sprinkled with holddowns in prices and wages. To save one percentage point on the basic inflation rate through policies that restrain total spending, we lose more than five points—easily $100 billion—of our annual real GNP.

The recession and slack of 1974–77 have exacted a toll of $500 billion in lost production of capital goods and consumer goods that could have added to our productivity and our standard of living. That cost should

---

"We cannot count on our current policies to pull us out of the stagflation swamp. The evidence of recent years has accumulated and become overwhelming. The time has come to face the likelihood that we have a losing hand, and to deal a new one."

---

be clearly recognized, although it must be equally recognized that there was, and is, no toll-free route of escape from our problems. In fact, the toll keeps mounting. After thirty months of economic expansion, we

have moved only about half the distance from the depths of the recession to a reasonable and feasible level of prosperity or full employment. Serious statistical studies designed to estimate the unemployment rate associated with reasonably balanced—neither slack nor tight—labor markets converge on a range between 5 and 5.5 percent. They demonstrate that with today's structure of labor markets, full employment certainly cannot be defined as a 4 percent unemployment rate. But neither can it be pegged anywhere near our recent 7.1 percent. Since unemployment has come down from 9 percent at the worst of the recession to 7.1 percent, we are about halfway to a reasonable cyclical target in the zone of 5 to 5.5 percent.

The excess of nearly two percentage points in the unemployment rate is not a structural phenomenon; it is not concentrated in "unemployables," secondary workers, or groups especially affected by government benefit programs. It is instructive to compare the unemployment rates of eminently employable groups today with their 1973–74 average:

	August 1977	1973–74 Average
	(percent)	
Married men	3.5	2.5
Craftsmen	5.5	4.0
Factory workers	7.0	5.0
"Job losers"	3.4	2.1
	(weeks)	
Average duration of unemployment	13.5	9.8

Unemployment remains high because production has not grown enough to generate the jobs required to get us back to prosperity. The behavior of the unemployment rate in recent years poses no mystery. Indeed, it has moved remarkably true to form in relation to the growth of production. Between 1973 and 1977, our annual growth rate has averaged 2 percent, and such a substandard growth performance entails a much increased rate of unemployment. Economists can disagree about whether the nation's "potential growth rate"—the rate of growth of real GNP that maintains a constant unemployment rate—is as low as 3.3 percent or as high as 4 percent, but it surely is not 2 percent. If I use my favorite number, 3.75 percent, for the potential growth rate, the 2 percent average actual growth rate since 1973 would be expected to raise the unemployment rate by 2.3 percentage points, in line with a rule-of-thumb formula that I developed in 1961. That would point to an unemployment rate a little above 7 percent currently, and that is where we are.

The potential growth rate of the economy is influenced by trends in productivity and in labor force participation. In the seventies, a rising fraction of women and young people have chosen to enter the labor force. That increase in "work ethic" permits the economy to enjoy greater growth without encountering tight labor markets. Indeed, in its absence, the rather disappointing trend in productivity would have significantly lowered our trend of potential growth. To be sure, if women and teenagers stopped hunting for jobs and went back to their knitting and ball-playing, respectively, our unemployment figures would be lower. But our labor markets would be tighter, and the potential of the economy would be reduced. The increased labor force participation of these workers is correctly viewed as an opportunity and not as a burden.

At the level required to bring the unemployment rate down to the middle of the 5-to-5.5 zone, our real GNP would be about $100 billion, or 5.5 percent, above its present level. The evidence suggests that our plant capacity could accommodate that extra output without strain, so long as it was broadly spread across sectors. Such a judgment must rest on estimates of operating rates, which are admittedly imperfect. But they are not likely to be seriously biased, either upward or downward. The estimate of capacity may inappropriately include some outmoded facilities, but it is just as likely to omit some rehabilitated facilities.

In short, idle resources and sacrificed output continue to represent an enormous national extravagance. Economists ought to be devoting more of their efforts and ingenuity to correcting that waste and less to talking it away or defining it out of existence.

The Costs of Inflation

Just as 7 percent unemployment is not full employment, so 6 percent inflation is not price stability. For the past two years, inflation has been reasonably steady and relatively well predicted, yet it remains domestic Public Enemy No. 1 in the view of a majority of the American people. I find that entirely understandable. In a system that rests on the dollar as a yardstick, a scorekeeping device, and a basis for planning and budgeting, the instability of the price level adds enormously to uncertainty and risk.

In our institutional environment, most people cannot hedge their wealth or their incomes against inflation. The single-family home has been the only major asset that has served as an effective inflation hedge during the past decade; and it obviously is not a feasible outlet for steady flows of saving. Common stocks have been miserable failures as inflation hedges; savings deposits

and life insurance offer no effective inflation protection. A small minority of Americans have obtained cost-of-living escalators that effectively protect their real incomes against inflation. But their escalated wages are passed through into prices and thereby destabilize the real incomes of the majority whose earnings are not indexed. Escalators are a means of passing the buck among groups within our society, not of protecting the buck for the whole of society.

This country has not adapted, and is not adapting, to 6 percent inflation. The tolerable rate of inflation in this society is considerably below 6 percent. In the early sixties, 1.5 percent inflation was generally regarded as tolerable; in the early seventies, a 3 percent rate was widely accepted. If we were now to label 6 percent inflation as acceptable, who could believe that such a decision was the final turn of the ratchet? This country needs an effort to restore the reliability of the dollar, not a set of innovations to replace it; it needs an effort to curb inflation, not a program to learn to live with it.

With current prospects and policies, the basic inflation rate is not likely to drop below 6 percent during the remainder of the present economic expansion. To be sure, the inflation rate fluctuates from quarter to quarter, and minor wiggles and jiggles tend to generate vain hopes and groundless fears. Recent declines in farm prices and a downward blip in mortgage interest rates have generated favorable news. That is genuinely reassuring evidence that the jump in inflation to an 8 percent rate earlier this year was transitory. But the latest figures do not signify a fundamental improvement that is likely to be sustained.

Our chance for some net relief from inflation has been reduced by a new wave of congressional actions that add to particular costs and prices. Employers' hourly labor costs will be raised by hikes in payroll taxes in January 1978 for both social security and unemployment insurance. Further increases in payroll taxes are contemplated to finance proposed reforms of social security. The minimum wage seems slated to move up from $2.30 to $2.65. The first installment of the wellhead tax on crude oil is scheduled to take effect in 1978. Government farm programs have reinstituted acreage cutbacks, deliberately reducing the productivity of our agriculture. Many of these cost-raising measures have some justification. No one of them spells the difference between price stability and rampant inflation. But, in combination, they may well add 1.5 percent to the inflation rate by late 1978.

This wave of cost-raising measures deserves far more attention and scrutiny than it has received. Reliance on such measures is nothing new, but their total magnitude does set a new record. The Congress may have been tempted to load costs on the budgets of consumers and employers in order to avoid loading more onto the federal budget. In several of these areas, the President initially advanced proposals that were admirably restrained, but then compromised in the face of strong political opposition. (When some of the press welcomes such instances as evidence of the President's education in the ways of Washington, I cannot share the enthusiasm.) Meanwhile, the financial and business community has been so preoccupied with Thursday afternoon reports on the money supply and reestimates of the federal deficit that it has missed the big new inflationary game in town.

All things considered, my best guess is that between now and 1979, inflation is more likely to accelerate than to decelerate—and not because of overly rapid growth or excess demand.

With that inflation forecast, a good growth performance in 1979 and 1980 seems unlikely. Bad news on inflation would turn into bad news for prosperity in several ways. First, it would mean higher interest rates. Short-term interest rates cannot responsibly be held below the inflation rate indefinitely. To me, an interest rate on Treasury bills above 7 percent would sound an alarm; it would lead to disintermediation and create a mortgage famine that would starve homebuilding. Second, in an environment of stubborn and intensifying inflation, the makers of fiscal policy would be understandably reluctant to provide any stimulus to the investor or consumer that might be needed to sustain growth. Third, bad news on inflation would heighten consumer anxiety and once again weaken discretionary household spending.

The connection between worsening inflation and a subsequent recession is not magic or automatic, but it is genuinely built into the attitudes and expectations of our public and our policymakers. "Inflation backlash" is a reality. Given that reality, we simply cannot take the risk of doing what comes naturally and hoping for good luck.

Thus, my principal message is that we cannot count on our current policies to pull us out of the stagflation swamp. The evidence based on the experience of recent years has accumulated and become overwhelming. "Patience and fortitude" is no longer an acceptable response to our disappointments. The time has come to face the likelihood that we have a losing hand, and to deal a new one.

A Fiscal-Monetary Cure?

Some who accept my grim verdict about current policies call for a new monetary-fiscal strategy. And they point in opposite directions. On one side, the argument takes these lines. If a slack economy is not curing inflation, then why take the high costs of slack? Why not try to grow out of the inflation with stimuli, such as large permanent tax cuts backed up by a monetary policy committed to low interest rates, that have reliably spurred growth every time they have been applied in the past?

On the other side, the reverse case is made. If inflation is not abating with 5 percent real growth, isn't it clear that we need more restrictive policies to slow the economy down until inflation responds?

These polar-opposite proposals have in common the justified anxiety that our current act of juggling two eggs may lead to both getting broken. But I fear that they have one other thing in common that is less admirable. They are asking us to kid ourselves. The expansionists are right in that production and jobs are good things—but not because they alleviate inflation. Any major stimulative strategy, taken alone, will hasten the day that inflation accelerates and that inflation backlash sets in. The restrictionists are right in that a big enough dose of restraint would curb inflation—but only at the price of some $100 billion in output per point of inflation reduction.

Some groups in the business and financial community no doubt would applaud a hypothetical announcement that the government was cutting its spending by, say,

$30 billion and that the Federal Reserve was now setting monetary targets aimed at, say, only 7 percent growth of nominal GNP. But when government contracts were rescinded, when banks began closing loan windows, when cash registers stopped ringing, the responses would be entirely predictable: new waves of layoffs, new slashes in capital budgets, a collapse in productivity, and new demands that the government stop imports, shorten workweeks, and launch programs of makework jobs.

Perhaps the most appealing variant of the restraint prescription is the call for a *very gradual*, but consistently maintained, slowing of monetary growth and reversal of fiscal stimulus. As far as I can see, that strategy —taken alone—offers us a long, dull headache instead of a short, severe one, but no smaller total amount of pain. Moreover, its plan to curb demand gently enough to avoid a recession surely sets a new record for fine-tuning. It reminds me of the story about the Greek boy who thought he could pick up a full-grown bull if he started with a newborn calf and lifted it every day. The first little trimming of total demand is a mere baby calf. It would not do production and employment much harm (nor would it do our inflation performance much good). But, as time progressed, that calf would grow into a bull —and we could not count on lifting it.

A Program for Prosperity and Price Stability

We need an anti-inflation program that is not an anti-growth program, and that goes beyond traditional fiscal and monetary measures. In the past three years, I have assembled long menus of measures that might hold down costs and prices without holding down production and employment. Now I offer a specific set of proposals. I do so uncomfortably—I left the business of packaging four-point programs nearly a decade ago, and I prefer to stay out of it. I do so diffidently—because the facets of the program have not been polished by staff work or constructive criticism. But I do so enthusiastically because I am convinced that the general approach it embodies represents our best hope for getting out of the stagflation swamp.

No net federal cost-raising. First, the administration should set a target of zero net cost-raising measures for 1978, and should report quarterly to the American people on the achievement of that target. Any new cost-raising governmental action that imposed higher labor costs on employers or higher prices on consumers would have to be neutralized by a federal cost-reducing measure—lightening the burden of regulation or providing

a cost-cutting subsidy. Thus we would be insured against an encore of the cost-raising actions of 1977.

Sales tax–cut incentive. Second, the federal government should institute a grant-in-aid program that would defray half the revenue loss of any state or city that reduced or repealed its sales taxes during 1978. Mayors and governors obtaining federal aid for sales tax cuts would pledge not to increase other cost-raising taxes during the period (but could raise income taxes). An allocation of $6 billion of federal outlays for this program would fund a 1 percentage point cut in the consumer price index. Sales taxes are part of the cost of living, both genuinely and statistically. Reductions in those taxes would hold down consumer prices and have anti-inflationary effects on wages that are linked, formally or informally, to the cost of living.

Tax relief for price-wage restraint. Third, a tax relief incentive should be offered to workers and businessmen who enlist in a cooperative anti-inflationary effort. To qualify for participation, a firm would have to pledge, at the beginning of 1978, to hold its employees' average rate of wage increase below 6 percent and its average rate of price increase below 4 percent (apart from a dollars-and-cents passthrough of any increases in costs of materials and supplies) during the course of the year. In return for participation, employees of the firm would receive a tax rebate (generally through withholding) equal to 1.5 percent of their wage or salary incomes with a ceiling of $225 per person; the firm would receive a 5 percent rebate on its income tax liabilities on domestic operating profits.

Any firm covered by a collective bargaining contract would be obliged to consult with union representatives before deciding to participate in the program. Typical workers who were counting on before-tax wage increases of 8 percent or less would benefit from participation.

I would hope for strong moral suasion, led by the President himself, to enlist participants in the program. But nonparticipation would be a matter of free choice and not subject to penalty. At the end of the year, each participating firm would file a statement of compliance that would be subject to audit by the Internal Revenue Service.

The total cost in federal revenues of the cooperative restraint program might approach $15 billion; with the sales tax grants, it could total $20 billion. Tax cuts of that magnitude are being widely espoused in the context of the forthcoming tax reform program. I would postpone the tax cuts in the reform package in the conviction that a pro-growth, anti-inflation program deserves a more urgent priority on the nation's agenda.

Obviously, the increase in purchasing power and profitability provided by the anti-inflationary tax cuts would stimulate consumption and investment. Indeed, the prospect of a credible attack on inflation could reduce the uncertainty that now constricts capital budgeting. If the program achieved its objective of a mutual and balanced de-escalation of wages and prices, there would be no overhang of "catch-up" wage and price increases in 1979. But opportunities should be held open for renewing the program (or phasing it out more gradually) in an effort to cut inflation once again.

New GNP targets. Fourth and finally, the administration and the Federal Reserve in cooperation should set forth revised fiscal and monetary targets designed to ensure full recovery *and* lower inflation. For 1978 those targets should aim for an encore of the increase in *nominal* GNP of 1977—about 10.5 percent—with more real growth and less inflation. For 1979 and 1980 they should aim to bring the growth of nominal GNP progressively into single-digit territory. Thus they will call for declining federal deficits and slowing money growth (appropriately adjusting for any further significant shifts in velocity). Such a fiscal-monetary strategy should strongly reinforce the credibility of the anti-inflation program and help to ensure that we don't slide back into the swamp.

Still, the first requirement is to get out of the swamp. My program is neither a panacea nor a long-run insurance policy against inflation and stagflation. But its approach offers a good chance of bringing about a mutual de-escalation of prices and wages, and an end to the insidious wave of governmental cost-raising actions. It recognizes that traditional monetary-fiscal policies are powerful tools to promote full recovery and to prevent a resurgence of excess-demand inflation. But it also recognizes realistically that they cannot by themselves cure stagflation. That new problem requires the additional help of new remedies, which of necessity are unconventional and unproved. Whether the new remedies become politically feasible will depend on whether knowledgeable Americans face up to the reality that we are likely to remain stuck in the stagflation swamp with current policies, and whether they are willing to consider seriously—and to criticize constructively—alternative routes to noninflationary prosperity.

23

Testimony to the Joint Economic Committee

Statement by Henry C. Wallich, Member, Board of Governors of the Federal Reserve System, before the Joint Economic Committee, U.S. Congress, February 8, 1978.

It is a pleasure to appear before the Joint Economic Committee to present my personal views in the area of incomes policies.

Disruptive inflation has plagued our economy for something like 12 years. During that period its virulence has varied, as high as 12.0 per cent in the fourth quarter of 1974 and as low as 1.5 per cent in the second quarter of 1967. But the experience has made clear that we are not "learning to live" with inflation. Increasingly, inflation is seen for what it is—a serious addiction that gradually undermines the vitality and even the viability of the addict.

While inflation is being forecast for the indefinite future at a rate close to that of the present, there is no reason at all to believe that inflation will stabilize if left alone. Inflation has shown itself in recent years to be highly inflexible downward. It has shown no similar inflexibility upward. Any one of a number of factors could send inflation spiraling again. Pressure of demand on limited manufacturing capacity, a major wage breakthrough resulting

Reprinted from Federal Reserve *Bulletin*, February, 1978.

from special circumstances that nevertheless could set a pattern, food prices, oil prices, all could trigger higher inflation that would then work its way into wages and become resistant to any decline. Such a ratchet mechanism is a tangible threat.

Further acceleration of inflation almost certainly would, after some not very long interval, lead to renewed increases in unemployment. Thus, there is no other choice but to try to bring down unemployment and inflation simultaneously.

It is largely because of concerns like these that a consensus has developed that the economy must be allowed to grow at only a moderate rate. Idle resources, human and material, can be absorbed only gradually. Moreover, the noninflationary limits to that absorption leave a distressingly high margin of unused resources even in the longer run.

Incomes policies have been suggested as a means of winding down inflation more rapidly. In the general view, however, incomes policies are associated with wage and price controls, or at least are seen as a step in that direction. This concern has helped to create an interest in a tax-oriented incomes policy (TIP) that cannot be charged with that defect because it is specifically designed to give full effect to market forces. While numerous versions of TIP exist, their common characteristic is a reliance on the tax system as a means of inducing more moderate behavior of wages and prices. With the committee's permission, I would like to discuss a variant that was developed by Professor Sidney Weintraub of the University of Pennsylvania and myself.

OUTLINE OF PLAN

The essence of the plan consists of a tax penalty on firms granting wage increases in excess of a guideline. The restraint is on wages rather than on prices. But the tax is paid by the firm. In this way, evenhandedness is maintained. The plan can be extended to include a restraint on profits if that is regarded as necessary. To begin with, however, I would like to

set forth why a plan focusing on wages combined with a tax paid by corporations seems adequate.

A considerable body of research indicates that prices in the long run are basically determined by wages. Nonwage factors such as those mentioned earlier—demand pressures, nonwage costs—may play an initiating role in price movements. But with wages and other compensation of labor amounting to 75 per cent of gross national product, wages unavoidably are the principal factor in prices. A slowing in wage increases, therefore, will necessarily bring about a slowing in price increases.

If prices follow wages, wage restraint will not lead to any reduction in real wage increases. Given productivity gains of, say, 3 per cent, labor will get the same increase in real wages with a 5 per cent wage increase and 2 per cent inflation as with a 9 per cent wage increase and 6 per cent inflation. The gains from productivity are all that the economy can give to labor, unless it is to be taken away from something else. These gains will go to labor at any level of inflation, so long as the gap between wages and prices, as it normally does, equals gains in productivity. Wage restraint, therefore, imposes no sacrifice upon labor in real terms. On the contrary, by reducing the threat of inflation, wage restraint would permit the economy to move to lower levels of unemployment and to move there more rapidly, thereby benefiting both labor and all others who share in the national income.

TECHNICAL ASPECTS

A tax to be imposed on firms granting excessive wage increases could take one of several forms. It could be imposed as an increase in the corporate income tax, as a payroll tax, through disallowance for income tax purposes of the deduction of any excess wage increases paid, and perhaps others. The plan could also be structured in the form of a tax reduction for firms avoiding excess wage increases.

Disallowance of excess wage increases as tax deductions has the advantage of having already been on the statute books after World War II and after the Korean war. An increase in the corporate income tax has the advantage that it could be scaled easily in proportion to the magnitude of the excess. This would help to make the penalty or threat of a penalty effective while largely eliminating controversies over marginal excesses. A rise in the corporate income tax, moreover, would be less easily shiftable than a payroll tax or denial of deductibility. On the other hand, it might more adversely affect the ability of the firm to invest.

Guideline

The setting of the wage guideline requires a governmental decision. A maximum wage increase equal to long-run productivity gains plus half of the current rate of inflation might be appropriate. The guideline would in no way interfere with the functioning of the market since firms and unions would be entirely free to make settlements above or below it. Thus, the concern that the guideline would become a first step on the way to a system of controls would be unwarranted. Likewise there seems to be no good reason for expecting the "maximum to become a minimum" since the guideline would not represent a maximum. The guideline would be lowered periodically as inflation was being reduced.

Coverage

A good case can be made for subjecting only a limited number of large corporations to the guideline and tax. In an inflation such as the present, which is kept going because one high wage settlement leads to another but in which there is no excess demand for labor, moderation in the settlements of large firms and some consequent slowing of the price trend would probably lead to moderation for most employers. Limiting the plan to large firms would greatly ease administrative complexities. However, an alternative and opposite procedure could also be envisaged—to cover not only all incorporated but also all unincorporated business.

Administrative Problems

The fact that laws disallowing excess wage increases under the post-World-War-II and Korean-war wage and price control legislation have been on the books suggests that the technical problems of measuring excess wage increases have been considered by the legislature and not found to be intractable. There is, of course, a wide range of technical problems to be resolved of which the following are indicative.

In an economy characterized by multicorporate enterprises, how is the tax-paying unit to be defined—a plant, a corporate entity, or an entire conglomerate? How are the excesses to be measured—by total payroll and total employment, or by individual categories of workers, with allowance for overtime, for fringe benefits including deferred compensation, cost-of-living adjustments, and health insurance and all the rest? How are new firms, firms with losses, with multiyear labor contracts, with numerous subsidiaries to be dealt with? Should the TIP penalty be applied for 1 year only, for a fixed multiyear period, or for a lengthy or indefinite period?

A large number of decisions will have to be made in writing the tax regulations. This is the same analysis, however, that firms and unions engage in during wage bargaining sessions and that at the present time the Council on Wage and Price Stability must also undertake. Furthermore, the initial evaluation of a wage package, which would form the basis for a pay-as-you-go approach to the tax, can be revised upon eventual audit by the Internal Revenue Service. Since the tax penalty would be proportionate to the degree of infringement of the guideline, minor differences between the taxpayer and the tax authorities would not involve large amounts of tax and could be compromised as many differences arising in tax audits are.

A TAX TO RESTRAIN
THE SHARE OF PROFITS

It was noted earlier that the wage guideline proposal does not contain a corresponding restraint on prices because prices can be expected to follow wages. However, if the evidence supporting this view is not generally accepted, a supplementary device could be introduced that would serve to restrain, not prices, but profits. A failure of prices to move with wages would tend to show itself in a corresponding change in profits. Labor would have a legitimate right to expect that no special benefits for profits should emerge from an acceptance by labor of a wage guideline. To ensure that this expectation is not disappointed, the corporate income tax could be raised so as to prevent the rise in total after-tax profits from exceeding some historical relationship to GNP. This would be a tax proportionate to the "excess profits" of the corporate sector as a whole, but not related to the profits of any particular corporation.

As a practical matter, such a tax increase probably would never be triggered at all. But if it were, the increase in the corporate tax could hardly amount to more than a few percentage points. Such a tax would be an "incomes policy" in the proper sense of the term since it would specifically be designed to deal with income shares. The setting of a profit share, presumably in the light of historical experience and the need for business capital expenditures, would be one of the difficult decisions to be made under this approach.

TAX REVENUES

To the extent that the tax measures proposed here are cast in the form of tax increases for exceeding a guideline, rather than tax reductions withheld, some incremental revenues would be collected. Their magnitude would depend on the nature of the guidelines set and on the magnitude of penalties in relation to violations. These additional revenues could be utilized to reduce the income tax burden. Given the uncertainty of these additional revenues, however, a precise link could probably not be established.

EXPECTED DURATION
OF THE PLAN

Since inflation is expected to come to an end under the plan, the arrangements, insofar as they do not involve carryovers from the operative period of the plan, should be terminated when success has been achieved. It might be better to reintroduce the scheme if inflation should revive thereafter rather than to perpetuate it at a time when it is not needed. Even after termination of the plan, a better understanding of the role of wage increases in price determination should prevail and should make it easier to avoid renewed bursts of inflation.

Alternatively, the arrangements could be kept alive even during a period of stable prices as a means of permanently facilitating lower rates of unemployment. It is the pressure of strong demand for labor that, at low levels of unemployment, tends to give rise to excessive wage increases. The threat of such increases, implying demand–pull inflation, in turn prevents the adoption of fiscal and monetary policies that would lead to such lower levels of unemployment. If the wage-increasing effect is restrained by a tax-oriented incomes policy, the achievement of permanently lower levels of unemployment should be within reach.

It should be clear, however, that TIP cannot serve as a counterpoise to, or justification for, overly stimulative fiscal and monetary policies. The rate of growth of the money supply would have to be reduced in line with diminishing inflation and eventually would have to be stabilized at a level consonant with the rate of real growth and the trend in velocity. Fiscal policy would have to limit the government's demands on the credit markets to whatever could be financed with that rate of money growth at stable prices and interest rates consistent with full employment.

24

A Tax-Based Incomes Policy (TIP):
What's It All About?

NANCY AMMON JIANAKOPLOS

SUBJECT corporations to higher corporate income tax rates if they give pay raises which are too large. This is the essence of a plan devised by Governor Henry C. Wallich of the Federal Reserve Board and Sidney Weintraub of the University of Pennsylvania.[1] Their proposal to use the tax system to curb inflation is called "TIP," an acronym for tax-based incomes policy. As inflation continues to plague the economy, many economists feel that the traditional tools of monetary and fiscal policy are inadequate to handle the situation and have recommended direct measures to stop wage and price increases.[2] The Wallich-Weintraub plan has received considerable attention as a policy measure which might be capable of dealing with the problem of inflation.[3]

Before adopting a program such as TIP, it is important to understand clearly how the proposal would operate and, more importantly, whether it would achieve the desired results. The first part of this article describes the functioning of TIP and the rationale for such a program as envisioned by Wallich and Weintraub. The rest of the article is devoted to an assessment of whether TIP would accomplish its stated objectives.

HOW WOULD TIP OPERATE?

According to the plan presented by Wallich and Weintraub, TIP would be centered on a single wage guidepost established by the Government.[4] The acceptable percentage wage increase could be set somewhere between the average increase in productivity throughout the economy (asserted to be around 3 percent) and some larger figure which incorporates all or part of the current rate of inflation. The ultimate aim of the guidepost is to bring wage increases in line with nationwide productivity increases.

The TIP guidepost is directed at wages only, although the tax is levied on corporate profits. The basic assumption behind TIP is that monetary and fiscal policies have been ineffective because they have not been able to prevent labor from obtaining wage increases in excess of productivity gains, even when there is significant unemployment in the economy. Furthermore, Wallich and Weintraub contend that empirical evidence supports the view that price in-

[1]Wallich and Weintraub first collaborated on this idea in Henry C. Wallich and Sidney Weintraub, "A Tax-Based Incomes Policy," *Journal of Economic Issues* (June 1971), pp. 1-19.

[2]See, for example, "Another Weapon Against Inflation: Tax Policy," *Business Week*, October 3, 1977, pp. 94-96; "Debate: How to Stop Inflation," *Fortune* (April 1977), pp. 116-20; Lindley H. Clark, Jr., "Uneasy Seers: More Analysts Predict New Inflation Spiral or Recession in 1978," *Wall Street Journal*, December 2, 1977.

[3]See, for example, U. S. Congress, Congressional Budget Office, *Recovery With Inflation*, July 1977, p. 40; U. S. Congress, Joint Economic Committee, *The 1977 Midyear Review of the Economy*, 95th Cong., 1st sess., September 26, 1977, p. 76; "Well-Cut Taxes Should Be Tailored," *New York Times*, December 21, 1977.

[4]Unless otherwise noted, all descriptions of TIP in this article are based on Wallich and Weintraub, "A Tax-Based Incomes Policy"; Henry C. Wallich, "Alternative Strategies for Price and Wage Controls," *Journal of Economic Issues* (December 1972), pp. 89-104; Henry C. Wallich, "A Plan for Dealing With Inflation in the U.S.," *Washington Post*, August 21, 1977; Sidney Weintraub, "An Incomes Policy to Stop Inflation," *Lloyds Bank Review* (January 1971), pp. 1-12; and Sidney Weintraub, "Incomes Policy: Completing the Stabilization Triangle," *Journal of Economic Issues* (December 1972), pp. 105-22.

Reprinted from Federal Reserve Bank of St. Louis *Review*, February, 1978.

creases have been a constant markup over unit wage increases. Therefore, if wage increases can be kept down, price increases will also be held down.

The corporate income tax system would be employed to enforce the TIP guidepost. Corporations which grant wage increases in excess of the guidepost would be subject to higher corporate income tax rates based on the amount that wage increases exceed the guidepost.

In order to understand how TIP would operate, consider the following example. Suppose the guidepost for wage increases is set at, say, 5 percent for a particular year. In the base year, Corporation A had a total wage bill of $100,000 and in the following year granted increases which brought its total wage bill to $108,000 — an 8 percent increase. Assuming no change in either the number or composition of the employees, this 8 percent increase is 3 percentage points above the guidepost. This excess would then be multiplied by a penalty number. If, for instance, the penalty was set at 2, the corporate tax rate of Corporation A would be increased by 6 percentage points (3 percentage point excess times penalty number of 2). Thus, instead of paying 48 percent of its profits in taxes, the existing corporate tax rate, Corporation A would have to pay 54 percent of its profits, as a penalty for acceding to "excessive" wage demands.

Wallich and Weintraub argue that because of competitive forces this additional tax could not be shifted forward to prices.[5] They, therefore, believe that such a tax penalty would cause corporations to deal more firmly with labor. In their view the penalty would ultimately restrain the rate of wage increases and, hence, reduce the rate of inflation.[6] Since wage increases would be curbed, corporations would not have higher costs to pass through in the form of price increases, thereby eliminating a major "cost-push" element of inflation. Furthermore, since the increases in incomes of workers would more closely approximate increases in productivity, there would be smaller increases in spending, reducing the "demand-pull" aspect of inflation.

Wallich and Weintraub acknowledge certain difficulties in computing the corporation's wage bill. One method which they believe would overcome many of these difficulties would be to construct an index of wages, rather than using the gross dollar figure. Using this method, wages, fringe benefits, and other related payments would be computed for each job classification and skill level and divided by the hours worked at each level. These wage figures would then be combined into an index weighted by the proportion of each of these classifications in the entire corporation. Changes in this index would then be compared to the guidepost in order to assess whether the corporation would be penalized.

Administrative problems are not neglected by Wallich and Weintraub. They recognize that the tax laws must be specific and "airtight" in order to avoid loopholes. However, it is argued that TIP would not involve establishing a new bureaucracy. Most of the data necessary to administer TIP are already collected for corporate income tax and employee payroll tax purposes.

One of the principal merits of TIP, in the view of Wallich and Weintraub, is that it would not interfere with the functioning of the market system. They argue that there would be no direct controls or distortions to the pricing mechanism. Firms would still be free to grant large wage demands, but would face the penalty of a higher corporate tax rate.

Rather than a short-term plan to curb inflation, TIP is envisioned to be a long-term means of reducing the rate of price increase. However, TIP is not intended to function by itself. Both Wallich and Weintraub see it as a supplement to "appropriate" monetary and fiscal policies. In addition, if labor contends that TIP would hold down wages while allowing profits to increase, Wallich proposes the implementation of an excess profits tax. This could be accomplished by increasing the basic corporate tax rate to keep the share of profits in national income constant.[7]

WOULD TIP WORK?

The TIP proposal has two principal objectives:

(1) to curb inflation, and

[5]See Richard A. Musgrave and Peggy B. Musgrave, *Public Finance In Theory and Practice* (New York: McGraw-Hill Book Company, 1973), Chapter 18, pp. 415-29, who contend that empirical evidence is inconclusive in determining whether the corporate income tax is shifted.

[6]Studies by Yehuda Kotowitz and Richard Portes, "The 'Tax on Wage Increases': A Theoretical Analysis," *Journal of Public Economics* (May 1974), pp. 113-32, and Peter Isard, "The Effectiveness of Using the Tax System to Curb Inflationary Collective Bargains: An Analysis of the Wallich-Weintraub Plan," *Journal of Political Economy* (May-June 1973), pp. 729-40, analyze the effect of TIP on an individual firm and conclude that theoretically TIP should lead to lower wage settlements for an individual firm.

[7]Other adjuncts proposed for TIP include a payroll tax credit designed to entice workers to accept lower wages. See Lawrence S. Seidman, "A Payroll Tax-Credit to Restrain Inflation," *National Tax Journal* (December 1976), pp. 398-412.

(2) to avoid interfering with the functioning of the market.

Given these aims of TIP, one can analyze whether TIP will, in fact, be able to accomplish its goals. Other issues raised by TIP, such as the costs of implementation and the ability of firms to avoid the tax penalty of TIP, will not be discussed here.[8]

Would TIP Curb Inflation?

TIP is based on the assumption that most of the inflation in the economy is of a "cost-push" nature. Inflation occurs, according to this framework, because labor is able to attain wage increases in excess of increases in productivity. Business is not capable of resisting, or finds it does not pay to resist, labor's demands. Faced with higher costs, businesses pass these costs through in the form of higher product prices. As prices rise, further wage increases are granted, forming the basis of a wage-price spiral. TIP is proposed as a measure which will intervene in this process and bring inflation to a halt.

As the Congressional Budget Office stated in a recent study, the assumption that inflation is the result of "cost-push" is "a conjectural notion at best."[9] A major challenge to the concept of "cost-push" rests on empirical evidence supporting an alternative theory of the cause of inflation. According to this other view, ongoing increases in the general price level (inflation) are primarily the result of excessive increases in the rate of monetary expansion.[10] Lags exist between the time when the money stock is increased and when prices rise. In this framework, the observed relationship between the rate of wage increase and the rate of price increase is explained as part of the adjustment process through which prices increase in response to increases in the money stock. This view does not deny the "cost-push" phenomenon,

but contends that it is consistent with the view that inflation is ultimately caused by money growth.[11]

When the stock of money is increased faster than the rate of increase in production, people find themselves with larger cash balances than they desire to hold. In order to bring their cash balances down to desired levels, they will spend the money, thereby bidding up prices on goods and services, and the general price level will rise. As long as the stock of money increases faster than the demand for money, inflation will persist, even if TIP manages to hold down wages temporarily.

Conversely, just as inflation is caused by excessive growth of the money stock, the only way to stop inflation is to reduce the growth of the money stock. As the rate of monetary expansion is reduced, people will have cash balances below their desired levels. They will reduce their rate of spending in order to build up these balances. As spending (demand) falls, the rate of inflation will decrease. Prices are "sticky," and just as it took several years to build up the current rate of inflation, it will take several years for inflation to wind down. One of the by-products of reducing inflation is a temporary idling of resources, since prices do not tend to be flexible in the short run. This is a cost of reducing inflation which must be borne, just as there are costs imposed on society as inflation mounts.

The idea that there are certain "key" wages in society, such as union wages, to which other wages and prices adjust, confuses the *motivation* for increasing the money stock with the *cause* of inflation.[12] If certain unions are able to attain large wage increases, even in the face of falling demand, the prices of the products produced by this labor will increase. As prices increase, less of this product will be demanded and the use of the resources (labor and capital) which produce this product will be decreased. Unemployment will rise as resources are freed to work in the production of other products whose prices are lower. The relative prices of products will change, but the average price level will be unchanged.

[8]For a discussion of implementation problems, see Gardner Ackley, "Okun's New Tax-Based Incomes-Policy Proposal," Survey Research Center, Institute for Social Research, The University of Michigan, *Economic Outlook USA* (Winter 1978), pp. 8-9. Although Ackley deals with the anti-inflation proposal put forward by Arthur Okun, he notes that the critique also applies to the Wallich-Weintraub proposal.

[9]Congressional Budget Office, "Recovery With Inflation," p. 41.

[10]Empirical support of this view for the period 1955 to 1971 is presented by Leonall C. Andersen and Denis S. Karnosky, "The Appropriate Time Frame for Controlling Monetary Aggregates: The St. Louis Evidence," *Controlling Monetary Aggregates II: The Implementation,* Federal Reserve Bank of Boston, Conference Series No. 9, September 1972, pp. 147-77. Additional evidence for the period 1971 to 1976 is found in Denis S. Karnosky, "The Link Between Money and Prices — 1971-76," this *Review* (June 1976), pp. 17-23.

[11]See Leonall C. Andersen and Denis S. Karnosky, "A Monetary Interpretation of Inflation" in Joel Popkin, ed., *Analysis of Inflation: 1965-1974,* Studies in Income and Wealth, Vol. 42, National Bureau of Economic Research, Inc. (Cambridge, Massachusetts: Ballinger Publishing Company, 1977), pp. 11-26.

[12]This argument draws on Armen A. Alchian and William R. Allen, *University Economics: Elements of Inquiry* (Belmont, California: Wadsworth Publishing Company, Inc., 1972), pp. 684-85.

However, if the Federal Reserve policymakers keep a close watch on these "key" industries and see an increase in idle resources (unemployment) in these industries, they may take actions to alleviate the unemployment by increasing the money stock. The increases in spending resulting from monetary expansion will bid up average prices and return relative prices to a position similar to that prior to the granting of the wage demands. It was as a consequence of the excessive wage demands that policy actions were *motivated*, but it was monetary expansion which *caused* the subsequent inflation.

Some proponents of TIP base their support on the belief that TIP will reduce *expectations* of inflation. Lower expectations of inflation in the future, according to this view, will lead to lower demands for wage increases and eventually lower prices. However, expectations of inflation do not cause inflation.[13] It is ongoing inflationary forces in the economy, excessive rates of monetary expansion, which lead to expectations of future inflation. Curbing inflationary expectations requires curbing the underlying forces which cause them.

Wallich and Weintraub agree that TIP is a supplement to, not a substitute for, "appropriate" monetary and fiscal policy. However, the character of their "appropriate" monetary policy is questionable. In the basic article which outlined TIP, Wallich and Weintraub stated, ". . . the proposal is conceived as a supplement to the familiar monetary-fiscal policies so that the economy might operate closer to full employment without the inflationary danger of excess demand and 'overheating.' "[14] Indeed, in a later article Weintraub is more specific: "Given a suitable incomes policy to align wages (and salaries) to productivity, monetary policy would be released to make its contribution to full employment. . . Full employment requires ample money supplies for its sustenance."[15] Thus, it appears that "appropriate" monetary policy, in the view of Wallich and Weintraub, is expansionary; however, a restrictive monetary policy is necessary to curb inflation.

This disparity in determining the appropriate character of monetary policy points out another problem with TIP. Given the lag time involved in the functioning of monetary policy, it might appear in the short run that TIP is, at least temporarily, holding down prices. If, at the same time, the Federal Reserve increases the rate of monetary expansion, inflationary pressures will actually be augmented. An incomes policy, such as TIP, gives policymakers the illusion of taking corrective measures against inflation when, in fact, reducing the rate of monetary expansion is the only way to accomplish that goal. In summary, it appears that TIP would not be effective in reducing inflation and could make matters worse by fostering inappropriate monetary policy.

Would TIP Interfere With the Market?

Wallich and Weintraub argue that TIP would not interfere with market pricing because no ceilings are placed on any wages or prices. TIP operates through the tax system, yet it is based on a *single* guidepost for every firm and industry. They contend that a single guidepost is appropriate because in competition all comparable workers would earn the same wage. TIP, therefore, is only imposing what competition would achieve.

The problem with this argument is that it is only true if all industries are in equilibrium and remain there. In a growing, changing economy, equilibrium prices and wage rates are changing. Prices and wages are constantly moving toward new equilibria; hence, there is no reason to believe that each sector in the economy would be at equilibrium when TIP was imposed or would remain there afterward. In the U. S. economy, demands and tastes of consumers are constantly shifting and the technology and products offered by business are also changing. As a consequence, the equilibrium prices of some goods are rising (houses, for example) while others are falling (electronic calculators). In addition, some firms are growing, making large profits, and seeking additional labor, while others are declining, earning very little profit, and contracting their labor forces.

Imposing a single wage guidepost would distort the price system. It does not matter whether the guidepost is imposed through the tax system or by direct fines and penalties. Those firms which are growing or are adapting to changing consumer tastes have an incentive to hire scarce resources (capital and labor) away from other firms, but they would be penalized either through a lower rate of return, if they grant "excess" wage demands, or by a barrier to growth if they adhere to the guidepost. Consequently, in some instances labor would not be compensated in accord

[13]Weintraub supports this contention in Weintraub, "Incomes Policy: Completing the Stabilization Triangle," p. 116.

[14]Wallich and Weintraub, "A Tax-Based Incomes Policy," p. 1.

[15]Weintraub, "Incomes Policy: Completing the Stabilization Triangle," p. 110.

with the demand for its services. In other cases, firms would not be able to attract all the labor they desired. Relative prices would, therefore, be distorted by the establishment of a single guidepost for all firms and industries.

The TIP proposal would lead to a misallocation of resources. Prices, when allowed to operate freely, offer signals of where demand is increasing and where demand is falling. Resources move to those industries or firms where they will receive the highest compensation. The TIP proposal would obscure these price signals and, hence, resources would not move to where they would be used most efficiently. The economy would suffer since production would be lower than it would be otherwise.

The distortions in the economy caused by TIP could have a very long lasting effect. Capital (plant and equipment) is allocated by the market to those firms which have the highest rate of return. The TIP proposal would reduce the rates of return of those firms which are growing, and capital would not be adequately allocated to them. Capital generally tends to have a relatively long life. Once it is misallocated, as a result of TIP, it would not be easy to reallocate it to a more efficient use. Thus, TIP could have serious long-term consequences, as a result of the distortions it would cause in the price system.

CONCLUSION

TIP is an incomes policy designed to reduce inflation without interfering with the market system. The essence of the proposal is to subject corporations to higher corporate income tax rates if they granted pay increases in excess of a single Government-mandated guidepost.

TIP would not be successful in reducing the rate of inflation because it is based on the premise that inflation is largely a "cost-push" phenomenon — higher wages leading to higher prices, which lead to still higher wages. Inflation, however, is caused primarily by excessive growth of the money stock. The TIP proposal, therefore, deals only with the symptoms of inflation, rather than attacking inflation at its root.

TIP would distort the market pricing system because the imposition of a single wage guidepost would not allow relative prices to adjust fully to change. This would lead to inefficiencies and a lower level of production than would be otherwise attainable.

Inflation is a serious problem, and there are no magic solutions. There may be a temporary reduction in the apparent rate of inflation with TIP, but eventually leaks will develop in the system and prices will rise anyway. The only way to stop inflation is to reduce the rate of monetary expansion.

25

FULL EMPLOYMENT AND BALANCED GROWTH ACT OF 1978
(THE HUMPHREY-HAWKINS BILL)

Dennis Roth
Economics Division

ISSUE DEFINITION

The "Full Employment and Balanced Growth Act of 1978" (H.R. 50, S. 50), better known as the Humphrey-Hawkins bill, is a culmination of years of effort by several Members of the House and Senate to develop legislation for achieving a full employment economy by expanding on goals set forth in the Employment Act of 1946. The current November 1977 compromise version is a revision of the bill introduced by Congressman Hawkins in the House and Senator Humphrey in the Senate in January 1977, and represents a revision of earlier versions introduced by them in the 93d and 94th Congresses. The main purpose of the bill remains to establish a procedural framework for setting national economic goals and policies, with particular emphasis on achieving a "full employment" economy with reasonable price stability. On Nov. 14, 1977, President Carter formally endorsed this revised compromise version of the bill.

This brief offers a short summary and comparison of some of the provisions of that compromise version.

BACKGROUND AND POLICY ANALYSIS
CHANGES IN THE COMPROMISE BILL

Title I—Goals and Policies

A comparison of the January 1977 version of the Humphrey-Hawkins bill and the proposed November 1977 version indicates that few, but not insignificant, changes have been made to the major provisions of the bill. The compromise version retains wording dealing with a "right to useful employment paying decent wages for every American able, willing, and seeking work." However, while the compromise version no longer "establishes" this right, it does mandate that the right be "translated into practical reality" and that the fulfillment of the right be set as a national goal.

In the lastest version, the economic planning process has been streamlined and additional macroeconomic goals have been made explicit. Specifically, the two planning documents called for in the January 1977 version (the Economic Report, and the Full Employment and Balanced Growth Plan), have been consolidated into a single document now called the Economic Report. The Report is given more structure and is to contain, among other elements: (1) a summary of the current and foreseeable status of the economy including factors such as employment and unemployment, production, real income, productivity, and prices, and is to give an analysis of recent developments affecting these economic variables (similar to January 1977 version with the addition of unemployment, productivity, and prices); (2) annual numerical goals for five years (the first and second year goals are termed short-term goals and the goals for the remaining three years medium-term goals) for employment and unemployment, production, real income, and productivity, and the programs and policies necessary to achieve these goals and to achieve reasonable price stability as rapidly as feasible (the number of years and numerical goals for production, real income, and productivity have been made explicit); (3) an interim unemployment goal of 3% for those 20 years old and over, and 4% for those 16 years old and over, which is to be achieved within five years after the first Economic Report (the 4% interim goal is now explicit rather than implicit and the time frame for achieving the unemployment goals was extended one year); and (4) policies and programs for reducing the differences between the rates of unemployment among teenagers, women, minorities, and other labor force groups and the overall rate of unemployment (also in January 1977 version).

Regarding the annual goals and timetable for the reduction of unemployment, the compromise bill now gives the President the flexibility to propose modifications, subject to congressional approval, to these goals and timetables in the third year after enactment and in any later year. This is one of the major additions to the bill.

Though the anti-inflation policies of the January bill remain intact, several specific provisions regarding goals have been changed: The January 1977 objectives "of holding the annual rate of consumer and other price increases to levels consistent with other reasonable price stability" and "of preventing a rise in the annual rate of consumer and other price increases *above such rates on the date of enactment of this Act*" (emphasis added) have been deleted. Instead, the achievement of "reasonable price stability" as rapidly as feasible is established as a major goal. A significant change has also been made regarding the interplay between the unemployment and reasonable price stability goals. The January 1977 version stated that the achievement of reasonable price stability should "not be sought through any weakening of the goals and timetable relating to the reduction of unemployment." The compromise version mandates that the means chosen to reduce unemployment and to achieve reasonable price stability be mutually reinforcing so as not to sacrifice one goal for the sake of achieving the other.

The role of the President's budget in the scheme of economic planning is clarified in the compromise bill. The President's budget is to be consistent with the short- and medium-term goals of employment and unemployment, production, real income, and productivity. The basic elements of the budget are to be included in each Economic Report and are, on both the expenditure and tax sides, to be geared to achieving the goals of the Act. Thus, the Administration's budget is to be supportive of the numerical goals of full employment.

The compromise bill has retained the requirement that the Federal Reserve Board submit an independent statement declaring its intended policies for the year and their relationship to the Economic Report's short-term goals. However, under the compromise version the statement goes only to the Congress and not also to the President as in the January 1977 version. Consequently, Congress, not the President, would be expected to initiate any necessary action to insure closer conformity to the purposes of the Act.

The compromise version also keeps the provision that primary emphasis is to be put on the expansion of private employment and that all programs and policies under the Act should be directed toward this purpose. And, while the Federal Government is mandated to plan and coordinate its own goals, policies, and programs to achieve full employment, no provisions of the Act are to be used to provide for Government control of production, employment, allocations of resources or wages and prices in the private sector, except to the extent authorized under other legislation.

The compromise version retains the provisions mandating that the President's Economic Report include certain "priority policies and programs" that are to be used to achieve the goals established in the Report. Encouraging job creation in the specified priority program areas is to serve the dual purpose of increasing employment and alleviating the specific supply problems that exist in these areas. These "priority" areas include energy, mass transportation, environmental improvement, human and product needs in the farm and rural sectors, health care, education and training, child care and other human services, housing, Federal aid to State and local governments, and national defense and other needed international programs.

Title II—Supplementary Employment Policies and Capital Formation

Unchanged in the November version is the recognition that fiscal and monetary policies alone may not be able to lower unem-

Library of Congress, Congressional Research Service, Major Issues System, Issue Brief Number IB77204, March 31, 1978.

ployment to the goals to be established by the President and approved by Congress. Consequently, in the President's Economic Report there are to be supplementary government employment programs and policies to help reach the overall unemployment goals. The compromise version has, however, dropped the requirement that the President use all of the policies and programs listed, and that he send messages to the Congress on all the policies and programs within a few months of enactment of the Act. The compromise version requires only that the President use the various policies and programs to the extent needed to reach the mandated goals and timetable for the reduction of unemployment and the other goals of the Act. The mix of policies and programs is to be included in the Economic Report to the extent that this will not unduly delay the report. The flexibility gained by this change was a major point of the Administration in negotiations.

The compromise version added section 207 to the bill regarding public and private capital formation. The provisions of this section mandate the President in his Economic Report to review and assess Federal Government programs and policies that affect business investment decisions and also those that affect the adequacy, composition, and effectiveness of public investments. If necessary, the President is to recommend new programs or modifications for improving existing programs to stimulate private capital formation and public investment.

In the compromise version changes were made in the implementing machinery but not in the role of the Federal Government as an employer of last resort. The compromise version states that if Americans aged 16 and over who are able, willing and seeking work are not and in the judgement of the President, cannot find private job opportunities nor find job opportunities under other programs and actions in existence, the President in accord with the goals and timetables set forth in the Act and/or the Employment Act of 1946, "shall establish reservoirs of public employment and private nonprofit employment projects, to be approved by the Secretary of Labor, in the form of expansion of CETA and other existing employment and training projects and/or through such new programs as are determined by the President to be needed and *which the Congress authorizes and provides funds for*" ((emphasis added) section 206 (c)). Similar to the January 1977 version, those new programs requiring authorizations are not to be put into operation until two years after

enactment of the Act, nor without a finding by the President, transmitted to the Congress, that other means of employment are not yielding enough jobs to be consistent with goals and timetables for the reduction of unemployment established in the Act. Different from the January 1977 version is the language mandating the expansion of CETA and other employment and training projects in existence. Expanding these projects to create last-resort jobs does not require any new authorization by Congress. Thus, the change in the jobs-of-last-resort provisions establishes a closer relationship between the reservoir and last-resort projects and CETA and other job efforts.

Title III—Congressional Review

With the consolidation of all the planning reports into the Economic Report, it was possible to make the language in this title, regarding the policies and procedures for Congressional review, more concise. The timetable for Congressional review has been shortened. The compromise version notably drops the establishment of a Division of Full Employment and Balanced Growth within the Congressional Budget Office.

Title IV—General Provisions

There are no major changes in this title. The section on definitions has been dropped and the clause dealing with differential unemployment rates (between women, minorities, and other labor force groups and the overall national rate) has been transferred to Title I.

SUMMARY OF THE BILL

The November version of the Full Employment and Balanced Growth Act of 1978 is a negotiated compromise based on the January 1977 version. The overall purpose of the bill is still to establish an orderly framework for formulating national economic goals and policies with particular emphasis on achieving a specifically defined "full employment" economy along with "reasonable price stability," and for co-ordinating the programs to achieve these goals and policies between the executive (including the Federal Reserve Board) and legislative branches of the Federal Government. The purpose of establishing such a framework and procedures stated in the preamble is "to translate into practical reality the right of all Americans who are able, willing, and seeking work to full opportunity for useful paid employment at fair rates of compensation."

26

Will Full Employment Cause Inflation?

by Charles C. Killingsworth

The persistence of extremely high levels of unemployment after months of recovery from the recent recession has stimulated new interest in proposals for a stronger and more effective effort by the federal government to achieve full employment. The Humphrey-Hawkins Full Employment Bill, at first widely regarded as little more than a political gesture, by a year ago was considered quite likely to pass both houses of Congress, in revised form, by the close of the 94th Congress. Now its prospects are clouded, and the reason is a series of strongly worded attacks on the alleged inflationary potential of this proposal—or indeed any proposal for reducing the reported unemployment rate as low as 3 or 4 percent. These attacks have come from respected economists, some of whom wear the liberal label and some of whom are called conservative. Congress is necessarily and properly concerned with inflation as well as unemployment. The repeated assertions that full employment (at least as defined in Humphrey-Hawkins) would certainly cause ruinous inflation—perhaps as high as a 15 percent annual

CHARLES C. KILLINGSWORTH is university professor of economics and labor and industrial relations, Michigan State University, and chairman of the National Council on Employment Policy. This article was first presented at hearings before the U.S. House Committee on the Budget, Task Force on Economic Projections, July 27, 1976.

rate—have greatly reduced the momentum and support that the effort to guarantee full employment once seemed to have.

The thesis of this article is that the predictions of disastrous inflation as a result of 3 or 4 percent unemployment lack support either in past experience or analysis. Such predictions rest, either implicitly or explicitly, on a controversial doctrine generally known as the ''Phillips curve,'' which holds that low unemployment rates cause high inflation rates, and vice versa. To the extent that the Phillips curve doctrine rests upon analysis of past experience, that past experience is fundamentally different from the approach to full employment that is proposed in the Humphrey-Hawkins bill. In the past, generally speaking, low unemployment rates have (arguably) resulted from the generalized pressure of aggregate demand. Usually, at least a part of the pressure of aggregate demand has been produced by fiscal and monetary policy. It is the reaction to that approach to full employment—general stimulation of aggregate demand—which the Phillips curve formulation purports to measure.

But our past experience does not include any period of low unemployment rates induced primarily, or even substantially, by the kinds of *focused demand* and *supply improvement* programs that are envisaged by the Humphrey-Hawkins bill. There are persuasive reasons for believing that these *specific* kinds of programs

would be much less inflationary than the generalized stimulation of aggregate demand which has been our primary, and nearly exclusive, weapon against excessive unemployment in recent decades.

Most or perhaps all of the economists who have made the alarming predictions of disastrous inflation as a result of full employment have assumed, either explicitly or implicitly, that full employment would be achieved primarily by generalized stimulation of aggregate demand. If we grant the validity of that assumption, then possibly the warning is justified. I say ''possibly'' because the Phillips curve analysis is not universally accepted, even by mainstream economists. But a judgment about the effect of the Humphrey-Hawkins bill on inflation need not await a resolution of the Phillips curve controversy, which may be a long time in coming. Those who apply the Phillips curve analysis to the Humphrey-Hawkins bill have misread that bill and have misunderstood the nature of the labor market problems to which it is addressed.

There is a role for fiscal policy in the Humphrey-Hawkins scheme. Even those economists who are most alarmed about inflation grant that our unemployment rate of nearly 8 percent could be reduced significantly without adding to inflationary pressures. Most of the inflation warnings place the danger zone in the range of 5 to 6 percent unemployment. Hence, many economists see some room for further stimulation of aggregate demand, and the Humphrey-Hawkins bill explicitly states that fiscal policy measures must be an important part of full employment policy. Since 1960, however, fiscal policy has come to be almost synonymous with tax cutting. I believe that this orientation of fiscal policy has led to unfortunate consequences and that the time has come to redirect fiscal policy. The Humphrey-Hawkins bill provides the vehicle for such a redirection, although the details are not spelled out in the bill.

PUBLIC SERVICE JOBS VS. TAX CUTTING

Humphrey-Hawkins explicitly provides for a major role for public service employment (PSE) in full employment policy. The bill also provides for increased emphasis on other labor market measures, such as training, relocation, placement, and so on. It should be obvious that an expenditure of $10 billion (for example) on such programs with no offsetting tax or other budget changes should provide at least as much of an addition to aggregate demand as a tax cut of $10 billion. But the impact of these two approaches to demand stimulation would be quite different. An understanding of the differences is a key to the current analysis of the potential impact of Humphrey-Hawkins on inflation.

In the first place, expenditures on PSE are much more cost-effective than tax cuts of equal magnitude in reducing unemployment. The Congressional Budget Office has prepared impact estimates of these two approaches to unemployment reduction.[1] The findings of this study imply that the net cost per job created by tax cuts after 24 months is in the range of $17,000 to $21,000. The findings also imply a net cost per PSE job after 24 months in the range of $2,600 to $3,500. In other words, dollars spent on a PSE program produce five to eight times as many jobs as an equal

[1] Congressional Budget Office, *Temporary Measures to Stimulate Employment: An Evaluation of Some Alternatives* (Washington: Government Printing Office, 1975), Summary Table 1.

number of dollars dedicated to tax cutting. This is a fact of fundamental importance to the correct evaluation of the Humphrey-Hawkins proposals. Even if one allows for a substantial margin of error in the Congressional Budget Office estimates, the superior cost-effectiveness of the PSE program compared with tax cutting is large and obvious. The lower cost per job means that many more jobs can be created with much less inflationary pressure by means of the PSE program than by tax cutting.

In the second place, the purchasing power effects of a tax cut are generally diffused throughout the economy, and its effect in terms of job creation is indirect and somewhat attenuated. When consumers and businesses find that they have to pay less

Economic forecasting has become a bad joke, and the influence of the profession on policy making has greatly diminished—except, perhaps, when the advice is, Don't do it.

money in taxes, they will spend more on goods and services. Some of this increased demand will be met by increasing hours of work for those already employed, some may be met by increasing productivity. Only part of the increased demand will be met by the creation of new jobs. And the new jobs that are created will not necessarily fit the skills and geographical distribution of the unemployed labor force.

In sharp contrast, the job-creation effect of the PSE program is direct and focused. (The "substitution" argument will be dealt with shortly.) Virtually all of the dollars in the PSE program are earmarked for payrolls. Eligibility requirements can be shaped in such a way as to insure that

the hiring is concentrated among labor force groups and geographical areas where the unemployment rates are highest.

The PSE program is sometimes criticized on the ground that it enlarges government payrolls rather than private employment, but the charge is something less than half-true. It ignores the "multiplier effect" of adding people to payrolls, whether public or private. Those added to payrolls spend their earnings, and most of the spending is for goods and services produced in the private sector. To the extent that goods and services are produced in the geographical areas where they are purchased, this spending of PSE earnings helps further to relieve localized unemployment problems. Hence, the PSE program can be sharply focused on particular groups and areas, and to some extent, the secondary spending resulting from PSE hiring will also be focused where unused capacity is likely to be greatest. In time, of course, the effects of PSE spending will be generally diffused through the economy, and a point generally overlooked is that most of the jobs *indirectly* created by the PSE program will be in the private sector.

ANSWERING THE "SUBSTITUTION" ARGUMENT

The PSE program has recently been subjected to strong criticism on the ground that its effectiveness is greatly diminished by the so-called substitution effect. The charge is that money allocated to state and local governments for new hires under the PSE program will actually be used to avoid layoffs of present employees or to staff programs that would otherwise have been undertaken with state and local funding. Members of the Council of Economic Advisers (CEA) have repeatedly argued that "after three years only one or two net new jobs remain out of 10 supposedly created originally."[2] This assertion is said to be supported by several studies of the job-creating effects of the present

[2] Testimony of Paul W. MacAvoy to Joint Economic Committee, reported in *New York Times*, January 29, 1976. See also a Letter to the Editor by Mr. MacAvoy, *ibid.*, March 10, 1976.

PSE program. However, the fact is that none of the studies relied upon is based on direct observation of the PSE program. All of them are largely theoretical analyses of state and local expenditure patterns under other kinds of federal grant programs, and the authors assume that the behavior of state and local governments will be the same under the PSE program.

As evidence, the studies on which the CEA and others rely are remarkably weak. One of the most careful and thorough of these studies ends with these words: "Clearly, far more analysis will be required before our numerical estimates can be taken as anything more than preliminary guides in the analysis of the practical problems we have examined."[3] Three of the authors of such studies have publicly conceded their weakness as evidence, saying, "A set of estimates ranging from 40 to 90 percent is hardly a 'smoking gun.'"[4] Despite these obvious weaknesses, these studies are frequently cited as indisputable fact—which is surely a disservice to rational discussion of an important issue in public policy. Furthermore, these critics usually ignore a significant corollary of the substitution hypothesis: if there is substitution, as alleged, the money does not simply vanish: it permits state and local tax reduction, or purchases by state and local units which otherwise would not have been made, and the final effect on aggregate demand is at least as great as from a federal tax cut, an increase in federal spending, or a revenue-sharing program.

A more general answer to the substitution argument is that it is based on the present administrative arrangements of the PSE program, under which the federal government grants funds to state and local units of government with only rather general restrictions on the ways in which the funds may be spent. If substitution can be shown to be a significant prob-

lem, several remedies are readily available: the federal government could take over the administration of some or all of the program; provision could be made for emphasis on specific projects which would not be carried out without a PSE program, instead of permitting the hiring of workers for the performance of ongoing functions of state and local governments; and greater emphasis could be placed on grants to nonprofit nongovernmental institutions. All of these would be possible under Humphrey-Hawkins.

The foregoing discussion is not intended to suggest that a PSE program is a panacea for unemployment, or that no problems of significance will ever arise in the administration of this kind of program. Rather, the argument is that increased reliance on PSE would be much less inflationary and more cost-effective than the tax-cutting version of fiscal policy. As I read the Humphrey-Hawkins bill, it contemplates the continued use of conventional fiscal policy tools (including tax cuts) under appropriate circumstances, but it would broaden and shift the emphasis in employment policy to include more reliance on direct job creation, humanpower training, and similar kinds of direct intervention in the labor market to achieve full employment.

Neither is the foregoing discussion intended to suggest that the inflation problem will disappear if the Humphrey-Hawkins bill is enacted. My personal view is that recent inflationary pressures have not originated in the labor market, although some labor market institutions may have contributed, directly or indirectly, to the maintenance of the inflationary spiral. To the extent that inflation has resulted from energy and raw materials shortages, crop failures, and other developments unrelated to the state of the labor market, it will still be with us even if we are able to devise and install a noninflationary full employment policy. I resist the dogma that unemployment and inflation are functionally related entities. Nevertheless, I am willing to concede some merit to the arguments of those who believe that the anti-inflation

provisions of the Humphrey-Hawkins bill should be expanded and strengthened. It is my understanding that amendments for that purpose are presently under active consideration.

HUMANPOWER TRAINING—A FULL EMPLOYMENT TOOL
Humanpower training and related labor market programs deserve more extended attention than they can be given in a relatively brief space. Certain observations are essential. It has become fashionable to assert that humanpower training has failed. In two senses this assertion is correct. Humanpower training has never been

> To the extent that inflation has resulted from energy and raw materials shortages, crop failures, and other developments unrelated to the state of the labor market, it will still be with us even if we are able to devise and install a noninflationary full employment policy.

a large enough program to have any significant effect on the general level of unemployment. Obviously, this is not an inherent shortcoming of this approach to labor market problems. Second, some particular programs have shown disappointing results, especially those directed at the most disadvantaged labor force groups or geographical areas. Neither of these facts justifies the generalization that humanpower training and similar programs cannot contribute to a full employment policy.

In fact, the great majority of the careful studies of humanpower training conclude that the monetary returns (to enrollees and to government)

[3] Orley Ashenfelter and Ronald Ehrenberg, "The Demand for Labor in the Public Sector," in *Labor in the Public and Nonprofit Sectors*, ed. D.S. Hamermesh (Princeton N.J.: Princeton University Press, 1975).
[4] Letter to the Editor, *New York Times*, March 26, 1976, signed by George E. Johnson, Orley Ashenfelter, and Ronald Ehrenberg.

from such programs exceed their costs, sometimes by very wide margins. The number of studies with this kind of conclusion is now an impressive total. Nevertheless, some methodological purists have attacked the validity of these studies. Some of the studies are crude, but many of them, particularly those of more recent vintage, compare not unfavorably with other evaluation studies in the social sciences. Some of the purists seem to ignore the basic fact that investigations in the social sciences can only rarely, if ever, be carried out under conditions as carefully and precisely controlled as in, say, a chemistry laboratory. Some of the critics have concluded that methodological weaknesses in the humanpower training cost-benefit studies compel the conclusion that the truth is exactly the opposite of what the studies report; the critics say that since the studies fail to demonstrate conclusively that benefits exceed costs, we must all conclude that the costs exceed the benefits and, therefore, that the programs have failed. Merely stating that argument, I think, sufficiently exposes its fallacy.

I am fond of quoting the observation of Justice Oliver Wendell Holmes that "certainty is generally illusion." In our daily lives all of us constantly base decisions on reasonable probabilities rather than absolute certainty, and I believe that we must do the same in many areas of public policy, including humanpower training. My conclusion is that the great preponderance of reasonably reliable evidence shows that most humanpower programs improve the earnings and employment potential of their enrollees. I conclude further that we have consistently underutilized this tool in the past, and that the Humphrey-Hawkins design would require greater emphasis on this particular tool as one of the many needed to achieve full employment.

LABOR FORCE COMPOSITION AND FULL EMPLOYMENT
Some of those who question or deny our ability to achieve full employment cite changes in the composition of the labor force in support of their

view. George L. Perry of the Brookings Institution was perhaps the first to advance this line of argument,[5] which runs as follows. The relative numbers of young people and women in the labor force have increased greatly in recent years. Because these groups, for various reasons, have persistently high rates of unemployment, their presence in greater numbers makes lower rates of unemployment more difficult to achieve than in earlier years. Perry provided a mathematical demonstration which may be described in simplified terms by saying that he applied the unemployment rates for specific age-sex groups in an earlier year to the same groups for the current year to illustrate the effect of changed age-sex composition. He found a relatively small but significant effect. His technique was followed (with enthusiasm, one surmises) by the Council of Economic Advisers two years after the publication of his original article. By using different years, the CEA was able to show that changing age-sex composition of the labor force has added approximately 0.5 percent to the unemployment rate in recent years. This has become one of the more durable fallacies in labor market discussions.

It is a fallacy because age and sex are only two of the relevant dimensions of the labor force. There are others of at least equal significance, and when they are considered, it is clear that the effect described by Perry is more than offset. Thus, if education and race are added to Perry's formulas, the result is a substantial *reduction* in the unemployment rate in more recent years resulting from changes in the composition of the labor force.[6] In addition, there were several changes in the Bureau of Labor Statistics—Bureau of the Census definitions of employment and unemployment in 1967 which had the net effect of reducing the reported unemployment rate by about 0.2 percent. Adding together all of these factors, we can conclude that defini-

5 In "Changing Labor Markets and Inflation," *Brookings Papers on Economic Activity,* March 1970, pp. 411–441.
6 See Sonia Conly, "Education and Labor Market Tightness," *Monthly Labor Review,* October 1974, pp. 51–53.

tion changes and changes in the age-sex-race-education composition of the labor force have *reduced* the unemployment rate in recent years by about 0.7 percent. From this standpoint, and using Perry's reasoning, full employment is now somewhat more easily achieved than it would have been 20 years ago.

WAGES, INFLATION, AND THE WORKING POOR
There is another major aspect to the argument that Humphrey-Hawkins is inflationary which I have not yet addressed. This is the contention that the so-called prevailing wage provisions in the bill would themselves be highly inflationary, entirely apart from the overall effect of the legisla-

I would be surprised if it turned out that most municipal governments (regardless of size and regardless of geographical area) pay higher wage rates than private industry for comparable jobs.

tion on the unemployment rate. Let me oversimplify a little by saying that the argument is that the wage provisions governing the PSE program would compel the payment of wage rates much higher than those now being paid on large numbers of jobs in the private sector, and that these higher wage rates would create a powerful "suction effect" that would draw into the PSE program a large number of low-paid workers, or would compel the upward adjustment of many wage rates in the private sector.

This line of argument deserves close attention because it poses a question of social policy that is of fundamental importance. It also poses some factual questions, and perhaps it is best to deal with those first. The Humphrey-Hawkins wage rate standard which is likely to be most generally applicable for public bodies provides for "the prevailing rates of pay for persons employed in similar public occupations by the same employer." Hence, the requirement is for equal pay for equal work *within the employing unit.* Charles L. Schultze, among others, has asserted that this wage standard "is bound to be highly inflationary."[7] He states that the wage for a low-skill or semiskilled municipal job is "often" far higher than the rate for the same job in private industry. He then predicts a mass exodus of workers from the low-pay jobs in private industry to the "last resort" jobs in the public sector, or a rapid rise in the wage scales for the low-level private industry jobs. Schultze cites median hourly wages for a few occupations in a handful of cities as factual support for his generalizations. I do not think the data presented are conclusive. No doubt what he says is true of *some* occupations in *some* cities, but we need a much broader information base than he provides to make a confident judgment. I do not pretend to know, in advance, what further investigation will reveal. I would be surprised, however, if it turned out that most municipal governments (regardless of size and regardless of geographical area) pay higher wage rates than private industry for comparable jobs.

Let us assume, for the sake of argument, that PSE hourly wage rates would be higher than for some significant percentage of jobs in private industry. The policy question which we must answer is: How much do we want to do for the working poor by means of the full employment program? My respected colleague, Sar Levitan, has criticized the Humphrey-Hawkins bill for doing too little for the working poor; Schultze seems to criticize it for doing too much for them. I think the intention of the bill is not clear, and that we should

[7] Testimony before U.S. Senate Subcommittee on Unemployment, Poverty and Migratory Labor, May 14, 1976 (mimeographed), p. 8.

make a conscious choice. It would not be difficult to find ways and means to exclude most of the working poor from the Humphrey-Hawkins programs, as I will show shortly. However, we could consciously choose to put at least some degree of pressure on the private sector to improve the worst jobs, both in terms of working conditions and wage rates. I doubt that the inflationary impact would be nearly as severe as Schultze fears. Even with a higher hourly rate available, some workers would choose to remain in the lower-paid jobs; one labor market phenomenon that has been documented by many studies is the long-run persistence of large pay differentials in the same labor market for comparable work. Some low-paid jobs in the personal service category would probably remain unfilled—for example, rest room attendants, domestic servants, shoeshiners—and people would simply do more for themselves. Some low-paid workers would be replaced by machines, as has been the case with many kinds of agricultural harvest labor. Perhaps more generally, employers would learn to utilize the formerly low-paid workers more efficiently; one of the lessons of many studies is that when labor is cheap it is often used wastefully, and vice versa. If we choose to follow this kind of social policy, of course the impact would depend partly on the speed of change. If we tried to remake the low-wage labor market in a very short period of time, the strains would be far greater than if we moved more slowly.

On the other hand, if we wished to exclude or drastically limit the participation of the working poor in any PSE program, we could easily find ways to do so. The WPA (Works Progress Administration) program of the 1930s and many job programs of the 1960s limited the hours of work available to enrollees. The hourly rate, of course, is only one of the factors determining earnings; the other is hours worked. We could require equal pay for equal work but provide only 30 or 32 hours of work per week, thus considerably reducing the incentive for the job changing that Schultze and others fear. We could

require a substantial period of unemployment to establish eligibility for a PSE job. We could greatly increase the number of PSE jobs in the nonprofit sector, assuming that wage rates there are generally lower than in government. One lesson of the 1960s is that it is not difficult to exclude people from social programs, if that is what we choose to do.

TAKING UP THE CHALLENGE
Let me conclude on a personal note. Many people of my generation were attracted to the study of economics because we had lived through the Great Depression and we knew personally the soul-shrinking agony of endlessly looking for a job that did not exist. Many of us thought that economics had to provide the solution to mass unemployment. The revolutionary ideas of J.M. Keynes strengthened that hope. For a time in the 1940s, and perhaps for a briefer time in the 1960s, we thought that economics had finally solved the problem of achieving full employment and that we could even conquer the ancient curse of poverty. The early 1960s were the golden age of the economist, but the eminence was brief and the fall was rapid. For much of the past decade, economics—once called the dismal science—has become the frightened science. Economic forecasting has become a bad joke, and the influence of the profession on policy making has greatly diminished—except, perhaps, when the advice is, Don't do it. In the animal world a frightened and confused creature often freezes into immobility. And we have had a virtual paralysis in employment policy in recent years, partly because almost every proposal has been greeted by cries of *Inflation!* from our frightened economists.

I refuse to believe that this nation has lost its adaptability and its capacity to learn from experience. As even its authors recognize, the Humphrey-Hawkins bill is not perfect. If it is adopted, experience will reveal unsuspected problems that will need correction. But consider what happened under the Manpower Development and Training Act. Congress monitored that legislation closely. Major improvements in the law were enacted in every session of Congress, and the whole system was fundamentally revised after a dozen years of experience with the passage of the Comprehensive Employment and Training Act. But improvement is not possible if the program is never even started. The Humphrey-Hawkins bill sets an ambitious— some would say a daring—goal. But large achievements seldom come from small ambitions. We have learned much about the difficulties of achieving full employment in the past decade. The Humphrey-Hawkins bill builds upon that experience and calls upon us to renew our faith that full employment is attainable. If we reject the challenge without even trying, we insure bitterness and misery in millions of lives, and we edge closer to the fortress society. If we try and succeed, we will have less crime in the streets, less ignorance, less disease, less madness, more simple justice, more strength as a nation, and more security for all of us. ∎

27

That Humphrey-Hawkins won't do what its sponsors promise is a small matter. What it will do is expand the pork barrel; it will create more inflation; and it will take the U.S. one more step in the direction of national planning

What Humphrey-Hawkins Won't Do

YALE BROZEN

THE MUCH REVISED Humphrey-Hawkins Full Employment and Balanced Growth Act (HR-50 and S-50) provides that the President must include in his annual Economic Report:

1. Current and future economic trends in the U.S.;

2. Five-year numerical goals for employment, production, real income, productivity, and balanced growth;

3. Programs to achieve "reasonable" price stability.

These, plus an annual monetary policy statement from the Federal Reserve, are the only specific actions mandated by the bill.

Title I declares that Humphrey-Hawkins' goal is to fulfill "the right of all Americans able, willing, and seeking to work to full opportunities for useful paid employment at fair rates of compensation." Now, no one quarrels with this goal. And that is *why* the bill should be opposed: because it starts us on a road that leads in the opposite direction.

Dangerous Relationship

The bill sets an interim goal of 3 per cent adult unemployment, and 4 per cent total unemployment; these numerical goals are ridiculous. The required statement from the Federal Reserve on monetary policy and the relationship of that policy to the short-term goals in the President's Economic Report are dangerous. And the numerical goals to be set in the Economic Report itself are potentially lethal.

I think the unemployment goals are ridiculous for two sets of reasons. The first set derives from the fact that

Congress does not mean to do what is truly required to meet them. If Congress were serious about unemployment, it would not be enacting another law. Instead, it would *repeal* some laws.

First, it would repeal the minimum-wage provisions of the Fair Labor Standards Act. That in itself would, within two years, halve the unemployment rate among minority teenagers, which now stands at almost 40 per cent.

Second, it would repeal the Davis-Bacon Act, which requires proportional minority hiring. That Act inflates the cost of federal and federally assisted construction projects by 10 to 15 per cent. Also, it indirectly inflates the cost of private construction by about 5 per cent. Repeal of Davis-Bacon would eliminate the $5-billion drain that is currently placed on capital markets in order to finance the excessive portion of the cost of federal projects. The new availability of this $5 billion in the capital market would directly create an additional 250,000 jobs in private-sector capital-formation industries (e.g., the machinery and construction industries).

Current rates of purchase of plant, equipment, and homes are about $20 billion below what would normally be expected at the end of a third year of recovery from a cyclical low. Normally, we would be at a rate of capital formation 10 per cent above the previous peak (fourth quarter of 1973). Instead, we are 2 per cent below that peak. The reason for this is the unprecedented behavior of the Federal Government. It is running a bigger deficit in this third year of recovery ($60 billion) than it did in the

second year ($45 billion). Normally, the deficit should by now be vanishing, and the capital that had been absorbed by the deficit should be becoming available for private capital formation. Instead, the rising deficit has forced up interest rates, and funds are being drained from the financial markets that otherwise would go into capital-goods industries. Repealing Davis-Bacon isn't the whole answer, of course, but that one action alone would cut the drain by $5 billion—*without* any reduction of federal activity!

A Goal Already Met

Third, if Congress were really interested in reducing the unemployment rate, it would mandate the enforcement of eligibility standards for receiving unemployment compensation. That one action would reduce the unemployment rate by one to 1.5 percentage points, bringing it down to 5 per cent.

The second set of reasons that make a 4 per cent unemployment goal ridiculous is that the reported unemployment rate is partly fictitious and partly a consequence of changes in demographics. The fictitious portion is contributed by the relatively new job registration requirements for people receiving food stamps and Aid to Families with Dependent Children. Under

Mr. Brozen is a professor of Business Economics at the University of Chicago's Graduate School of Business and an adjunct scholar of the American Enterprise Institute. This article is adapted from a recent speech to the Chicago Association of Commerce and Industry.

these requirements, all able-bodied persons between the ages of 18 and 65 in families receiving such aid must register for employment in order to continue their eligibility. Ninety per cent of these compulsory registrants never take a job or enter a training program. This contrasts with the normal experience of unemployed persons, who generally find a job within eight to ten weeks after starting to look for one. These compulsory registrants have, within the past few years, added up to 2 percentage points to the reported unemployment rate. If there were no compulsory registration requirements, the current reported unemployment rate would be at a level which today would be regarded as showing full employment.

More Unemployment

The current full-employment unemployment rate, removing the fictional element, is approximately 4.9 per cent. The full-employment unemployment rate in 1960 was 4 per cent. The difference between those two figures is where the changes in demographics come in. A higher proportion of jobseekers today are new entrants or re-entrants into the labor force than was the case in 1960. Those newly entering or re-entering the labor force take more time searching for a desirable job and

receive more job offers before finally selecting one than people who have voluntarily quit or who have been permanently laid off. There is always some unemployment in a full-employment economy in America, because each year about one-fifth to one-quarter of all workers voluntarily quit to search for better jobs. On the average, they take six to eight weeks between jobs. That in itself creates an average unemployment rate of 3 per cent at full-employment levels. Add in workers who prefer to take seasonal employment and then report themselves as unemployed in the off-season so as to collect unemployment compensation; workers permanently laid off who take time to choose among alternative jobs; and the new entrants and re-entrants —and we have a full-employment unemployment rate of 4.9 per cent. That is why a 4 per cent target is ridiculous. Such an imprudent goal will only give Congress and the Administration an excuse to add more government employment programs and to fund more useless public projects such as the water projects which President Carter tried, and failed, to kill last year.

Humphrey-Hawkins' provision that the Federal Reserve must issue an annual statement on monetary policy and on the relationship of that policy to the goals in the President's Economic Report is exceedingly dangerous. It

perpetuates the fiction—enshrined in the Phillips Curve, which has been totally discredited by modern economic research—that unemployment can be cured by creating a little more money and a little more inflation. In fact, the result will be a lot more inflation and probably more, not less, unemployment.

The Camel's Nose

Finally, the addition of five-year numerical goals to the Economic Report is potentially lethal. It is another step down the road to national planning. Why we should take such a step when five-year plans have earned such ill repute in other countries surpasses all understanding. Even the Russians have, semantically at least, abandoned five-year planning: they have shifted to six-year plans in the hope that this will wipe the egg off their faces.

The trouble with five-year plans is that people, or at least politicians and bureaucrats, will come to believe that they should try to make them come true. What little planning the government has done for some industries has already led to several disasters. For years, the government set goals for agricultural output, applied various controls to try to make these goals come true—and was constantly surprised by what actually happened. It applied indicative planning in tin and aluminum and then tried to make its indications come true by supplying financing subsidies, special tax breaks, and stand-by purchase contracts. We ended with a glut of tin-smelter and aluminum capacity. Our government, alarmed by a potential shortage of helium, again applied indicative planning. It signed purchase contracts for helium on the basis of its projections. Now it has more helium on its hands than anyone knows what to do with and has been trying to wriggle out of its contracts for years.

Indicative planning or the setting of goals is the camel's nose under the tent. It has created havoc nearly every time we have done it. It's easy to bet the taxpayer's shirt on some presumed national need. But why not let the people who are betting their own shirts do the planning? Their mistakes are self-limiting, and their vision is more realistic.

28

THE MINIMUM WAGE CONTROVERSY

by Christopher Jencks

Do minimum wage laws increase unemployment? Do they assure poor families a decent income?

Minimum wage laws have enjoyed the support of both liberals and radicals for at least a generation. This unusual unanimity probably explains why President Carter rejected the advice of both business executives and economists last year and endorsed legislation that raised the minimum from $2.30 to $2.65 an hour. According to the Coalition for a Fair Minimum Wage and other supporters of the increase, it represents a victory for the working poor, albeit less than they deserve or need. This view may, however, be too optimistic.

Economists have traditionally opposed any increase in the minimum wage on the ground that it will reduce employment. The argument is simple. Workers, they say, vary dramatically in skills, work habits, and attitudes toward their employers. As a result, firms are willing to pay far more for some workers than for others. Congress has traditionally set the minimum wage at about half the average wage for all nonfarm employees. But Congress cannot guarantee that every would-be worker is half as valuable to his or her employer

Christopher Jencks, a visiting professor at the University of California, Santa Barbara, is a senior editor of Working Papers.

as the average worker. Some don't understand much English. Some quarrel with their fellow employees, their bosses, or their customers. Some drink too much. Some frequently fail to show up. Employers will hire these "undesirable" workers only if they are much cheaper than the average worker. If the law requires a firm to pay all employees at least half the national average, most firms will avoid hiring the least desirable workers. Even if the labor market is tight, firms will find it more profitable to lure desirable workers away from other jobs with premium wages than to hire the least desirable workers at the statutory minimum.

How plausible is this argument? There is no question that some people have characteristics that make them undesirable employees and are chronically unemployed as a result. It is not clear, however, that these workers would have an appreciably easier time finding work if there were no minimum wage. Many are probably undesirable employees at *any* price. Conversely, many poorly paid workers have precisely the same characteristics as workers earning higher wages. These workers hold poorly paid jobs not because they lack the attributes needed to perform competently in a better paid job, but because they have not actually applied for such a job when there happened to be a vacancy.

Assessing the actual effect of minimum wage legislation on employment therefore requires historical evidence. America began collecting reliable employment statistics only after World War II. Since then the statutory minimum has generally ranged between 45 and 55 percent of the average wage. Such modest variations inevitably have modest effects on employment compared to other factors. Virtually every economist who has studied the matter has concluded that raising the minimum has *some* negative effect on employment, but the size of the estimated effect varies from one study to the next, depending on the years covered and the other factors taken into account.

If one is simply interested in maximizing Gross National Product, *any* reduction in employment is undesirable. But if one's goal is to increase the annual earnings of low-wage workers, a higher minimum wage may make sense. It will lower the number of hours "undesirable" employees work, but it will increase what they earn when they work. (Except during serious recessions, virtually everyone who looks for a job persistently is employed at least part of every year.) The net effect of changing the minimum wage is thus hard to assess, especially since many employers simply ignore the law.[1]

But even if minimum wages improve the annual earnings of low-wage workers, they may not serve their larger purpose. The original rationale for a minimum wage was that every worker should be paid enough to support himself (sic) and his family at what society regards as a decent level. Survey data suggest that this is still the main reason why the public favors minimum wage legislation.[2] Those who advocate raising the minimum also emphasize this argument. Before the recent increase, for example, the minimum was $2.30 an hour. A person earning $2.30 an hour at a steady job with no overtime could expect to gross about $4,600 a year. Congressional testimony in support of raising the minimum repeatedly stressed the fact that a family of four with only $4,600 falls below the federal poverty line.

The difficulty with this argument is that only a small minority of low-wage workers are trying to support a family of four entirely on what they earn. In May 1974, for example, the minimum wage rose from $1.60 to $2.00 an hour. Fifteen percent of all workers reported earning less than $2.00 an hour in 1973. Less than a quarter of these low-wage workers were the only earners in their families.[3] Furthermore, nearly half the sole earners with low wages were not supporting anyone but themselves.[4] Thus only about one low-wage worker in eight was actually trying to support a family on his, or more often her, earnings. Another eighth were supporting themselves. Thirty percent were teenagers, virtually all of whom lived with their parents. Thirty-seven percent were adult women who lived either with their parents or with a working husband. Ten percent were adult men who

lived either with their parents or with a working wife.

Because three-quarters of all low-wage workers were pooling their resources with relatives, low-wage workers' family income was not very different from the family income of Americans in general. Table 1 shows the distribution of 1972 family incomes for workers who reported earning less than $1.60 an hour and for those earning between $1.60 and $2.00 an hour in May 1973. Some of the workers earning less than $1.60 were in jobs not covered by minimum wage legislation. Some doubtless misreported their wages. The rest were simply paid less than the law required. On the average, these workers' families were slightly poorer than families in general. But since they were paid less than the statutory minimum in 1973, it is not obvious that raising the minimum to $2.00 in 1974 increased their wages, let alone their annual earnings. Workers earning between $1.60 and $2.00 an hour were presumably more likely to benefit from increasing the statutory mimimum to $2.00. Yet their 1972 family incomes were generally *higher* than the incomes of typical American families. Only 15 percent lived in families with incomes below $4,000 a year, for example, whereas Table 1 shows

that 22 percent of all families fell in this category.

This finding is so counterintuitive as to require some explanation. Part of the explanation is that many low-wage workers are teenagers. Low-wage teenagers come from families with incomes well above the national average. That is partly because the heads of families with teenage children are at the peak of their earning power, partly because a working teenager boosts family income, and partly because working teenagers, whatever their wages, are an elite group. The less desirable teenage workers, many of whom come from low-income families, are simply unemployed. Applying minimum wage legislation to teenagers therefore has quite perverse effects. It boosts the wages of those who find jobs. But the teenagers who find jobs are not those who most need the money.[5] At the same time, raising the minimum encourages firms to hire adults instead of teenagers. The burden of unemployment falls primarily on the poorest teenagers.

But even if we confined minimum wage legislation to adults, raising the minimum might not improve the distribution of family income. Table 1 shows that adults earning less than $1.60 an hour came from families somewhat worse off than the average. But workers earning between $1.60 and

TABLE 1: PERCENTAGE OF LOW–WAGE WORKERS WITH VARIOUS FAMILY INCOMES

All workers earning:	0–$4,000	$4,000–$8,000	$8,000–$15,000	$15,000 or more	Total
$1.60 or less	23.4	26.9	32.0	17.7	100
$1.61 – $2.00	14.6	24.5	37.9	23.0	100
All adults earning:					
$1.60 or less	31.8	30.9	26.4	10.8	100
$1.61 – $2.00	17.9	28.9	39.2	14.0	100
All families	21.8	21.8	32.4	24.0	100

"Family income" includes all earnings, property income, and transfer payments received in 1972 by related individuals living together in 1973. Single individuals are included as "families." Unrelated individuals living together are treated as separate "families." Lines 1-4 are from Edward Gramlich, "Impact of Minimum Wages on Other Wages, Employment, and Family Incomes," *Brookings Papers on Economic Activity,* 1976, Table 10. Row 5 is from *Current Population Reports,* Series P-60, no. 105, June 1977, Table 9. The CPS distribution for all families differs from Gramlich's distribution for all families, since Gramlich's distribution is weighted by the number of wage earners per family.

$2.00 were living primarily in middle-income families. Raising their wages therefore shifted resources away from the rich and the poor toward those in the middle. Given the relatively desperate position of poor families, that is probably not a progressive change.

The motive behind minimum wage legislation is clearly humane. The law seeks to restrict the ravages of a competitive economic system by ensuring that every family has enough money to get by, regardless of its members' bargaining power in the labor market. But the law does not achieve this. It does not guarantee every worker a job at the statutory minimum. It merely forbids employers to hire workers at less than the minimum. Partly as a result, many families have no earners at all. Others have earners who can only find sporadic work. Furthermore, even if a family has one wage earner who gets the statutory minimum on a regular basis, its overall income will not be adequate for raising children. The new minimum of $2.65 ensures, for example, that a family of four with one regularly employed earner who gets no overtime will receive about $5,300 a year before taxes and deductions. Nobody really believes that $5,300 is enough to make ends meet. The mean income of four-person families in 1976 was about $19,000. The typical citizen now thinks that a family of four needs at least $10,000 to "get along" in his or her community.[6] Bureau of Labor Statistics budgets that estimate the cost of basic necessities support this popular judgment. According to these budgets, a worker supporting three other people would need to earn at least $5.00 an hour to sustain a minimal standard of living. Families with wages below this level need either two earners or some kind of outside help. Yet virtually no one is pushing for a $5.00 minimum, which would probably increase unemployment substantially.

Minimum wage legislation tries to alter the distribution of family incomes by altering the distribution of hourly wages. But the link between individuals' hourly wages

The typical citizen feels that a family of four needs at least $10,000 to "get along" — but no one is pushing for a $5.00 minimum

and their families' annual income is extremely weak, especially at the bottom of the wage distribution. Boosting minimum wages ends up helping many families that are not unusually needy while ignoring the problems of other families that are in serious financial trouble. A better solution might be to drop the idea of minimum wages in favor of guaranteed public employment at a substantially higher wage for any individual who is the sole support of his or her family. Wages for such workers (a minority of those who are unemployed) could be scaled to family needs—say $2.50 an hour for a single individual and $5.00 an hour for the sole support of a family of four. A second alternative would be to develop a system of publicly financed wage subsidies for workers in the private sector who are the sole support of their families. Neither alternative is perfect. But they at least have the virtue of facing a widely felt problem directly, instead of trying to deal with it indirectly. ∎

---

1. Edward Gramlich discusses the extent of noncompliance in "Impact of Minimum Wages on Other Wages, Employment, and Family Incomes," *Brookings Papers on Economic Activity*, 1976, vol. 2. Orly Ashenfelter and Robert Smith discuss the same issue using data supplied by firms in "Compliance with the Minimum Wage Law," a 1974 paper prepared for the Labor Department's Office of the Assistant Secretary for Policy, Evaluation, and Research.

2. See Lee Rainwater, *What Money Buys*, Basic Books, 1974.

3. The Census Bureau began its wage surveys in 1973. The bureau has not published tabulations from these surveys, but Gramlich's paper, cited above, allows one to make rough estimates of the percentage of low-wage workers who are the sole support of

their families. Gramlich's tables show almost 9.6 million workers earning less than $2.00 an hour in 1973. Of these, 2.9 million were teenagers, 1.5 million were adult male family "heads," 0.4 million were adult male nonheads, 1.1 million were adult female "heads," and 3.7 million were adult female nonheads. Virtually all the teenagers were presumably living with at least one other earner. The same holds for the males who were not classified as heads. Among male heads, *Current Population Reports*, Series P-60, no. 105, Table 44 indicates that 68 percent of those with 1975 annual incomes below $5,000 were married, and Table 28 indicates that 55 percent of those who were married had working wives. If these percentages also apply to low-wage males in 1973, about 0.9 million male heads were sole earners. Among female nonheads, *Current Population Reports*, Series P-60, no. 105, Table 28 indicates that about 7 percent of all married women earning less than $5,000 in 1975 had husbands with no earnings at all. If the same were true for married women earning less than $2.00 an hour in 1973, about 0.2 million female nonheads with low wages would have been the sole earners in their families. Finally, virtually all the 1.1 million female heads with low wages were the sole earners in their families (though a few presumably lived with teenage children or some other relative who worked). Overall, then, 0.9 + 0.2 + 1.1 = 2.2 million of the 9.6 million individuals with low wages were the only earners in their families.

4. *Current Population Reports*, Series P-60, no. 105, Table 44 shows that of individuals with incomes less than $5,000 per year in 1975, 28 percent of all male heads and 64 percent of all female heads (using Gramlich's broad definition) were "unrelated individuals," i.e. families of one. If these ratios also held for individuals with low wages in 1973, 1.1 million of the 2.2 million sole earners would have been unrelated individuals. The actual number could have been somewhat lower, since the ratios for low-income individuals are probably inflated by inclusion of retired widows and widowers and by exclusion of some low-wage workers with children who also received AFDC and thus had total incomes over $5,000.

5. Raising the low wages of teenagers could still help reduce inequality if low-wage teenagers from low-income families worked more hours than low-wage teenagers from high-income families. This seems likely, since the latter are often students. But even teenagers working full time in May 1973 had family incomes above the national average.

6. Extrapolated from data in Rainwater's *What Money Buys* (p. 53).

29

A talk given at
Fairleigh Dickinson University,
Hackensack, New Jersey, on
Wednesday, March 2, 1977

Monetary Objectives and Monetary Policy

Richard G. Davis
Senior Economic Adviser
Federal Reserve Bank of New York

Since the spring of 1975 the Federal Reserve has been announcing projected growth ranges for several measures of money and bank credit. The use of such monetary "targets" raises a wide range of issues in monetary economics, from the rather narrowly technical to the more broadly philosophical. Since the subject is vast and time is limited, I shall have to be content with a terse and selective summary of some of the main issues posed by the use of monetary targets. Specifically, I want to (1) describe the procedures for setting projected monetary growth ranges currently in use, (2) try to suggest some historical reasons for the evolution of these procedures, (3) describe the broad strategic considerations that enter into the setting of the monetary growth ranges, (4) discuss some general problems in determining just what numerical values should be chosen under given circumstances, and (5) discuss some problems in realizing projected growth ranges once they are set.

Under the current procedure, the Chairman of the Federal Reserve Board announces projected growth ranges for the coming four-quarter period in quarterly presentations to (alternately) the House and Senate banking committees. These presentations are made in response to a joint Concurrent Resolution of the House and Senate passed in March 1975.

At the outset I should perhaps note that the term "targets", often applied to these monetary growth ranges, actually has no particular official standing. Indeed in some respects the term is misleading since it may seem to imply that particular numerical values for the money supply, rather than the general health of the economy, is the "target" of policy. And it may seem to imply a degree of rigidity with regard to the pursuit of these money supply ranges that does not exist. Notwithstanding these difficulties, I will frequently use the term "target" for lack of a more convenient alternative.

The ranges themselves are defined in terms of upper and lower limits for growth rates in three definitions of the money supply (and one of bank credit) as measured from the most recent quarterly average levels to the prospective levels four quarters ahead. The current target period thus covers growth over a one-year period ending with the fourth quarter of 1977. The group of monetary measures that are targeted at the moment includes M_1 (currency plus demand deposits), M_2 (M_1 plus commercial bank time and savings deposits other than large negotiable CDs), and M_3 (M_2 plus deposits and shares at mutual savings banks and savings and loan associations). Chart 1 shows the current growth rate ranges for M_1 and M_2 and compares them with actual growth rates over some recent past periods. While the targets are stated in growth rate terms, given the base period levels, these growth rates can of course also be translated directly into upper and lower limits on the dollar levels four quarters hence. A translation into dollar levels is sometimes useful as a means of following how the aggregates may be tracking relative to the targets. Chart 2 shows the growth path of M_1 over the four quarters of 1976 relative to the upper and lower limits implied by the target growth rates at the beginning of 1976.

Excerpted from Federal Reserve Bank of New York *Quarterly Review*, Spring, 1977.

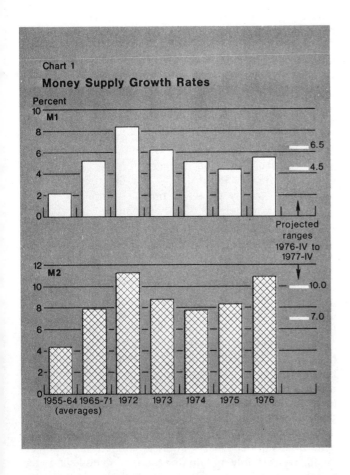

Chart 1
Money Supply Growth Rates

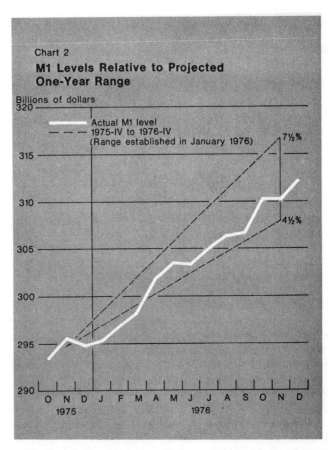

Chart 2
M1 Levels Relative to Projected One-Year Range

Historical evolution

Quite apart from the immediate impetus to publicly announced monetary targets provided by the Congressional Concurrent Resolution, the present targeting procedure represents the product of a long evolution in thinking over the postwar period. When active countercyclical monetary policy first got under way in the postwar period, the Federal Reserve faced a new situation and new objectives for which the experience of earlier decades really offered little guidance. Clearly, one of the main objectives of policy was to provide countercyclical ballast. This meant "tightening" when expansion threatened to become unsustainably exuberant and "easing" when the economy became soft. At first, it was pretty much universal practice both inside and outside the Federal Reserve to calibrate policy in terms of money market conditions or the behavior of short-term interest rates. Policy was said to be "easing" or "easy" when short-term rates were falling or low and to be "tightening" or "tight" when rates were rising or high.

After some experience with this framework, however, it became evident that the behavior of interest rates

was not always a good way to calibrate the impact of policy. The trouble was that, even in the short run, interest rate movements depend only in part on what the Federal Reserve does and much more on what the economy itself does by way of generating demands for money and credit. As a result, interest rates can give off misleading signals of policy's impact at crucial junctures in the business cycle, with the movements in rates reflecting the effect not of policy but of cyclical developments in the economy itself.

Perhaps the *locus classicus* of such situations occurred in early 1960 when the economy went into recession and interest rates fell even though bank reserves and the money supply continued to contract until the middle of the year. The conjunction of a falling money supply and bank reserves along with falling interest rates made it quite clear that declining rates reflected weakening credit demands at a time when the economy was going into recession. Under such conditions, it didn't seem to make much sense to describe monetary policy as "easy" simply because interest rates were falling. The feeling spread in the 1960's that this kind of situation might not be at all rare and indeed might be a systematic feature of business-cycle behavior. As a result, wariness about identifying monetary "tightness" and "ease" with interest rate movements increased. At the same time, the advantages of identifying policy directly by the behavior of movements in the money supply and bank reserves seemed to become more apparent.

This trend in thinking was clearly also spurred by a roughly concurrent increase in the popularity of "monetarism"—a view that claims a dominant importance for the behavior of the money supply in determining a wide range of short and longer run economic developments. Nevertheless, there is little intrinsic connection between the question of what indexes to use in measuring and guiding monetary policy and the larger issues posed by monetarism about the behavior of the economy as a whole.

In any case, the accelerating rates of inflation we began to experience in the late 1960's undoubtedly further undermined confidence in the use of interest rates and increased the appeal of monetary aggregates as measures of policy. With the relatively high rates of inflation that emerged in the late 1960's, an old idea resurfaced, namely, that actual market rates of interest really consist of two parts: (1) a so-called "real" rate of interest which equals the market rate adjusted for any depreciation in the purchasing power of the principal over the life of the loan and (2) an inflationary component to compensate for this depreciation.

With high and variable rates of inflation, given market interest rates obviously will not have a constant meaning in terms of the real "tightness" or "ease" they imply about financial markets. Under these conditions the behavior of market rates becomes a rather elastic measuring rod. Moreover, even if the monetary authorities could in theory control at least some nominal interest rates by pegging the prices of some debt instruments, they have no control at all over the "real" interest rate, i.e., the nominal rate adjusted for inflation. Finally, the emergence of inflation over recent years as an absolutely first-rank economic problem has tended to reemphasize the long-run strategic importance of monetary growth rates.

The strategy of setting monetary targets

To return to the current practices regarding monetary targets, it is easy, at least on one level, to describe how the numerical monetary target ranges are set. Procedurally, the result is the outcome of a vote by the Federal Open Market Committee (FOMC). In choosing among alternatives, the individual Committee members obviously vote for that set of target numbers they think is most likely to produce good results for the economy

over the coming year *given the information at hand.* For each member, this decision depends upon two elements: (1) his preferences among possible outcomes for the economy and (2) his views about what outcomes are in fact likely to result from the choice of particular target ranges. The economics staffs at the Board of Governors of the Federal Reserve System and at the Reserve Banks try to provide some assistance on this latter aspect of the problem by trying to project the consequences for the economy of alternative target ranges. These projections may be made in a variety of ways, ranging from the use of econometric models to purely judgmental projections, with various combinations in between. Obviously, however, the various staff judgments will not always agree, will not always be right, and will not always be accepted by the Committee members.

Immediate circumstances aside, Chairman Arthur F. Burns and other senior Federal Reserve officials, including President Paul A. Volcker of the New York Reserve Bank, have frequently emphasized that the overall process of setting monetary aggregate targets has been influenced since its inception by a longer run strategy: This strategy is one of gradually bringing down growth rates in money to levels that in the long run may prove compatible with price stability.

The linkage suggested by this strategy between the longer run behavior of money and price stability, however, does not necessarily imply a "monetarist" view of inflation—certainly not in the sense of believing, as Milton Friedman has put it, that inflation is "always and everywhere a purely monetary phenomenon". The events of the past few years, it seems to me, should have made it clear that, in the short run, inflation can lead a life of its own quite independent of current or past monetary development. The 12 percent inflation of 1974, for example, was clearly traceable in a large part to special factors and cannot be explained by monetary growth alone.

But on a longer term basis, it doesn't take much massaging of the data to suggest a general if imperfect parallelism between monetary growth and inflation (Chart 3). Even over this longer run, there is a serious question under present day conditions as to whether the causality doesn't run as much from prices to money as from money to prices. Central banks and governments all over the world have often found themselves under intense pressure to validate price increases stemming from nonmonetary sources because the short-run alternatives have seemed to be pressures on interest rates and employment. Consequently, although in a narrow, purely economic view of the inflation problem, rapid monetary growth might be regarded as the "cause" of long-run inflation, a more comprehensive view of the entire process must put the blame on a multitude of political, social, and economic pressures. These pressures have given an inflationary bias to modern economies, one that has often been accommodated by monetary expansion simply because in the short run this has seemed to be the least undesirable among available alternatives.

Yet despite reservations about purely monetary theories of inflation, economists do generally agree that avoidance of excessive monetary growth is at least a necessary—though not necessarily a sufficient—condition for long-run price stability. Thus, it was evident by 1972 that a long-term strategy of gradually slowing monetary growth rates had become desirable. As Chart 1 shows, growth rates did in fact slow in 1973 and 1974 but, beginning in 1975, the pressing immediate problem of ensuring an adequate economic recovery became a factor. Nevertheless, the longer term objective of gradually lowering monetary growth rates has continued to be reaffirmed—most recently in February by Chairman Burns in his regular quarterly testimony to the Congress. As Chart 4 shows, all but one of the eight individual changes in monetary target

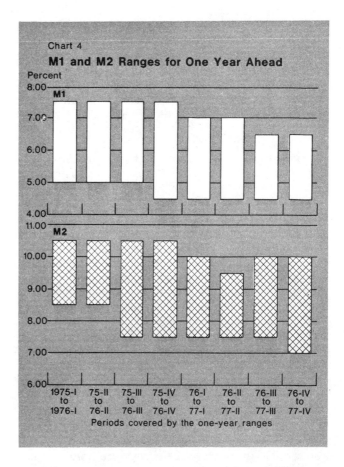

Chart 4

M1 and M2 Ranges for One Year Ahead

ranges for M_1 and M_2 that have been made over the past two years have been in the direction of modest downward adjustments in the upper or lower ends of the ranges of one or more of the money supply measures.

The current targets are clearly still well above the levels that would be likely to prove consistent with long-run price stability. To be sure, no one can say with certainty just what these growth rates are, but the historical record seems to suggest rough estimates of about 1 to 2 percent for M_1 and about 3 to 4 percent for M_2.

Movements to such levels could not be made all at once, however. Inflation, once set in motion, tends to be extremely persistent under modern conditions, even after demand pressures have disapppeared. Thus at least *some* inflation seems inevitable, no matter what monetary policy does, for a certain period ahead. If monetary growth rates do not take this fact into account, they risk being insufficient to finance adequate growth of real economic activity. This consideration provides a strong reason for setting monetary targets under these conditions above levels appropriate for

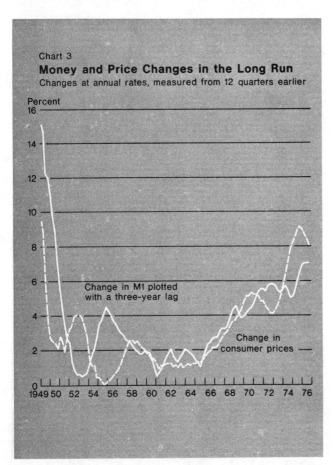

Chart 3

Money and Price Changes in the Long Run

Changes at annual rates, measured from 12 quarters earlier

long-run price stability, moving down to those levels as inflation recedes.

Problems in setting targets

A major problem in setting targets is that there can be slippages in the relationship between money and the economy over periods of time and in orders of magnitude substantial enough to be important to policymakers. To the extent that such slippages exist, determining target levels needed to achieve any given economic result will have to involve a significant amount of judgment. The existence of slippages means that appropriate target ranges simply cannot be mechanically deduced from past behavior—as would be implied, for example, by a literal and uncritical use of projections from an econometric model.

The relationship between the growth of money and the growth of GNP can deviate from past patterns, for example, if the public's desire to hold money balances under given conditions—the "demand for money function" in the parlance of economists—changes. No one thinks the demand for money under given conditions is absolutely stable, but there are substantial differences of opinion as to just how important shifts in money demand may be. We have recently had highly suggestive (to me) evidence that the demand for money can in fact deviate far enough from the norm to have quite significant policy implications. Thus, over the first year of the current economic expansion, the income velocity (turnover) of M_1 balances rose very rapidly, by almost 8 percent. It is normal for velocity to rise at above-trend rates the first year of economic expansion, but the 1975-76 rise was abnormally rapid even so— the rate of increase exceeded the average for the four preceding upturns by nearly 60 percent. What is most striking about this abnormally rapid rise in velocity is that it occurred despite some net downward drift in the yields on a wide range of financial instruments (including common stocks) that are alternatives to holding money. Economists assume that declines in such yields ought to *reduce* the incentive to economize on noninterest-bearing M_1 balances. Thus they would normally expect interest rate declines to *reduce* velocity or at least slow its growth, not to produce the unusually rapid increase that actually occurred.

That velocity did, nevertheless, increase so rapidly suggests a weakened desire to hold money balances under given conditions. And there have been some institutional developments recently that could explain a shift of funds out of M_1 balances. These developments —including the spreading use of NOW accounts and the opening-up of savings accounts to business, for example—could explain the apparent reduction in the demand for M_1 balances that the figures on velocity

seem to imply. The point of all of this is simply that anyone looking ahead at the very beginning of the recovery and trying to guess an appropriate rate of M_1 expansion for the year ahead would have had a real problem. Relying on past statistical relationships alone would have led him to a serious overestimate of the M_1 growth needed to finance the rather vigorous 13 percent growth of nominal GNP that actually occurred.

A second technical problem that complicates setting aggregate targets has to do with the changing relationships among the various monetary measures that are targeted. Over the years, M_2 and M_3 have on average grown more rapidly than M_1 (Chart 5). Thus under normal circumstances we would expect the M_2 and M_3 target ranges to be above the corresponding M_1 ranges —as they have over the past two years. Complicating the problem, however, is the fact that the differentials between the growth rates of M_1 and the other two measures have at times varied sharply.

The explanation for these shifting relative growth rates lies mainly in the sensitivity of the time and savings deposits included in M_2 and M_3 (but not in M_1) to competition from open market instruments, such

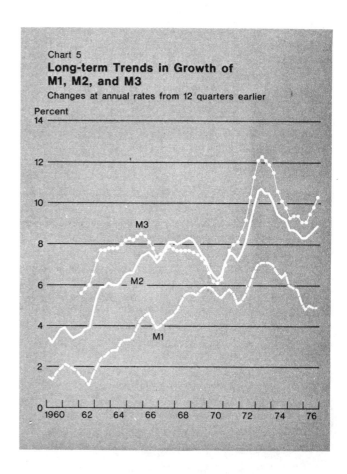

Chart 5

Long-term Trends in Growth of M1, M2, and M3

Changes at annual rates from 12 quarters earlier

as Treasury bills and commercial paper. This sensitivity in itself might cause no particular problem if interest rate differentials between time and savings deposits and open market instruments were roughly constant. But, in fact, these interest rate differentials show rather sizable changes. These changes, in turn, follow roughly the overall average level of interest rates as it varies with the business cycle. In part, the changes in interest rate differentials result from Regulation Q, which puts limits on deposit interest rates and thus may prevent them from following market rates up when the latter are rising. But Regulation Q is only part of the story. For various reasons, deposit rates tend to be slow to adjust to changes in competing market rates even when market rates are relatively low and the legal ceilings are not a consideration.

The result of the sluggish adjustment of bank deposit rates to rising open market rates is often a flow of funds out of interest-bearing deposits along with a corresponding slowdown in M_2 and M_3 growth relative to M_1. Conversely, when market rates are falling, funds tend to flow back into time and savings accounts, resulting in abnormally rapid M_2 and M_3 growth relative to M_1. These movements clearly can create some dilemmas in setting targets. Over the past year, for example, M_1 grew 5.5 percent, about the middle of the 4½ to 7½ percent target range set early in the year, while M_2 grew by about 10.9 percent, somewhat above the upper end of its 7½ to 10½ percent range. The unusually wide spread between M_1 and M_2 growth in 1976 undoubtedly did reflect in large part the unusual declines in open market interest rates during the year. These declines clearly encouraged massive flows of funds out of market instruments and into the various types of time and savings deposits.

What is the proper attitude to take toward the unusually rapid growth rates of M_2 and M_3 in these circumstances? One possibility is simply to make some allowances for the fact that interest rate relationships between deposits and market instruments are out of line with their long-run equilibria and adjust upward the target ranges for M_2 and M_3 relative to M_1. This in fact is what the FOMC did at its October meeting. (The change was subsequently modified in January as bank time and savings deposit rates seemed to be adjusting downward to a more normal relationship with market rates.)

.   .   .

Conclusion

Even this short review of monetary aggregate targets clearly indicates that there are many problems connected with them: problems in setting the targets, problems in hitting the targets, and indeed limits to what the approach can accomplish in improving the performance of the economy. In no sense has the use of monetary targets been able to turn what used to be called the "art" of central banking into a rigid mechanical process for controlling and monitoring the flow of money and credit. Judgment is required in determining at what levels the targets should be set and under what conditions and in what ways they should be changed. Judgment is also required in making the week-to-week and month-to-month decisions with regard to open market operations appropriate to achieving the targets. And, finally, judgment is required in deciding how to respond when monetary performance seems to be getting out of line with what had been expected and intended.

Nevertheless, despite all these caveats, the setting of monetary objectives covering fairly long time spans —however provisional and subject to change—seems to me one of the more constructive innovations in macroeconomic policymaking of recent years—not just in this country, but in others as well. It is a development, moreover, that seems especially useful in a period when high and variable rates of inflation have become one of our most serious problems.

30

MONEY—A CHANGING CONCEPT IN A CHANGING WORLD

By Carl M. Gambs

> *It is a singular and, indeed, a significant fact that, although money was the first economic subject to attract men's thoughtful attention, and has been the focal centre of economic investigation ever since, there is at the present day not even an approximate agreement as to what ought to be designated by the word. The business world makes use of the term in several senses, while among economists there are almost as many different conceptions as there are writers upon money.*
>
> A. P. Andrew[1]

The money stock has been given increasing attention in recent years. Both the Federal Reserve and the public currently closely observe the rate at which the quantity of money is growing. Accompanying this increased attention to money is a recognition that there is considerable disagreement as to how money should be defined. As the above 1899 statement by A. P. Andrew demonstrates, this disagreement is far from new.

While the nature of the disagreement over the definition of money has changed since 1899, disagreement seems always to have been present.[2] In 1974 the Board of Governors of the Federal Reserve System, recognizing the importance of this problem, appointed the Advisory Committee on Monetary Statistics (generally termed the Bach Committee after Professor G. L. Bach, the chairman) to examine some of the issues involved. The Bach Committee's report was released in June 1976,[3] but given the extent of disagreement on the subject, its conclusions are unlikely to greatly reduce the controversy over the definition of money.

An increasing source of difficulty in defining money is the rapid change taking place in the nation's payments system.[4] Payments system change was also a major factor at the time that Andrew was writing, but has not been an

---

[1] A. P. Andrew, "What Ought to be Called Money," *Quarterly Journal of Economics*, Vol. 13 (January 1899), p. 219.

[2] For an excellent discussion of both historical and current controversies regarding the definition of money, see Milton Friedman and Anna J. Schwartz, *Monetary Statistics of the United States* (New York: National Bureau of Economic Research, 1970), pp. 93-189.

[3] Board of Governors of the Federal Reserve System, *Improving the Monetary Aggregates, Report of the Advisory Committee on Monetary Statistics*, Washington, D.C., June 1976.

[4] It is probably more accurate to refer to "payments systems," as there are currently a number of alternative ways of making funds transfers. The term "payments system" is used here to include all systems for making funds transfers, including those which may only be implemented in the future.

Reprinted from Federal Reserve Bank of Kansas City *Monthly Review*, January, 1977.

important source of controversy since the 1930's. The final third of the 19th century saw radical changes in the monetary system of the United States, particularly in the domestic payments system. On the eve of the Civil War (January 1860), the American money stock—defined to include specie, bank notes, and bank deposits—consisted of $186 million in gold, $184 million in bank notes, and $241 million in bank deposits.[5] During and after the War, the composition changed drastically. Bank deposits increased from 38.6 per cent of money holdings in 1860 to 54.7 per cent in 1867, and to 68.6 per cent in 1875. By 1899, deposits had risen to 81 per cent of all money holdings.[6] While we do not have data on either the quantity of demand deposits or the volume of payments by check during this period, this movement from currency to bank deposits was indicative of the shift that took place in the payments system toward the making of payments by check.

In spite of this shift, there was a general reluctance to include demand deposits in the money supply. It is not clear to what extent late 19th century economists realized that this change was taking place. Since they did not have published figures on the money stock, they were not aware of the precise degree to which changes were occurring. Perhaps the changes taking place were recognized, but a kind of intellectual inertia caused the economists of the day to prefer the traditional definitions which excluded deposits. At any rate, there seems to have been a general reluctance to expand the definition of money to include bank deposits,[7] just as many economists are reluctant to modify today's commonly accepted definitions.

There is at least some reason for believing that changes in the payments system currently taking place will be every bit as significant as the changes of the 19th century. It is widely believed that the United States is in the early stages of movement toward an electronic funds transfer system (EFTS)—a system where many—perhaps most—payments would be made in response to electronic instructions rather than instructions written on a paper check.

While there are very wide differences of opinion as to the likely speed and extent of EFTS development, there seems to be very little reason for doubting that another change in the payments system is well underway. Until recently, with the minor exception of traveler's checks, payments could be made only with currency and commercial bank checking accounts. It is now increasingly possible to make payments from other types of accounts—commercial bank savings accounts, accounts at savings and loan associations (S&L's), mutual savings banks (MSB's), credit unions (CU's), and even certain mutual fund accounts. In addition, an increasing proportion of purchases is being made with credit cards.

In light of these developments, it seems useful to attempt to consider whether these changes, like the changes of the late 19th century, will require modifications in our

---

5 Jack Lewis Rutner, "Money in the Antebellum Economy: Its Composition, Relation to Income and Its Determinants" (unpublished Ph. D. dissertation, University of Chicago, June 1974), pp. 182-83.

6 Post-Civil War monetary statistics, as compiled by Friedman and Schwartz, are in U.S. Bureau of the Census, *Historical Statistics of the United States, Colonial Times to 1970, Bicentennial Edition, Part 2* (Washington, D.C.: Government Printing Office, 1975), pp. 992-93.

7 "On the other hand, the stretching of the word (money) to make it cover such means of trade as bank deposits and bills of exchange presents itself as even more objectionable, primarily because it is in the highest degree discordant with the traditional way of employing the term, and must inevitably tend therefore to arouse suspicion, provoke antagonism, and entail misunderstanding, and because at the same time there are plenty of other expressions, such as 'currency,' 'circulating medium,' and 'means of payment,' which can be used quite as effectively to represent the same all-inclusive concept," Andrew, p. 226.

H. Parker Willis, one of the leading monetary economists of the day, was contending as late as 1925 that even bank notes were not money. H. Parker Willis and George W. Edwards, *Banking and Business* (New York: Harper and Brothers, 1925), pp. 96-97.

concept of money. This article discusses the implications of payments system changes for the various definitions of money published by the Federal Reserve System. Also considered is the degree to which the usefulness of current definitions is likely to be reduced and the extent to which simple modifications of these definitions can restore that usefulness.

CURRENT DEFINITIONS
OF MONEY

Three approaches to the definition of money have been widely used. The traditional approach has been to define money as those assets which can be used to purchase goods and services or to pay debts—that is those assets which serve as media of exchange. A second approach, suggested by Milton Friedman, would define money as those assets which serve as a "temporary abode of purchasing power"— that is assets which are held during relatively brief periods when an individual or firm has receipts exceeding expenditures. The third approach is not always explicitly stated, but has been widely used in monetary research and seems to have been extremely important to the Bach Committee. This approach would define money as the aggregate or aggregates which are highly correlated with gross national product or some other measure of economic activity. Presumably this approach rests on the belief that the money stock thus defined would be of greater value in the formulation of stabilization policy.

The Federal Reserve System regularly publishes data for five alternative money stock definitions. Multiple measures are published because there are differences of opinion as to what is the appropriate basis for defining money and because there is a good deal of uncertainty as to what empirical definition best fits the various theoretical approaches. Since the Federal Reserve has only limited access to data for many nonmember institutions, the money stock definitions are inadequate in some instances.

M1, which consists of currency and demand deposits other than those held by commercial banks and the U.S. Government, corresponds to the traditional medium of exchange approach to the money supply. It does not, however, include one familiar medium of exchange, traveler's checks.[8]

M2 is M1 plus time and savings deposits of commercial banks other than large negotiable certificates of deposit (CD's) at weekly reporting banks. M3 is M2 plus deposits at MSB's, S&L's, and CU's. M4 is M2 plus large negotiable CD's and M5 is M3 plus large negotiable CD's. These four definitions reflect to some extent the "temporary abode of purchasing power" approach, as well as the belief of many economists that one or another of these magnitudes is more closely related to GNP than is M1.[9]

The "temporary abode of purchasing power" approach seems to have been more discussed than used in formulating M2 through M5. These definitions all contain certain components which are ordinarily held for long periods of time and exclude other items which fulfill the "temporary abode" function. It seems

---

[8] The largest U.S. issuer of traveler's checks is not a commercial bank and thus does not report to the Federal Reserve (or any other bank regulator). At one time, bank-issued traveler's checks were a part of the money supply. The two major banks in the traveler's check business now use holding company subsidiaries to issue them. Thus, they are not liabilities of the bank and not part of the money supply.

[9] There has apparently never been an exhaustive study of the numerous possibilities to determine empirically which definition of money has been most closely related to economic activity in the past. There have, however, been a number of limited attempts in this direction. See Milton Friedman and David Meiselman, "The Relative Stability of Monetary Velocity and the Investment Multiplier in the United States, 1897-1958," in Commission on Money and Credit, *Stabilization Policies* (Englewood Cliffs, N.J.: Prentice-Hall, 1963), pp. 242-46; Frederick C. Shadrack, "An Empirical Approach to the Definition of Money," in Federal Reserve Bank of New York, *Monetary Aggregates and Monetary Policy* (New York, 1974); Edward F. Renshaw, "A Note on Economic Activity and Alternative Definitions of the Money Supply," *Journal of Money, Credit and Banking,* Vol. 7 (November 1975), pp. 507-13.

clear, for example, that long-term bank CD's do not serve as a temporary abode of purchasing power, yet, with the exception of CD's larger than $100,000 they are included in all of the broader definitions. Moreover, the similar instruments of S&L's and MSB's are included in M3 and M5. On the other hand, large negotiable certificates of deposit clearly serve as a temporary abode of purchasing power for large corporations, but have been excluded from the most widely used definitions.[10] Since existing definitions do not consistently reflect the "temporary abode of purchasing power" approach, this article concentrates on the implication of changes in the payments system for the medium of exchange and correlation with economic activity approaches to the money stock.

It should be noted that there are other changes taking place which have implications for the definition of the money supply which are beyond the scope of this article. Perhaps the most important of these is the change in the composition of the time deposit portion of M2, which once consisted entirely of household savings deposits but now includes large quantities of business savings deposits and long-term time deposits.[11]

MAJOR CHANGES IN THE PAYMENTS SYSTEM

The Extension of Payment Accounts To New Institutions

Historically, commercial banks have been the only financial institution to provide a deposit account which could be used to pay third parties. From 1933 to 1972 these payments could be made only from noninterest bearing demand deposit accounts.[12] Since 1972, there have been a number of innovations which have allowed other institutions to offer close substitutes for bank checking accounts.

NOW Accounts. In 1972, following a favorable court decision, MSB's in Massachusetts began offering NOW accounts to their customers. These accounts are legally savings deposits but allow the customer to withdraw funds by writing a "negotiable order of withdrawal (NOW)." Since a NOW looks, and more importantly, functions like a check, NOW accounts are—from the point of view of the customer—an interest bearing checking account.

Since their legal status was similar to that of Massachusetts MSB's, savings banks in New Hampshire followed the Massachusetts example within a few months. A 1973 act of Congress limited interest bearing NOW accounts to these two states and extended the power to offer them to commercial banks and savings and loan associations. More recently, the power to issue NOW accounts was extended to financial institutions in the rest of New England (Maine, Vermont, Rhode Island, and Connecticut), effective March 1, 1976, and there is some Congressional sentiment for extending them nationwide. The maximum interest rate which can be paid on NOW accounts is uniform for all offering institutions at 5 per cent, ¼ per cent less than thrift institutions are permitted on regular savings accounts and the same as commercial bank savings accounts.

The evidence from Massachusetts and New Hampshire suggests that the introduction of NOW accounts into a market does not lead to

---

10 This exclusion appears to be due to the influence of Milton Friedman (Friedman and Schwartz, pp. 170-71), who argues that negotiable CD's are more like commercial paper than like other types of time deposits. Accepting this argument might, however, imply including commercial paper in money, rather than excluding large CD's.

11 For a detailed discussion of this point see Steven M. Roberts, "Developing Money Substitutes, Current Trends and Their Implications for Redefining the Monetary Aggregates," Board of Governors of the Federal Reserve System, Advisory Committee on Monetary Statistics—Staff Paper No. 8 in Staff Papers to accompany the *Report of the Advisory Committee on Monetary Statistics* (forthcoming).

12 A limited number of MSB's were also authorized to offer demand deposit accounts.

consumers immediately moving their funds en masse from checking to NOW accounts. However it does suggest that NOW accounts are likely to eventually become the predominant type of household payment account. Since ownership of NOW accounts is limited to individuals, sole proprietorships, and nonprofit organizations, only the approximately $2 billion in demand deposits owned by these groups (of $6 billion in total demand deposits) in the two states was eligible for conversion to NOW accounts.[13] By June 30, 1976, total NOW account deposits in Massachusetts and New Hampshire had reached $1.2 billion, and were still growing at the rate of more than 70 per cent per year. Unfortunately, it is impossible to accurately estimate the extent to which these funds came from demand deposit accounts and the extent to which they came from savings accounts at commercial banks or thrift institutions.[14]

The inability to estimate the sources of funds which have gone into NOW accounts has serious implications for any attempt to include them in money stock estimates. Under current practice, NOW accounts are not included in M1. Thus, to the extent that funds have moved out of demand deposits into NOW accounts, current M1 data underestimate the growth of medium of exchange money. NOW accounts at commercial banks are in M2, while M3 includes NOW accounts held at thrift institutions. If all NOW balances had come from demand deposits, adding total NOW account balances into M1 would give a series which would be historically consistent. To the extent that NOW deposits have come from savings accounts, this procedure would lead to an exaggerated picture of the rate of growth of M1, since some of the growth would merely represent a transfer of funds from savings to NOW accounts without any change in the character or activity of the funds. Treating NOW accounts as demand deposits would also affect the rate of growth of M2, since some NOW funds have moved from thrift savings accounts to NOW accounts. Only M3 is unaffected by the existence of NOW accounts.

It should be noted that NOW account totals are not yet large enough to create a serious problem. Total New England NOW accounts were only $1.5 billion as of July 30, 1976. Since NOW balances have built up gradually over a 4-year period, their effect on the rate of growth of the monetary aggregates has been extremely small. However, if NOW accounts are legalized for the entire nation, it would present serious complications for money stock measurement. Consumers now hold approximately $80 billion in demand deposits, much of which—based on the New England experience—is likely to be converted to NOW accounts along with some portion of consumer savings accounts.

Credit Union Share Drafts. Many credit unions have recently begun offering their customers the ability to make funds transfers with a check-like instrument called a "share draft." In August of 1974, the Administrator of the National Credit Union Administration granted three Federal CU's temporary authority to begin offering share drafts. These three CU's were joined by two state CU's in a 6-month pilot program. While the authority to offer share draft accounts is still officially temporary, additional CU's were allowed to offer share draft accounts following the end of the pilot program. As of July 1976, 193 Federal

---

[13] John D. Paulus, *Effects of "NOW" Accounts on 1974-75 Commercial Bank Costs and Earnings,* Staff Economic Study No 88, Board of Governors of the Federal Reserve System, 1976, p. 2.

[14] Paulus estimates that about 80 per cent of NOW balances have come from demand deposits. This estimate is probably too high, as it rests on the assumption that all funds in active NOW accounts (those on which drafts are drawn) came from demand deposits. However, some active NOW accounts almost certainly represent the combination of what were previously separate checking and savings accounts and others are known to be the funds of households who previously had accounts only at thrift institutions and purchased money orders in lieu of using a checking account. See Paulus, *Effects of "NOW" Accounts . . . .*, pp. 9-12.

credit unions and a substantial number of state CU's were offering share drafts.

Share draft accounts are usually interest bearing. However, "dividends" (interest) are most commonly paid on the minimum account balance. Thus, while credit unions paying dividends in the fourth quarter of 1975 had an average stated rate of 5.67 per cent, the average rate paid was only 2.04 per cent of total share draft balances.[15] Legally, share drafts are a payable through draft like the drafts widely used by insurance companies and other corporations. Unlike NOW account drafts, which clear like checks and are eventually returned to the account holder, share drafts normally do not move beyond the bank through which they are payable. That bank, in the majority of cases, is not the bank at which the credit union keeps its regular working balance. The funds are subsequently transferred from the credit union's account at its own bank to the paying bank. The information on the draft is processed electronically and transmitted to the CU or its servicing organization on magnetic tape. Thus, the customer receives only a statement rather than a cancelled check, although he does make a carbonless paper copy at the time of writing the draft.

As of July 1976, the 193 Federal CU's offering share draft accounts had $72 million in these accounts. While this is a miniscule amount compared to commercial bank demand deposit accounts or even NOW accounts, the total in both state and Federal credit unions probably exceeds $100 million. As roughly 99 per cent of credit unions are not yet offering these accounts, there is clearly room for considerable expansion.

The American Bankers Association and several state bankers associations and individual commercial banks have recently filed law suits asking that share drafts be prohibited on the grounds that there is no legal authority

for them to be offered. The NOW account experience would seem to suggest that if these legal actions are successful, credit unions may still be able to obtain the legislative authority necessary to continue offering share drafts.

The money supply implications of share draft accounts are precisely the same as for NOW accounts. Since they provide a substitute for demand deposits, their continued exclusion from M1 and M2 underestimates the growth of medium of exchange money. Simply adding them to demand deposits will not, however, be fully satisfactory, since some portion of these funds would otherwise have been in savings accounts at CU's or other institutions. Unfortunately, there is currently not enough data to include total share draft accounts in any money stock definition narrower than M3, since there are no available estimates of share draft accounts at state credit unions.

Thrift Institution Checking Accounts. In several states, MSB's have long had the power to issue checking accounts. Recently, state chartered MSB's and S&L's have been granted the authority to offer checking accounts in Connecticut, Maine, and New York, and state chartered S&L's have been given the authority to offer noninterest bearing NOW accounts in Illinois. The long-run importance of these accounts will obviously depend on the future status of NOW accounts, although in Connecticut, thrift checking account balances on June 30 were nearly double NOW account balances. There is ample reason to believe that thrift institutions might eventually acquire a substantial share of household checking-type accounts in the states where they are allowed to issue them. The fact that a very large portion of households choose to bank on the basis of locational convenience suggests that, in the long run, thrifts might obtain a market share proportionate to their share of offices.

Thrift checking accounts clearly should be included in M1, although it is difficult to do so as long as the necessary data are not regularly reported. These deposits are like thrift NOW

15 CUNA Research Division, *Share-Drafts vs. NOW Accounts*, Credit Union Research Bulletin No. 182, Madison, Wisc., April 1976, p. 7.

accounts in that they currently are in neither M1 nor M2. In the past it has been impossible to determine the size of checking account balances at mutual savings banks because both checking accounts and escrow accounts at many institutions have been identically reported as demand deposits. Continued growth of thrift checking accounts will imply a shifting of funds from commercial banks to thrifts and will lead to M1 and M2, as currently reported, growing at slower rates than they would otherwise.

Money Market Mutual Funds. One of the more interesting financial innovations of the 1970's has been the development of the money market mutual funds. These funds hold portfolios of short-term corporate and government securities and bank CD's. Individual buyers of these funds can thus obtain returns which are not available without a substantial investment (as in the case of CD's larger than $100,000). Small businesses and institutions which might be large enough to acquire the types of instruments held by money market funds apparently find that it is less costly to use a fund than to manage their own holdings of such instruments.

Since 1974, an increasing number of these funds have allowed fund owners to redeem their shares by writing a check. These checks, which are drawn on a bank account arranged by the fund, typically can be written for any amount in excess of $500. As of June 30, 1976, funds with this option had $2.1 billion of the $3.4 billion in assets of all money market funds. Most of the rest of the funds allowed withdrawals by wire transfers, a method which may be superior for many holders.

Money market funds benefited during their early history from the unusually high rates then being paid on short-term money market instruments. These funds have not, contrary to the expectations of some observers, experienced extremely sharp declines with the subsequent fall in short-term interest rates, although they are currently experiencing little or no growth.

Their inherent advantages—allowing small holders to obtain returns not directly available to them and providing diversification with low transactions costs—make it seem likely that they will continue to grow over the long run. Furthermore, there is no technical reason why these funds could not allow checks to be drawn on them in much smaller amounts. Nor is there any reason why the check-writing option need be restricted to money market funds. Even with current restrictions, these funds would seem to meet most criteria for money. The liabilities of money market funds are not, however, included in any of the currently published definitions of money, although their holdings of bank deposits are. If the minimum size check which can be drawn should be reduced, the case for treating them as money would be strengthened.

While these accounts have received much less attention than NOW accounts and share drafts, they are currently more important quantitatively. Incorporating them into money stock estimates would be considerably more difficult, however, since these institutions, unlike the issuers of NOW and share draft accounts, do not report regularly to the financial regulatory agencies.

The Increased "Moneyness" of Savings Accounts

It has been the traditional practice to include demand deposits, but not other deposits, as money when using a medium of exchange criterion. Changes occurring in the nature of savings accounts, both at commercial banks and at thrift institutions, are making this practice increasingly untenable. A number of regulatory changes in recent years have made it possible for households to use savings accounts for third party payments. These changes mean that funds transfers are increasingly being made with assets not included in M1, but rather with regular savings accounts at banks and S&L's. Thus, the medium of exchange criterion for defining money is becoming increasingly difficult to apply.

Bill Paying Services. In April 1975, S&L's were given the power to offer bill paying services from savings accounts. A similar power was granted to commercial banks in September 1975. While these services have generated relatively little activity to date, they are serving as partial substitutes for checking accounts where in use.

Telephone Transfers. In April of 1975, the Board of Governors of the Federal Reserve System reversed a long-held position and allowed banks to transfer funds from an individual's savings account to a checking account on the basis of a telephone authorization. This action followed the development of telephone transfer services by some thrift institutions and nonmember banks. While telephone transfers are not widely used, they are being offered by a number of banks and they are clearly reducing the barriers between savings and checking accounts.

Automatic Transfers to Cover Overdrafts. A proposal currently under consideration by the Board of Governors might make the distinction between savings and demand deposits much less important—except for the lower reserve requirements on the former. This proposal would allow an arrangement whereby funds would automatically be transferred in multiples of $100 from a savings account to a checking account when the balance in the checking account reached zero or some other predetermined level. Were it not for the restriction that transfers be in $100 multiples, depending on the pricing of transfers, the transfer privilege might well lead to the use of zero balance checking accounts, with funds being transferred to cover every check. Such a procedure would allow banks to reduce the quantity of funds which must be held in required reserves. Under the regulation proposed, 30 days' interest would be lost on any funds transferred, so these accounts would have a much lower yield than do NOW accounts. The yield would probably be more like the yield on CU share draft accounts.

The transfer privilege would also reduce the usefulness of the traditional M1 definition, because substantial quantities of demand deposits would likely move into savings accounts. Simply including savings accounts in M1 would not be totally satisfactory, because the majority of funds in savings accounts would not have come from demand deposits. This is not a problem with M2 when the savings accounts are at commercial banks. However, such accounts might be set up at thrift institutions (especially since it might not be necessary to forego 30 days' interest on transfers from thrift accounts). To the extent that thrift accounts are used in this way, only M3 would be unaffected.

Savings and Loan EFTS Projects. Thrift institutions outside of New England are generally prohibited from offering checking or similar accounts. The prohibition has led a number of S&L's to attempt to develop electronic substitutes. The Federal Home Loan Bank Board has authorized S&L's to set up "remote service units" (RSU's) on an experimental basis. RSU's are off-premise terminals which may be used by either one or several institutions. They may be located in a public area such as an airport, but most commonly have been placed in supermarkets. S&L's probably gained an early lead over commercial banks in this area because most S&L's already were handling their savings accounts "on line" and because of their strong desire to tap the checking account market. More recently, commercial banks have been prevented from setting up similar operations in a number of states because of court decisions that remote terminals were subject to state branching laws. (Federal S&L's, unlike national banks, are not subject to state branching laws.)

The Federal Home Loan Bank Board reports that as of May 1976, 85 Federal S&L's were operating RSU's at 234 different locations.[16] (Some locations have several terminals, as at least one S&L is placing them at individual supermarket check-out counters.) These RSU's handled more than 56,000 transactions in May, with approximately three-quarters of the transactions being withdrawals and the remainder deposits. The dollar volumes of deposits and withdrawals were approximately $2.7 million and $2.0 million, respectively. While RSU's have not turned S&L savings accounts into checking accounts, they have made these accounts much more accessible.

The effect of S&L EFTS projects on the various money stock concepts is similar to the other innovations already discussed. To the extent that these projects allow people to substitute an account with an S&L for a checking account, it reduces the usefulness of the current M1. And since S&L accounts are not in M2, this aggregate is also reduced in usefulness.

Credit Cards and Check Credit Plans

The fact that increased credit facilities reduce the demand for money has long been recognized.[17] Traditionally, credit facilities have been treated as a factor which could lead to shifts in the demand for money, but which need not be explicitly taken into account when estimating a demand for money function. Keynes suggested incorporating credit facilities directly into the analysis. Under his alternative treatment, unused lines of credit at commercial banks would be included in the money stock.[18] This suggestion has, from time to time, been reiterated by others. Until relatively recently, overdraft accounts such as those long prevalent in Great Britain were virtually unknown in the United States. Over the last decade, however, "check credit" plans, as overdrafts are commonly called, have been set up by a large

number of banks. Furthermore, the introduction of the bank credit card has provided bank customers with an alternative payment mechanism and the functional equivalent of overdrafts.

Unfortunately, at least for those who would like to take Keynes' approach, no data are available on total credit lines on either bank credit cards or check credit accounts. A reasonable estimate for bank credit cards is that credit lines total approximately $30 billion.[19] Commercial banks had $9.5 billion outstanding on credit cards (as compared to $2.8 billion outstanding on check credit accounts) as of June 30, 1976. This implies unused bank credit card lines of about $20 billion. While this quantity is certainly substantial, it would probably be unwise to attempt to incorporate unused lines into the money stock. These lines of credit are in many cases granted and increased unilaterally by the credit card bank and may have little relationship to the amount of credit that the card holder is likely to use. Furthermore, these lines frequently serve merely as a signal to reexamine the card holder's credit standing before increasing the line rather than as a constraint on the amount of credit available.

That adding unused credit lines to the money supply would be a dubious practice can be seen by looking at the ratio of total debits to estimated unused lines on bank credit cards. In the year ending June 30, 1976, there was $22.9 billion extended on bank credit cards and $4.5 billion of credit extended on check credit plans. Dividing the $22.9 billion in debits on bank credit card plans by the $20 billion in estimated unused credit card lines gives a ratio of about 1.1, as compared to the ratio of debits to average balances in household checking accounts which is believed to be in the range of 20-25. Nevertheless, the continued growth and

[16] Fifty-one state chartered institutions are also involved in these projects. The institutions with the largest operations are, however, generally federally chartered.

[17] Irving Fisher, *The Purchasing Power of Money* (rev. ed.; New York: MacMillan, 1922), p. 81.

[18] J. M. Keynes, *A Treatise on Money,* Vol. 1 (London: MacMillan, 1930), pp. 41-43.

[19] The two major national bank credit cards reported a total of 42 million accounts as of March 31, 1976. If the average account has a credit line estimated to be about $700, total lines are approximately $30 billion.

use of credit card and check credit accounts is likely to make the relationship between any money stock measure and the level of economic activity less stable. Since the evidence suggests that both check credit and credit cards are widely used during periods of tight credit,[20] it is quite likely that the degree to which they substitute for money will vary cyclically.

Electronic Funds Transfer

Electronic funds transfer (EFT) developments are probably the most widely discussed innovations in the payments system today. While EFT is likely to have a substantial effect on the demand for money, its impact on the nature of money will likely be confined to the areas already discussed, particularly by facilitating the growth of overdraft accounts and by reducing whatever barriers remain between noninterest bearing checking accounts and interest bearing accounts.

If thrift institutions in most of the country continue to be barred from offering checking (or NOW) accounts, they are likely to attempt to gain entry into the payments system through an EFT system, since the legal barriers to their participation in electronic payments seem to be much less of a factor than they are in the area of paper payments. It has also been widely suggested that an EFT system will lead to a substantial increase in the use of overdrafts

(check credit). The fact that float will be reduced or eliminated, it is argued, will increase the demand for overdrafts. And to the extent that EFT gives banks better control over overdraft accounts, it is likely to lead them to market them more aggressively.

To the extent that EFT developments lead to thrift accounts being used as transaction accounts, the volume of transactions conducted with M1 and M2 as currently measured will be reduced. If the development of an EFT system increases the use of overdrafts, it will strengthen the case for including them in the money stock. It will not, however, eliminate the problems with this approach.

CONCLUSIONS

Just as the 19th century changes in the way that payments were made required a broadened definition of the money stock, the changes currently underway will require a broadening of any definition based on which assets can serve as media of exchange. Only the broadest definitions, those which include the deposits of thrift institutions as well as those at commercial banks, are likely to be unaffected. Many policymakers and scholars prefer to use a narrower definition. They are likely to be increasingly faced with a dilemma as it is unlikely that it will be possible to develop any narrow money stock series which can be extended very far into the past and still be conceptually consistent. The problem that Andrew noted in 1899 seems likely to become more rather than less serious.

---

[20] Richard L. Peterson, "Factors Affecting the Growth of Bank Credit Card and Check Credit" (paper presented at the meeting of the American Finance Association, Atlantic City, N.J., September 16, 1976).

Behavior of the income velocity of money

. . . consideration of the stock of money alone is not sufficient for assessment of the adequacy of the economy's liquidity. Money has a second dimension, namely, velocity, or—in common parlance—the intensity with which it is being used.[1]

Monetary policy decisions are based on the likely impact future money supply growth will have on the nation's economic activity. How much of an increase in the volume of money is needed to achieve the desired level of activity depends, however, on how intensively the stock of money is used—its velocity. If the rate of money use is expected to change from what it has been in the past, a different quantity of money will be needed to maintain the past level of economic activity. As each dollar is used more often, fewer dollars are needed to facilitate the same amount of transactions. As a first step in determining future velocity movements, it is useful to analyze the past.

Postwar behavior of velocity

Of the several measures of the velocity of money, the one most commonly used is the income velocity of M-1 (V-1) defined as the ratio of GNP to M-1[2]. Since the end of World War II the income velocity of M-1 has been on a generally rising trend. Over the past 30 years V-1 has risen at a 3.5 percent average annual rate—from a ratio of 2.05 in the first quarter of 1947 to 5.82 in the second quarter of 1977.

Quarter-to-quarter rates of change in V-1, however, have been quite volatile. They have ranged, in compounded annual rates, from a 5.9 percent decline in the first quarter of 1949 to a 22.4 percent gain in the third quarter of 1950. Over the past decade quarter-to-quarter rates of change in V-1 ranged between extremes of –3.7 percent in the fourth quarter of 1970 to 11.5 percent in the third quarter of 1975.

During the postwar period movements in V-1 have had a discernible cyclical pattern. From the peak to the trough in the first five of the six postwar recessions, V-1 declined. In the 1973-75 recession the average annual rate of change in V-1 slowed to 1.5 percent from the 3.4 percent average gain in the 1971-73 expansion.

During the recovery phases of the six business expansions since 1947, V-1 has generally risen at a rapid rate. From the first quarter of 1975 to the first quarter of 1976, the first year of the current expansion, V-1 rose at a rate of 8.3 percent, faster than in any other first year of recovery since the 1950-53 expansion. As the economy moves from recovery to expansion, the rate of increase in V-1 tends to slow and then to pick up again as the expansion proceeds. In the second year of the current expansion, V-1 grew at a rate of 3.5 percent, somewhat above the 3.1 percent rate observed in the second year of both the 1961-69 and 1971-73 expansions but below the 4.0 percent average second-year pace of the five previous expansions.

The seemingly erratic short-term movements in measured velocity and its pro-

[1]Arthur F. Burns, Chairman, Board of Governors of the Federal Reserve System, statement before the Committee on Banking, Housing and Urban Affairs, U.S. Senate, May 3, 1977.

[2]GNP represents the current value of annual spending on final goods and services. M-1 is defined as currency and demand deposits held by the public. While the income velocity of M-1 is most commonly used, similar income velocity measures exist for other measures of income and/or money.

Reprinted from Federal Reserve Bank of Chicago *Economic Perspectives*, September–October, 1977.

118

Velocity has been on a rising trend over the postwar period

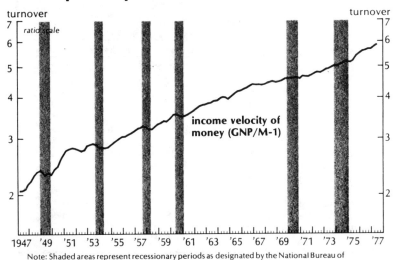

Note: Shaded areas represent recessionary periods as designated by the National Bureau of Economic Research.

SOURCES: M-1—Board of Governors, Federal Reserve System; GNP—U.S. Department of Commerce.

A major economic factor influencing the postwar rise in velocity is the general rise in interest rates that has occurred. Individuals, businesses, and state and local governmental units hold checking account balances and currency primarily to facilitate expenditures. As interest rates rise, the opportunity cost of holding noninterest-earning M-1 balances increases. To the extent that highly liquid interest-earning investment alternatives are available, money-holders have an incentive to shift funds in excess of transactions needs out of M-1 balances into earning assets.

nounced cyclical pattern may suggest that the relationship between monetary growth and GNP is extremely loose and unpredictable. However, it is generally recognized that there are substantial lags between changes in money and changes in GNP. Indeed, most studies indicate that the primary impact of a monetary change on GNP is not felt for six months to a year, with the total effect being distributed over an even longer period. When this lagged relationship is taken into account, the money-GNP relationship—though far from perfect—is much tighter than the variable behavior of measured velocity would suggest. Nevertheless, the relationship is subject to gradual modification over time, as payments habits and basic economic conditions change, and these changes show up as secular, or longer-term, trends in velocity.

Factors affecting velocity

The postwar rise in V-1 indicates that the public has been reducing its holdings of M-1 balances relative to GNP. This economization of cash balances has been influenced by economic, institutional, and technical factors.

Over the postwar period investment alternatives have been greatly expanded. For example, the increased desire of corporations to reduce cash balances led to the expansion of existing market alternatives—such as commercial paper—and the development of new instruments—such as certificates of deposit. The introduction by thrift institutions of a wider variety of consumer-type time and savings accounts and the development of money market mutual funds enhanced individuals' access to interest-bearing substitutes for M-1 balances. More recently, regulatory changes permitting businesses and state and local governments to hold savings accounts at commercial banks and the development of NOW (negotiable orders of withdrawal) accounts in New England have induced smaller businesses, state and local governments, and individuals to shift additional funds out of M-1 balances.

An increase in the technical efficiency with which funds can be transferred is another factor tending to increase velocity. Thus, such developments as wider use of wire transfer of funds and, more recently,

Rates of change in velocity differ over the business cycle

Recessions		Expansions				
				Rate of change in V-1		
Period	Rate of change in V-1	Period	Trough-to-peak	First year	Second year	Third year
(Peak-to-trough)	(percent)	(Trough-to-peak)		(percent)		
48-IV to 49-IV	-2.7	49-IV to 53-III	5.9	14.2	5.2	1.8
53-III to 54-II	-2.9	54-II to 57-III	5.0	5.3	4.3	4.9
57-III to 58-II	-3.1	58-II to 60-II	5.4	6.6	4.1	—
60-II to 61-I	-1.7	61-I to 69-IV	3.1	5.9	3.1	3.5
69-IV to 70-IV	-0.3	70-IV to 73-IV	3.4	2.7	3.1	4.6
73-IV to 75-I	1.5	75-I to 77-II*	5.7*	8.3	3.5	4.6**

Average annual rates of change in the income velocity of M-1 (V-1 = GNP/M-1).
*Current expansion continuing.
**Rate of change in V-1 in 77-II, the first quarter of the third year of expansion.
SOURCE: M-1 data—Board of Governors, Federal Reserve System; GNP data—U.S. Department of Commerce; Business cycle turning points—National Bureau of Economic Research.

telephonic transfer of funds between savings and checking accounts at commercial banks also help explain the postwar rise in velocity.

Since M-1 balances are held primarily to facilitate expenditures, the increasing availability of overdraft facilities and the more widespread use of credit cards have probably reduced the average amount of M-1 needed for transactions purposes and thus influenced the rise in velocity.

Prospects for future velocity movements

These factors in different combinations affect velocity in a complex fashion. Over the first two years of the current expansion, rates of change in the income velocity of M-1, though unaccompanied by the rise in interest rates observed in previous expansions, have generally been consistent with past patterns. Technical and institutional factors, however, have increased the ability of individuals, businesses, and state and local governments to reduce M-1 balances without sacrificing liquidity. In addition, cash management techniques once implemented are likely to be continued even though interest rates fall.

History suggests that, as the economy proceeds through the third year of expansion, velocity will continue on an upward trend at perhaps a faster pace than observed in the second year of expansion. The expectation of continued real economic growth, together with the likelihood that interest rates may rise as credit demands strengthen later in 1977, tends to reinforce this conclusion.

Anne Marie Laporte

32

The President's Address on Energy Problems

THREE BASIC ELEMENTS

By JIMMY CARTER, *President of the United States*

Delivered to the American People, November 8, 1977

GOOD EVENING: More than six months ago, in April, I spoke to you about a need for a national policy to deal with our present and future energy problems, and the next day I sent my proposals to the Congress.

The Congress has recognized the urgency of this problem, and has come to grips with some of the most complex and difficult decisions that a legislative body has ever been asked to make. Working with Congress we have formed a new Department of Energy, headed by Secretary James Schlesinger. We now have the ability to administer the new energy legislation, and Congressional work on the national energy plan has now reached the final stage.

Last week the Senate sent its version of the legislation to the conference committees, where members of the House and Senate will now resolve differences between the bills they have passed. There, in the next few weeks, the strength and courage of our political system will be proven. The choices facing the members of Congress are not easy. For them to pass an effective and fair plan, they will need your support and your understanding — your support to resist pressures from a few for special favors at the expense of the rest of us and your understanding that there can be no effective plan without some sacrifice from all of us.

Tonight, at this crucial time, I want to emphasize why it is so important that we have an energy plan, and what we will risk as a nation if we are timid, or reluctant to face this challenge. It's crucial that you understand how serious this challenge is. With every passing month, our energy problems have grown worse. This summer we used more oil and gasoline than ever before in our history. More of our oil is coming from foreign countries. Just since April our oil imports have cost us $23 billion—about $350 worth of foreign oil for the average American family.

A few weeks ago in Detroit an unemployed steelworker told me something that may reflect the feelings of many of you. "Mr. President," he said, "I don't feel much like talking about energy and foreign policy. I'm concerned about how I am going to live. I can't be too concerned about other things when I have a 10-year-old daughter to raise and I don't have a job, and I am 56 years old."

Well, I understand how he felt, but I must tell you the truth, and the truth is that you cannot talk about our economic problems now or in the future without talking about energy.

Let me try to describe the size and the effect of the problem. Our farmers are the greatest agricultural exporters the world has ever known, but it now takes all the food and the fiber that we export in two years just to pay for just one year of imported oil—about $45 billion.

This excessive importing of foreign oil is a tremendous and rapidly increasing drain on our national economy. It hurts every American family.

It causes unemployment. Every $5 billion increase in oil imports costs us 200,000 American jobs. It costs us business investments. Vast amounts of American wealth no longer stay in the United States to build our factories and to give us a better life.

It makes it harder for us to balance our Federal budget and to finance needed programs for our people. It unbalances our nation's trade with other countries. This year, primarily because of oil, our imports will be at least $25 billion more than all the American goods that we sell overseas.

It pushes up international energy prices because excessive importing of oil by the United States makes it easier for foreign producers to raise their prices. It feeds serious inflationary pressures in our own economy.

From *Vital Speeches of the Day*, December 1, 1977.

If this trend continues, the excessive reliance on foreign oil could make the very security of our nation increasingly dependent on uncertain energy supplies. Our national security depends on more than just our armed forces. It also rests on the strength of our economy, on our national will, and on the ability of the United States to carry out our foreign policy as a free and independent nation. America overseas is only as strong as America at home.

The Secretary of Defense said recently, "The present deficiency of assured energy sources is the single surest threat to our security and to that of our allies."

Yesterday, after careful consideration, I announced the postponement of a major overseas trip until after Christmas because of the paramount importance of developing an effective energy plan this year. I have no doubt that this is the right decision, because the other nations of the world—allies and adversaries alike—await our energy decisions with a great interest and concern.

As one of the world's largest producers of coal and oil and gas, why do we have this problem with energy, and why is it so difficult to solve?

One problem is that the price of all energy is going up both because of its increasing scarcity and because the price of oil is not set in a free and competitive market. The world price is set by a foreign cartel—the governments of the so-called O.P.E.C. nations. That price is now almost five times as great as it was in 1973.

Our biggest problem, however, is that we simply use too much—and waste too much—energy. Our imports have more than tripled in the last 10 years. Although all countries could afford to be more efficient, we are the worst offender. Since the great price rise in 1973, the Japanese have cut their oil imports. The Germans, the French, the British, the Italians have all cut their oil imports. Meanwhile, although we have large petroleum supplies of our own and most of them don't, we in the United States have increased our imports of oil more than 40 percent.

This problem has come upon us suddenly. Ten years ago, when foreign oil was cheap, we imported just two and one-half million barrels of oil a day—about 20 percent of what we used. By 1972 we were importing about 30 percent. This year when foreign oil is very expensive, we are importing nearly nine million barrels a day—almost one-half of all the oil we use. Unless we act quickly, imports will continue to go up, and all the problems that I just described will grow even worse.

There are three things we must do to avoid this danger: first, cut back on consumption; second, shift away from oil and gas to other sources of energy; and third, encourage production of energy here in the United States. These are the purposes of the new energy legislation.

In order to conserve energy, the Congress is now acting to make our automobiles, homes, and appliances more efficient, and to encourage industry to save both heat and electricity.

The Congressional conference committees are now considering changes in how electric power rates are to be set in order to discourage waste, to reward those who use less energy, and to encourage a change in the use of electricity to hours of the day when demand is low.

Another very important question before Congress is how to let the market price for domestic oil go up to reflect the cost of replacing it, while at the same time protecting the

American consumers and our economy.

We must face an unpleasant fact about energy prices. They are going up, whether we pass an energy program or not, as fuel becomes more scarce and more expensive to produce. The question is who should benefit from those rising prices for oil already discovered. Our energy plan captures and returns them to the public, where they can stimulate the economy, save more energy, and create new jobs.

We will use research and development projects, tax incentives and penalties, and regulatory authority to hasten the shift from oil and gas to coal, to wind and solar power, to geothermal, methane and other energy sources.

We've also proposed, and Congress is reviewing, incentives to encourage production of oil and gas here in our own country. This is where another major controversy arises.

It's important that we promote new oil and gas discoveries and increase production by giving adequate prices to the producers.

We've recommended that the price, for instance, of new natural gas be raised each year to the average price of domestic oil that would produce the same amount of energy. With this new policy, the gross income of gas producers would average about $2 billion each year more than at the present price level.

New oil prices would also rise in three years to the present world level and then be increased annually to keep up with inflation. This incentive for new oil production would be the highest in the whole world.

These proposals would provide adequate incentives for exploration and production of domestic oil and gas, but some of the oil companies want much more—tens of billions of dollars more. They want greatly increased prices for "old" oil and gas—energy supplies which have already been discovered and which are being produced. They want immediate and permanent deregulation of gas prices, which would cost consumers $70 billion or more between now and 1985. They want even higher prices than those we've proposed for "new" gas and oil, and they want the higher prices sooner; they want lower taxes on their profits.

These are all controversial questions, and the Congressional debates, as you can well imagine, are intense. The political pressures are great because the stakes are so high — billions and billions of dollars. We should reward individuals and companies who discover and produce new oil and gas, but we must not give them huge windfall profits on their existing wells at the expense of the American people.

Now, the energy proposal I made to Congress last April had three basic elements to insure that it is well balanced.

First, it's fair both to the American consumers and to the energy producers, and it will not disrupt our national economy.

Second, as I've said before, it's designed to meet our important goals for energy conservation, to promote a shift to more plentiful and permanent energy supplies and encourage increased production of energy in the United States.

And third, it protects our Federal budget from any unreasonable burden.

These are the three standards by which the final legislation will be judged. I will sign the energy bills only if they meet these tests.

During the next few weeks, the Congress will make a

judgment on these vital questions. I will be working closely with them. And you are also deeply involved in these decisions.

This is not a contest of strength between a President and the Congress, nor between the House and the Senate. What is being measured is the strength and will of our nation—whether we can acknowledge a threat and meet a serious challenge together.

I'm convinced that we can have enough energy to permit a continued growth of our economy, to expand production and jobs, and to protect the security of the United States, if we act wisely.

I believe that this country can meet any challenge, but this is an exceptionally difficult one because the threat is not easy to see, and a solution is neither simple nor politically popular.

I said six months ago that no one would be completely satisfied with this national energy plan. Unfortunately, that prediction has turned out to be right. There is some part of this complex legislation to which every region and every interest group can object. But a common national sacrifice to meet this serious problem should be shared by everyone—some proof that the plan is fair. Many groups have risen to the challenge, but unfortunately there are still some who seek personal gain over the national interest.

It's also especially difficult to deal with long-range future challenges. A President is elected for just four years, a senator for six, and our representatives in Congress for only two years. It has always been easier to wait until the next year or the next term of office, to avoid political risk.

But you do not choose your elected officials simply to fill an office. The Congress is facing very difficult decisions, and we have formed a good partnership. All of us in government need your help.

This is an effort which requires vision and cooperation from all Americans. I hope that each of you will take steps to conserve our precious energy, and also join with your elected officials at all levels of government to meet this test of our nation's judgment and will.

There are serious problems, and this has been a serious talk. But our energy plan also reflects the optimism that I feel about our ability to deal with these problems. The story of the human race is one of adapting to changing circumstances. The history of our nation is one of meeting challenges, and overcoming them. This major legislation is a necessary first step on a long and difficult road.

This energy plan is a good insurance policy for the future, in which relatively small premiums that we pay today will protect us in the years ahead. But if we fail to act boldly today, then we will surely face a greater series of crises tomorrow—energy shortages, environmental damage, ever more massive government bureaucracy and regulations, and ill-considered last-minute crash programs.

I hope that perhaps 100 years from now the change to inexhaustible energy sources will have been made, and our nation's concern about energy will be over. But we can make that transition smoothly—for our country and for our children and for our grandchildren—only if we take careful steps now to prepare ourselves for that future.

During the next few weeks, attention will be focused on the Congress, but the proving of our courage and commitment will continue, in different forms and places, in the months and the years, even generations ahead.

It's fitting that I am speaking to you on an Election Day, a day which reminds us that you the people are the the the rulers of this nation—that your government will be as courageous and effective and fair as you demand that it be.

This will not be the last time that I as President present difficult and controversial choices to you and ask for your help. I believe that the duties of this office permit me to do no less.

But I am confident that we can find the wisdom and the courage to make the right decisions—even when they are unpleasant—so that we might, together, preserve the greatness of our nation.

Thank you very much.

33

The Nature and Origins of the U.S. Energy Crisis

JAI-HOON YANG

AGGREGATIVE economic policy is designed to stabilize the general price level and the growth in output and employment. Monetary policy, as a general tool of aggregate demand management, seeks to achieve these goals by affecting the volume of total spending in the economy. Whether ultimate goals of this policy are achieved depends to a large extent upon the external shocks to which the economy is subjected. Regardless of the sources of these shocks — weather, foreign actions, or changes in institutional conditions — they must be taken into consideration in the process of monetary policy planning and execution. One of the recent shocks has been the sudden and dramatic increase in the relative price of energy, which has significantly affected U.S. productive capacity.[1] This article traces and analyzes the underlying factors which were instrumental in rendering the U.S. economy vulnerable to the energy shock.

In the wake of the Arab oil embargo in 1973-74 and the weather-induced natural gas crisis in the winter just passed, concern about an energy crisis has spread across the U.S. The crisis often has been identified as an *energy gap* manifested as shortages of gasoline in 1974, and of heating oil and natural gas last winter. The emergence and the prospective persistence of such an energy gap often have been diagnosed as being the result of rising demand for energy and dwindling supplies of oil and natural gas. However, such a perception of the nature and the roots of the energy crisis is based on an uncritical acceptance of the "lump-of-energy" conception and on a denial of the laws of demand.

An alternate view of the energy crisis rejects the identification of the energy problem as a growing imbalance between the absolute quantity of energy demanded and supplied. Rather, the energy problem is diagnosed as the apparent "failure" of the energy market to accommodate the amount of energy demanded at policy-mandated prices, and the seemingly progressive deterioration in the capacity of the energy market to adjust to man-made and weather-induced shocks.

The history of U.S. energy markets reveals that the roots of the current crisis have been nurtured by past public policy measures. These policies were adopted in response to demands by segments of the energy industry for protection from the rigors of market competition. The crisis is rooted in the supplanting of the market mode of competition by the political mode. From this perspective, it is difficult to avoid the conclusion that past public policies (pursued to shelter some segments of the energy industry) have been, in large measure, responsible for the energy crisis.

THE NATURE AND ROOTS OF THE U.S. ENERGY CRISIS: TWO VIEWS

A Prevalent View

A widely accepted diagnosis of the nature of the U.S. energy crisis is one of growing imbalance in the nation's energy budget. Such a diagnosis is based on the premise that the amount of energy demanded will continue to increase, while the amount of oil and natural gas supplied will diminish.[2] The "crisis" the U.S. faces is often said to be a grave threat to the nation's economic security and the American way of life.

This conception of the energy crisis is, thus, that of an inexorable emergence and worsening of an *energy gap*, unless dependence on nonrenewable fossil fuel in general, and on oil and natural gas in particular, is not reduced. In estimating the length of the "grace period" during which plans for an oilless future must be made, the projections of energy "demands" are based upon alternative assumptions of the rate of growth in energy usage in the form of oil consumption. Such projections are typically made by extrapolating the historical

---

[1]Robert H. Rasche and John A. Tatom, "The Effects of the New Energy Regime on Economic Capacity, Production, and Prices," this *Review* (May 1977), pp. 2-12 and "Energy Resources and Potential GNP," this *Review* (June 1977), pp. 10-24.

[2]S. David Freeman, Director, *A Time to Choose*, Final Report by the Energy Policy Project of the Ford Foundation (Cambridge: Ballinger Publishing Co., 1974).

Reprinted from Federal Reserve Bank of St. Louis *Review*, July, 1977.

rates of growth in energy usage and by assuming different (lower) rates of growth under alternative conservation plans.[3] Then, given geological estimates of potentially recoverable oil reserves, the computation of the grace period becomes routine.

For example, some estimates of the grace period use as a benchmark the estimate of about 2 trillion barrels of total world recoverable oil. Even using a "conservative" projection of a 3 percent rate of growth in oil demand, as contrasted to the 8 percent rate of growth in the 1960s, the world's presently estimated recoverable oil resources would be exhausted before 2020. The arithmetic is unassailable and, hence, the spectre of freezing in the dark arises if the U.S. is not weaned away from its dependency on oil in time.[4]

The policy prescriptions that often follow from such a view of the energy problem are mandated conservation and the pursuit of technical energy efficiency during the transition into a new energy regime.[5] Such a transition is deemed to be facilitated by a mix of standby and regular ·excise and consumption taxes on energy, subsidies, tax credits, "reform" of the utility rate-making procedures, a system of incentive pricing for *new* oil and natural gas, and by a set of mandatory allocations and conversions to coal — the more plentiful "interim" fuel.

An Alternate Market-Based View

The essence of the energy problem from the alternate view is that the problem is one of apparent (or potential) "malfunction" in the market for energy. This view focuses squarely on the capacity of the energy market to respond to unforeseen shocks, such as the recent oil embargo and severe weather, and to accommodate foreseeable changes in the quantity of energy demanded. When the energy problem is framed in this manner,[6] the accumulated stock of knowledge regarding the functioning of markets can be used to diagnose the nature and the origins of the energy problem.

Despite its importance, energy must be viewed as a commodity not unlike any other commodity that competes for a share of limited budgets. Hence, the amounts of energy demanded and supplied are both determined by laws that govern consumer and producer behavior.

According to the *first law of demand*, the lower the price (that is, the lower the sacrifice incurred in terms of other goods that have to be given up to purchase energy), the higher is the quantity demanded, other things being equal.[7] And, according to the *second law of demand*, the longer the elapsed time after a price fall, the greater will be the extent of substitution toward the commodity which has become cheaper. As prices fall, increases in the quantity demanded occur, first, because more is demanded by the *present* users and, second, because *new* users enter the market.

Such an adaptive behavior on the part of consumers is mirrored in a similar behavior on the part of producers in an exchange system organized within a general private property framework. Thus, a greater quantity of energy will be supplied as prices rise because more energy will be supplied by the *present* producers and *new* (higher-cost) producers will be enticed to enter the market.

The nature of the energy problem from the market view is the "inadequate capacity" of the energy market to adjust to unexpected shocks, such as the man-made oil embargo and nature-induced severe weather conditions. Such a conception of the nature of the energy problem leads one to heed Santayana's dictum that, "those who do not learn from history are condemned to ·repeat it," and to study the history of energy markets in the U.S. for a clue to the roots of the current energy crisis.

Such a study of the history of energy markets, especially the markets for oil and natural gas, reveals some general characteristics of the energy market which have circumscribed its adjustment capacity, such as the exceptionally long (three-to five-year) lead

[3]Ibid., pp. 19-25.

[4]For a graphic illustration of the apocalytic vision of the dismal energy future evoked by the recent discussions of the energy crisis, see Isaac Asimov, "Essay," *Time* (April 25, 1977), p. 33.

[5]Such a regime is characterized by renewable and essentially inexhaustible energy sources, such as solar and wind energy, and viable nuclear fusion technology.

[6]For a statement of this approach, see Armen A. Alchian, "An Introduction to Confusion," in *No Time to Confuse* (San Francisco: Institute for Contemporary Studies, 1975). Also see Edward J. Mitchell, *U.S. Energy Policy: A Primer*

(Washington, D.C.: American Enterprise Institute (AEI), 1974); Hendrick S. Houthakker, *The World Price of Oil* (Washington, D.C.: AEI, 1976), Washington, D.C.; and Douglas R. Bohi, Milton Russel, and Nancy McCarthy Snyder, U.S. Congress, House of Representatives, Committee on Banking, Currency, and Housing, *The Economics of Energy and Natural Resource Pricing*, A Compilation of Reports and Hearings, 94th Congress, 1st Session, Parts 1 and 2, March 1975, pp. 1-230.

[7]Armen A. Alchian and William R. Allen, *University Economics,* 3rd. ed. (Belmont, California: Wadsworth Publishing Company, 1972), pp. 60-66.

times for end-use delivery and the common pool problem.[8] More importantly, a historical inquiry, which will be discussed in greater detail in later sections, also reveals that deep government involvement in the past has greatly attenuated the adjustment capacities of the energy market.

For example, the legacy of the demand prorationing system,[9] which arose in the 1920s, and the subsequent voluntary and mandatory import quotas on oil products (on national security grounds) in the 1950s, is evident in the current problem. Indeed, the formation of the oil producers' cartel (OPEC) in 1960 was proximately caused by the imposition of mandatory import quotas in the U.S. in 1959.[10] The Supreme Court's ruling on the Phillip's case in 1954 also was one of the roots of the current energy problem.[11] The more recent price controls on energy imposed in mid-1971 also have had adverse effects.

The unifying thread in the apparently disparate set of causes of the energy problem, is the replacement of the market mode of competition by the political mode of advocacy politics. The more successful were those who sought relief from the rigors of competition through political means, the less robust became the adjustment capacity of the energy markets to unforeseen shocks.

Comparison of the Two Views

The market-based view of the energy crisis denies the usefulness of the prevalent conception of the energy crisis as that of an ever accelerating shortfall in the amount of BTUs (British Thermal Units) embodied in finite and nonrenewable oil and natural gas. The fatal flaw in the prevalent view is the failure to perceive the fundamental distinction between (1) rising prices in response to changes in underlying schedules of demand and supply, and (2) the phenomenon of rising shortages in quantity supplied relative to quantity demanded, because prices *do not* or *are not allowed* to adjust fast enough to equate the quantity demanded to quantity supplied.

According to the market view, the adherents of the prevalent view, in advancing their various scenarios of impending disaster, ignore adaptive human behavior under perceived changes in scarcity and opportunities. They base their scenarios instead on the arbitrary projections of quantity demanded relative to estimates of fixed "recoverable" reserves of oil and gas.[12] Such a mechanistic conception of the problem neglects the roles which changes in price and technology play in inducing revisions in the estimates of recoverable reserves, as well as in altering the quantity demanded of oil and gas *and* the quantity supplied of alternate sources of energy. Such neglect reflects two underlying false premises.

The first premise is that energy is an "essential resource." According to this premise, the demand for energy is insensitive to changes in its price. The premise, in essence, denies the fundamental laws of demand. This premise is falsified by the available evidence which indicates that the quantity demanded of energy is sensitive to both its price and consumer income.[13] More importantly, the price sensitivity of demand for energy is greater in the long run than in the short run.

---

[8]The common pool problem is similar to the fishery problem in that both arise due to the ill-defined property rights over the common resource at issue. Typically, the applicable law with regard to property rights is the rule of capture. That is, the exclusive property rights are created at the instant of capturing fish or drawing oil from the pool. There exist, therefore, incentives for co-owners of the pool to extract as much of the oil as they singly can. Such an unrestrained behavior on their part, however, tends to reduce the ultimate amount of oil recoverable by drilling, relative to the more paced rate of drilling known as the "maximum efficient rate of production (MER)." Hence, the logic of joint maximization would call for a rate of production not to exceed MER. The problem involved in striking an agreement to promote joint maximization is similar to the one in forming a cartel of producers to coordinate production decisions. See U.S. Congress, Senate, Committee on the Judiciary, *Governmental Intervention in the Market Mechanism: The Petroleum Industry*, Hearings before the Subcommittee on Antitrust and Monopoly, 91st Congress, 1st Session, Part 2, 1969, pp. 1070-71.

[9]Market demand prorationing refers to the system of allocating production quotas to individual oil producers. It arose in response to the common pool problem in the production of crude oil. Since the transaction costs (inclusive of negotiation and enforcement costs of agreed upon output shares) involved in determining the oil to be drawn from a common pool by co-owners are substantial, such determination was done through the mediation of various state regulatory commissions. Rationing of the quota was specified in terms of the allowable percentage of MER (maximum efficient rate of production), with a view to controlling total production such that the targeted market price of oil could be sustained. Ibid., pp. 1069-73.

[10]See Kenneth W. Dam, "Implementation of Import Quotas: The Case of Oil," *The Journal of Law and Economics* (April 1971), pp. 1-60.

[11]The Supreme Court ruled that the Federal Power Commission *must* regulate the wellhead price of natural gas flowing in interstate commerce. Phillips Petroleum Company V. Wisconsin, 347 U.S. 622, 1954. See Edmund W. Kitch, "Regulation of the Field Market for Natural Gas by the Federal Power Commission," *The Journal of Law and Economics* (October 1968), pp. 243-80.

[12]For a discussion of various concepts of (mineral) reserves and the problems in estimating them, see U.S. Congress, House of Representatives and Senate, Joint Economic Committee, *Adequacy of U.S. Oil and Gas Reserves*, 94th Congress, 1st Session, 1975, pp. 14-27.

[13]Dale W. Jorgenson, ed., *Econometric Studies of U.S. Energy Policy* (Amsterdam: North-Holland, 1976); Also Houthakker, *The World Price of Oil*, p. 8.

The second premise is that the reserves of oil and gas in particular, and other nonrenewable energy resources in general, are a predetermined, fixed "lump" which is independent of both price and technology. This premise ignores the fact that reserves are essentially adjustable inventories which the energy producers hold in order to safeguard their market positions. The amount of reserves (inventories) producers want to hold, then, is dependent upon the perceived cost of holding them relative to the expected returns from such holdings.

The prevalent view of the nature and origins of the energy crisis is, thus, based on twin fallacies: the lump of energy fallacy and the denial of the fundamental laws of demand. Such a view tends to ignore the following facts: (1) that the demand for energy is a derived demand,[14] (2) that energy produces valued output in conjunction with other scarce factors of production (such as labor and capital), (3) that other factors are substitutable for energy in the production process (hence other factors are valuable, as is energy), and (4) that the substitution of one form of energy for another depends on the relative cost of alternative forms of energy.[15]

Underlying the prevalent view is a concept that could be characterized as the "BTU theory of value." A strict BTU theory of value would hold that energy is the *only* scarce resource and, as such, is as fallacious as the Marxian labor theory of value, which holds that labor is the sole source of value. If the issue is presented so starkly, one would be hard put to find an advocate of such a BTU theory of value. However, the theory, at least in its applied forms, appears to have substantial adherents.

A variant of the BTU theory of value imputes an inherent, independent value to a specific source of BTUs, such as oil or natural gas. This variant denies the proposition that a dollar's worth of energy (in whatever form) is equal in value to a dollar's worth of labor or capital. Therefore, a question regarding the cost of conserving energy in terms of non-energy factors of production is seldom raised explicitly in assessing the comparative merits of various energy programs.

For example, some proposals to conserve the BTUs embodied in natural gas would use taxation and other measures to induce conversion to coal of electric power and industrial plants, designed to operate on natural gas. The question of cost-effectiveness in terms of the *total* resource use, relative to the desired output forthcoming from the production process, is seldom fully addressed. Implicit in this view is either a belief in the inherent value of the BTUs embodied in natural gas and the denial of the scarcity value of other cooperating factors, *or* a lingering belief that the price of natural gas does not, or will not be permitted to, reflect its true scarcity value.[16]

The market-based interpretation of the energy problem implies that the urgent task of public policy is to make the energy market *more* responsive to *unexpected* shocks and *expected* changes in market demand and supply conditions. Such a goal is likely to be achieved only if tinkering in the energy market by self-serving domestic power groups, acting through the government, is effectively curtailed.[17] Public pol-

---

[14]Demand for energy is a derived demand in the sense that an energy resource is not wanted for its own sake but for the output of the objects of more immediate consumption, such as comfortable temperatures and transportation services, which energy helps to produce.

[15]For recent articles which document the "abundant" availability of energy at higher market prices (from such sources as untapped natural gas reservoirs, Devonian shale and geopressured methane), see *The Wall Street Journal* editorial pages, 27 April 1977 and 14 June 1977. For an account of a series of substitutions of alternate fuels used for illuminants as the price of whale oil (the dominant lighting fuel in the U.S. in the early 1800s) rose drastically, see Murray L. Weidenbaum and Reno Harnish, *Government Credit Subsidies for Energy Development* (Washington, D.C.: American Enterprise Institute, 1976), pp. 4-5.

[16]Should the price indeed reflect the true scarcity value of natural gas, and, even given that, should some industrial users decide to use natural gas in conjunction with the natural gas powered capital goods already put in place (presumably because the total resource cost is lower than the alternative of enforced capital replacement), the only basis for questioning such a decision appears to be a BTU theory of value.

[17]In case of a discrepancy between direct private costs and total social cost of using energy resources in the presence of pollution externalities, an intervention through excise taxes could be appropriate. It may also be appropriate to attempt to induce changes in the discount rate that market participants use to optimize the time distribution of extraction and consumption of energy resources, if a demonstrable basis exists for a bias in the market interest rate. For a classic discussion of the problem of social cost, see Ronald H. Coase, "The Problem of Social Cost," *The Journal of Law and Economics* (October 1960), pp. 1-44. For a voluminous literature inspired by the Coase work, see William J. Baumol, "On Taxation and the Control of Externalities," *The American Economic Review* 62 no. 3 (June 1972), pp. 307-322 and various comments on the article together with "Reply," *The American Economic Review* 64 no. 3 (June 1974), pp. 462-92. For a discussion of the "proper" social discount rate for capital deepening decisions, see Kenneth J. Arrow, "Discounting and Public Investment Criteria," in *Water Research*, A. V. Kneese and S. C. Smith, eds. (Baltimore: Johns Hopkins Press, 1966), pp. 28-30; Jack Hirshleifer, James C. DeHaven, and Jerome W. Milliman, *Water Supply* (Chicago, The University of Chicago Press, 1960), pp. 139-41; Stephen A. Marglin, "The Social Rate of Discount and the Optimal Rate of Investment," *The Quarterly Journal of Economics* 77 no. 1 (February 1963), pp. 95-111; Gordon Tullock, "The Social Rate of Discount and the Optimal Rate of Investment: Comment," *The Quarterly Journal of Economics*, 78 no. 2 (May 1964), pp. 336-45.

icy becomes questionable if it is based exclusively on conserving particular forms of energy, such as oil and natural gas, without an explicit regard to the total cost of that policy, including the capital cost, relative to the demonstrable total benefits.

PAST PUBLIC POLICIES AS THE ROOTS OF THE ENERGY CRISIS

The Natural Gas Market

The controls on the wellhead price of natural gas, which were imposed in the 1960s, were below the market clearing level in the 1960s. According to the first law of demand, mentioned above, the expected result was an increase in the quantity of natural gas demanded by existing users of natural gas. According to the second law of demand, as the lower price persisted, there entered a new class of users, such as electric utilities. At first glance, it would appear that there should have been a "shortage" of natural gas, as the quantity demanded outstripped the quantity supplied when prices are held down artificially. This was not the case, however.

It appears paradoxical that an "artificially" low price of natural gas led to an *actual* increase in consumption, rather than to a mere increase in *attempted* consumption. Why did producers supply enough gas to accommodate the increase in quantity demanded at the artificially low price? The resolution of this puzzle holds a key to unravelling the nature of the fallacy imbedded in the prevalent view of the energy problem.

The technological nature of the natural gas (and oil) industry is such that the industry maintains a relatively high inventory-to sales ratio.[18] The inventories are held in the form of *proved reserves*. The existence of inventories helps to dampen fluctuations in the current price and facilitates quantity adjustments to fluctuations in demand. The amount of reserves (inventories) sellers want to hold is systematically related (1) to the expected future market price relative to the current price, and (2) to the cost of holding inventories.

To understand what we observed in the 1960s — (1) the simultaneous lowering of the regulated price of natural gas below the market clearing level *and*

increased consumption and production of natural gas, and (2) the conversion to natural gas by utilities and industrial users — it is necessary to review the history of regulatory control on the wellhead price of natural gas since the Phillips case of 1954.

The Federal Power Commission (FPC) approached its Supreme Court mandated task of regulating the wellhead price of natural gas on a case by case basis until the early 1960s. The case by case approach, however, put such a strain on the FPC's resources that the commission itself estimated that its 1960 case load would not be completed until the year 2043.[19] Faced with such a backlog of case load, the FPC introduced in 1961, the Permian Basin method of area-wide rate-making.[20]

Under the Permian Basin methodology, the FPC would establish a "just and reasonable" ceiling price for all natural gas produced within a broadly defined producing area such as the Permian Basin in Texas or Southern Louisiana. This method of price control resulted in the practice of basing the permitted price on the historical cost of a low cost producer in a given area. Therefore, the new method was instrumental in inducing a downward revision in the expected *future* price of natural gas.

Chart I indicates that the hypothesized downward revision in the expected price was in fact borne out by the actual price behavior. The relative price of natural gas declined on balance in the post-Permian 1960s, in sharp contrast to its rising trend between the late 1940s and the early 1960s. Chart I also shows that the actual thrust of regulation after the Phillips case of 1954 and prior to the Permian Basin proceedings, was such that the price of natural gas was permitted to continue its rise relative to both the price of oil and other prices in general.

In terms of the interpretation offered above of reserves as business inventories, one would expect that the downward revision in the expected future price of natural gas would have induced an accelerated

---

[18]This is because of the long lead time between exploration and production. See Paul W. MacAvoy and Robert S. Pindyck, *Price Controls and the Natural Gas Shortage* (Washington, D.C.: American Enterprise Institute, 1975), pp. 16-19.

[19]Ibid., p. 12.

[20]The area-wide rate making procedure, based on an adaptation of the public utility rate-making approach, tended to impart a downward bias to the regulated wellhead price. The FPC attempted to arrive at an area-wide composite average cost estimate based on a survey of cost data. Confronted with the logically impossible problem of joint cost allocation between oil and gas, the FPC systematically chose the figures at the lower end of the choice set. The Supreme Court once again ruled, in 1968, that it was within the discretion of the FPC to adopt the area-wide rate-making procedure, however arbitrary the rate may be. Permian Area Rate Cases, 390 U.S. 747 (1968).

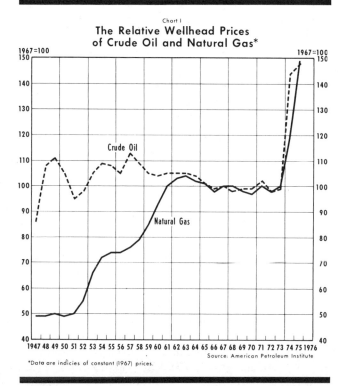

Chart I
**The Relative Wellhead Prices
of Crude Oil and Natural Gas***

*Data are indicies of constant (1967) prices.

Source: American Petroleum Institute

Chart II
Ratio of Natural Gas Reserves to Production [1]

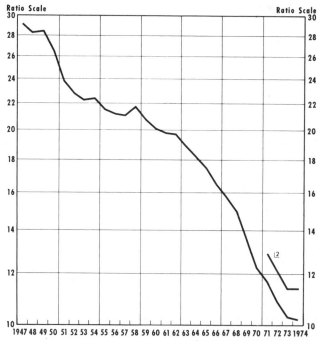

Source: American Gas Association

[1] Measured as the ratio of: the beginning and end of year figures for proven reserves of natural gas to the production of natural gas during that year.
[2] Includes 26 trillion cubic feet at 14.72 psia and 60°F in Prudhoe Bay, Alaska.

downward revision in the desired reserve-to-production ratios. Such an expectation is borne out by the behavior of the reserve-to-production ratios shown in Chart II. The chart shows that the reserve-to-production ratio was falling even before the Permian Basin proceedings in the early 1960s, indicating that the actual ratio was above the desired ratio. However, the downward adjustment proceeded at a slower rate of 1.8 percent per year after the Phillips case of 1954 but prior to the Permian proceedings in 1961, compared to the 3.7 percent per year rate in the earlier 1947-54 period. Such behavior is consistent with the earlier finding that regulation permitted a relative increase in the price of natural gas prior to the early 1960s.

The decline in the reserve-to-production ratio accelerated after the Permian proceedings began early in the 1960s. The ratio fell at the rate of 6 percent per year from 1963 to 1970. Such an acceleration in the decline of the ratio reflects the downward adjustment in the desired reserve-to-production ratio induced by the adoption of the Permian methodology.

Chart III indicates that the accelerated downward adjustment in the reserve-to-production ratio in the 1960s took the form, first, of decelerating growth of reserves, and then of outright reduction in reserves since 1968. Chart IV indicates that this slowing in

reserve accumulation and the eventual reduction in reserves, can be attributed squarely to the slowing in the search for reserves as a direct consequence of policy-induced souring in the prospective returns on exploration and development activities. The Chart shows that there has been a secular improvement in the success ratios in exploratory and development efforts, possibly due to technological progress.[21] Therefore, the marked reduction in the number of successful gas well drillings since 1962, as shown in Chart IV, is primarily due to the reduction in the search activities. Production of natural gas, however, did not start decreasing absolutely until 1973.

The drawing down of reserves (inventories) by producers reconciles the apparent puzzle of an "artificially" low, controlled price and the observed increases in the quantity supplied. It is ironic that the peculiarities of the market for natural gas masked the policy-induced disequilibrium in the market, so that many new industrial and electric utility users switched over to natural gas from coal. They were attracted to natural gas because of its apparent "bargain" price

---

[21] The conclusion regarding the success ratios also holds individually for new-field wildcats, total exploratory wells and development wells.

Chart III
Changes in Natural Gas Reserves*

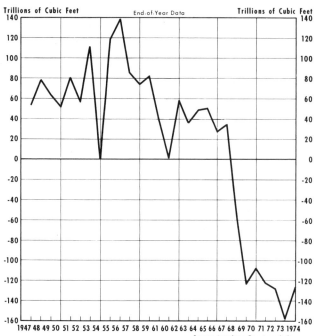

Source: American Gas Association
*This series is generated by subtracting estimated production of natural gas during the year from the reserve revisions, extentions, and discoveries during the same year.

and the higher cost of using coal occasioned by the passage of various environmental legislations.

Chart IV
Natural Gas Drilling and Production

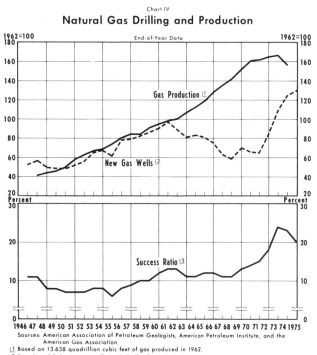

Sources: American Association of Petroleum Geologists, American Petroleum Institute, and the American Gas Association.
|1 Based on 13.638 quadrillion cubic feet of gas produced in 1962.
|2 Based on 5,848 new gas wells in 1962. This figure includes exploratory and development wells.
|3 Measured as the ratio of new gas wells to total wells drilled.

In view of the eventual emergence *at the controlled price* of a shortage in the market for natural gas, which led to supply curtailments, the decisions of new users to convert to natural gas must be judged with hindsight to have been ill-advised. It is doubly ironic that these victims of the unintended side-effects of public policy could now become targets of elaborate tax and administrative measures.

The Oil Market

The preceding analysis of the nature and origins of the natural gas crisis is applicable to the market for oil, the other endangered specie of energy. The adjustment capacity of the market for oil also has been attenuated as a consequence of past public policy. In contrast to the unintended shortage policy followed in the market for natural gas, a deliberate surplus policy was followed in the market for oil. As noted earlier, various state regulatory agencies followed a demand pro-rationing policy to cope with the common pool problem in the industry, which arose from the rule of capture doctrine in existence. This, in turn, arose from incompletely defined property rights over oil in the ground.[22]

In the absence of a demand pro-rationing system and of consolidation of an oil field under one or joint control, violent fluctuations arose in the price of crude oil that producers received as developed fields were intensively mined and new discoveries made.[23] The demand pro-rationing system evolved to protect the joint interests of the producers.[24] Under the demand pro-rationing system the state regulatory agencies, such as the Texas Railroad Commission, sought to alleviate this condition by setting total production targets for the particular state, and by distributing the production quotas according to a formula which favored small and usually higher-cost producers. The ever-present stripper wells — producing less than 20 barrels per day — were usually exempted from quota regulation altogether. The economic consequence of this form of allocation was higher than necessary

[22]Since oil is mobile in underground reservoirs, it is difficult to define and enforce property rights when the field is owned jointly.

[23]Morris A. Adelman, "Efficiency of Resource Use in Crude Petroleum," *Southern Economic Journal* 31 (October 1964), pp. 101-22.

[24]This system is a classic case of "acquired regulation." In such a situation, regulation is supplied by the state in response to the demand by the incumbents (mainly to restrain entry). For the original statement of the hypothesis of acquired regulation, see George Stigler, "The Theory of Economic Regulation," *The Bell Journal of Economics and Management Science* (Spring 1971), pp. 3-21.

resource costs of domestic oil, as higher-cost producers were rewarded.

Prior to 1948, the U.S. was a net exporter of oil, holding 31 percent of the then proven world reserves. Thus, the U.S. occupied a position of dominance, even greater than the position of Saudi Arabia today. But an accelerated pace of discovery and development by the major international oil companies of low-cost reserves in the Persian Gulf states began to make inroads into the U.S. position. Threatened by the competition from low-cost foreign oil imported mainly by the U.S. based major integrated international oil companies, other domestic oil producers and refiners, who had not developed foreign sources of oil, succeeded in persuading the government to institute a voluntary oil import program in 1957.[25]

The voluntary program failed, mostly due to the attempts of non-major U.S. producers to import from their recently developed wells in the Persian Gulf area. Unlike the international majors, which had already developed extensive networks of markets outside the U.S., these late-comers from the U.S. seized the opening under the voluntary import program to increase their market share at home. As a consequence, total imports as a percent of domestic production jumped from 19.7 percent in 1957 to 22.4 percent by 1959. Yielding to the intense pressure by a coalition of domestic producers and refiners, who demanded protection from cheap foreign oil on "security of supply" and other grounds, the voluntary import program became a mandatory import quota system in 1959.[26] As a result, a segment of the domestic oil industry was insulated from the rigors of competition in the market place. The mandatory program was to last until April 1973.

Under the Mandatory Oil Import Program, the overall import quota was set so as to freeze the share of imports at the level achieved in 1959. The distribution of import licenses among refiners was skewed in favor of smaller refiners. Such refiners received a disproportionately larger share of import licenses (in effect, subsidies), which had a market value per barrel equal to the difference between the higher-priced, regulated domestic oil and the cheaper, market-priced foreign oil.

The conventional method of arriving at the cost of the mandatory quota system is to add the estimated additional consumer costs of oil products to the cost of domestic resources unnecessarily used up to produce oil that could have been imported more cheaply. The real cost of the Program, however, would far exceed the conventionally estimated sum. The Program had sown the seed of the current energy crisis by sharply reducing the capacity of the oil market to respond to external shocks such as the effective cartelization of the Organization of Petroleum Exporting Countries (OPEC), and the Oil Embargo of 1973.

The Program set in motion a chain of events that culminated in the birth of OPEC in September 1960. The imposition of the U.S. import quota, based on a fixed share of the U.S. oil market, meant that imports could grow only at the rate of growth of U.S. production. This meant that the increased production that was just coming on stream from foreign wells developed by non-major U.S. producers had to be diverted away from the U.S. market. Precipitous price declines ensued in the world oil market and price competition forced the major international oil companies (majors hereafter) to match the decline.

It so happened, however, that the profit-sharing arrangement which the majors had with the oil producing countries was on the basis of the *posted price* rather than on the *market price*.[27] Therefore, in order to lighten the squeeze on their profits, the majors unilaterally cut posted prices in 1959 and once again in August 1960, despite strenuous protests and explicit warnings from the exporting countries.[28] The quota-induced cut in posted prices by the majors provided the spark for the exporting countries to form an organization to safeguard their common interest.

It is a moot point whether such an organization would have formed in the absence of the Mandatory Oil Import Quota Program. The point is that the quota system adopted in 1959 had a direct causal effect on the formation of OPEC, and such an untoward effect should be considered as a significant component of the cost of import programs.

The surplus policy on domestic oil, pursued by both state and Federal authorities at the instigation of some segments of the industry, reduced the incentives of the oil industry to improve efficiency and to add to

[25]See Dam, *Implementation*, pp. 5-8. Also see Morris A. Adelman, *The World Petroleum Market* (Resources for the Future, Inc.; Baltimore: The Johns Hopkins University Press, 1972), pp. 150-55.

[26]Dam, *Implementation*, pp. 9-14 and pp. 58-60.

[27]Yoon S. Park, *Oil Money and the World Economy* (Boulder: Westview Press, 1976), pp. 27-35.

[28]Bohi, Russel, and Snyder, *Economics of Energy*, p. 47, (p. 57 of the *Compilation*).

its stock of oil reserves. Public policy then delivered another blow to the oil market in the form of a series of price freeze and control programs instituted in 1971 to fight inflation. The domestic oil price control program had the unintended effect of killing off the mandatory import quota system. While the domestic price was being held down, the foreign price of oil increased and surpassed the U.S. level, thus wiping out the value of import licenses.

The familiar scenario of one control begetting another, in order to deal with the unintended distortions produced by the previous control, was repeated many times.[29] For example, under Phase IV of the price control program, the Cost of Living Council (CLC) adopted the technique of "vintaging" to the pricing of crude oil. A two-tier price system, with a ceiling price on "old" crude and a market-determined price on "new" and "released" domestic crude oil, was designed to encourage new exploration and production.[30] The program, while encouraging domestic exploration and development, created predictable problems of its own, due to the fact that not every refiner had equal access to *old* and *new* domestic crude oil, nor to domestic and imported crude oil.

Complaints of discrimination and charges of evading the two-tier pricing system through tie-in-sales, were often raised.[31] As a consequence of the two-tier pricing, substantial price differentials appeared in refined products reflecting different access to lower and higher-priced crude oil. The crude oil program was instrumental in creating artificial, policy-induced competitive advantages and disadvantages where none existed. A coalition of refiners, who had not developed their own domestic sources of old crude oil, lobbied actively for a crude oil allocation program under which they would receive their "equitable share" of lower-priced old crude oil.[32]

When the OAPEC (Organization of Arab Petroleum Exporting Countries)[33] embargo unexpectedly hit the U.S. in October 1973, the energy markets, particularly those of oil and natural gas, were tied up in knots due to the effects of the past policies, such as demand pro-rationing, the mandatory import quotas, and price controls on oil and natural gas. The U.S. dependence on foreign oil was to become larger than that which would have resulted in a world of open markets for natural gas and oil.[34]

The public policy response to the embargo exacerbated the adjustment problem. The Federal Energy Office — instead of focusing on the level of stocks of crude oil and refined products (which was the technique used to allocate production quotas by the Texas Railroad Commission) — focused on an anticipated reduction in U.S. oil imports, which was repeatedly overestimated. The amount of oil allocated for consumption consistently fell below the sum of domestic production and imports. As a consequence, the U.S. ended the embargo period with a higher stock of petroleum products than it started.[35]

In the wake of the embargo and the quadrupling of the crude oil price, a coalition of refiners without access to cheaper domestic old oil finally succeeded in having the newly organized Federal Energy Administration adopt the crude oil cost equalization program in December 1974.[36] The program was designed to allocate lower-priced domestic crude oil subject to price controls proportionately among refiners, and was adopted in response to the pressures to allow *all* refiners to have the equal access to cheaper domestic oil.

The principal part of the program was designed to distribute low-cost "old" domestic crude oil proportionately to *all* U.S. refiners through the issuance of tickets or entitlements. The entitlements represented rights to purchase lower-priced "old" domestic crude just as the import licenses during the mandatory oil import quota period represented rights to purchase the then cheaper foreign oil. Although the situation is reversed, the principle of resorting to political com-

---

[29]For an authoritative and revealing account of the utter frustration experienced by a former Federal Energy Office (FEO) administrator, see William A. Johnson, "The Impact of Energy Controls on the Oil Industry: How to Worsen an Energy Crisis," in *Energy: The Policy Issues*, edited by Gary D. Eppen (Chicago: University of Chicago Press, 1975), pp. 99-121.

[30]Ibid., pp. 109-110.

[31]Ibid., pp. 110-111.

[32]U.S. Congress, House of Representatives and Senate Subcommittee on Consumer Economics of the Joint Economic Committee, *The F.E.A. and Competition in the Oil Industry*, 93rd Congress, 2nd. Session, 1974, p. 17 and pp. 52-53.

[33]OAPEC was founded in 1967 by the Arab members of the OPEC.

[34]The price control on natural gas was having a delayed impact on the quantities supplied relative to the quantities demanded by then. Hence, the excess demand for natural gas spilled over into the market for oil. Bohi, Russel, and Snyder, *Economics of Energy*, pp. 81-7.

[35]Richard B. Mancke, *Performance of the Federal Energy Office* (Washington, D.C.: American Enterprise Institute, 1975), pp. 4-7.

[36]See "Allocations: F.E.A. Adopts Regulations Designed to Equalize Crude, Fuel Oil Costs," *Energy Users Report* no. 69 (Washington, D.C.: The Bureau of National Affairs, Inc., 5 December 1974), p. A-7. Hereinafter, *Energy Users Report*.

petition to alter economic outcomes remained invariant. Once again, as in the import licensing and the demand pro-rationing systems, smaller refiners (with less than a 175,000 barrel per day capacity) were to receive proportionately more entitlements than larger refiners.[37]

The system of entitlements, in conjunction with the multi-tier pricing of crude oil that was introduced earlier, had the unintended effect of increasing U.S. dependency on foreign oil.[38] The increase in foreign dependency was due to the joint effects of the "uncontrolled" price of "new" domestic oil being set below the world (the OPEC cartel) price, and the entitlement program. The former reduced the domestic production below the level that would otherwise have been attained under free (open) market pricing, while the entitlement program had the perverse effect of encouraging imports by, in effect, taxing domestic production and subsidizing imports.[39]

Figure I illustrates how a public policy, designed to deal with one set of problems through intervention in the market place, created another problem. The rise in the world (cartel) price of oil and the domestic price control on crude oil led to a demand by some refiners for crude oil allocation and cost equalization programs. Such a demand was eventually answered by the Emergency Petroleum Allocation Act of 1973 and Crude Oil Equalization Program of 1974. In Figure I, one can contrast the amount of imports that would have prevailed under free market pricing and the entitlement programs as evolved. Pw denotes the "world" price set by OPEC.[40] OPEC is assumed ready to supply all the "residual" oil demanded by the U.S. at Pw. In the absence of any domestic price control, the domestic production would be OB and the imports BC. However, under the price controls on both the "old" and the "new" domestic oil at P1 and P2 respectively, the U.S. producers would supply OE of "old" oil and EA of "new" oil. The total domestic production would now be OA and the amount of

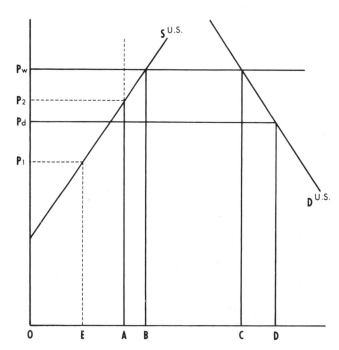

Figure I
The Effects of Price Controls and Entitlements

Pw: World Price (set by OPEC)
P1: U.S. "Old" Oil Prices
P2: U.S. "New" Oil Price
Pd: Weighted Average of Domestic and Foreign Oil*
*Assume Controls on End-Product Prices Using Pass-Through Provisions

imports would be AC, which are purchased at price Pw. The dependence on foreign oil increases by AB.

The introduction of the entitlement system worsens the situation further, especially when one assumes the existence of controls on end-product prices through pass-through provisions, for example, on utility rates. If we assume that the pricing of oil products is based on the weighted average price, denoted by Pd, of domestic and foreign oil, imported oil now increases to AD whereas the domestic production is still at OA. In view of the avowed objective at that time to achieve energy self-sufficiency by 1985 (Project Independence), it is indeed ironic that the policies chosen militated against the professed goal.

Aside from the adverse effect on foreign dependency, the crude oil cost equalization program raises a fundamental question regarding the role of public policy in the market place. Those who first asked for allocation and, then, for cost equalization of crude oil were those refiners who had not integrated backward

[37]*Energy Users Report*, p. A-8.

[38]See Hans H. Helbling and James E. Turley, "Oil Price Controls," this *Review* (November 1975); Also Robert E. Hall & Robert S. Pindyck, "The Conflicting Goals of National Energy Policy," *The Public Interest* no. 47 (Spring 1977), p. 3.

[39]See Milton Friedman, "Subsidizing OPEC Oil," *Newsweek* June 23, 1975, p. 75, and Hall and Pindyck, "The Conflicting Goals," p. 3 and p. 5.

[40]The analysis abstracts from the question of how the Pw has been chosen. Presumably, if the objective is to maximize the joint profits (or wealth) of the OPEC members, a dominant-firm price leadership model would be relevant.

to production of crude oil.[41] Their argument was that it was unfair for them to be deprived of the supply of crude oil by the integrated producers in times of crude oil "shortage." They argued that the price to society of impending failures, due to their inability to secure crude oil in times of "tight" supply, would be a reduction of competition in the market. They sought, through political actions, access to crude on the same terms as the integrated producers.

However, the reasoning advanced above for political intercessions runs counter to the concept of competition in the market place. The cardinal rule of competition is that individual participants in the market place bear the full consequences of their own market decisions, inclusive of those decisions regarding the future supply of raw materials. One possible strategy for an oil refiner, regarding the future source of raw materials, is to depend on the spot market for a supply of crude oil. This tends to be a higher risk strategy than the alternative one of integrating backward to the production of crude oil. A higher risk strategy is associated in the long run with a higher expected return than the alternative lower risk strategy.

In terms of this "new view" of industrial organization, then, the demands of some refiners for equal access on competitive ground is difficult to defend.[42] Furthermore, expected accommodations of their pleas tend to have effects beyond the mere redistribution of wealth from the integrated companies to those who were not integrated. It would tend to reduce the integrated oil companies' incentives to explore and develop new reserves of crude oil.

---

[41]See Eppen, *Energy*, pp. 106-107.

[42]For a systematic statement of the "new view" of industrial organization, see Oliver E. Williamson, *Markets and Hierarchies* (New York: The Free Press, 1975). For an application of the new view to the U.S. oil industry, see David J. Teece, "Vertical Integration in the U.S. Oil Industry," in *Vertical Integration in the Oil Industry*, edited by Edward J. Mitchell (Washington, D.C.: American Enterprise Institute, 1976).

An exploration into the history of two major energy markets in the U.S. reveals that the overriding uncertainty regarding the thrust and direction of public policy on energy has shrouded the energy markets. Under these circumstances, decision-makers in the energy industry were distracted from the business of securing, processing and marketing energy products in response to the perceived "energy consumption policies" of individual consumers and "energy supply policies" of fellow competitors. Instead, they have had to play the socially unproductive game of trying to anticipate and influence shifts in public policy.

CONCLUSIONS

The growing concern about an energy crisis has resulted in a repeated call for a national energy policy. Unfortunately, there are widespread misconceptions about the nature and origins of the U.S. energy problem. Past attempts by various segments of the energy industry to avoid the rigors of competition have resulted in public policies which have emasculated the energy market's ability to adjust to man-made and nature-induced shocks. It is ironic that those who now call for deregulation of the energy market are the ones that had successfully sought most of the existing regulations.

We are now faced with a "crisis," which calls for policy-mandated conservation measures that may be costly in terms of economic utilization of existing capital resources. And we seem to forget that an unfettered energy market could, and still can, bring forth ever expanding supplies of energy from higher-cost conventional sources and more exotic, alternate sources. Also, an unencumbered energy market could, and still can, induce effective conservation on the part of consumers, through the working of the first and second laws of demand. The question that remains, however, is whether the various elements of the energy industry will accept competitive market outcomes in totality or demand protection from the rigors of competition when the sledding gets tough.

34

Energy: Where Did the Crisis Go?

By STEVEN RATTNER

WASHINGTON — It is just a year since Jimmy Carter launched his national energy plan, under the banner, "the moral equivalent of war." As it turned out, a more propitious year could have been chosen.

Instead of wrenching shortages to provide a political push, there were surpluses large enough to be embarrassing. Instead of soaring prices, there was stability, and even some decline. The energy plan has faded almost as quickly as the natural gas crisis that had given the plan an early, glorious springboard.

For critics of the plan, the events of the year served as vindication of their proposition that forces already in motion could solve the nation's energy problems.

"The year has shown that without any super package — without any part of it passed — we have been able to conserve energy, reduce oil imports and maintain natural gas production," said John Lichtblau, executive director of the Petroleum Industry Research Foundation.

The Administration has been taking pains, however, to dismiss talk of gluts and price cutting, seeing them as a diversion momentarily hiding the vast energy upheavals it believes must surely lie ahead. Others agree with that view. "I think the whole world two years from now will not look anywhere as good," said an oil industry executive.

Energy Secretary James R. Schlesinger, in an interview last week, endorsed that view. "The fact that you don't have a visible shortage tends to mask the longer-range shortage. The things you cite have been used as an excuse for postponing until tomorrow what we ought to do today."

Among the developments:

• The abundance of natural gas this winter, despite unusually cold weather. At the same time, a three-year decline in natural gas production appears to have been halted and several gas utilities are once again accepting new residential customers.

• Imports of crude oil from the Organization of Petroleum Exporting Countries are down sharply — nearly 9 percent this year — as a result of new supplies from the North Sea, Alaska and elsewhere. Prices, particularly after adjustment for inflation, are also down.

• Coal production rose last year despite the long strike, and industry and utilities have begun to convert to coal in droves. Electric power remains ample, partly as a result of increased nuclear supplies.

• Energy consumption and gross national product in the United States formerly increased at almost the same rate. The relationship between the two has been changing and last year, energy growth totaled less than 65 percent of economic growth.

To be sure, not all the signs were hopeful. There were increased indications of production problems in Saudi Arabia and of an inclination among Saudis to limit their oil production. And the dollar plummeted on foreign exchange markets, in part reflecting a European perception that America had failed to deal with its energy problems.

"The long-term things all look worse now than we thought they would," said Alvin L. Alm, Assistant Secretary of Energy Policy.

The principal force behind the self-correction cited by a number of energy experts is higher prices; oil prices are up fivefold since 1973 and natural gas prices have more than tripled during the same period. At the same time, the effect of several pieces of legislation enacted by Congress in the wake of the Arab oil embargo — such as automobile mileage standards — is now beginning to be felt.

Perhaps the most dramatic demonstration of the shift involves natural gas. Hundreds of companies across the Middle West in the winter of 1976-77 lost their gas because of the short supply and residential priority. Hundreds of thousands of workers were temporarily unemployed.

This winter, which was equally cold on a national basis, saw not a single layoff due to gas supply problems. Moreover, the Texas Railroad Commission, which regulates energy production in the state, was forced to order a cutback because of excess supply. Prices in several gas-producing states were extremely weak.

In part, this reflects increased storage by the natural-gas utilities to prepare for any future shortages. In part, it represents widespread efforts by industry to speed conversion to other fuels, including coal.

But it also is indicative of the early effects of quickly rising prices. In 1973, 7,466 wells were drilled in the United States in search of oil and gas. By 1977, the total had climbed to 9,961.

The impact of all this drilling on gas production has become evident. From 1973 to 1976, natural gas production declined by 12 percent but last year it did not decline at all and several companies expect it to rise in 1978.

The improved gas outlook has also led a number of utilities to accept new customers. New hookups have been tightly restricted for the most part since the early 1970's, when a coming gas shortage became apparent. Last year, about 550,000 new customers were hooked up, according to industry estimates.

"We've always thought there would be plenty of gas available for residential use if we could limit industrial use," said Theodore R. Eck, chief economist of the Standard Oil Company (Indiana).

The oil industry has experienced similar changes. Imports are down 16 percent for the first two months of this year while production is up 7.4 percent, chiefly reflecting the flow of Alaskan oil, which recently topped 1.1 million barrels a day. The upsurge in drilling has also helped oil production. Domestic production not including Alaska has continued to decline, but at a slower rate.

The improved domestic oil picture has actually led to a glut on the West Coast as Alaskan oil arrives by tanker. Crude oil supplies there are more than double year-ago levels and California, which produces nearly a million barrels a day, is warning that some of its wells may be forced to shut down.

Similar conditions pervade Europe. Oil imports hardly grew last year, reflecting weak economies, increased oil production from the North Sea and larger supplies of gas from Northern Europe.

As a result, demand for OPEC oil was down nearly 9 percent during the first two months of this year, to less than 30 million barrels a day. By comparison, OPEC production at its peak in 1973 totaled 31 million barrels a day.

The worldwide glut has in large part been responsible for an increasingly moderate stand on prices by the OPEC cartel. Prices appear to be frozen for 1978 and substantial quantities of oil have been moving at discounts as high as 30 cents a barrel.

To all appearances, supplies of other fuels are equally ample. In spite of the coal strike, coal miners were still able to produce 673 million tons last year, up from 665 million tons a year earlier, according to the National Coal Association. The frantic rush by coal users last fall to increase stockpiles before the

> *The primary force for the turnaround, some experts claim, has been a price rise.*

strike pushed production in some weeks to 16 million tons a week, an annual rate of 840 million tons.

Moreover, industry and utilities, fearful of an eventual shortfall of oil and gas, appear to be moving of their own accord toward coal. A survey by the National Electric Reliability Council turned up plans by utilities to install 241 coal-fired boilers by 1985, which are expected to consume 400 million tons of coal a year.

Electric power is similarly abundant, partly because of increased nuclear supplies. According to the Atomic Industrial Forum, nuclear power increased its share of total generation by two-

Steven Rattner is a reporter in the Washington bureau of The New York Times.

tenths of 1 percent last year, to 9 percent. Meanwhile, nuclear generation will nearly triple over the next decade as a result of power plants already under construction.

Perhaps more important is the pronounced shift toward conservation. Once energy consumption and the economy grew in lockstep; now, thanks to higher energy prices, that relationship appears to have been broken, or at least bent.

According to Mr. Lichtblau, the oil industry expert, the energy-to-G.N.P. ratio fell to between 60 and 65 percent last year from 70 percent in 1976.

Another calculation, by Henry S. Rowen, former president of the Rand Corporation, showed that G.N.P., after adjustment for inflation, has grown by 11 percent since 1973, while energy consumption increased by only 3 percent.

"In short," Mr. Rowen told an American Petroleum Institute seminar recently, "we are using 8 percent less energy than we would have if energy consumption had grown proportionately with G.N.P. as it did in the period from 1956 to 1970."

Conservation has taken a variety of forms: Homes have been insulated, industry has switched to more energy-efficient processes, improved airplane engines are coming into use, lights are being turned off.

Some of this conservation is being achieved by legislation. Sharp increases in automobile efficiency — to 27.1 miles à gallon on average by 1985 — are expected to send gasoline consumption into decline by the early 1980's. Last year, gasoline demand was up by only 2.4 percent from a year ago, according to the American Petroleum Institute. This has kept gasoline prices essentially unchanged and in the Northeast they are even down by about 2 cents a gallon.

John G. Buckley, vice president of Northeast Petroleum Industries, calculated that 2.7 million homes were insulated in 1976 and six million last year. This year insulation is off to a slower start, Mr. Buckley said, because home owners are waiting for Congress to approve tax credits for the job.

"The market is working," he said. "Prices are high enough to encourage people to do it without tax credits."

Despite all these favorable develop-

ments, energy officials insist that the need for a national energy plan has not diminished.

For example, although many nuclear reactors are now under construction, few are on order and a number of energy experts believe it is nearly impossible to win approval today for a new nuclear facility. Similarly, the Administration believes that the potential for industrial coal conversion is not being realized.

Most important, the outlook for world oil supply is cloudy. The official Administration position is that a severe oil shortage will strike in the early 1980's, causing oil prices to double, not including increases to match inflation. Private economists are skeptical of this early date, although they agree that oil supplies are certainly limited.

For example, the Exxon Corporation's domestic subsidiary this year cut its estimate of United States oil imports in 1985 to 11.4 million barrels a day from last year's forecast of 11.7 million barrels a day.

"When exactly the oil crunch is going to strike is one of those incalculables," Schlesinger said, "but you know it's coming."

The slowdown in real wages: a postwar perspective

*Recent modest gains in productivity
and high inflation cast doubt on
whether real earnings will regain
the pre-1962 average rate of increase*

H. M. DOUTY

Adjusted for inflation, the average rates of pay of American workers have risen only half as fast since 1962 as during the decade and a half beginning with 1947. Is it likely that real pay will return to the early postwar rate of increase? This article traces the influence of productivity and price changes on real wages during the two halves of the postwar period, compares the postwar real wage experience with historical experience, and concludes with some comments on the outlook for resumption of a higher rate of real wage advance.

The division of the postwar period into approximately equal parts, 1947–62 and 1962–76, is not arbitrary. In 1962, the United States was on the eve of developments of profound economic importance. In particular, our involvement in the Vietnam war would increase substantially, while a variety of domestic social programs would be inaugurated or expanded. Beginning in 1966, inflation became a continuing and pervasive problem. The social costs of industrial output began to receive increased attention, and, notably with Edward Mishan's powerful polemic in 1967, the desirability of economic growth itself was called into question.[1] In ways difficult to measure, the operation of the labor market was affected by antidiscrimination hiring and promotion programs designed for minority groups and women, and to some extent by changing attitudes toward

H. M. Douty is a former Assistant Commissioner for Wages and Industrial Relations, Bureau of Labor Statistics.

work. Beginning in late 1973, the impact of the Arab oil cartel on crude petroleum prices had marked effects on our energy-intensive society.

Real wage trends

During the 15 years from 1947 to 1962, the real hourly earnings of production or nonsupervisory workers in the private nonfarm economy, adjusted for overtime (in manufacturing only) and for interindustry employment shifts, increased at an average rate of 2.5 percent annually; the advance during the 14-year period from 1962 to 1976 averaged only 1.2 percent annually.[2] This finding for the second half of the period is buttressed by statistics derived from two entirely different types of wage surveys. Effective general wage rate changes in major collective bargaining agreements show an average annual advance, in real terms, of about 1.2 percent for the years 1962 to 1976.[3] The average rate of increase in the salaries of professional, administrative, technical, and clerical employees in private industry, when adjusted for cost-of-living changes, was less than 1 percent annually during the second half of the postwar period.[4] Unfortunately, neither of these series extends back to 1947.

Other earnings measures that can be expressed in real terms include average weekly earnings, average spendable weekly earnings, and average compensation per hour. All are appropriate for some purposes, and the differences among them are discussed in a useful article by Thomas W. Gavett.[5] Although in-

Reprinted from *Monthly Labor Review*, August, 1977.

fluenced by factors additional to those affecting the movement of adjusted average hourly earnings, each of these measures exhibits a lower growth rate during the second half of the postwar period. Table 1 shows a variety of real wage indexes for the postwar period, or, where complete data are not available, for the second half only.

The focus of this article is cn the index of adjusted average hourly earnings of production or nonsupervisory workers (shown in the first column of table 1). This measure is available for the entire postwar period. Its labor force coverage is comprehensive—about 53 million workers in 1976. Most importantly,

it provides a rough indication of change in the level of wage rates.[6]

Postwar productivity and real wages

It has long been recognized that productivity experience constitutes the major underlying condition for change over time in the real wage position of the working population. Thus, Paul Douglas, in his pioneering study of wage trends between 1890 and 1926, wrote: "It has been the increase in physical and in value productivity which fundamentally has made possible the increase in real wages."[7]

Productivity, or output per hour, tends to fluctuate from year to year and is particularly sensitive to changes in output and labor input associated with cyclical behavior in business activity. It is longer term movements that are of major interest for real wage analysis. Table 2 shows the index of output per hour for the private business sector during the postwar years.[8] For 1947–62, the average annual rate of increase was 3.1 percent, compared with 2.1 percent for 1962–76. As in the case of real wages, the average rate of increase in productivity was distinctly higher in the first half of the postwar period.

The reasons for the slowdown during the second half in the rate of productivity increase are undoubtedly complex. One factor involves the decline in the magnitude of the shift of manpower from agriculture to nonfarm industries where, for the most part, output per hour is higher. Another factor appears to relate to the changing composition of the labor force, notably the influx of new entrants from the "baby boom" of the immediate postwar era and the increased labor force participation rate of women. However, the capital/labor ratio, a major determinant of productivity, does not appear to have fallen during the second half of the postwar period.[9] But other and perhaps more subtle factors probably have helped shape the productivity trend of these years. Some of these influences are considered briefly in the final section of this article.

Inflation and real wages

Much more visible than postwar productivity experience has been the difference between the inflation rates in the first and second halves of the period. Table 3 shows the year-to-year percentage changes in money and real earnings and in the Consumer Price Index for 1947–76.

During the first half of the period, except for the sharp increases from 1947 to 1948 (the end of the World War II inflation) and from 1950 to 1951 (the short-lived price explosion that accompanied our entrance into the Korean conflict), the year-to-year increase in the level of consumer prices exceeded 3 percent only for 1956–57. In fact, for 9 of the first 15

Table 1. Indexes of real wages: adjusted average hourly earnings and other measures, 1947–76

[1967 = 100]

Year	Adjusted[1] average hourly earnings[2]	Gross average weekly earnings[2]	Spendable average weekly earnings[3] (worker with 3 dependents)[2]	Compensation per hour[4]	White-collar salaries		General wage changes effective in major labor contracts[6]
					Professional, administrative, and technical workers[5]	Clerical and clerical supervisory workers[5]	
Average annual rate of increase:[7]							
1947–62	2.5	2.2	1.6	3.3	-------	-------	-------
1962–76	1.2	.6	.5	2.1	0.7	0.6	1.2
1947	63.7	66.9	73.4	52.5	-------	-------	-------
1948	63.8	66.7	74.0	52.9	-------	-------	-------
1949	67.5	69.1	76.7	54.4	-------	-------	-------
1950	69.3	72.4	79.4	57.7	-------	-------	-------
1951	69.0	73.0	78.9	58.6	-------	-------	-------
1952	70.9	74.9	80.1	61.1	-------	-------	-------
1953	74.4	78.2	82.9	64.6	-------	-------	-------
1954	76.6	78.7	83.2	66.5	-------	-------	-------
1955	79.4	82.9	86.9	68.5	-------	-------	-------
1956	82.3	85.3	89.0	72.0	-------	-------	-------
1957	83.4	85.4	88.4	74.2	-------	-------	-------
1958	84.5	85.1	87.8	75.6	-------	-------	-------
1959	86.8	88.6	90.6	78.5	-------	-------	-------
1960	88.4	89.3	90.5	80.5	-------	-------	-------
1961	90.2	90.5	91.5	82.8	-------	-------	-------
1962	92.2	93.1	93.5	85.7	92.3	94.9	93.2
1963	93.7	94.7	94.3	88.0	94.2	96.1	95.0
1964	95.1	96.5	97.8	91.6	96.0	97.3	96.2
1965	96.9	98.8	100.5	93.6	98.0	97.9	97.9
1966	98.1	99.8	100.4	97.3	98.6	98.1	98.6
1967	100.0	100.0	100.0	100.0	100.0	100.0	100.0
1968	102.0	101.5	100.6	103.3	101.3	101.0	101.2
1969	103.2	102.5	100.2	104.8	101.6	101.1	101.0
1970	103.9	101.0	99.0	106.0	101.9	101.3	102.3
1971	106.7	103.0	102.0	108.4	104.3	103.5	105.9
1972	110.0	106.7	106.4	110.8	106.5	106.3	108.7
1973	110.1	107.3	105.4	112.9	105.7	105.5	109.8
1974	107.4	102.7	100.1	111.2	101.3	101.2	108.3
1975	107.1	99.8	99.6	111.8	100.5	101.6	107.9
1976	108.3	101.4	100.9	114.3	101.4	103.2	110.0

[1]Adjusted for overtime payments (in manufacturing only) and for interindustry employment shifts.
[2]Production or nonsupervisory workers in the private nonfarm sector.
[3]Adjusted for Federal income and social security tax changes as well as for consumer price changes.
[4]Includes supervisory workers, self-employed persons, and farm employees in the private business sector. Fringe benefits are included in the compensation series.
[5]Data collected in annual surveys of salaries in selected occupations in major divisions of private industry, excluding agriculture.
[6]Collective bargaining agreements covering 1,000 workers or more.
[7]Computed by the compound interest rate formula.

Table 2.   Index of output per hour, all persons, private business sector, 1947–76

[1967 = 100]

Year	Output per hour	Year	Output per hour
1947	52.3	1961	80.6
1948	54.4	1962	84.4
1949	55.3	1963	87.7
1950	59.7	1964	91.3
		1965	94.7
1951	61.5	1966	97.8
1952	63.0	1967	100.0
1953	65.3	1968	103.3
1954	66.5	1969	103.7
1955	69.2	1970	104.5
		1971	107.8
		1972	110.8
1956	70.2	1973	113.1
1957	72.3	1974	109.2
1958	74.2	1975	111.3
1959	76.8	1976	115.7
1960	78.1		

years the increase was 1.5 percent or less; actual decreases occurred in two of these years. The average annual rate of increase from 1947 to 1962 was 2 percent. Clearly, this experience did not provide fertile ground for the growth of strong inflationary expectations.

The 1962–76 period was decisively different. The level of consumer prices began to edge up after 1962, and by 1966 an 8-year period of relative price stability ended—primarily because of the way in which our participation in the Vietnam war was financed. The inflation thus begun had its origin from the side of demand; once underway, however, it attained a momentum of its own. This is strikingly shown by the behavior of money wages during the economic downturn of 1970–71, the fifth postwar recession. In the first four recessions, the rate of increase in money wages declined. During the 1970–71 recession, although the rate of price increase moderated, money wages rose almost as rapidly as during the expansion phase of the cycle, until controls were instituted in August 1971.[10] A much more severe recession began in late 1973, and during 1974 rates of price and wage increase accelerated. By 1976, inflation rates were still high by normal peacetime standards.

In sum, there has been no respite from rises in the general price level since 1962, and notably over the 10 years since 1966. This contrasts with the first half of the postwar period, when inflationary episodes were brief and temporary. The average annual rate of increase in consumer prices for 1962–76 was 4.6 percent, more than twice the rate experienced during the first half; if measured from 1966, the annual rate was 5.8 percent.

Year-to-year changes in real wages also varied significantly between the two segments of the postwar period. In 8 of the 15 years between 1947 and 1962,

real rates of pay increased by 2.5 percent or more. During the second half of the postwar period, this rate of increase occurred only in the 2 years which coincided with the first two phases of the wage-price control program beginning in August 1971. Real rates actually declined over 2 years, and the increase was negligible in a third.

The major gains in real wages during the first half of the postwar period occurred during years of substantial price stability, notably 1948–50 and 1951–56. When prices moved upward as in 1956–58, the rate of real wage increase tended to fall. The major variations in year-to-year changes during the second half occurred after 1966, when the complex interaction of demand and cost factors produced the inflation which we still experience.

Real wage expectations

Almost from the beginning, the American experience has fostered expectations of secular gains in real wages, and hence in living standards, among the working population. Available statistics indicate that

Table 3.   Year-to-year percentage changes in money and real earnings, production and related workers, private nonfarm economy, and in Consumer Price Index, 1947–76

Year	Adjusted[1] average hourly earnings		Consumer Price Index
	Money	Real	
Average annual rate of increase:			
1947–62	4.6	2.5	2.0
1962–76	5.8	1.2	4.6
1947–48	8.0	.2	7.8
1948–49	4.8	5.8	−1.0
1949–50	3.7	2.7	1.0
1950–51	7.4	−.5	7.9
1951–52	5.0	2.8	2.2
1952–53	5.7	4.9	.8
1953–54	3.5	3.0	.5
1954–55	3.2	3.6	−.4
1955–56	5.2	3.7	1.5
1956–57	4.9	1.3	3.6
1957–58	4.1	1.4	2.7
1958–59	3.5	2.7	.8
1959–60	3.4	1.8	1.6
1960–61	3.1	2.1	1.0
1961–62	3.3	2.2	1.1
1962–63	2.9	1.7	1.2
1963–64	2.8	1.5	1.3
1964–65	3.7	2.0	1.7
1965–66	4.1	1.3	2.8
1966–67	4.8	1.9	2.9
1967–68	6.3	2.1	4.2
1968–69	6.6	1.3	5.3
1969–70	6.6	.7	5.9
1970–71	7.1	2.8	4.3
1971–72	6.5	3.2	3.3
1972–73	6.3	.1	6.2
1973–74	8.9	−2.1	11.0
1974–75	8.8	−.3	9.1
1975–76	7.0	1.3	5.7

[1]Adjusted for overtime (in manufacturing only) and for interindustry employment shifts.

in most periods the economy has yielded higher real rates of pay and, in the long run, impressive gains in leisure. Increases in real wages generally have been achieved through rising money rates coupled, especially during the 19th century, with essentially stable or falling prices. Inflation, even during the 20th century, has been episodic, at least until recent years.

It seems fair to say that until the period following World War II these expectations were basically unstructured. That is, gains in money and real wages were largely achieved through the operation of unorganized labor markets. Expectations, even in the comparatively small unionized sector, were not tied to annual wage bargains, but were more general and long term in character. This began to change with the great surge in union organization beginning in the mid-1930's. Other developments also altered the economic climate and the complexion of economic decisionmaking. For example, the Federal Government's role in economic management greatly expanded. This was accompanied by the growth of statistical systems that provided infinitely more, and more timely, information on output, employment, prices, and other economic magnitudes than had hitherto been available.[11]

During the postwar period, expectations of gains in real wages became at least partially institutionalized. Workers began to perceive such gains as accruing regularly and as related to a measurable trend in national productivity. This expectation was formalized, perhaps at the time fortuitously, in the celebrated 1948 contract between General Motors and the United Automobile Workers.[12] This 2-year agreement provided for an annual 3-cent-an-hour wage increase (about 2 percent), together with a cost-of-living escalator clause, to assure the GM worker "that the buying power of his hour of work will increase as the Nation's industrial efficiency improves."

The long-term collective bargaining agreement, defined as a contract extending for 2 years or more, was a social invention of considerable importance. It spread with comparative rapidity. By 1974, only 5.6 percent of major collective bargaining agreements, accounting for 3.2 percent of the workers covered by such contracts, were of less than 2 years' duration.[13] As developed through collective bargaining, the wage provisions of long-term contracts took many forms. They typically provided, however, for annual increases in money wages and the expectation, with or without escalator arrangements, that real wage gains would result. Annual pay adjustments also became common in the private nonunion sector. In the Federal white-collar civil service, the Federal Salary Reform Act of 1962 provided for annual review of Federal salary scales and for annual adjustments, subject to Executive Branch recommendations and Congressional action. The voluntary wage-price guideposts of 1962–66 focused on wage change in relation to the national productivity trend rate. The accompanying discussions of pay policy broadened anticipations of annual wage gains.

During the second half of the postwar period, as we have seen, the average annual increase in real rates of pay was approximately half the rate of increase obtained during the first half. Over the same period, the average annual rate of increase in output per hour in the private business sector fell by about one-third; the decline computed from 1966 was even more decisive (about one-half). Aside from shifts in income distribution toward wage earners, increases in productivity provide the basic source for real wage gains.

The highly favorable real wage experience during the first half of the postwar period created expectations that these gains would continue. However, the decline in the rate of productivity increase reduced the extent to which these expectations could be realized, at least for nonsupervisory workers as a class. Although this was not immediately apparent, it was clear that the upward movement of consumer prices beginning in 1966 threatened to erase further gains in real wages or even to lower living standards. Consequently, a cost-of-living factor increasingly began to accompany annual adjustments in money wages which, given the trend in productivity during the second half of the postwar period, were not fully sustainable in real terms. Thus, workers under major collective bargaining contracts with escalator provisions increased from 2.5 million in 1968 to 6.0 million in 1976.[14] Aside from formal escalation, efforts to compensate for cost-of-living changes through collective bargaining include "catch-up" adjustments and adjustments that attempt to anticipate the movement of living costs over the duration of the contract. In wage decisions in the much larger nonunion segment of the economy, substantial changes in living costs provide a powerful impetus for upward adjustments in money wages.

It is, of course, perfectly understandable that workers should attempt to protect their living standards from erosion by inflation. The point being made here is that during the second half of the postwar period the institutionalization of the annual wage increase, together with the effort to protect gains in money wages through an inflation factor, increased the difficulty of bringing an inflationary episode to an end. This is especially true when the effort is to protect the real value of wage increases that cannot be sustained by the recent trend in output per hour.

Historically, the winding down of wage-price spirals appears to have been greatly influenced by income lags built into the system.[15]

Historical growth in real wages

How does the postwar experience with real wages fit into the secular picture? A brief look at real wage trends in the United States from 1800 to the beginning of World War II may throw some light on recent experience.

Measures of the trend of money wages and of the cost of living for much of this long period are not entirely satisfactory. Stanley Lebergott presents "highly speculative" estimates of change in real wages for 1800–60 which represent an average annual increase of about 0.8 percent.[16] For 1860–90, Clarence Long estimates that average daily wages in manufacturing increased by 51 percent in real terms, or at an average annual rate of 1.4 percent.[17] Albert Rees estimates that real average hourly earnings in manufacturing increased 39 percent from 1890 to 1914, which also works out to an average annual rate of about 1.4 percent.[18] From 1914 to 1926, the Paul Douglas "all industry" index of real hourly earnings rose by 30 percent (an average annual rate of 2.2 percent); the Douglas figures for manufacturing alone are the same.[19] For the longer period from 1914 to 1939, the BLS average hourly earnings series for manufacturing shows a real increase at an average annual rate of 2.9 percent. Omitting the World War I years, the average annual increase was 2.8 percent if measured from 1920 and 2.7 percent if measured from 1922 (that is, after the postwar deflation).[20]

Although they must be interpreted with considerable caution, the above figures indicate that, at least prior to World War I, average annual gains in real wages over long periods have been under 2 percent. However, within the periods cited, sizable variations undoubtedly occurred in the rate of increase. Thus, Lebergott's estimates for 1800–60 indicate that practically the entire gain in real wages took place during the 30 years from 1820 to 1850. Long's 1860–90 estimates, when broken into 5-year intervals, show a very large increase for 1865–70, presumably in part a catch-up for a decline experienced during the Civil War, and thereafter rather uniform gains except for 1875–80, when practically no increase in real wages occurred. In Rees' estimates for 1890–1914, most of the increase occurred after 1898. For the period after World War I to 1939, the average annual rate of increase, in excess of 2.5 percent, appears high. It is interesting to note that the rate of increase was considerably greater during the depressed 1930's (for those with employment) than during the prosperous 1920's.

This variation in the rate of real wage increase reflects many factors, including labor market changes, technical innovations and their diffusion, the rate of capital formation, and money wage and price behavior. Aside from shortrun changes relating to the business cycle, there may be long swings in the rate of productivity growth which contribute to trend variations in real rates of pay.

Outlook for real wages

This review of the historical record of real wage increases raises a significant question. Is it possible for the United States to resume the rate of increase achieved during the first half of the period following World War II?

A return to the real wage trend of 1947–62 means that the trend rate of output per hour will have to approach that attained during the same period. This rate appears high by what limited insight we have into the historical productivity record.[21] Several factors were cited earlier as contributing to the lower trend in productivity during the second half of the postwar period; namely, a marked decline in the shift of manpower from farm to nonfarm activities, and changes in the age-sex composition of the labor force.

These labor force changes may have been accompanied by others, more complex and less quantifiable. Productivity depends in part on the willingness of the work force to produce, on factors of worker motivation and morale. It may be that, among some segments of the labor force, the 1960's witnessed shifts in attitudes toward jobs and work that were not conducive to high standards of performance. These shifts might have reflected the increasing affluence of the population; the fact that jobs were, in general, more readily available than in the past; the relaxation of hiring standards in response to both labor market and government pressures; the spread of government transfer payments, so that, to some extent, alternatives to work were created; and social discontent, particularly in regard to our involvement in Vietnam.

The persistent inflation of the past decade also may have contributed to the decline in the rate of productivity growth. Inflation adds to the uncertainties inherent in business planning and can inhibit capital formation and equity investment. It contributes to social unrest, which has repercussions in the labor market and on attitudes toward work.

Finally, the comparatively high productivity performance of the first half of the postwar period may reflect, in part, the flowering of technological innovations that had their roots in the dismal 1930's and the war years. Thus, the economy, exploiting a number of connected techniques, may have raised its productivity along an S–shaped curve and may not be able to carry the rise of real incomes beyond a certain level unless major technological advances occur.[22]

These various considerations—the interindustry shift of workers, the complex changes occurring in labor market composition and attitudes, the intricate and disturbing consequences of persistent inflation, and perhaps a break, or at least a slowing down, in technological innovation—may all bear on the ability of the economy to sustain a high rate of increase in output per hour. This in turn affects both the rate of increase in real wages that can emerge from the complex process of money wage determination and the expectations that workers realistically can entertain about the rate of improvement in their standard of living. ☐

-------FOOTNOTES-------

[1] E. J. Mishan, *The Costs of Economic Growth* (London, Staples Press, 1967). A somewhat more popular version appeared as *Technology and Growth: The Price We Pay* (New York, Praeger Publishers, 1969).

[2] For a description of the adjusted hourly earnings index, see Norman J. Samuels, "New hourly earnings index," *Monthly Labor Review,* December 1971, pp. 66–67.

[3] Computed from *Handbook of Labor Statistics 1975—Reference Edition,* Bulletin 1865 (Bureau of Labor Statistics, 1975), table 89, p. 202, for 1962–74; "Major Collective Bargaining Settlements, 1976" (Bureau of Labor Statistics release, Jan. 28, 1976), table A, for 1975–76.

[4] Computed from *National Survey of Professional, Administrative, Technical, and Clerical Pay, March 1976,* Bulletin 1931 (Bureau of Labor Statistics, 1976), table 1, p. 2.

[5] Thomas W. Gavett, "Measures of change in real wages and earnings," *Monthly Labor Review,* February 1972, pp. 48–53.

[6] A definitive measure would require a more rigorously constructed wage rate index, or, in view of the complex modern wage bargain, an index that also measures employer payments for supplementary benefits. The Bureau of Labor Statistics is now compiling such a measure, but the data published to date begin in the final quarter of 1975 and only relate to wage rates. See "The Bureau of Labor Statistics Introduces the First Measure of Wage and Salary Rate Trends From Its New Employment Cost Index" (Bureau of Labor Statistics, June 18, 1976).

[7] Paul H. Douglas, *Real Wages in the United States, 1890–1926* (Boston, Houghton Mifflin Co., 1930), p. 557.

[8] This measure covers the entire market sector of the economy. See J. R. Norsworthy and L. J. Fulco, "New sector definitions for productivity series," *Monthly Labor Review,* October 1976, pp. 40–42.

[9] Jerome A. Mark, *Current Developments in Productivity, 1973–74,* Report 436 (Bureau of Labor Statistics, 1975), pp. 7–14.

[10] See *Economic Report of the President,* 1972, table 8, p. 48, and table 9, p. 49.

[11] See the forthcoming study by Joseph W. Duncan and William C. Shelton, *Revolution in U.S. Government Statistics, 1926–76,* conducted under the auspices of the Statistical Policy Division, Office of Management and Budget.

[12] Nelson M. Bortz, "Cost-of-Living Clauses and the UAW–GM Pact," *Monthly Labor Review,* July 1948, pp. 1–7. See also Joseph W. Garbarino, *Wage Policy and Long-Term Contracts,* (Washington, The Brookings Institution, 1962), especially ch. 2.

[13] *Characteristics of Major Collective Bargaining Agreements, July 1, 1974,* Bulletin 1888 (Bureau of Labor Statistics, 1975), table 14, p. 7.

[14] Douglas LeRoy, "Scheduled wage increases and escalator provisions in 1977," *Monthly Labor Review,* January 1977, p. 23.

[15] For an elaboration of this point, see H. M. Douty, "Living costs, wages, and wage policy," *Monthly Labor Review,* June 1967, pp. 1–7.

[16] Computed from Stanley Lebergott, *Manpower in Economic Growth: The American Record Since 1800* (New York, McGraw-Hill, 1964), p. 154.

[17] Computed from Clarence D. Long, *Wages and Earnings in the United States, 1860–1890* (Princeton, N. J., Princeton University Press, 1960), table A–1, pp. 121–24, table B–1, p. 156, and table B–2, p. 157.

[18] Computed from Albert Rees, *Real Wages in Manufacturing, 1890–1914* (Princeton, N. J., Princeton University Press, 1961), table 44, p. 120.

[19] Computed from Douglas, *Real Wages,* table 73, p. 205, and table 24, p. 108. Although relating only to manufacturing, the Rees rather than the Douglas real wage index was used for the period 1890–1914 primarily because the Rees cost-of-living index for deflating money wages appears superior to the Douglas index. For 1914–1926, Douglas used, with some weighting modifications, the BLS index. See Douglas, pp. 43–59.

[20] Computed from *Handbook of Labor Statistics 1975—Reference Edition,* Bulletin 1865 (Bureau of Labor Statistics, 1975), table 98, p. 248, and table 122, p. 313.

[21] *Historical Statistics of the United States: Colonial Times to 1957* (Bureau of the Census, 1960), tabular series W1–3, p. 599.

[22] I am indebted for this formulation to ideas expressed in a letter from Sir Henry Phelps Brown, Professor of Economics, Emeritus, London School of Economics.

36

How tax policy dampens economic growth

While the mid-April tax deadline will give millions of Americans the worst kind of Saturday night fever, signs are hinting at a refreshing new swing in tax policy. The House Democratic Caucus voted last week to defer next year's scheduled increases in Social Security taxes, passed only six months ago. And Congress is increasingly receptive to the evidence, now being marshaled by many economists, strongly supporting tax cuts but arguing that to spur economic growth and employment the Administration should pitch these cuts more heavily toward the business sector.

These economists are concerned about what they call "the wedge." They argue that over the years, increased taxes have driven a larger wedge between the cost of labor or capital—as measured by the price paid by the employer or borrower—and the aftertax receipts of the worker or investor. "The decision whether or not to work or invest depends on aftertax income," says the University of Southern California's Arthur B. Laffer, a prominent spokesman for this new wave in public tax policy. "And more precisely, it's a matter of the effective marginal tax rate. That's the one people base their decisions on, the rate at the margin."

So the bigger the bite taken by taxes, the less incentive there is for working, saving, or investing. These reduced incentives result in slower economic growth and higher unemployment, Laffer argues.

Effect on savings. The sheer magnitude of the federal sector's tax needs—amounting to some $400 billion in fiscal 1978—means that the impact of the wedge on total output could be enormous. Michael J. Boskin of Stanford University, in an analysis soon to be published in the prestigious *Journal of Political Economy*, estimates that the tax wedge in capital markets alone—the difference between what it costs companies to raise capital and the aftertax income to those who save and provide the capital—cuts saving and capital accumulation by a mind-numbing $40 billion to $50 billion a year. Boskin's estimate of this wedge amounts to some 20% of business investment. "My model is the first to show that taxes have a significant effect on the saving rate," he notes. Since higher-income groups save more than lower-income groups, to the extent that the Administration's tax proposals empha-

size taxing higher incomes, they could further magnify the nation's capital shortage. "The investment tax credit and accelerated depreciation are usually thought of as breaks for big business," Boskin says, "but that's drastically off the mark. They narrow the capital-market wedge, spurring productivity and employment."

Boskin is not alone in arguing that the tax wedge hits saving and capital formation hardest. "We've got to get productivity up, and that takes capital forma-

Paul S. Conklin

Economist Laffer: Increased taxes reduce the incentive for saving and working.

tion," says Washington consultant Charls E. Walker. "But in this country we've taxed saving, what with all the layers of corporate and personal taxation, as if it were a sin." Walker, a former Treasury Under Secretary, hopes that Congress can be persuaded to approximately double the four-percentage-point cut in corporate tax rates proposed over the next three years by the Carter Administration.

Long-term goals. Congress may be open to persuasion because of a mounting body of evidence, derived from new data and improved statistical techniques, which indicates that many kinds of tax cuts would involve far smaller revenue losses to the government than had previously been thought. Indeed, in the case of tax cuts for capital, Walker suspects that it may be possible to

produce that Nirvana of economic philosophy—the free lunch. "I think we may well be on the upper part of the curve, where tax cuts on saving would actually generate higher government revenues," he says. In other words, the higher rates of return to business that result from tax cuts could stimulate so much more investment and output that total government receipts would ultimately rise above the level obtainable at the higher tax rates. As chairman of the American Council for Capital Formation, Walker recently hired Laffer to construct a revenue-forecasting model to capture such long-run effects.

Laffer, for his part, will also be looking closely at the effects of the tax wedge in labor markets, where the entire spectrum of employer and employee contributions for such items as unemployment compensation, workmen's compensation, and Social Security go hand-in-hand with income taxes to create a yawning gap between what it costs a company to employ a worker and what the worker actually gets in aftertax income. "I don't even want to say at this point that it's savings that are hit worst," Laffer says. "The disincentives for unemployed inner-city residents are really among the highest, because they often lose social welfare benefits by taking a job, as well as having to pay taxes on the earnings." Laffer maintains that jobs and output would receive a major direct stimulus if the employment wedge could be reduced, particularly for those currently receiving benefits and for teenagers, housewives, and others whose earnings are subject to high marginal rates because of the earnings of other family members.

But at least until midyear, when Laffer expects to obtain his preliminary results, the data seem clearest on

The wedge between costs and aftertax income limits investments and jobs

taxation of investment income. Another model recently completed under contract for the National Association of Manufacturers by Washington consultant Norman Ture, estimates that corporate tax reduction would result in significantly higher federal revenues 10 years later. Presenting his results to a recent hearing of the House Ways & Means Committee, Ture said that an effective rate reduction averaging 5.5% would cost the Treasury $8 billion in direct loss during its 10th year—but by that time would have generated sufficient growth in sales, investment, and employment to account for $17 billion in "feedback" revenue gains, netting out to a plus of $9 billion for Treasury coffers. Noted University of Chicago Economist Arnold C. Harberger, in an evaluation conducted for the NAM, has praised the model for breaking new ground and its ability to analyze the effects of tax changes.

Shortsighted estimates. Boskin, however, is not sure just how to interpret the gains claimed by Ture and anticipated by Walker and Laffer. "If 1988 revenues are higher," he asks, "how do you discount that back to 1978? How much is it worth right now?" But Boskin has no qualms about the fundamental message of the current research: The estimates of revenue loss that are presented to Congress by the Treasury concerning each year's tax reduction proposals have been seriously overstated. The estimates have generally been limited to first-year impacts, Boskin explains, and they simp-

Treasury estimates of revenue losses from tax cuts seem overstated

ly do not allow sufficient time for the full stimulative effects on the nation's economic activity and the size of the tax base to show up.

This is largely the result of a kind of limitation common to all of the major forecasting models now available for the U. S. economy, according to the new wave of federal tax theorists. As they see it, the models, from the oldest Wharton vintage to the latest from Chase Econometrics, have never outgrown their preoccupation with forecasting the next year or two of the current business cycle. This is no small challenge in itself, but it has led modelers to neglect longer-run interaction within the economy.

Congress' response. Broad data on the overall economy that show little detail about how individuals behave have usually been adequate for short-run forecasting purposes. This contributed, the wedgers argue, to such mistaken views as the insensitivity of savings to the interest rate. "In fact, the saving rate has looked pretty stable a lot of the time," Boskin concedes. "But that was brought about by a great number of offsetting developments." Boskin maintains that data covering the savings, work, and consumption decisions of different age and sex groups within the total population make it clear that saving does respond significantly to changes in the aftertax rate of interest.

According to Walker, whose own experience at the Treasury should be a guide, the evidence from the new models will have a major effect on the legislative outlook. "Congress puts a lot of weight in its tax decisions on the expected revenue effects," he says. "If the models show that past assumptions have been wrong, Congress will respond."

37

Long Swings II—Kuznets explains history

Massive immigration from Europe formed
the basis for the long swings discovered
by the Nobel laureate. But it's unlikely
that those unique events will recur—
though some other force could emerge.

Simon Kuznets, who won the Nobel prize for
economics in 1971, is not often in the public
eye. He has neither spearheaded a revolution
in monetary theory and policy nor written a
best-selling textbook. But his work on long
swings in the growth of population and related
economic activity takes on new relevance at
a time when it's more fashionable to be gloomy
than confident about the future.

Kuznets's work — both in substance and
style — contrasts sharply with that of the unfortunate Nikolai Kondratyev, whose claim to
discovery of 50-year supercycles was dissected
in last month's article.

First, Kuznets is a superb quantitative re-
searcher whose pioneering work on concepts
and measures of national income has changed
the way in which governments the world over
look at economic problems. Unlike Kondratyev,
he is meticulous, not only in estimating economic magnitudes, but in distinguishing between the seasonal, cyclical and longer-term
forces that impinge on them. Second, Kuznets's claims are both scientific and modest.
He contends only that several advanced industrial countries were affected by 20-odd-year
growth swings between the mid-1870s and
World War I. And what's more, he offers a
rationale, a theory, to explain his findings.
For unlike Kondratyev and his contemporary
followers, Kuznets does not rest his case on
faith in the mechanical unfolding of a super-
cycle.

Business cycles, which endure from two to
10 or so years, are highly visible and, save for

the cases where the recessions are exceedingly mild, inflict the pain of high unemployment, bankruptcies, credit crunches and inventory gluts on the body economic. But long swings — alternating periods of fast and slow growth — are unseen and unfelt until long after they've passed. And that's why it's important to have a theory and, in testing it, to distinguish carefully between the effects of a hypothesized long-swing mechanism and the statistical noise that's created by business cycles.

How not to

The exercise depicted in the first chart on page 13 shows how not to approach the long swings — or why time-series data shouldn't be indiscriminately cooked. By following some well-worn steps, first converting levels to first differences — changes from one year to the next — and then smoothing those changes with moving averages, it's easy to uncover a long swing in the real gross national product of the United States that runs from the later 1950s to the early 1970s.

But why does this long swing emerge? And what, if anything, does it mean? The long swing on the chart is the creature of the business cycle pattern that is indicated by the shaded areas. Two relatively deep recessions — 1957-58 and especially 1973-75 — were separated by a long period, particularly the 1960s, in which recessions were few and mild. And the result is a long swing, the precise shape of which hinges on the number of terms in the moving averages. Note that the dating of the peak occurs in 1963 in one case, and in 1969 in the other. Alternative methods of smoothing also yield long swings that are roughly similar. They are common products of the same business cycle pattern, and until it is demonstrated that there's a rationale lurking beneath the numbers, such swings are meaningless.

Now to contrast that mechanical exercise with Kuznets's long swings. What Kuznets argues is that swings in the growth of population generate long swings in closely related activities, such as home construction, and that from the mid-1870s to World War I their impact is to be seen in the pattern of GNP growth. And to explain those phenomena, Kuznets outlines a self-generating long-swing mechanism.

But before plunging forward, it's necessary to understand just what Kuznets means when he speaks of population-sensitive activities. The point can be most easily grasped by contrasting the impact of population change on the demand for homes and the demand for paper napkins. Consider a rigidly ordered community in which 1) the ratio of real income to the population is fixed and 2) prevailing social standards call for tying home construction and paper napkin production to population growth. Assume further that each addition to population is matched by the virtually instant construction of a new dwelling unit, and — unearthly paradise that it is — that existing homes need never be replaced or repaired.

Suppose that over a seven-year period the population grows as indicated in the accompanying table. If the paper-napkin-to-people ratio is set at 1 pound of napkins per person annually, napkin production increases from 4,950 to 5,700 pounds with annual percentage increases that are identical with those of total population, changes ranging from 1.0% to 5.0%.

Year	Population	Change in population	Percentage increase	Percentage change of increase
1	4,950	—	—	—
2	5,000	+50	+1.0	—
3	5,250	+250	+5.0	+500
4	5,390	+140	+2.7	−44
5	5,450	+60	+1.1	−57
6	5,600	+50	+0.9	−17
7	5,700	+100	+1.8	+100

But home construction is a very different matter. Homes, like diamonds, are forever, and so changes in the total stock depend not on the level of population, but on annual changes. And the result is that there are very wide swings in new housing construction, ranging from +500% to −57%. In short, home construction, unlike paper napkin production, is very sensitive to population change. So long as population rises, year-to-year percentage

Recipe for "long swings"
Begin with GNP levels. . .

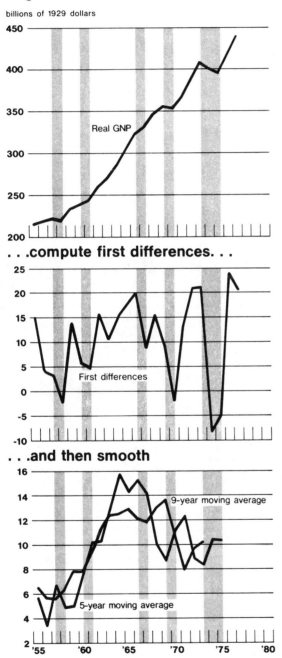

billions of 1929 dollars

. . .compute first differences. . .

. . .and then smooth

changes in home production will far exceed those of population.

What happens, though, if the community's population falls to 5,650 — or by 0.9% — in the 8th year? Napkin production will also dip by the same amount. But again, home construction is different. There are now 50 vacant homes and, since those structures have perpetual lives, production in year 8 is 0, not −50 as indicated by the presumptive demand. Now suppose that population turns around in year 9 and rises to 5,675. Napkin production begins to recover, but home construction remains at zero because of the overhang of 25 vacancies. And it continues to be dormant until population again exceeds 5,700.

Thus the basis for long swings in the output of long-lived commodities such as homes. Restrictive assumptions of the sort made here are not valid in the wider world. Real income isn't rigidly tied to population, nor is the stock of housing. Homes are destroyed, repaired and replaced. But the well-documented existence of long housing swings in a number of countries attests to the analytical pertinence of our parable.

Now, back to the main line. Population growth has never ceased to enchant Simon Kuznets. In his prize-winning book, *Secular Movements in Production and Prices* — published in 1930 but completed about three years earlier — he wrote: "The growth of population appears to us human beings as a self-generating process, itself independent, yet influencing all social phenomena. But in the industrial system of a country, population is just another productive factor and its size from year to year is of the same significance as, for example, the annual production of pig-iron. To treat the growth of population as an independent dynamic factor implies an anthropocentric delusion as to the specific function of man in his productive and procreative capacities." In a sense, all of Kuznets's subsequent work on long swings is an elaboration of this basic theme.

The gist of Kuznets's long swing schema is captured in the second chart, page 14, which shows 10-year moving averages of annual changes in total population, net immigration and gross construction. Note that the congruence of the three curves is greatest in the period from the mid-1870s to 1914 — the golden age of the Atlantic community when large masses of people, as well as goods and capital, migrated from Europe to the Americas.

Links in the chain

To explain that congruence, Kuznets posits a complex set of interrelationships. The links of the chain are as follows:

• Swings in the growth of the total U.S. population were dominated by waves of immigrants from Europe, people lured westward by the promise of higher living standards. Kuznets's measures of that lure or "pull" — one that he admits is imperfect — are per-capita changes in the flow of goods to consumers.

• The swings in population growth generate long swings in such "population-sensitive" components of capital formation as home and railroad construction. They accounted for more than 40% of total capital formation in the 1870s. The capital formation swings, in turn, gave rise to swings in the growth of GNP.

• During the period of highly congruent swings in population and the population-sensitive elements of capital formation, there were inverse swings in the other components of capital formation, such as producers' durables and nonresidential construction. So early on in the period from 1870 to 1914, there was a crowding-out effect within the United States that Kuznets attributes to capacity bottlenecks. And abroad — at least in some of the countries from which people were emigrating — there is evidence of swings in population and GNP growth that are the inverse of those in the United States.

Kuznets finds two long growth swings of about 20 years in duration in the U.S. GNP between the 1870s and World War I. The first turns up in 1873, reaches a peak in 1882 and troughs in 1893; the second peaks in 1908 and declines until 1916. And he postulates that they may be explained by a self-generating cyclical mechanism. In 1958, he wrote that: "The long swings in additions to per-capita

Swings in growth
Kuznets's basic elements

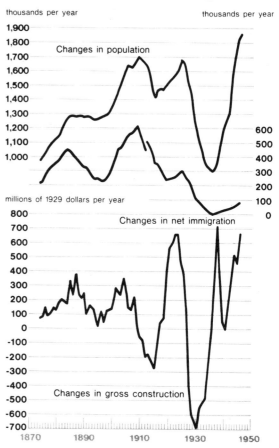

10-year moving averages.
Sources: Population: S. Kuznets *Capital in the American Economy* (NBER) 1961, 624. Immigration: S. Kuznets and E. Rubin, *Immigration and the Foreign Born* (NBER) 1954, 95-6-7. Gross Construction: M. Abramowitz, *Evidences of Long Swings in Aggregate Construction since the Civil War* (NBER) 1964, 142.

flow of goods to consumers resulted, with some lag, in long swings first in the net migration balance and then in the natural increase yielding swing in total population growth. The latter then induced, again with some lag, similar swings in population-sensitive capital formation, which caused inverted swings in 'other' capital formation, and in changes in per-capita flow of goods to consumers. The swings in the latter then started another swing in the net migration balance and in natural increase, and so on. This, however, is a tentative sketch — and does not claim even rough validity."

Later, in 1961, Kuznets concluded that "If there was such a self-perpetuating mechanism of long swings before World War I, it disappeared thereafter." And he cites, as reasons, restrictions on immigration to the United States, a short relative decline in the population-sensitive components of capital formation and a growth of production capacity that eliminated the inverse swings.

That ends the Kuznets story, but two loose ends remain. The first is whether there was in fact a self-perpetuating mechanism that produced the long swings. An affirmative answer might imply that similar self-generating mechanisms may generate long swings in the future. But it's an issue that's still unresolved despite the use of new — but perhaps not really sophisticated — statistical techniques that have been used in testing long-swing hypotheses. Other researchers — notably Milton Friedman and Anna J. Schwartz, who were Kuznets's colleagues at the National Bureau of Economic Research — believe that the long swings were episodic rather than cyclical. And that implies that they can be explained by fluctuations in the growth of the money stock, wars and deep recessions.

Another unresolved issue is whether the Kuznets cycle is really dead. A former student of Kuznets's, Richard Easterlin of the University of Pennsylvania, thinks not. He suggests that there's a new, self-perpetuating mechanism that may produce long swings in the growth of the domestic labor force, and cites in evidence the major upsurge in the number of 15-to-29 year olds, both absolutely and in relation to those aged 30 to 64. Because of the less than perfect substitution between younger and older workers, employment prospects for the 15-29 group aren't bright. Moreover, in attempting to combat higher youth unemployment through stimulative monetary and fiscal policy, the federal government is stoking inflation.

So what Easterlin contends is that the change in the age structure of the labor force is in part responsible for the current coupling of relatively high unemployment with inflation. At the moment the proportion of people in the 15 to 29 group is extremely high. But if Easterlin is right, counterforces are already in motion.

The current surfeit of young people has resulted in a deterioration of their labor market position and a relative decline of their well-being. As a consequence, they are marrying later and having fewer children. So about 20 years hence — in the 1990s — today's decisions will result in an abnormally low proportion of young in the population. And with the relatively smaller supply, their economic position will be enhanced. Affluence will then encourage earlier marriage and more children — thus launching a new baby boom.

It's an intriguing hypothesis that has yet to be tested. And while the critical evidence is not yet available, it seems likely that Easterlin will have greater success with his self-generating population mechanism — the line of causation that runs from economic well-being to age of marriage and childbearing — than with the link between that cycle and inflation.

The bottom line of any consideration of long swings and their impact on the economic future is their relevance. Are they something that most business managers and most investors ought to ponder in formulating plans for the future? The answer is a qualified negative. Kuznets's long swings — whether they were episodic or products of a self-generating mechanism — are phenomena of a past that's not likely to be reenacted. But some nagging doubts remain. That doesn't mean that decision-makers should take the popular scare stories with any more than a grain of salt. But like the aging agnostic who occasionally prayed — just in case — it's best to keep an open mind.

38

AMERICANS

The structure of a nation's economy, the problems it faces, and the solutions it devises for those problems are determined in large measure by the people who compose it. Everyone who will be a mature worker, pensioner, or executive in the U.S. in the next 20 years is already born. By looking closely at who these people are, what they will want, and what they can do, business and government can tell a great deal about what sort of country the U.S. will be in the next two decades and what sort of challenges it will face.

Even economists consider demographics—the study of populations—a rather unexciting and unrewarding branch of their science. Business executives, distracted by inflation, shifting markets, and increasing government intervention in the private sector, have had little time to listen to the demographers.

The U.S., however, is going through some fundamental demographic changes that forecasters and policymakers will have to take into account. The economy is already feeling the impact of these shifts, and there is more—much more—to come in the future. "Demographic statistics make dull reading," says economist Michael L. Wachter of the University of Pennsylvania's Wharton School, "but they helped lay the groundwork for our current economic problems."

The most obvious change in the U.S. population is simply that it is growing older. In 1970 the median age was just under 28. Within three years, it will reach 30, and by the turn of the century, it will hit 35. Such a change means a shift in patterns of consumption and incomes. And, inevitably, changes in social attitudes as well. "The growing mood of conservatism in American society is probably related to the maturation of the population and the waning of the youth culture," says Jeffrey Evans of the National Institute of Child Health & Human Development.

But the steady upward march of the median age gives a deceptive impression of orderly progression. Actually, the structure of the U.S. population is due for some sudden and disconcerting shifts, which have their origins in

How drastic shifts in

CHANGE

demographics affect the economy

changes in the birth rate years ago. The various age groups that make up the total population—the "cohorts," as the demographers refer to them—will expand dramatically and then shrink abruptly as these waves occur.

Baby boom, then bust

Three drastic shifts in the rate at which the U.S. population reproduces and increases itself have occurred in the past half century. The first was the "birth dearth" of the Depression years, when total births dropped to about 2.5 million from an average of close to 3 million a year. At the time, the fertility rate (the number of children born to the average woman in her lifetime) dropped close to 2.1—the replacement level that would lead to a stable population if maintained indefinitely.

The second shift was the well-publicized "baby boom" of the postwar era, which continued into the early 1960s. In the mid-1950s the fertility rate shot up to 3.8, and the number of births each year surged past the 4 million mark.

Then came the third shift—the "baby bust"—marked by a progressively steep decline in the fertility rate, which had fallen to 1.76 by 1976—far below the population replacement level. And this, in turn, brought the number of births down to 3.13 million in that year.

The unstabilizing effects of such a baby boom, preceded and followed by a very low birth rate, are the source of many of the problems the U. S. has faced in recent years. And the problems are by no means ended. "Because of the low birth rates both before and after its occurrence, this group of cohorts is like a melon being digested by a boa constrictor," says demographer Denis F. Johnston of the Census Bureau. "It will undergo strains and pose a succession of problems for the nation's institutions as it moves through the age cycle."

The baby boom cohorts made their mark on U. S. society and on U. S. markets long before they left home. School districts will be paying for years on the bonds they have floated to provide educational facilities that may or may not be needed in the future. Manufacturers of stereo sets and blue jeans will have to hope that tastes will not change with age.

The real impact of the baby boom on the U. S. economy, however, began to be felt in the late 1960s, when the first cohort entered the labor market. The problems were masked for a while by growing college enrollments and by the manpower needs of an overheated economy and the Vietnam war. But by the early 1970s, rising unemployment figures brought the issue into sharp focus: The U. S. economy must create jobs and incomes for a rapidly expanding mature labor force in the next decade. After that, it must adjust to a slower rate of growth and eventually, perhaps, to very modest growth by historical standards. Beginning after the year 2000, the economy must find ways to keep the mounting costs of pensions and retirement income from overwhelming the producing workers.

Declining population

The immediate problem—and the problem of the early 1980s—is to produce jobs that will absorb these new workers into the economic system. This may become somewhat easier as the baby boom cohorts grow older, since the tremendous acceleration in the growth of the working-age population will soon be behind us. The growth of the 18-to-24-year-old group is now slowing sharply, and by the 1980s, this cohort will be declining steadily—a process that will continue for another 15 years. Over the next 12 years, the most rapidly increasing element of the population will be 25 to 44 years old. On the whole, of course, this is the most employable age group in the U. S. labor force and the most productive. It is also the group with the highest spending profile. Its numbers will jump by 35% to 78 million in 1990 from 58 million today. After 1985, however, the 25-to-34-year-old segment will top out, and it will decline throughout the 1990s.

Meanwhile, the 45-to-54-year age group will shrink a bit until the second half of the 1980s, when it will enter a period of rapid growth. By 1995, the baby boom generation will begin to swell the ranks of the 55- to 64-year-olds. Throughout the 1980s and 1990s, the over-64 group will grow steadily, but as a percentage of total population, it will remain steady at 11% to 12%. The enormous increase in this group will start in the second decade of the next century, as the baby boom cohorts become senior citizens.

The 1980s, therefore, shapes up as a decade of enormous opportunities for growth as well as for severe strains on the economy. In the 1990s, with an older and more slowly expanding labor force, growth will come harder, but the quality of life may be easier to improve. After the year 2000, the U. S. will enter a new period of economic and social strain as the number of people no longer working increases in proportion to the number still on the job.

After the year 2000, however, the labor force will consist increasingly of people who are not yet born. And demographers, who failed entirely to foresee both the baby boom and the subsequent baby bust, are qualifying their predictions about the future of the birth rate with a lot of caveats. Most think that the birth rate will rise somewhat as the baby boom generation enters its 30s and as women who have postponed childbearing face a now-or-never choice.

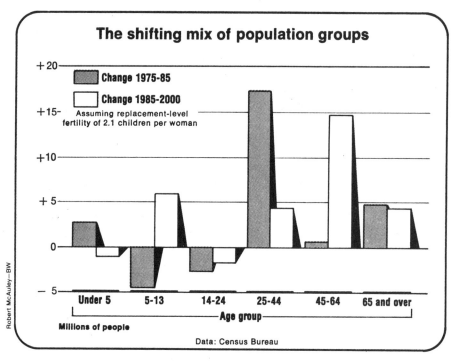

The shifting mix of population groups

- ■ Change 1975-85
- □ Change 1985-2000

Assuming replacement-level fertility of 2.1 children per woman

Age group: Under 5 · 5-13 · 14-24 · 25-44 · 45-64 · 65 and over

Millions of people

Robert McAuley—BW

Data: Census Bureau

But though birth and fertility rates did pick up a bit last year, few experts see a dramatic surge in fertility ahead.

The Census Bureau's official view is that the fertility rate will eventually move up and stabilize around the replacement level. But Robert L. Clark of the University of North Carolina thinks the figure will be even lower. "Of course, the picture could change overnight," he says, "but the current social and economic trends suggest that fertility will tend to stay somewhat below the replacement level."

Among the trends cited by Clark and others are such social phenomena as the falling marriage and rising divorce rates, deferred childbearing, the upswing in single-parent, two wage-earner, and individual households, and higher education levels. Add to that the increased work experience among young women and their greater career opportu-

nities, the high cost of rearing and educating children, and the ever-increasing usage of effective birth control techniques. Says Clark: "All of these trends tend to reinforce each other."

Given such powerful factors, demographers can draw some tentative conclusions about the future:

The over-all rate of unemployment should begin to drop in the 1980s as the rear guard of the baby boom generation enters its mature working years. Productivity should increase for a while, reflecting a more experienced work force. This, in turn, may help dampen inflation. By the mid-1980s, however, labor surplus will give way to labor scarcity. Economic growth will slow, and inflationary pressures are apt to rise.

Government spending on education and crime prevention is likely to slacken. In the wake of sagging birth rates, primary school enrollments have already plummeted in many localities and secondary school attendance is also beginning to decline sharply—both as a result of the baby bust and of the increasing number of dropouts. At the same time, college enrollment rates have also been declining, particularly for males. "If present trends continue," says the Census Bureau's Johnston, "the number of undergraduates will fall faster than the college-age population for at least another decade."

Similarly, crime rates are beginning to subside in many areas. More than 75% of such crimes as burglary, robbery, and auto theft are committed by youngsters under 25, and their numbers are beginning to wane. "Because crime is associated with unemployment, and because joblessness among teenagers may

Decades of successive strains as the postwar 'baby boom' generation matures

be expected to lessen as their numbers decrease, the crime rate could fall significantly in the 1980s," speculates psychologist Eugene Winograd of Emory University in Atlanta.

The aging of the baby boom group may eventually dampen the population shift from the Northeast and Midwest to the Sunbelt. "In the past," says Rand Corp. demographer Peter Morrison, "high birth rates often hid the fact that migration was occurring. But when rates dropped sharply in the 1970s, a lot of areas suddenly found themselves losing population." Since the young adult group most prone to migrate will be declining in size in the 1980s, Morrison expects the tempo of migration to slow somewhat—particularly if the trend toward two-paycheck families continues.

The baby boom cohorts are likely to experience continuing difficulties in satisfying career and income aspirations—simply because of the competitive pressures generated by their sheer numbers—just as they had faced heightened unemployment in their teens. To be sure, the lack of seasoned managers to oversee the flood tide of younger workers will create a problem for business (page 68). And it will provide rapid advancement for a lucky few (and delayed retirement for some managers). But most of the baby boom cohorts probably face the prospect of heightened competition as well as relatively depressed incomes and advancement opportunities during most of their working lives, particularly in the context of slow labor force growth.

Compounding the problem is the fact that this group is the best educated in the nation's history, with more than 40% of them estimated to have attended college by the time they are 30. At the same time, their ranks include a number of youngsters, primarily blacks and other minorities, whose educational attainments have been falling sharply in recent years. In both cases, the situation spells frustration: The college-educated are having to settle for lower-level positions than they anticipated, and the disadvantaged are having trouble finding any jobs at all.

As a result, some experts see "severe social disruptions" in the decades ahead, with little chance that the economy (which may then be on a permanent slow growth track) will ever supply enough high-level jobs to match the educational attainments and aspirations of the baby boom group. The Census Bureau's Johnston, however, is more sanguine, predicting a variety of responses to the new economic realities. "Many young people will work harder and seek more education in their adult years to boost their chances of advancement," he says.

"Others may downgrade material affluence and the work ethic. And a few may seek an outlet in efforts to change the system."

The Wharton School's Wachter feels that the chief problem may lie with the disadvantaged. "We are in danger," he says, "of creating a permanent group of marginal workers whose lack of skills and early job experience, combined with high welfare and jobless benefits, will keep them chronically unemployed."

Notwithstanding the frustrations of the job market, the outlook for consumer spending appears bright—at least during the near term. As Leon W. Taub of Chase Econometric Associates Inc. puts it: "The new consumers may feel poorer, but they will be better off in real terms as the economy continues to grow. And with fewer children to support and more two-wage-earner families, discretionary income will rise." To give some idea of the pending surge in purchasing power, Conference Board economist Fabian Linden estimates that the U. S. will add 7 million families in the 25-to-44-year age group in the decade ending in 1985. "By that year," he says, "the income of that group will have risen 80%, and it will account for half of all consumer spending."

Demographic trends suggest where much of that income will go. Housing demand should be particularly strong in the next few years, "both for the single-family homes that are typically purchased by young families in their early 30s, and for apartments that cater to the growing number of single-adult, one-child, and childless households," notes demographer James A. Sweet of the University of Wisconsin. Adds consumer economist Carol Brock Kenney of Loeb Rhoades, Hornblower & Co.: "Houses will be smaller, better-insulated, and will require smaller appliances with multipurpose functions. And their sales will spur demand for household durables, textiles, and do-it-yourself products."

For marketers, though, the trick will be to look beyond the gross age shifts in the population to changes in living patterns. For instance, to deal with a slowing birthrate and with increased competition for the food dollar from fast-food outlets and convenience stores, supermarket chains are now altering their product mixes and interior designs. And a recent study unveiled by the Coca-Cola Co. indicates that although teenagers consume more soft drinks than their elders, those in their 40s now consume more of the beverages than they did in their younger years. "This suggests that demand for many so-called youth products can continue to grow as

the population ages," says a Wall Street consumer analyst.

In general, the experts feel that demographic trends suggest a stress on quality, durability, and variety in future purchases, with more dollars going to small consumer durables, entertainment, travel, recreation, adult education, and other convenience- and experience-oriented goods and services.

A need for added capital

Behind such optimistic appraisals of tomorrow's markets, of course, lies the assumption that the government can devise and implement economic policies appropriate to the changing economic and demographic climate. And to economist Wachter, that means the recognition that aggregate demand stimulus will worsen, not solve, the stagflation dilemma currently facing the nation. Following the lead of George L. Perry of the Brookings Institution, Wachter argues that the failure to recognize that structural changes in the labor force—the influx of low-skilled teenagers and young women—had changed the unemployment-inflation trade-off in the mid-1960s permitted policymakers to overheat the economy, sparking a sharp rise in inflation. "We're all paying the penalty of that mistake now," he says.

What is more, the problem is still with us. Wachter and his economist wife Susan have calculated that structural shifts in the labor force, together with high jobless and welfare benefits and a rising minimum wage, have now pushed the noninflationary unemployment rate to the 5½% range, compared to 4% in 1955. "And due to a continuing lag in capital investment by industry," Wachter says, "it could be as high as 6%."

The solution as he sees it is clear. Because labor force growth is about to slacken as the baby boom completes its entry into the prime work force, structural unemployment can be expected to decline. But taking advantage of this favorable shift requires added capital spending, since a failure to expand physical capacity now could result in supply bottlenecks well before the economy reaches its new full employment potential. Thus, Wachter favors vastly expanded incentives for investment, far beyond what President Carter is proposing in his current tax package. "We should be thinking," Wachter says, "about things like a 12% tax credit, accelerated depreciation, and allowing companies to expense the added costs of new health, pollution, and energy usage regulations that may be imposed after a new plant is built."

At the same time, Wachter argues

that there is an immediate need for upgrading the skills of disadvantaged youngsters in the 16-to-24-year age group so that they will be in a better position to take advantage of improving job opportunities when the labor market tightens in a few years. "Time is running out for this group, which has suffered extraordinarily high rates of unemployment in recent years," he warns. Rather than public service employment, which takes youngsters off the streets but provides few skills that are transferable to the private sector, Wachter favors financial inducements such as wage subsidies and tax credits to encourage industry to hire and train the low-skilled. "Such programs would not only alleviate human suffering but would pay off for industry in the coming decade when labor supplies will tighten."

And what of the era beyond 1985? Assuming that the U. S. is now on a permanent path leading toward population stability, most economists who have looked at the implications of such a scenario are not overly concerned. "Higher immigration, delayed retirement, and increased labor force participation by women may well soften the blow of a reduced flow of domestic workers," says Larry Neal of the University of Illinois. Neal also points to the practice of such countries as West Germany and Switzerland in importing "guest laborers" to supplement their work forces.

Nor do economists worry—as they did during the depression—that the econo-my will suffer "secular stagnation" because of a lack of adequate demand to stimulate investment. "If there's one thing we've learned—perhaps too well— it's how to maintain aggregate demand," says Wachter. While overall economic growth will eventually slacken in line with slower labor force growth, Neal notes that per-capita income and the ratio of capital to labor would both tend to rise. "With zero population growth, productivity would tend to increase as the result of greater investment in physical and human capital, and we might even improve the rate of advance of technological progress," he speculates.

Intergenerational conflict

Perhaps the most serious problem in the current demographic scenario is the burden that a large retired group imposes on the working population when pensions are financed on a pay-as-you-go basis and when the ratio of retirees to workers increases. The hefty increases in Social Security taxes mandated by recent legislation are only the first taste of this problem, which will take on massive proportions in the next century—when the baby boom generation reaches retirement age.

In another 60 years, the so-called dependency ratio (the ratio of wage earners to beneficiaries) is expected to fall from its current level of 3.2 to 1 to less than 2 to 1. Many observers fear that the prospect of ever-escalating payroll taxes will spark a rebellion among younger workers, who will eventually balk at paying the tab for their elders. Since the political clout of the elderly will increase with their numbers, such a conflict could tear apart the nation's social fabric.

Even if the intergenerational conflict is contained, economists see the possibility of serious economic effects. Harvard University's Martin Feldstein believes that the scheduled rises in Social Security benefits will inspire workers to reduce their savings for retirement, resulting in less capital for business investment, and thereby slowing productivity gains and the advance in real wages.

Chase Econometric's Taub also worries about the impact of a growing tax burden on individual incentives. "At some point, people may simply stop working as hard," he says.

Weighty as these problems are, however, they are not intractable. Joseph J. Spengler, economics professor emeritus of Duke University, believes that one key answer is extending the retirement age. Another solution might be to scale back the growth of future retirement benefits, allowing the replacement of wages to decline on a percentage basis during a period when everyone is more affluent.

"The important thing," says Spengler, "is that analysis of demographic trends allows us to see clearly the dimensions of future problems, and that is the essential first step toward their solution."

39

Mediating Growth Tensions Daniel Bell

O ne of the more remarkable aspects of public policy debate in the United States, as Anthony Downs pointed out several years ago, is that "American public attention rarely remains sharply focused upon any one domestic issue for very long—even if it involves a continuing problem of crucial importance to society." Instead, as Downs continues, "a systematic 'issue-attention cycle' seems strongly to influence public attitudes and behavior concerning most key domestic problems. Each of the problems suddenly leaps into prominence, remains there for a short time, and then—though still largely unresolved—gradually fades from the center of public attention."

Negative Consequences

The *Limits to Growth* controversy is a prime example of the issue-attention cycle and its deleterious effects on public policy debate. There were three elements that conjoined to give this study, and the issue, undue attention. First, it was sponsored by a group of international businessmen, organized under the ambiguous name of the Club of Rome. Second, the results were presented as deriving from a presumably sophisticated computer simulation model that was developed by young colleagues of Jay Forrester at MIT. And third, its calamitous and apocalyptic warnings of the impending exhaustion of resources, or the drowning of the world in pollution and wastes, came fortuitously close in time with a worldwide Arab oil embargo.

This latter development shut down gasoline stations, reduced available fuel oil, and limited oil for energy and industrial power. Events became a Hollywood scenario of what the end of the industrial world might face *if*—it was quickly assumed *when*—the resources were depleted. The simple warning was evident: the world, particularly the advanced industrial countries, would have to cut back on economic growth if it were to survive, let alone provide an unspoiled environment.

Two crucial changes have made many of the recent issues quite different from similar policy problems of the past, even when the same issues reappear in a new guise. These changes are in the modes of presentation and the nature of the involvements.

The first is the impact of intensive media exposure. We now have, because of the revolutions in transportation and communication, a national society, and every issue now receives redoubled and national attention. National television networks seek out issues they can dramatize. The national newsweeklies seek to encourage public focus on policy problems. The difficulty is that the very nature of the media—the two-to-three-minute intensive set of photoflashes, or the anecdotal and human interest stories—tend to simplify, overdramatize, exaggerate (and usually seek to pin a question on good guys and bad guys). This increases the alarms and anxieties of the listeners and readers. It also provokes other individuals who want public attention to think up media events (such as burying an automobile to dramatize the ecology issue). In the end the effect is to distort the complexity of the problem and inhibit solutions.

From *Society*, January/February, 1978. Reprinted with permission, Edison Electric Institute.

The second difference is that these issues now mix economic and social questions with symbolic and expressive emotions that are derived from conflicting values. And while values underlie all public policy questions, what often happens is that the issues become dominated by heavy emotional charges that tend to absolutize the question and make it more difficult to attempt mediation and compromise. Any attempt at a trade-off is seen by one or another faction that is emotionally involved as a betrayal of principle, and thus the resolution of the issue is often more difficult than in the past.

Advanced Stage

The "limits to growth" issue has now become largely exhausted. It has not disappeared as a public policy issue; but it has run its course through the issue-attention cycle, and is now in a very different stage. On one level a fickle public and a fickle media have found new issues. But on the more serious level a debate was provoked that sought to disentangle the issues and to assess the consequences of one or another alternative course.

Under severe criticism from the academic community, most of the assumptions and the logic of analysis of the Club of Rome study were found to be faulty. The comprehensive, scholarly, and fair-minded assessments of the Edison Electric Institute have provided a basis for the establishment of relevant facts and the clarification of values. And, in a

If we are to deal with these two questions, we have to review the way the growth issue arose, and sort out the different assumptions (and misleading notions) that were entangled together. And then, on the social limits issue, we have to sort out the factual questions and the value assumptions and test both against a set of standards. In its emergence, and in the debates that swirled around it, the economic growth issue was more complicated than the usual single-dimension issue, because mixed up within it were three very different issues, different in their causal sources, sequences, and policy consequences. These were the pollution issue, the environmental spoliation issue, and the depletion of physical resources issue.

Physical Limits: Pollution

The pollution issue arose because alarmed observers pointed out that economic growth simply increased industrial wastes that were propelled into the air or tossed into the waters, thus creating smog and foul air or dirty lakes or rivers where fish could not survive or men and women swim. There was an obvious point to all this. As C.B. McCoy, then the president of Du Pont, once remarked wryly, "We used to have a mural in the Du Pont auditorium which showed our smokestacks belching smoke, and we all took that as a symbol of industrial prosperity. But now we have had to erase that picture from our wall."

The economic growth issue is an umbrella for a wide range of social discontents

---

meeting in Philadelphia in April 1976, the Club of Rome reversed itself almost completely. It virtually abandoned the argument regarding the extent of physical resources. It stated that its aim had been, primarily, to alert the worldwide public to environmental and resources problems, and that its chief concern was with the gap between rich and poor nations, a gap that, if widened, would lead to extended famines, social disturbances, and war.

Yet the logic of its reversal was clear. If one is to make the question of reducing the disparities between nations the central question for the world polity, then it is obvious that economic growth is a necessity in order to expand the wealth of the world and make it available for rising standards of living for the peoples of the world.

Two other different questions then arise. One is how to assure that economic growth is possible, both within resource constraints (principally rising costs of energy) and the maintenance of a livable environment. The other is the new question that the limits to growth are not physical or economic resources, but social. In recent years the issue of economic growth has become an umbrella for a wide range of social discontents: for those who have become antitechnology and want a return to nature; for those who believe that size, bigness, and complexity dwarf the human being and reduce the human scale; for those who have turned against materialism on the grounds that the possession of goods leads to alienation or dissolute ways, and so on.

Yet what was less obvious were three other factors. First was the lack of historical actuality in the alarm over the issue. Nineteenth century American cities were probably more polluted and the air worse to breathe than the present, largely because of the heavy use of coal as a fuel. The disappearance of coal-burning locomotives and their replacement by diesels, and the control of emissions from the great steel mills in Pittsburgh and Chicago, certainly made those cities cleaner and more livable. History does not point to the elimination of a social problem, but it does provide a better perspective on the nature of change.

The second fact was that a large part of the pollution was a trade-off for other gains. In the case of the automobile, this was the increase in personal mobility. But more important, and much less well known, was the fact that much of the pollution of the rivers and streams of the country resulted from the runoff of nitrates from fertilizers applied to the farms, and that it was this technological revolution on the farm that had resulted in the extraordinary increases in productivity which, before World War II, were about 1 to 2 percent a year, and in the quarter of a century after were averaging 6 to 8 percent a year. As a result of this productivity, about 4 percent of the labor force could feed the entire population of the United States and a large part of the world besides. The restriction of such fertilizers, in order to reduce water pollution, inevitably would mean some reduction in the supply of food.

The third fact, however, was the very belated realization that the reasons for the pollution lay less in the greed of industry, or the indifference of municipalities about the disposal of wastes, or the casual approach of the motorist to car emissions—though there was a basis of truth in all of this—than the simple fact that the market principle had never been applied to the use of air and water. In most economic textbooks, until recently, air and water were given as the illustrations of a free good, that is, a good that had no cost because of the very abundance of the resource.

Now, there is a simple economic principle that if something has no cost, it will be used recklessly and heedlessly. If you have some wastes, toss them into the water and let them be washed away or pumped into the air where they would be "blown" away. In effect, pollution increased because there were few costs. Or, to put it more precisely, the costs that did arise were externalized, since the individuals generating these costs did not have to pay for them. But if air and water are treated as scarce resources, one puts a price on their use, and the existence of a price forces a user to economize on the resource. To that extent the problem of pollution was a failure of economic imagination; and to the extent that a price becomes put on a resource, and has to be internalized by the person generating the costs, it becomes—like safety in the factory—a force for the reduction of pollution.

Environmental Spoliation

The issue of environmental spoliation was raised primarily in relation to unregulated patterns of growth, particularly in regard to land use. There was fear that the widespread strip mining of coal would scar large sections of the landscape, the speed-up in the cutting of timber lay bare large sections of forests, and the rapid spread of "ticky-tacky" houses lead to an ugly suburban sprawl that would disfigure the countryside, especially in coastal regions, and reduce the amenities available to the population as a whole.

Many of these fears were justified. But the fact was that by the time of alarmed discovery, both legislative and judicial regulative steps had been taken to control the reckless use of land, while the slowdown in population growth, as well as rising costs and inflation, had reduced the number of housing starts and, for many communities, had provided a breather to do more intelligent land use planning.

Resource Depletion

The resources issue has probably played the heaviest role in the attack on the idea of economic growth. In large measure this was because of the extraordinary publicity of the Club of Rome's *Limits to Growth* study, a publicity that was accentuated by the sudden embargo on oil by OPEC as a result of Arab initiatives. The sight of gas stations shut down, the fear of little fuel for winter heating, the alarms by utilities and government exhorting people to save on energy use, all reinforced the belief that somehow a resource limitation, or even the threat of exhaustion, was responsible for that situation. Of course it was not. The OPEC action was entirely political, the result of a cartel action rather than a response by the market to the fear of declining resources. But in the popular view the resources issue had become salient.

In quiet retrospect it is clear that the resources issue is a good example of the mishandling and misdirection of a public policy issue, and that the Club of Rome study is a fearful example of how badly social science can be misused to push a particular point of view. The first and most obvious fact is that no matter how elegant, complicated, abstruse, or dominating a computer model may be, its conclusions—in the working out of the interrelations of resources, population growth, and intensities of use—are only as good as the reliability of the initial data and the assumptions used. Yet in instance after instance the assumptions are questionable. The second, less obvious, fact is that few resources command a monopoly use, and once one puts price into a model (and more specifically in the real world) then the level of price will determine alternative patterns of use and substitutions.

Challenges to economic growth (often from upper-middle-class liberals) have come at the same time as an unprecedented sociological revolution

If one thinks only in physical terms, then it is likely that one does not need to worry about ever running out of resources. Reserves are almost infinitely greater than the 250-year supply that is assumed in the *Limits to Growth* model. But the crucial point is that economic development, while it does depend upon technology, has a wide range of alternative methods, each one being characterized by a different mix of capital, labor, and resource inputs. Society tends to adopt technologies that are compatible with existing resource endowments. When the resource pattern changes, new techniques are introduced, either for extraction and exploration, or by the introduction of substitutes, that provide a different pattern of organization.

Sociological Revolution

In the public policy debate on economic growth there is, however, a far different issue, and a paradox: the challenge to the idea of economic growth (often from upper-middle-class liberals) has come at the very time when there has been an unprecedented sociological revolution, what I have called the "revolution of rising entitlements." Over the past twenty-five years we have seen the expansion of the welfare state and the spread of a normative social policy. Central governments in all societies, but in particular the industrial democracies, have made an irreversible commitment to redress economic and social inequalities and to provide for a range of services and support for large sections of the society, particularly the disadvantaged. In the United States federal spending for what is defined as "social welfare purposes" rose from $14 billion in 1950 to $180 billion in 1975, or from less than one-fifth of the federal budget to more than one-half.

The sociological revolution has been more, though, than

the expenditure of money. It has taken the form—a basic shift in the values of the society—that what was once considered to be an individual effort is now a claim on the government, a claim for protection against societal hazards and, in effect, an entitlement, something that a person is entitled to by virtue of being a citizen of that society.

Now, these large new expenditures can be financed only in two ways: either out of economic growth or by direct redistribution of incomes. In the 1960s the philosophy of government was to finance the expansion of these services out of the rising revenues created by economic growth. The simple fact is that economic growth is a political "solvent." While growth invariably raises expectations, the means for financing social welfare expenditures have come essentially from economic growth. In a trillion dollar economy, an increase in the economic growth rate of 1 percent means a net addition of $100 billion by the end of a decade. And as the Kennedy and Johnson administrations found out (until Vietnam War expenditures began to escalate), the Congress was more willing to vote for the social welfare costs of the New Frontier or the Great Society, so long as economic growth provided additional fiscal revenues, than to reform the tax structure or shift the weight of taxes in the society. Given the continuing demand for social expenditures, the only other means of financing these, other than economic growth, would be through direct income redistribution—a political fact that invites not only obvious social conflicts, but special dysfunctions as well.

Social Limits

Economic growth is desirable, possible, and necessary. It is necessary to meet the social demands on the society and, as the Edison Electric Institute has written, "to increase extractive and processing capacity, to develop new, more efficient technologies, and to develop fuels and processes which are more consistent with the stringent environmental standards being set for the nation."

What, then, of the question of social limits to growth? Here the institute concludes, "On the question of psychological and organizational limits to growth, it is concluded that there are *no inherent limits* to man's capacity to adapt and cope with complexity. Given the will to do so, man can devise evermore intricate organization forms and make them work. It is a matter of social choice whether this will be done." Such a sweeping and unqualified statement reflects a lack of appreciation for the complexity of the problem. It does not allow us to even consider in what way there may or may not be social limits.

It is a fundamental sociological theorem that growth involves a change in scale. But a change in scale is not simply a linear extension in size of any existing organization. No institution that undergoes a change in size does so, *if it is to survive and adapt*, without changing its form and shape. It was Galileo, more than 350 years ago, who laid down this principle.

Every organization theorist knows this, and the corollary principle is that a change in size necessitates a change in structure—if the organization, or the society, is to continue functioning. To put it less abstractly, the continued growth of an organization, or a society, involves a necessary decentralization of structure and operations, as the scope and scale of the enterprise or the society itself, which involve more centralization of control and policy, continue to expand.

The Club of Rome study is a fearful example of how badly social science can be misused to push a particular viewpoint

---

The management of scale is one of the major difficulties besetting a modern society—and the reasons for these difficulties are largely political. Let me revert to an earlier point. We have become in the past thirty years, because of the revolutions in transportation and communication, a national society. Yet we do not have the institutions to match the new scales; the scales of function and administrative operation simply do not match. As a result we get escalating costs of state and local government and fewer and fewer services as some tax bases shrink and others exempt themselves from the costs of government. In short, we have here a structure of vested interests that are resistant to change and that, increasingly, levy more and more of a charge on the society.

The point has to be expanded. The question of social limits is not a technological or organizational question, but a political one. And those who raise it, rhetorically, as an argument against economic growth rarely face up to the problems they themselves create. Thus, for example, there *is* an inherent conflict between participation and efficiency. One of the more important facts about American life in the last two decades has been the enormous expansion of citizen involvement in all aspects of public policy debate. Yet while much of this is highly desirable, it also has a cost. For the multiplication of citizens groups also leads to the multiplication of veto groups and to a politics of stymie.

Yet this, too, creates a further curious paradox. Many persons claim today that government has grown too large and that they are unable to have a voice in its decisions. And they believe, therefore, that political apathy is on the rise. Yet the converse is true. There is much more participation than ever before, but because, in the clash of multiple interests, each group may not get its way, it feels helpless and alienated.

Necessary Trade-offs

The answer to these situations is not a technocratic solution of ever more intricate organization forms, but the simpler recognition by every segment of the society that no single group can ever wholly have its way, that one cannot absolutize a position, and that bargaining and trade-offs are necessary. Any solution to a political issue involves differential costs, and that is the principle of public government that has to be recognized and accepted. An increase in public services for the disadvantaged means an increase in taxes and a reduction of personal consumption. Tightened environmental restrictions may lead to plant shutdowns and loss of jobs for communities. These are, inevitably, differences in values and, short of war, they have to be mediated.

One other point needs to be confronted: the argument that technology is dehumanizing and reduces the human scale. The facts are simply quite different. There are two characteristics to technology that have to be established. The first is that, basically, technology is instrumental. It is a machine, a design, or a technique that can be used in many different ways, according to the social purposes or the social system in which it is embedded. The second fact is that technology tends to become more simplified rather than more complicated in design, in the ability to use and understand it.

Question of social limits is not technological or organizational, but political. There is a tendency to ideologize the question and for positions to harden

The idea, then, that there are social limits to growth does not derive from technology, or even organizational size—if it is adaptive to the requirements of new functions and scale—but to the differing fears, vested interests, and value conflicts of individuals and groups. But this is the oldest of all problems of human organization and is resolvable if one accepts the "rules of the game," that is, the procedures of open debate, compromise, and acceptance of the rule of law.

Fred Hirsch's recent book *The Social Limits to Growth* has been hailed by a number of reviewers as indicating the limitations to economic growth. But the moral of Hirsch's book is vastly different. Hirsch correctly states a theorem that goes back to Ricardo: that certain kinds of goods, privileges, or services (what he calls "positional goods") are inherently limited because they are relatively unique—that is, only one person can have a house at the top of the mountain—so that economic growth reduces the number of and increases the competition for such positional goods.

The goods clearly would be reduced; but with the expansion of transportation and the multiplication of new kinds of goods, the absolute number increases. Yet as a *principle* the point remains true. Inevitably there will be a *relative* scarcity of positional goods. But what follows most sharply from this is the increasing difficulty of *equality* because of the limitation of positional goods, rather than social limits—unless one adopts a principle of lottery or rotation in the distribution of such unique goods. It would be interesting to hear a complete egalitarian argue the position.

Clear Thinking

The issue-attention cycle has negative and positive features. The negative ones have tended to dominate. Issues flare up, are posed in striking rhetoric, gain emotional adherents, receive exaggerated attention, are resolved often by "fiat" (that is, legislation is passed and an agency is created to "do something" about the problem), and then attention fades. Yet there are obvious positive values as well. An industry shows that it is willing to face an issue squarely, rather than back off and engage in propaganda or rhetorical debate. There is an emphasis on factual inquiry. The different points of view are weighed and tested, and there is an emphasis on both the different values involved as well as the costs and trade-offs of the different policies that are proposed.

One of the dangers of the issue-attention cycle is that because the issues are often symbolic as well as economic, there is a tendency to ideologize the question and for contrary positions to harden. If there has been a strength to the American approach to social policy, it has been that its emphasis has been on what is primarily instrumental (that is, possible), though this has at times neglected the underlying values at stake in an issue. What emerges from all this is the implicit acceptance by all parties of the legitimate right of government to raise issues of public interest and to demand a public accounting from all interested parties. What has been less evident is the willingness of the parties to break away from "prejudged" or stereotyped conceptions that often have an ideological flavor.

There is a legitimacy to the liberal view of governmental concern, on the level of values and policy, and there is a utility to the industry view of the market as an instrumentality. The market *is* a useful instrument for regulation because the price mechanism is impersonal and forces compliance by an individual on himself, since a rising price will usually force him to economize, and in such instances the market is clearly preferable to bureaucratic intervention. Yet the point is that the market can be used for social purposes as well, by government.

What is at stake is the need to think creatively and clearly on public policy questions and, on a factual basis and within the values that are consensually accepted, come to agreements that allow us to meet these questions in an open and democratic way. This is what we are doing.□

READINGS SUGGESTED BY THE AUTHOR:
Beckerman, Wilfred. *Two Cheers for the Affluent Society: A Spirited Defense of Economic Growth.* New York: St. Martin's Press, 1975.
Downs, Anthony. "Up and Down with Ecology—The 'Issue Attention Cycle.'" *The Public Interest*, no. 28 (Summer 1972): 38–50.
Hirsch, Fred. *The Social Limits to Growth.* Cambridge, Mass.: Harvard University Press/Twentieth Century Fund, 1976.
Maddox, John. *Beyond the Energy Crisis.* New York: McGraw-Hill, 1975.

Daniel Bell is professor of sociology at Harvard University. He has served on the President's Commission on Technology, Automation, and Economic Progress and as cochairman of the Panel on Social Indicators for the Department of Health, Education, and Welfare. He is the author of many works, and his sociological writings are among the most important in the field.

40

MARTIN REIN and LEE RAINWATER

How Large Is the Welfare Class?

Data from a ten-year survey show that a relatively small percentage of welfare recipients is committed to welfare as a "way of life."

The growing cost of this country's welfare programs —the so-called "welfare crisis"—has prompted a great deal of discussion, much of which adds up to a theory that there is a large proportion of people on welfare who have been dependent on it for such a long period of time that they can be said to constitute a welfare class.

The three main popular views about families in the welfare class are all based on the assumption that welfare has become a way of life for a great many of its recipients. The most common of these views is that members of the welfare class are victims of social, psychological, or physical pathology. They are referred to as "multi-problem" families who must remain on welfare because they are "unemployable." This kind of family, it is often felt, has become so committed to a life on welfare that it remains on welfare even when some of its problems have been ameliorated.

Another opinion is that the welfare class is an exploited group that functions in the economy like a modern reserve army, responding to cyclical changes in the demand for labor. A certain proportion of the population, therefore, is at the mercy of the ups and downs in the employment cycle, and the vagaries of the low-wage labor market.

Finally, there is the view that a substantial number of welfare clients are "cheats." People with long-term

MARTIN REIN is Professor of Urban Studies, Massachusetts Institute of Technology. LEE RAINWATER is Professor of Sociology, Harvard University.

Reprinted from Challenge, copyright © 1977 by M. E. Sharpe, Inc. Reprinted by permission of M. E. Sharpe, Inc.

dependency on welfare are seen not as the exploited, but as the exploiters. They use the public transfer system as entrepreneurs, and make their living by manipulating the system, rather than by finding work.

Whatever one's opinion as to the reason for a family's long-term attachment to and dependence on the welfare system, it would seem important to determine just how large this welfare class really is. For what policy-makers believe about the size and characteristics of this class will significantly affect what they do in the area of welfare reform.

Our investigations suggest that the welfare class is not nearly so large as people think it is.

The Panel Study

There have been a number of attempts to estimate the size of the group with a long-term dependence on welfare, but the task has proved difficult because it has been based on routine administrative welfare statistics, which deal only with particular cases at particular times. The best way to determine the size of the welfare class is to follow a sample of families over a period of years to see how high the probability is that they will go on welfare, stay there for a considerable time, and derive a major proportion of their income from welfare. So far as we are aware, there is only one survey that provides the kinds of data which enable those probabilities to be assessed—the Panel Study of Income Dynamics, conducted by the University of Michigan Survey Research Center.

For a decade now, a national sample of over 10,000 American adults, who are members of over 5,000 families, have been interviewed to determine how their family income has been obtained. It has become clear from much previous research that the life careers of women and their children are central to the welfare experience. We therefore chose for analysis from the Panel Study women who were between the ages of 18 and 54 in 1968, the first year of the survey. We followed the patterns of their welfare experience through 1974, developed a model of that experience, and projected the model over a ten-year period. Our aim was to determine the incidence of welfare class membership. Our operational definition of such membership was attachment to the welfare system for at least nine out of ten years, and at least 50 percent dependence on the system for family income during that period. This definition is consistent

with the conception of a welfare class held by researchers, policy-makers, and the general public.

We wanted to know, for a given group of women, how many were likely to become members of the welfare class. This involved three basic component questions: How many would go on welfare at all? How long would they stay on welfare? How dependent would they be on welfare for family income? (This last component is an important one. The Panel survey data reveal, for example, that a number of families on welfare for long periods derive only a small portion of their income from it, and this income consists of welfare payments on behalf of foster children being cared for by couples—hardly a situation that would qualify them for membership in the welfare class.)

The data show that from 1968 to the present, the probability that a woman between the ages of 18 and 54 would go on welfare has been about 1.5 percent. That is, of every 1,000 women who have not been on welfare during the previous year, about 15 will join the rolls. Since there are roughly 50 million women in this age range in the United States, this means that about 750,000 of them will become welfare recipients each year.

Once a woman goes on welfare, the data show, the probability of her staying on it for a second year is 60 percent; for a third year, 70 percent. The probability rises to a plateau of 80 percent for the fifth year and beyond. At any given time, about 5.5 percent of women from 18 to 54 years of age are members of families which obtain at least part of their income from welfare. The analysis suggests that the average woman who goes on welfare at all spends about four out of ten years in that position. Her four years is the sum of two consecutive years on welfare, and two years' "cycling back" to welfare, after having left it for one or more years. But this four-year period does not conform to the concept of a member of the welfare class, which requires a much longer-term dependency. If we estimate the various stages of welfare participation for 18- to 54-year-old women, we can arrive at an estimate of the size of the group which is dependent on welfare for a period of at least nine out of ten years.

Of the 50 million women in the country in that age range, 43 million, or 86 percent, will have had no welfare experience at all over the ten-year period 1968-1977. But 7 million, or 14 percent, will have had some welfare income in at least one of those years. Here is a breakdown of the welfare experience of those 7 million women:

Total women 18-54 years old in first year	50,000,000
Have been on welfare at least once in 10 years	7,000,000
On welfare for 4 or fewer years	3,500,000
On welfare more than 4 years	3,500,000
On welfare 5 to 8 years	2,730,000
On welfare 9 or 10 years	770,000
Of those on welfare 9 or 10 years, Less than 50 percent dependent on welfare	154,000
50 percent or more dependent on welfare	616,000

Thus the size of the welfare class comes to 616,000 women out of the total of 50 million. Since in any one year some 2.7 million women are likely to be on welfare, we find that only slightly over 20 percent of those on welfare at any one particular time are members of the welfare class, by our definition. The other 80 percent have short- or medium-term welfare careers. And of the 7 million women who go on welfare in any year, the welfare class represents only 10 percent. It is true, however, that although the welfare class constitutes only a fifth of those on welfare at any given time, its members consume more than a fifth of the welfare dollars. In fact, our data suggest that they consume as much as 60 percent of all welfare dollars going to the families of women between the ages of 18 and 54.

Overall, one can conclude that the welfare class is a definite minority among welfare recipients. The patterns of welfare careers, which have been studied by Susan Anderson-Khleif, who read the cases discussed here, suggest that it might be useful to think of two other categories of welfare recipients as more typical.

Common patterns among welfare clients

One of the more common groups of welfare clients is composed of those who make use of welfare in the course of some kind of family transition—usually marital breakup. These families go on welfare with every expectation of leaving it as quickly as possible; they use welfare as a resource in "digging out" of the financial hole the marital disruption puts them in. As the new female household head gets on her feet, she begins to work, sometimes after having finished her schooling, and eventually earns enough to discontinue her welfare payments.

Another common group is made up of families in which job problems, rather than marital disruption, produce the financial crisis to which welfare is a solution. Male or female heads of households lose their jobs and have a hard time finding others, or else they have jobs in the marginal labor market and are therefore subject to recurrent unemployment. They go on welfare for a short period of time. They may, however, be "cyclers," coming back to welfare in some later period of unemployment.

Then there is a small group (perhaps as large as the welfare class) for whom welfare represents a transition to other public transfers. It consists of household heads who receive welfare while they are establishing their eligibility for workmen's compensation, or widow's or survivor's benefits. To some extent, this shifting from means-tested to social insurance benefits may lead to an underestimation of the size of the welfare class. It is quite possible that enterprising welfare departments shift cases with marginal eligibility off the welfare rolls and onto some form of social insurance program as a way of minimizing costs to the states and localities.

We have described life situations which are common among welfare recipients. Is there any pattern that might be called common among welfare class members? It is possible to discern a "locked-in" pattern in many of these families, a situation where everything is going wrong at the same time. Families like this are bereft of a social support network to which they can turn for help. They may not, as other welfare families do, have access to friends, neighbors, relatives, or their own economic resources from reported or unreported work. They may also face serious psychiatric problems. They do, in fact, conform to the image of the "multi-problem" family which many people have of the typical welfare client. But one must be cautious in attributing a hard-and-fast pattern to families in the welfare class. Their situations are actually heterogeneous, as a close reading of their case records will reveal, and some of them indicate a readiness to leave the welfare system, though, of course, they may have to come back on welfare at some future time.

Implications for welfare reform

At present, welfare seems to serve primarily as a way for society to cope with two of its problems—family disruption and labor market inadequacy. The dominant issues in welfare reform, therefore, should be those having to do with the life situations, needs, and incentives of the larger group of welfare recipients.

Since there is next to nothing that government policy can do to reduce the level of family disruption, a proper goal of family social policy would be to design income maintenance systems that smooth out the financial difficulties now accompanying marital breakup. Since as many as half of today's children will live at some time in a single-parent family, usually headed by the mother, a principal goal of welfare reform should be to provide security for that family, without at the same time discouraging mothers and other family members from pursuing work careers.

In the long run, however, a full-employment policy designed to provide more jobs and greater job security for both men and women is the key to solving welfare problems. It is likely that the effect of the so-called disincentives to work contained in present and proposed programs has been considerably exaggerated in discussions of welfare problems and welfare reform. If there were more opportunities for employment, there would be more incentive to work.

In light of these considerations, the principal goal of welfare reform should be to reduce the number of occasions when people going through the common crises of family breakup and unemployment require means-tested programs. A program of universal benefit for the working as well as the nonworking poor (for example, child allowances or tax credits), supplemented perhaps by the development of a new form of social insurance to diminish the economic risks for single heads of households, should go a long way toward reducing the number of people who use means-tested programs at all, and should also decrease the number of people who stay on welfare for even a moderate period of time.

41

FOOD STAMPS: WHO GETS THEM AND WHAT DO THEY ACCOMPLISH?

One of the controversial components of the Carter Administration's new welfare reform proposal—the *Better Jobs and Income Program*—is the cashing out of the Food Stamp Program. Among other changes, this proposal would convert $5 billion now going to low-income persons in the form of food stamps into a cash minimum income for all.

It is noteworthy that the U.S. Congress has never enacted into law a universal cash benefit program. We have, however, had a guaranteed minimum income for all in this country since 1974. It is not in cash, but in food purchasing power.

Why is the only universal guaranteed minimum income program in the U.S. provided in food stamps? Is it simply a result of historical circumstances, or is it because society places a special value on providing food purchasing power rather than general purchasing power? If the answer is the latter, what objectives did people have in mind and are these objectives being met?

Let us take stock, as Maurice MacDonald does in his book *Food, Stamps, and Income Maintenance.*

Early History

Food assistance to the needy in this country was initiated in legislation with the interesting title "The Potato Control Act of 1935." Nobody thought its primary aim was to help the poor. Rather, it was to dispose of surplus commodities in order to support farm prices—that is, to help the farmers. This initial objective is why the program was made the responsibility of the Department of Agriculture, and why its descendent is still administered by that department today—rather than the Department of Health, Education, and Welfare, as one might expect of a program that aids the poor.

In line with its main objective, the program took the form of direct distribution of those commodities that happened to be in surplus each month. This stimulated opposition from two sources: the recipients and their supporters, and the food retailers and their supporters. The former group complained that (1) the once-a-month distribution (even perishables were distributed monthly) created insuperable difficulties in terms of eating needs, and (2) what happened to be available determined what people ate, irrespective of nutritional need. The latter group had a predictable grievance: that normal trade channels (and therefore the food distributors' markup) were bypassed by direct commodity distribution.

The lobbying efforts of the food distributors were successful; and 1939 saw the authorization of a food stamp plan whose purpose was to increase domestic food consumption through regular business channels. The foods that could be purchased with the subsidy were, however, still restricted to the monthly list of surplus commodities designated by the Secretary of Agriculture. The first food stamp program served four million people a year at an annual average cost of $65 million. At its height in 1939, direct commodity distribution reached 12.7 million people at a cost of $66 million. By 1943, the farm surplus had disappeared and the unemployment rate had dropped. Food stamps were terminated and direct commodity distribution, though formally retained, became extremely limited.

The conflict between disposing of surpluses to help the farmer and providing subsidies for food consumption to help the needy arose again after the war with the reappearance of farm surpluses. The direct commodity distribution program again expanded, continuing to grow until the disappearance of farm surpluses at the end of the 1960s—its scale largely determined throughout by the availability of surplus foods, and not the extent of need. Liberals made continuing efforts throughout the 1950s to revive food stamps, and in 1958 authorization was passed for a two-year pilot food stamp program. President Eisenhower, however, declined to take advantage of this invitation, and it was left to John F. Kennedy and the famous West Virginia primary to elevate the nutritional needs of the poor to high political priority.

The 1960s

The year 1961 witnessed Kennedy's executive order to institute 8 (which later grew to 43) pilot food stamp programs, in which all domestic foods could be purchased at participating retail outlets. By March 1964 these programs were serving nearly 400,000 people at a federal cost of $29 million. New pilots continued to be added. Evaluations showed that the food consumption and nutrition of the poor increased; they also showed that, since the foods being bought were not predominantly what happened to be on the surplus commodity list, such programs could not eliminate the prevailing farm surplus.

A bill to authorize a nationwide program was introduced and ran into the familiar conflict, as MacDonald relates: "Southern Democrats and Republicans (especially farm bloc members) were reluctant to endorse a public assistance effort in the guise of an agricultural program. This obstacle was overcome by a willing arrangement between backers of wheat and cotton price supports and proponents of food stamps. The result was the Food Stamp Act of 1964."

With regard to helping the poor, the 1964 Act had loopholes (which undoubtedly helped its passage). Whether or not to establish a food stamp project was left to the discretion of the state agencies authorized to administer local public assistance. The act prohibited the operation of food stamps and commodity distribution in the same locality. The amount of subsidization varied by income level—the poorer the participant, the lower the purchase price of a given quantity of stamps—and was uniform throughout the country. But setting the cutoff income level (above which people were no longer entitled to any subsidy) was left to the states.

These provisions predictably led to wide geographic variations in the amount of help the poor could get from the program. Even after taking eligibility variations into account, however, it became apparent as the sixties progressed that there were other unidentified sources of variation. It also turned out that when counties shifted over from commodity distribution to food stamps, the number of participants declined, on average, by 40%.

Food stamp proponents began to ask what was going on. In 1967, members of the Senate Subcommittee on Employment, Manpower, and Poverty traveled to the Mississippi Delta to investigate. The 1968 report *Hunger U.S.A.,* which was released by the self-appointed Citizens Board of Inquiry into Hunger and Malnutrition in the United States, was given wide publicity in a CBS television special. The ensuing controversy led Ralph Abernathy and the Poor People's Campaign to confront the Department of Agriculture directly. And the Senate established a Select Committee on Nutrition and Human Need, chaired by George McGovern.

In the 1968 elections, hunger in America was a major campaign issue, and in May 1969 Nixon pledged "to put an end to hunger in America itself for all time." He recommended several reforms in the food stamp program which, along with additional improvements, were passed by the Congress in 1971.

The 1971 Amendments included free stamps for the most needy, a ceiling of 30% of income for the purchase price for food stamp allotments, and uniform national eligibility standards dependent only on income and family size. This combination of reforms effectively doubled the average food stamp benefit. The federal share of the administrative costs of the program incurred by the states was also increased to 50%. Further amendments in 1973 mandated that all counties switch over from food distribution to food stamps by July 1974. "Thus by conscious congressional design," states MacDonald, "the food stamp program finally became available to all eligible low-income persons." It had taken nearly 30 years since the first efforts to distribute surplus food to the needy during the depression.

The food surpluses had disappeared, and so had any serious talk about food programs as a way to help agriculture. In fact, universalization of the food stamp program probably passed in partial response to the generally recognized need for welfare reform and some kind of guaranteed minimum for the poor—evidence of this general recognition being the narrow margin by which Nixon's Family Assistance Plan (FAP) was defeated in 1972.[1]

The Present Food Stamp Program: Whom Does it Reach?

So we now have a guaranteed minimum income in food which is available to all low-income Americans. That it is available, however, does not mean that everyone takes advantage of it. In fact, as of 1976, less than half the eligible population availed themselves of food stamps. Who are the people who can but don't use food stamps? Why don't they? And what can be done about it? MacDonald addresses all these questions with the help of state participation rate estimates and a multivariate study of the household characteristics that are associated with low probabilities of food stamp use, using national survey data from the Michigan Longitudinal Panel Study of Income Dynamics.

Individual states differ strikingly in their participation levels, ranging in 1974 from a low of 14.9% in Wyoming to a high of 55.7% in California. The ten with the lowest rates are all midwestern states with substantial farming activity. The ten highest are coastal and/or highly industrialized states. These differences lead one to suspect that geography, social attitudes toward public assistance, and the historical influence of the farm lobby (in favor of commodity distribution rather than food stamps) may account for the difference. And certainly these factors are important.

But participation differences appear at the local level as well. MacDonald points out, for instance, that "the counties along Wisconsin's northern border . . . have markedly different participation rates [from one another]. There is even substantial variation across Wisconsin [urban] areas, ranging from a low of around 25% in Madison to 40% in Milwaukee and over 45% in Superior." Similar variation has been found in other states. Such differences among localities with highly similar eligible populations suggest that administrative practices (including outreach activities) vary from jurisdiction to jurisdiction.

What about the argument that low participation rates really reflect relative need—that those who qualify but whose incomes are not much below the cutoff point (and who do not, in consequence, qualify for much of a bonus) do not apply because the bother is greater than the value of the bonus? MacDonald finds that this does not entirely explain the existing situation. Although half the nonrecipients are missing out on less than $200 a year by not participating, over 11% are missing out on more than $800 and 7% are missing out on more than $1,000 a year.

Why do people fail to take advantage of these relatively substantial sums? Until MacDonald's study, answers to this question have been based mainly on conjecture, supplemented by rudimentary survey information. The major reasons usually advanced are (a) the stigma associated with using the stamps, (b) the time and trouble it takes to get certified for, purchase, and use food stamps (user costs), and (c) ignorance of how to apply for and use the stamps.

MacDonald's study has found (using 1971 data) that all these factors probably play substantial roles. First, households receiving welfare had a high probability of purchasing food stamps. These households, of course, have already had to overcome the stigma and user costs associated with welfare. And because they are on welfare their access to information about the food stamp program is likely to be good.

Second, those over 65 were distinctly less likely to use food stamps than other age groups. Older people are generally more conservative, leading us to expect them to feel the stigma costs associated with food stamps more than younger people whose social values may be changing. They are also less likely to be receptive to information about new programs.

Third, those households whose heads were not in the labor force had much higher participation rates (47%) than those with a head either employed or looking for work (35%). This supports the view that the "working poor" are a low-participation group and is consistent with the view that stigma is an inhibiting factor—an important point when it is remembered that food stamps constitute the only income support program for which most of the working poor are eligible.

How Can Participation Be Improved?

To the extent that nonparticipation stems from ignorance of one's eligibility, increasing participation entails that the Department of Agriculture strictly enforce its own guidelines for outreach, namely, "inform all low-income households eligible to receive food stamps of the availability and benefits of the program." MacDonald also finds that access to sources of general information does not help explain participation, suggesting that outreach should provide very specific information about benefit entitlements and how to get stamps.

To the extent that it stems from the time and trouble involved, streamlining the efficiency of local agency operations should help somewhat, although having to go to the food stamp outlets to get the stamps constitutes an irreducible user cost. (The need for having the money on hand to buy the stamps has been eliminated by the very recent food stamp amendments.)

To the extent that it stems from stigma—and the evidence is consistent with the view that stigma is important—it is difficult to predict what policy reforms might increase participation. "Stigma is a question of attitudes and personal perceptions of how one is viewed by others." We know little about how attitudes become ingrained or about how they change.

The most straightforward way to remove all these barriers, of course, would be to abolish the *food stamp* component altogether and simply replace it with cash. A cash entitlement is easy to advertise, could be readily mailed to recipients, and would not identify recipients as they purchased food. But efforts in this direction have failed thus far.

Why this opposition? It seems to stem from three possible sources, which all come down to using food stamps to *restrict* the benefits to food purchases: (a) taxpayers wanting to prevent "welfare bums" from wasteful spending, (b) liberals wanting to ensure adequate food consumption by the poor, and (c) food distributors wanting the sale of food to be subsidized to their benefit.

Do food stamps influence food buying patterns? That is the question to which we now turn.

Do Food Stamps Get People to Eat More? Eat Better?

Research on food consumption and income levels is in general agreement that, at least up to relatively comfortable income levels, increases in income are accompanied by increases both in calorie intake and in the nutritional quality of the food consumed. The question becomes, therefore: Do food stamps stimulate food consumption and nutritional intake *more* than an equivalent cash benefit would?

MacDonald addresses this issue in some detail, reviewing evidence from other studies as well as examining data himself, and he concludes that neither the quantity nor quality of the food consumed by food stamp recipients is very different from those of people at the same income level who do not get food stamps.

First, MacDonald pursues the question of the amount of food purchased by dividing food stamp users into three groups—those whose food expenditures exceed their food stamp allotment, those whose food expenditures are equal to their stamp allotment, and those whose food expenditures are less than their stamp allotment. The first group is clearly unconstrained in their expenditures by the existence of food stamps. They buy the food they would anyway, using the full food stamp bonus and only adding extra cash as necessary—saving an amount equal to the bonus, which they can then spend on anything they like. The second group may or may not be constrained, depending on whether the food stamp bonus exactly equals what they would have spent without it or whether it has made them buy more food than they otherwise would. The third group is clearly constrained. They may not buy more food than they otherwise would, but they would certainly use the unused bonus on nonfood items if it were cash. Using the Michigan data, MacDonald finds that 71.3% are in the first category, 4.7% in the second, and 24% in the third. For more than two-thirds of recipients, therefore, food stamps are clearly synonymous with cash.

MacDonald also examines the extent to which the constrained households spent *more* on food than they would out of a cash transfer equivalent (as opposed to simply leaving some stamps unused, thereby forgoing the bonus). His lower-bound estimate is that only ten cents of every bonus stamp dollar spent by these households actually goes for food they would not buy if they got the benefit in cash. Accounting for the unconstrained households as well yields the estimate that only eight cents of every bonus food stamp dollar goes for food that would not be purchased otherwise—meaning that 92% of the total food stamp bonus is in fact equivalent to cash for the recipient households.

If total expenditures on food are not affected much, what about the kinds of food bought? The food stamp program has no provisions directing food purchases toward better nutrition. But does having more purchasing power directed toward food lead to better nutrition in any case? The evidence reviewed by MacDonald allows no such conclusion. A study of California shows some nutritional improvement among food stamp recipients as compared with nonrecipients. But this finding is suspect because there were many other ways in which the two groups differed from each other—including the fact that the total incomes (cash and in-kind) of the nonparticipants were on average $43 a month less than those of participants. A study of rural Pennsylvania—with better research controls—showed no effect, except in temporary periods of unusual cash shortages on the part of the families. In contrast, interestingly enough, evidence from the North Carolina sample of the rural negative income tax experiment (strictly a cash transfer program) showed that the group receiving the cash transfers did significantly improve the nutritional quality of their diets. This is probably because the North Carolina families were distinctly poorer than most other groups that have been studied and may, therefore, have had a greater margin for dietary improvement (which could as conceivably have come about with food stamp bonuses, instead of cash).

Conclusion

Food stamps constitute America's only universal minimum income program. There is distinct variation according to demographic group in the proportion of eligible households that avail themselves of these benefits. The aged and the working poor use them less than other groups, which is consistent with the view that the stigma associated with the program is holding people back.

To the extent that public support for a minimum income in the form of food stamps, rather than an equivalent one in general purchasing power, stems from a desire to constrain the purchases of the poor and/or to increase the quantity and quality of the food they consume, the program is largely unsuccessful. Less than ten cents per bonus dollar seems to go for food that would not otherwise be purchased.

Then why not give cash and eliminate the hassle and unpleasantness of the stamp negotiation process? The answer must lie in the politics of income support. Perhaps the time will soon come when we no longer have to ask it.

---

[1] FAP would have cashed out food stamps and provided a guaranteed minimum income in cash to all families with children.

42

TAMING A 148-BILLION-DOLLAR FEDERAL GIANT: WILL ANYTHING WORK?

Special Report

Not yet three decades old, the Department of Health, Education and Welfare is still growing relentlessly—and stirring increasing criticism. Now reform is being planned for an agency that touches nearly everyone.

The U.S. Government's No. 1 spender, the Department of Health, Education and Welfare, is promising under new leadership to control the massive problems of the nation's fastest-growing bureaucracy.

If there is success, it will come where other efforts have failed. Bringing to rein the headlong growth of a Department that now oversees more than one third of all federal spending has not proved possible so far.

With a budget of nearly 148 billion dollars this year and forecast at 164 billion in 1978, HEW has been accused of a broad range of misguided efforts. Among them: ignoring welfare graft, abetting excessive red tape, creating a top-heavy layer of administrators and allowing heavy-handed enforcement of policies.

There are widespread demands for vast changes in the Department, including a breakup of a sprawling bureaucracy that has grown in the 24 years since its founding from a staff of 37,000 to 157,000.

Declares Senator Lawton Chiles (Dem.), of Florida: "HEW is out of control. We must decide how to harness it, and do so as quickly as possible."

The Department's new Secretary, Joseph A. Califano, Jr., agrees that some programs have been mismanaged. He has taken steps to attempt to simplify procedures and make HEW more efficient.

At the same time, he has pledged to expand other programs—such as Head Start, which provides preschool training for low-income youngsters—initiated by the late President Lyndon Johnson in his Great Society efforts with the help of Califano, who was then a White House adviser. Critics contend that the expansion of projects will cost many millions more and increase the bureaucracy still further.

The heat generated by the controversy has spilled into the private lives of HEW officials. Califano has been widely criticized for such actions as hiring a cook for his personal use in the Department, even though many officials in other Government branches also have chefs. The practice is defended on the ground that long hours on the job make private in-house dining necessary.

Few critics of HEW are opposed to its over-all aims. Such programs as Social Security, medicare for the elderly and disabled and aid to the nation's schools are widely acclaimed for having raised living standards of millions of Americans once overlooked by the Government. It is the excesses and abuses arising out of various programs—inevitable, some say, in such massive efforts—that have caused most of the furor.

A dominating force. The burgeoning of HEW in just over two decades has been spectacular. Created in 1953 under a Republican Administration, the Department began with a relative handful of research and service programs aimed largely at helping people in need. Total spending in the first year was 1.9 billion dollars.

Since then, HEW's annual budget has risen almost 7,700 per cent. Employment has climbed 326 per cent. In terms of personnel, it has become the fourth-largest Department of the Federal Government.

In a single stroke, spending more than quadrupled in 1963 when Social Security was folded into the Department. With some 33 million beneficiaries of its medicare and cash-benefits programs, Social Security still dominates the HEW budget.

More than 105 billion dollars will be paid out in the current fiscal year in Social Security cash and medical benefits. Another 36 billion dollars will be spent, much of it in grants to States, in programs such as aid to families with dependent children, medicaid for the needy, social services, supplemental-security income and black-lung benefits. Spending under these programs is considered virtually uncontrollable because everyone meeting certain eligibility requirements is entitled by law to receive benefits.

Only about 17 billion dollars in the entire HEW budget is subject to annual review by Congress and, therefore, considered controllable.

Today the Department administers 381 statutory programs that, in one way or another, touch every American. Its rainbow of interests ranges from the care of pregnant women to feeding the elderly. Even the children's TV program "Sesame Street" is sustained partly with HEW funds.

The Department's wide-ranging responsibilities include operation of one of the world's leading health-research centers, the National Institutes of Health, in Washington, D.C. The Center for Disease Control in Atlanta, which played a major role in the swine-flu program, is another HEW branch with a global reputation. HEW's Food and Drug Administration has a long and controversial record of protecting the interests of consumers.

In the 1960s and 1970s, HEW has been in the forefront of some of the most complex and controversial issues of the times: the human upheaval caused by a changing economy, legalized abortion, genetic research, disintegration of family living, the cost and quality of education, the welfare explosion and attempts to end discrimination by race, national origin, sex or age.

Whether the Department is advocating busing of children to achieve racial balance in schools or ordering a ban of saccharin to protect people's health, it seldom has failed to arouse the passions of its friends and enemies alike.

Programs added willy-nilly. Hundreds of expensive and noble-sounding social programs—some actively sought by the Department, some created almost willy-nilly by Congress—have been handed to HEW in recent years.

Some goals that sounded feasible in the abstract have proved difficult to achieve. In many cases, funds simply have not been available to carry out the grandiose aims set forth by Congress in the authorizing legislation.

Former HEW Secretary Elliot Richardson has said that the dollar gap between what Congress authorizes and what it actually appropriates to run a program is "a political shell game." Hopes are raised only to be dashed, he noted in a blistering critique of HEW at the time of his departure from the Department in 1973.

To stay within spending limits set by Congress, program managers often have to pick and choose who among the needy will be helped or to spread programs so thin that they have almost no impact. Inevitably, said the former Secretary, the result has been disappointment and anger directed at the Department, usually followed by demands from special-interest groups for more funding.

The cost of extending the present range of HEW services equitably, Richardson asserted, would require additional spending "roughly equivalent to the entire federal budget."

Once started, programs at HEW almost never die.

They tend to live on, with their own growing constituencies and entrenched bureaucracy, after they are no longer needed, and even after their failure may have been amply demonstrated. "Programs are only put in; we don't take them out," says Senator Chiles, who advocates much closer periodic evaluation of HEW's activities.

Some programs that may be of questionable value are supported by organized interests that Congress does not want to antagonize. Other programs are perpetuated because they have become the pets of powerful members of Congress, whose names the enacting legislation often bears.

Secretary Califano told *U.S. News & World Report* that he would not hesitate to recommend abolishing "programs that

don't work." But, he added: "I guarantee you that over the next four years, the problem in getting rid of those programs will be more on Capitol Hill than with the executive branch. That has been the experience throughout."

For 20 years, Presidents and HEW Secretaries have urged Congress to eliminate or reduce funding for impact aid to school districts where there are federal installations. In theory, the money compensates local areas for the extra burden of having to educate children of federal employes. The Federal Government does not pay local taxes.

But to critics of the program, impact aid is just another term for pork barrel. It "is not an effective or equitable way to distribute federal education funds," argued Califano before a House Appropriations subcommittee.

"Sacred cows." The Carter Administration has proposed cutting impact aid by about half next year—to 370 million dollars. The White House also has asked Congress to chop spending for nurses-training programs, which the Administration says are no longer needed, and to suspend new appropriations for direct student loans, which officials say are already adequately funded.

When Califano outlined these proposals to the House Appropriations Subcommittee on Health, Education and Welfare in March, Chairman Daniel J. Flood (Dem.), of Pennsylvania, warned the Administration that it was tinkering with "sacred cows."

"Now, you do not seriously think that Congress is going to accept those proposals, do you?" Flood asked.

Pressure groups long ago learned that Capitol Hill is a rewarding place to come to when they want to involve the Federal Government in new social endeavors or to expand the size and scope of existing ones. Says a House member: "Everybody is running [for re-election] every two years, and he is contacted by every pressure group under the sun."

Experts in social legislation say that Congress keeps on creating new programs, often with scant regard to how they will be administered, who will benefit from them or how they will be financed.

There is confusion, too, because Congress seems to speak to HEW in many different voices. Legislation affecting the Department is controlled by more than 30 separate congressional committees and subcommittees. Each seems to have its own priorities and approach to how the Department should be run.

Some programs technically within

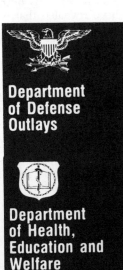

OUTSTRIPPING DEFENSE SPENDING

$164.1 bil.

$150 bil.

$110.6 bil.

$100 bil.

Department of Defense Outlays

$47.5 bil.

$50 bil.

Department of Health, Education and Welfare Outlays

$1.9 bil.

0

1953 '54 '55 '56 '57 '58 '59 '60 '61 '62 '63* '64 '65 '66 '67 '68 '69 '70 '71 '72 '73 '74 '75 '76 '77 '78
(HEW Founded)   (est.) (est.)

As recently as 10 years ago, HEW accounted for just over $1 of every $5 spent by the U.S. Government. Today, it spends more than $1 of every $3. The upward trend shows little sign of turning around.

*Social Security programs added to HEW outlays in 1963.

Note: Years ended June 30, except 1977 and 1978, ending September 30. Estimates are latest official forecasts.

Source: U.S. Office of Management and Budget

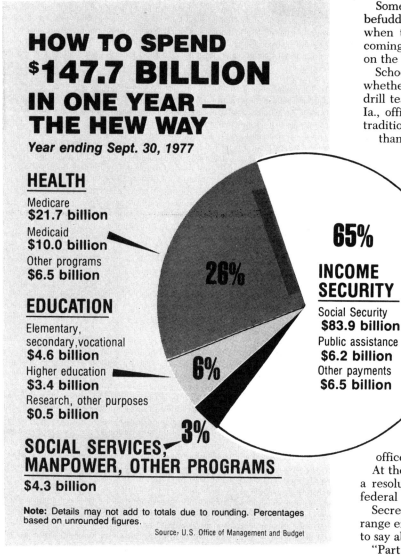

HOW TO SPEND $147.7 BILLION IN ONE YEAR — THE HEW WAY

Year ending Sept. 30, 1977

HEALTH

Medicare
$21.7 billion

Medicaid
$10.0 billion

Other programs
$6.5 billion

EDUCATION

Elementary,
secondary, vocational
$4.6 billion

Higher education
$3.4 billion

Research, other purposes
$0.5 billion

SOCIAL SERVICES, MANPOWER, OTHER PROGRAMS

$4.3 billion

26%

6%

3%

65%

INCOME SECURITY

Social Security
$83.9 billion

Public assistance
$6.2 billion

Other payments
$6.5 billion

Note: Details may not add to totals due to rounding. Percentages based on unrounded figures.

Source: U.S. Office of Management and Budget

TAMING A WELFARE GIANT
[*continued from preceding page*]

HEW's jurisdiction have been set up by Congress to operate largely outside the HEW Secretary's direct control. For example, the Secretary cannot review the budget of the National Cancer Institute, which by law reports directly to the President.

Former HEW Secretary David Mathews was asked last year if the Department is "out of control." He replied that the problem is not that it is out of control but that it is "controlled by a variety of different forces."

It is HEW's highly structured bureaucracy, spewing out a seemingly endless flow of rules and questionnaires, that infuriates many people who must deal with it.

A proliferation of programs, many of which overlap and duplicate others, has led to "a ridiculous labyrinth of bureaucracies, regulations and guidelines," according to former Secretary Richardson.

In 1973, Richardson found that there were 1,200 pages of HEW regulations dealing with human-service programs. For each page of regulations, there were 10 pages of interpretative guidelines. Rules were being laid down without coordination with other branches of HEW. "In general," Richardson noted, "confusion and contradictions are maximized."

Sometimes a law is interpreted in ways that anger and befuddle the average citizen. Such was the case last year when the Department's Office for Civil Rights implied a coming crackdown on schools that supposedly discriminate on the basis of sex.

School officials around the country were left wondering whether they would be forced to open up boys' choirs, girls drill teams and the like to the opposite sex. In Des Moines Ia., officials at Roosevelt High School decided to abolish a traditional father-daughter St. Valentine's Day dinner rather than risk violating HEW's regulations against discrimination by sex.

New regulations have since cleared up much of the confusion, but not before one newspaper editorialized that HEW was inflicted with something it called "rulemania."

"People were hopping mad." At times, HEW seems to be drowning in a sea of paper and unnecessary red tape.

An uproar developed last fall when a lengthy civil-rights questionnaire was mailed out to some 10,000 school districts across the nation. In order to continue getting federal funds, school officials were required to fill out a series of complex questions on a nine-page form. Soon, members of Congress were hearing loud complaints from school officials who said they could not understand the questions, or the reasons for asking them. Small districts said they lacked the time and expertise to provide the answers.

"People were hopping mad about those forms," said a Senator. "They were bringing them into my office in wheelbarrows."

At the height of the furor, the Georgia State senate passed a resolution condemning "bureaucratic monstrosities from federal agencies."

Secretary Califano, who has given high priority to a long-range effort to simplify the paper work at HEW, has had this to say about bureaucratic forms in general:

"Part of the problem is we designed every form for the lowest common denominator . . . as though it has to be filled out by a 6-year-old. But we made it so long and so complicated, nobody can fill it out."

Critics have come down especially hard on HEW in recent years for allowing fraud and abuse to flourish in many of the programs it manages. Investigations have revealed that billions of dollars are wasted annually.

For instance, experts estimate that as much as 3 billion dollars a year is siphoned out of medicaid funds by doctors, nursing homes, laboratories, beneficiaries and others in a position to cheat the program.

As much as 10 per cent of the nearly 6 billion dollars that HEW distributes annually through State programs under Aid to Families with Dependent Children (AFDC) reaches people who are not legally entitled to receive benefits.

It was discovered also that the new Supplemental Security Income program—which assures a minimum monthly income for aged, blind and disabled people—overpaid beneficiaries by almost 1 billion dollars in its first 18 months.

In one famous case involving HEW funds, a Chicago woman—dubbed the "Welfare Queen" of that city—collected thousands of dollars fraudulently under various programs. Federal and local officials refused at first to take action against her. It was only public pressure that resulted in her trial and conviction.

After much prodding by Congress, HEW has begun to

tighten up, especially on the huge grants and other payments to States for such State-run programs as cash welfare benefits and medicaid for the needy.

For years, HEW officials argued they had little authority to force the States to crack down on waste in welfare, even though more than half of the total funds for these programs comes from the Federal Government. There was no over-all policy to encourage State and local program administrators to hire more investigators and auditors or to computerize their growing lists of beneficiaries and service providers.

Until 1973, there was just one investigator responsible for policing almost all of the Department's multibillion-dollar activities. Only Social Security, which is administered from Washington and had its own well-regarded bureaucracy in place when it joined the Department in 1963, had maintained a steady record of ferreting out and prosecuting program fraud and abuse.

Although more investigators recently have been hired, Congress still is far from satisfied that enough is being done.

Last year, a House Government Operations subcommittee charged that the people at HEW were reluctant to reveal abuses and inefficiencies that might reflect unfavorably on the officials directly responsible for various programs. Said the panel: "Even when serious deficiencies became known to responsible officials, corrective action was sometimes not taken until literally years later."

Congress this year has ordered HEW to establish an Office of Inspector General, with an initial staff of 100 investigators and 900 auditors. To enhance his independence, the Inspector General will have a fixed term and will be directly responsible to Congress as well as the HEW Secretary. Califano says the new office is "an important self-policing mechanism that has been sadly lacking in the Department."

Under an agreement worked out between Califano and Attorney General Griffin Bell, agents from the Federal Bureau of Investigation have been assigned to assist HEW investigators until the Inspector General's office is operating at full capacity. "Today HEW has 270 cases in more than 140 cities ready for active investigation," Califano pointed out.

Thomas D. Morris, a former Assistant Comptroller General of the U.S., has been named to head the new office. Califano told Congress that he expects Morris to apply the same strict auditing procedures he installed at the Comptroller General's operation.

Has HEW grown too big for anyone to manage? Should it be broken up into two or more separate departments?

Some people think the combination of health, education and welfare functions is an unnatural marriage that will never work out. Others argue that the three vast fields should go hand in hand, since they share the same basic goal: improving the way people live. But in March, Senator

In a Small Midwest City

WHERE HEW MONEY BRINGS HELP—AND GROWING FRUSTRATION

ALBION, Mich.

In this southern Michigan city of 12,000, you can see at first hand the impact that one federal agency is having on American communities.

Albion is a turn-of-the-century-style town with a red-brick main street, quaint Victorian houses and stately farms just several blocks from the downtown area.

It is largely a blue-collar town with at least 35 factories that make everything from air conditioners to metal castings for auto companies. The population is 33 per cent black and 6 per cent Latino. The unemployment rate is 13 per cent, mostly because of the closing in 1975 of a glass plant that employed 1,000.

A lion's share. Some residents fear the growing dependence on the U.S. Department of Health, Education and Welfare and other agencies.

Albion gets a larger share of HEW funds than most cities its size because of its population and employment problems. Last year, HEW spent $600,000 here on public schools and a college.

In the last year, the agency provided the city schools—mainly through State or local agencies—a total of $272,000 for programs involving about half the district's 3,300 students.

A departmental grant of $70,000 is paying for a bilingual kindergarten for English and Spanish-speaking students and, in other grades, for programs in Latino history and culture.

Other HEW grants allocated to the

local schools a total of $202,000 for various reading programs, materials and laboratories for at least 1,400 students. In addition, the U.S. Department of Agriculture gave the schools $142,500 this year for free and reduced-price lunch programs for at least 1,200 students.

Superintendent Garth Errington of the Albion public-school system says that he occasionally is frustrated by HEW's red tape.

He observes: "Sometimes the paper work seems overwhelming. But then I realize that with HEW money, we've been able to help our students who are low achievers. At our level of State and local funding, we could never afford to do it alone."

Another major recipient of funds is Albion College, a private, liberal arts, Methodist-affiliated institution that has 1,700 students. It is the most expensive college in the State, with tuition, room and board at $4,540 this year.

During the current fiscal year, Albion College will receive $344,968 from HEW for campus programs. At least 250 students will get direct HEW aid.

Other campus projects getting HEW aid include the work-study program helping 60 students earn their way through school, grants to 160 students from low-income families and about $4,000 for new books and journals for the college library.

"HEW grants are good, but we draw the line when it looks like the Government may interfere with us and tell us

how to run this institution," says Bernard T. Lomas, president of the college.

The city government itself gets no HEW money. But it makes "extensive" use of other federal-agency grants, says Neal Godby, city manager. "We prefer to apply for other federal money, such as general revenue sharing, because there are fewer strings attached."

Other aid. The Federal Government spent at least 2.2 million dollars here in the last fiscal year alone on more than a dozen programs. The largest grant last year was 1.5 million dollars from the Environmental Protection Agency for a waste-water-treatment project.

Area residents also receive sizable amounts in other HEW funds, including more than $500,000 a month in Social Security benefits to about 2,600 individuals. Estimates are that local citizens are paid between 2 million and 3.5 million dollars in federal welfare funds—covering such activities as food stamps, medicaid and aid for dependent children.

Albion Community Hospital reports that 30 per cent of its patients received medicare benefits last year and 11 per cent were covered by medicaid.

HEW and other federal funds have been a big windfall, but civic leaders are wary of depending on them too much.

"If all federal funds were cut off tomorrow, I don't think anything in this town would have to shut down," declares Albion Mayor Charles Jones. "We're not leaning too heavily on the Federal Government."

A WHO'S WHO OF "CLIENTS"

It is a rare American family that goes untouched by one or another of HEW's programs. Among those who will get direct cash payments or other benefits this year—

- 33 million people on Social Security.

- 25 million low-income people receiving medicaid benefits.

- 15 million aged and disabled who get medicare.

- 12 million persons helped by Aid to Families with Dependent Children.

- 6 million schoolchildren benefiting from education programs.

- 5.4 million men and women with federally insured college loans outstanding.

- 4 million or more aged, blind or disabled who get supplementary-security income.

- 1.2 million handicapped receiving rehabilitation aid.

Of these and others, millions get help from two or more HEW programs.

THE HEW CONGLOMERATE OF AGENCIES WITHIN AGENCIES

The Department of Health, Education and Welfare, a conglomeration of agencies, reaches out through a myriad of arms. These well-known branches provide scores of social services across the country:

Social Security Administration. Handles Social Security payments and all other cash-assistance programs, including Aid to Families with Dependent Children and Supplemental Security Income.

Public Health Service. Includes the Health Services Administration, the Health Resources Administration, the Center for Disease Control, the National Institutes of Health, and the Alcohol, Drug Abuse and Mental Health Administration.

Food and Drug Administration. Part of Public Health Service, it sets standards for certain foods and drugs, licenses drugs for manufacture and distribution.

Health Care Financing Administration. Supervises medicaid and medicare, including policing of quality control and fraud and abuse.

Office of Education. Plans and supervises all federal-assistance programs to the nation's schools.

Office for Civil Rights. Works primarily to get school districts to ban race and sex discrimination.

Office of Human Development. Oversees all human-development and social-services efforts, such as the Head Start education program for low-income preschool children, programs for youth runaways and rehabilitation services.

TAMING A WELFARE GIANT
[*continued from preceding page*]

Abraham Ribicoff (Dem.), of Connecticut, and 28 of his colleagues introduced legislation to split off education as a separate department. Ribicoff, who headed HEW in the 1960s, said "the unmanageability of HEW is widely known." Because of the Department's immense size, he added, "leadership to handle the vast range of educational issues and programs is almost impossible."

In his campaign, President Carter endorsed the concept of a separate Department of Education, but there were indications he may be having second thoughts about it.

Califano has made it plain that he wants HEW to remain intact. "It is important that social and human services be closely related," he says, "and I think that they can be closely related."

The Secretary maintains that many if not most of HEW's problems can be solved through internal reorganization.

A design to "streamline." Califano has already announced one major reshuffling of responsibilities, calling these changes "the most far-reaching" in Department history. The restructuring, according to Califano, "will simplify and streamline HEW operations, and help make possible effective program management, sound financial control and coherent delivery of social services."

No legislation was necessary under the reorganization and much of it has already gone into effect. In the new arrangements, there are five operating divisions covering broad areas of endeavor, such as cash-assistance programs, previously handled by many offices. The system is supposed to eliminate needless spending, serve as a cross-check against fraud and abuse, and bring the Federal Government into closer interaction with State and local governments.

The surprise departure in late April of the man slated to be HEW's "top doctor" has cast a shadow over at least one phase of Califano's reorganization plan—that dealing with health policy. Dr. Christopher Fordham III, awaiting Senate confirmation, decided abruptly that he did not want the job of Assistant Secretary for Health and returned to his home in North Carolina. It was reported that Dr. Fordham, among other reasons, was dissatisfied with the reduced authority he would have under the new setup.

Despite such problems, Califano predicts that the reorganization package will produce a savings to taxpayers—mostly through a reduction of opportunity for fraud and abuse in programs—of 1 billion dollars in the first two years, and 2 billion a year by 1981.

It seems inevitable that the Department will continue to grow. Next year, President Carter plans to present his recommendations for a new national health-insurance program, which could have a major impact on HEW's future expansion.

Democrats also are talking about dusting off some of the old Great Society programs—such as Head Start and the Job Corps—which have been dormant, more or less, during eight years of Republican rule. Califano has proposed doing more in the area of child health. There has been discussion, too, about moving the food-stamp program over from the Department of Agriculture.

Meanwhile, debate continues on whether the Federal Government should take over from the States the direct financing and administration of welfare.

By and large, however, the new Secretary feels the immediate task is to prove that HEW can manage efficiently and fairly the programs it already has. He adds: "I want to make HEW a symbol of the manageability, not the unmanageability, of Government."

43

Interview With Joseph A. Califano, Jr., Secretary of Health, Education and Welfare

One More Plan to End Fraud in Welfare

How extensive is cheating in aid programs for the needy? What's being done about it? Can health costs be brought under control? For answers, *U.S. News & World Report* went to the Government's top official in welfare and medicine, who is considering far-reaching changes affecting millions.

Q Mr. Secretary, reports come in almost daily about massive fraud and waste in the welfare program. Just how bad have you found it to be?

A My estimate is that we lose to fraud, error and abuse something approaching 10 per cent of funds spent on the two large programs we administer: welfare and medicaid. That would amount to about a billion dollars a year in each program. Frankly, there is more of it than I anticipated coming into this job. It's unacceptable.

Q How many people are cheating the welfare system?

A Substantial numbers—in the tens of thousands. For example, we've come across about 26,000 present or recent federal civilian employes on welfare. Most of these are individuals at the lowest salary levels who have large families and are entitled to welfare. But many others either should not be on the welfare rolls, or they're getting more money than necessary.

We are still calculating the number of other persons who are improperly getting welfare payments. In medicaid, we have examined by computer some 250 million transactions, and discovered 47,000 doctors and pharmacists whose bills raise questions.

It would be difficult at this point to pinpoint an exact figure of individuals involved in actual fraud.

Q What are some examples of irregularities that you have found?

A Some doctors claim to have performed more than one appendectomy on the same person, or file claims for half a dozen tonsillectomies on the same individual in a year. Other cases involve women who supposedly have given birth three times in the same year, or doctors who list 70 house calls to the same address in a year.

Among pharmacists, the abuse is usually refilling prescriptions an inordinate number of times. One pharmacist we found had billed medicaid for 478 prescriptions for the same patient within one year.

Q How are you curbing these frauds?

A Many of the medical abuses can be found by searching the billing records of participating doctors and pharmacists with computers.

The welfare problems are more easily solved at the local level, using more-thorough investigations of people who apply for eligibility. We have experimented in San Francisco with a system in which we give welfare applicants a list of the official documents they will need, and tell them that we'll be running a check of every other application to make sure it is legitimate. Before the system was implemented, that office had approved more than 90 per cent of the welfare applications of individuals who walked in off the street. Now, only 70 per cent of the people who get that checklist ever come back to the office. We hope to expand this system nationwide.

Aside from these specific procedures, however, we need to tighten up the welfare system so that it will not allow abuses. The way it is now, we have a system that has been an invitation for anyone to rip it off.

If you put a cookie jar on the shelf and leave a kid in the room with a ladder, he's going to get at that jar. We've got a lot of people out there eating cookies. Under the Carter Administration's plan, we think that will change.

Q What are the key elements of the Administration's welfare-reform plan?

A Our chief goal is to target the money on the people who really need it—which the present system does not do. We also want to eliminate those aspects of the current system that are antijob and antifamily. In many industrial States in the Northeast and in the West, you're better off on welfare than you are working in a job that pays the minimum wage. That has to change.

Under the Carter proposal, it will always be more valuable to work than not to work, and it will always be more worthwhile to work in the private sector than it would be to work in a public-service job.

We also think the failure of 24 States to cover two-parent families encourages abuse. In many poor families, the most effective thing a jobless father can do to make money for his wife and children is to leave the house—and thus entitle the family to welfare and medicaid benefits. We think that the new system should try to keep families together and employed as much as possible.

The most glaring example of benefits that don't get to the proper people is the food-stamp program. There are millions of Americans entitled to food stamps who don't get them—largely because they're old or working and can't get to the disbursement offices. We would like to organize a new distribution system, so that all the people who are eligible for food stamps can get them easily.

Q Would Carter's welfare plan cover more people?

A We estimate that the plan will cut the number of

eligible Americans from 40 million to 36 million, but it will increase the number who actually receive benefits. Many who are now eligible—especially for food stamps—don't actually use the benefits. The three major benefits programs are Aid to Families With Dependent Children, Supplemental Security Income, and food stamps.

Q How much more would the new program cost?

A President Carter said it would cost 2.8 billion dollars a year more than the current program when it goes into effect in 1981. That would be added to the 28.3 billion dollars that is now being spent on welfare, jobs and related programs, and on outlays that will be offset by the new program.

Q Why do welfare costs seem to keep going up in good times and bad, despite Government reforms?

A Some programs—such as supplemental income for the aged, the blind and disabled—have a cost-of-living index that goes up automatically as inflation goes up. That population is going to continue to increase because of the "graying" of America, and because the courts are increasingly defining disability in a broader and broader context.

Although costs seem likely to level off in the medicaid program in the next 10 years, the costs of medicare for the elderly will go up sharply during that time. Why? Because this country is making a tremendous investment in its senior citizens, and those programs are going to go higher and higher as people live longer.

Q You seem to be saying that welfare costs are practically doomed to keep rising—

A "Welfare" is the wrong word. The costs of taking care of people who are not working in the American population are going to continue to rise. The most significant part of that rise will be the increasing proportion of older people in the population—a trend that will occur just as the relative size of the younger population declines.

Q Will it ever be possible to provide enough jobs for all the welfare recipients who want to work?

A I hope so. The jobs program in the President's welfare package provides 1.4 million jobs—more than 600,000 of which will go to welfare recipients. We have included as many public-service jobs as we feel we can honestly deliver. We didn't want to go out and overpromise on the jobs question.

Q Aren't a lot of people who are on welfare able to work?

A Yes, and the majority of people on welfare do work—at least part time or part of the year. We have this image of

somebody on welfare sitting back in a rocking chair, not working. Most work, but they don't earn enough to keep themselves above the subsistence level, and so they need to supplement their income with welfare.

You've got to remember something else: We're talking about a population with tremendous problems—mothers who are very poorly educated, people with serious health handicaps. A high number of these people will have to be supported by the common society.

Q Wouldn't it be better if the private sector, instead of the Government, provided the jobs?

A Of course it would, but that's not possible in areas of high joblessness, when the national unemployment rate runs very high. Back in 1968, when unemployment was running around 3.6 per cent, the gentlest kind of financial assistance from the Government would encourage business to reach out for this disadvantaged population. But that isn't possible in today's economy.

I want to make clear that, under the Carter plan, a person will always make more money in the private sector than in a public-service job—close to 10 per cent more—so there is a built-in incentive to move into a private-sector job.

Q What is the outlook for the welfare program in Congress?

A My own judgment is that we can get it through in 1978, but it won't be easy. It'll be tough. I think there are a lot of differences to be worked out, but I also think there is strong sentiment to overhaul the system on Capitol Hill.

Q On another topic: Both you and President Carter are against federal funds for abortions. What alternatives are there for poor women?

A I think there are ample private resources to deal with that problem. Private groups will arrange for abortions for women who feel they have no other option. We are carefully monitoring the health problems that arise out of abortions, and we have seen no significant increase in these problems since federal funding was reduced.

Q What is the best alternative to abortions?

A The most serious problem is teen-age pregnancy. We need to educate teen-agers about their responsibilities, and counsel them about the psychological problems that arise from an unexpected pregnancy.

Repeat pregnancies constitute another major problem. Unless prevention programs are available, about 18 per cent of teen-aged women who have had the first child become pregnant again within six months. At the end of one year, 44 per cent of those women get pregnant again, and 70 per cent after two years.

We want to get at this problem through family planning, counseling and the schools. Too often, a young girl is given 15 minutes of counseling and a choice of contraceptive devices, and then she's sent out on her own. There is very little follow-up. As a result, many of these girls are off the birth-control method within a few months and get pregnant.

We also want to make the schools understand this problem more sensibly. In too many schools, a pregnant student is removed from classes, and in some cases it would be better to allow her to finish the school year and remain with her classmates if she wants to have the baby in her own community. These women shouldn't be removed from the mainstream of learning. That just handicaps them further.

Q What about the rapid rise in costs of health care? Is national health insurance the answer?

A We need a nationwide, comprehensive health-insurance system, but I don't believe we can move to it until we change the nature of the medical system in this country.

The reason for the inflationary spiral is that there is essentially no competition for health care. There is no incentive to hold down costs or to be efficient. None of the ingenious competition that makes our industrial system work so well operates in the health industry—which is the third-biggest in the country, behind agriculture and construction.

Q How does the Administration propose to bring costs of health care under control?

A One part of our strategy is the hospital-cost-containment bill we have sent to Congress. It is designed to put a lid on hospital costs that are rising at 15 per cent a year. Such cost increases are inexcusable, because care coming out of them is getting no better. Hospitals are, in effect, a whole host of individual monopolies. The only way we can make them more cost-conscious in the short run is to put a ceiling on their fees.

The other area we feel shows great promise is the health-maintenance organization [HMO], in which a group of members pay a set fee every year. For that, they get virtually all their health-care needs from a central hospital or clinic. The HMO has a strong incentive to hold costs down while providing superior health care. HMO costs average at least 25 to 30 per cent less than conventional health-care delivery systems, and a person is 50 per cent less likely to be hospitalized under an HMO because unnecessary hospital care is discouraged.

We plan a major conference of top corporations and labor groups in March on this issue, and we think we will give the HMO idea a tremendous boost.

I should add that we have learned a tremendous amount about the behavior of doctors in the past few months as we have investigated medicaid fraud and abuse, and we will be able to use this information in devising systems to build in lower costs and more-efficient procedures to our proposals.

Q Should health insurance be run by the Government, or by private insurance firms?

A I don't know yet. We've had more than a hundred hearings on this matter around the country, and we are still forming our ideas. My current inclination is to use both the public and private sector, but I don't yet know what the proper mix should be.

This will involve a tremendous investment by the American people, and I hope it will be carefully thought through by all citizens. Our current aim is to get a national health program through by the end of President Carter's first term, so we still have some lead time on it.

Q You have indicated that you favor an overhaul of drug-safety regulations. What do you propose?

A First, all applications for new drugs should be treated in the same way, with no special categories for antibiotics or other prescription drugs.

Second, we need a better way of balancing the benefits and risks of a drug.

Third, we need to get some valuable drugs on the market faster—particularly when a drug might be lifesaving, or might provide a high degree of assistance to someone. One example of such a drug is sodium valproate, which has shown great promise in reducing epileptic seizures. It is used in Europe but hasn't been adequately tested in the U.S. because of the arduous procedures and paper work we require. We need to get such drugs out helping people, with carefully devised restrictions on their use, and I think everybody—including the pharmaceutical industries—is ready to revise the law.

Q There have been reports that your Department is going to conduct an antismoking drive—

A You bet. Just look at the figures and you see why. From the first cigarette, a person increases the danger of lung cancer on a straight upward line.

Now, the realities are that the tobacco industry has a very

strong lobby—in combination with agriculture interests—in Congress and the executive branch, so there won't be a change in the federal tobacco-subsidy programs. I don't intend to tilt at that windmill.

However, the Surgeon General and I have an obligation to educate the public—and particularly children and teenagers—to the dangers of smoking before they get hooked. People have a right, within obvious limits, to eat or drink or smoke whatever they like. But if you have a product like cigarettes that results in the premature death of thousands of people every year and adds billions to our national health bill, then people ought to be alerted to that fact.

We plan to announce a campaign early this year that will employ some very sophisticated advertising, telling people that smoking, by every statistical measure we have, is slow-motion suicide.

Q On another aspect of your office: What are the prospects for establishing a separate Department of Education, which President Carter seems to favor?

A I remain opposed to such a Department, but if the President decides to create it, I will do whatever is necessary to help it along.

Basically, as I said in my book, "A Presidential Nation"—written long before I became HEW Secretary—I think the President needs fewer, not more, people reporting to him. In addition, education is closely related to other federal programs within HEW, and it is easier to co-ordinate these programs within a single Department rather than creating another bureaucracy.

An Education Department would not be answering to its obvious constituency—students and parents—but to administrators and teachers who would assert an unwarranted degree of influence.

Q Should high schools require prospective graduates to pass minimum-standards tests on basic skills?

A I favor better and more-frequent testing in reading, writing and arithmetic at all grade levels, so that we can detect earlier when a student is slipping behind. However, it's my personal view that it's very dangerous for the Federal Government to start saying, "Every child ought to be able to pass this test," or have some kind of a national test. That's a frightening power.

Q Does your Department favor more school busing for racial desegregation?

A School busing is still where it has always been: in the hands of the federal courts. The thrust for busing in this

country invariably has come from the courts or from the school administrators, and rarely from HEW.

Busing will solve fewer and fewer problems as we go down the road, for two reasons:

One, we have overburdened the schools with all of the political freight of our failure to provide an economic system in which everyone has an equal opportunity. The schools are plagued by the same problems that any single institution would have in trying to integrate society.

Two, the school populations of the center cities are increasingly minority-dominated, with some urban school systems having more than 90 per cent minority enrollment.

It becomes very difficult to see how busing can resolve that kind of development.

Q Can we have quality education for all without racial integration?

A No. There's no question that the educational experience is better if it's a socially and racially integrated experience. But we can't expect the school system to take in two or three generations of elementary-school children, in just 16 to 24 years, and resolve a problem that has been with this country from the beginning.

Q What if the Supreme Court rules against special advantages for minorities in the reverse-discrimination case of Allan Bakke that it is now considering?

A If the Court decides that race-sensitive admissions programs are unconstitutional, access of minorities could be sharply curbed in a wide variety of areas. I hope that will not happen. There is a rational reason for establishing these special admissions programs, and I hope the Court will lay down some broad, thoughtful language of the kind they did in the original 1954 school-desegregation case that will set us off on the right track.

Q From the viewpoint of the man who heads one of the largest Departments in Government, what is the most difficult domestic problem the country faces?

A It is still racism. It astonishes me that, with all the progress we've made in the last 15 years, we still are plagued in almost every aspect of our society with issues of race. It exists in education, employment, health care and housing.

It manifests itself in many ways that I see every day. For example, if you're a black man, you've got less than a 50 per cent chance of reaching age 65, which means if you work and contribute to the Social Security system, the odds are you won't get anything out of it.

If you're a black woman and you're pregnant, you've got a 69 per cent greater chance that your baby will die in childbirth than if you were white. And there is a three-times-greater chance that you yourself will die in childbirth.

Q Does the answer lie in more federal intervention, more laws, more money?

A I don't think this kind of a problem is susceptible to massive federal funding or new programs alone. But it is susceptible to national leadership, and we need to continue to set a national moral tone in this country about blacks and their relationship to whites. That can still have a tremendous impact.

I think many blacks would agree that access to most key areas is now available to all minorities who have truly had equal educational and training opportunities. The problem for these individuals—as Jesse Jackson [civil-rights leader] says—is taking advantage of that access and helping them become aware of that access.

For the rest, it is the problem of assuring true equality of opportunity from the start.   ∎

44

National Health Care Planning

THE HEALTH MAINTENANCE ORGANIZATION

By JOSEPH A. CALIFANO, JR., *United States Secretary of Health, Education and Welfare*

Delivered before the LBJ Foundation Luncheon, New York, New York, October 27, 1977

IT means a great deal to me to be here today. This occasion gives me an opportunity to share with a distinguished audience some concerns about a major national issue. But I have more personal reasons for cherishing this moment.

For several years in the 1960's, it was my privilege to serve a President who had a shaping influence on my life — and more importantly, upon the life of this Nation. For Lyndon Johnson not only knew about government — he cared about people. This restless, endlessly striving, visionary man turned those two qualities, knowing and caring, into the greatest array of humanitarian programs since the New Deal: Programs like Head Start; the Elementary and Secondary Education Act; the Higher Education Act; Medicare for older citizens and Medicaid for the poor; dozens of other programs serving millions of citizens.

Lyndon Johnson was an emancipator in the tradition of Abraham Lincoln; a reformer in the tradition of Franklin D. Roosevelt, and a legislative craftsman in the tradition of — Lyndon Johnson.

He was one of the great Presidents.

He was fortunate, as he often told us, to have "outmarried himself," — to his great benefit — and ours. For Lady Bird Johnson was more than a graceful presence in his Administration; more than a wife who encouraged her husband when he needed encouragement, and who gently restrained him when he needed that.

Mrs. Johnson had her own clear convictions and her own career as a leader; it was she who planted the environmental movement on the front pages of America. Today, what she planted — a national concern for the quality of our landscape, our air and water — indeed, for the whole physical quality of life in America — has borne rich fruit. I'm honored to be here with her; to pay tribute to her inspired persistence and to her husband's.

Today, we honor — in their name — a man who exemplifies so much of the Johnsons' own energy, practicality, and uncommon social vision: Dr. Sidney Garfield, an authentic pioneer of health and medical care in America: a pioneer who, forty years ago on the construction site of the Grand Coulee Dam, under the leadership of one of America's great industrial families, founded what was to become The Kaiser Health Plan.

Dr. Garfield's life, it seems to me, illustrates two themes that have been on my mind since President Carter took office and I became Secretary of Health, Education and Welfare: Those twin themes are compassion — and competence.

The great challenge that President Johnson faced was persuading this Nation to tackle the unfinished business of a

From *Vital Speeches of the Day*, December 1, 1977.

generation — and to break a legislative logjam. He succeeded brilliantly — and the compassionate programs launched in these years are monuments to that success.

President Carter, his legatee, faces a challenge no less awesome: To build on that success; to answer the expectations created in the sixties for broad social justice and a higher standard of living; but to answer also another national demand that has arisen in America: a demand for prudent, efficiently managed government. Compassion, of course — but compassion informed and disciplined by competence. President Carter is determined to satisfy that demand.

Nowhere is that demand more insistent — or more exacting — than in the field of health care in America.

The hallowed, sacred symbol of health care has been the doctor with the little black bag, treating his patient — enshrined in *Saturday Evening Post* covers by Norman Rockwell and in the gentle TV image of Dr. Marcus Welby.

But health care in America is something vastly more complex than these old images conjure up. Doctor and patient are still central to health care in America — and always will be. But they are surrounded, in today's world, by something new: a vast health care industry — the third largest industry in the United States after construction and agriculture.

Consider, first, its size and complexity: more than 375,000 doctors; 7,000 hospitals; 16,000 skilled nursing homes; thousands of laboratories; hundreds of suppliers of drugs, expensive medical equipment and other medical products — with a $139 billion price tag in 1976.

The big, expensive decisions in this industry are too often not really made — they happen in a host of private and public institutions, with little coherent planning at the state and local levels.

It is, second, an industry that operates largely without the usual restraints that control costs and guarantee efficiency in other industries — notably competition.

In the health care industry, the consumer makes surprisingly few decisions beyond selecting his family doctor. Instead, the physician is the central decision maker for more than 70 percent of health care services — from selecting the specialists to ordering the laboratory tests to hospitalization.

Ninety percent of hospital bills are paid by third parties — private insurance companies, Medicare and Medicaid. This means that to a disturbing degree, those who provide health care — doctors — and those who consume it — patients — do not think about cost: someone else is paying.

Third, this vast, complex, largely non-competitive industry is increasingly based upon sophisticated and costly technology: a dazzling array of diagnostic and therapeutic devices: computerized axial tomography scanners; kidney dialysis machines; ultrasonic scanners, which are on the horizon.

In Atlanta, for example, there are 17 cat scanners for a population of 1.5 million; five of those machines are in doctors' offices. The whole state of Connecticut, by contrast, has only six cat scanners for a population twice as large: three million. And the experts tell us eight is sufficient for that population. There are enough cat scanners in Southern California for the entire western United States.

Doctors, hospitals and communities are so eager to install the latest equipment, so eager for the prestige and eminence that come from having the latest technology, that giant spending decisions are often made with little regard for necessity, efficiency, or sometimes even quality. Keeping up with the Joneses is understandable, even excusable, for neighbors spending their own money on lawnmowers or sprinkler systems, but we can no longer afford to indulge this wasteful medical arms race. We must devise ways to assure that when we spend for medical technology, we buy quality, no pointless luxury.

Fourth, the health care industry in America is, increasingly, an expensive industry whose appetite for private and public dollars is seemingly uncontrolled — and growing.

The median income of American families was $13,700 in 1975. In that same year, the average family expenditure for health care was nearly $1,600 . . . more than 10 percent of the median income.

An average hospital stay cost less than $350 in 1965. It now costs over $1,400.

Our fellow citizens paid $26.3 billion to doctors last year. Yet doctors' fees are going up — faster than incomes for the rest of the population.

Health care spending was 8.3 percent of our Gross National Product in 1975. At present inflation rates, it could reach 10 percent by 1980. Without some kind of restraint, health care spending by 1980 will have ballooned to at least $230 billion: $1,000 a year for each man, woman and child in America.

This rapid inflation imperils the ability of uninsured people to get health care at all. It gobbles tax dollars at such a rate that they are not available for other public purposes. The Federal Government now pays 12 cents of every taxpayer dollar to the health industry. The average American worker works one month each year to pay the health industry.

In health care we are driving the ultimate gas guzzler: heavy, expensive, laden with optional accessories. But we are not getting a perfect or entirely safe ride — far from it.

Our goal in America — a goal shared by doctors, patients and government; by all of us — is simple: high quality health care for all, at a reasonable cost.

If that is our goal, we must take seriously this problem of spiraling health care costs. For rising costs threaten quality; we are, as costs go up, in danger of getting less — for more. Rising costs threaten our goal of broad access, of quality health care for all; we are in danger, as costs go up, of having more expensive care — for fewer people.

Our system for delivering health care in America, despite its great achievements; despite the enormous amounts we spend in quest of quality, has some serious flaws: flaws in organization; flaws of inequity.

In our inner cities, minority citizens still lag far behind others in their access to physician care. Manhattan has 800 doctors per 100,000 citizens; Newark, New Jersey has only 60 per 100,000.

In our inner cities, the outpatient departments of large metropolitan hospitals are often the basic providers of care. Yet the cost of this kind of care is two or three times higher than the same services offered in other settings, such as Health Maintenance Organizations and community health centers.

Our present health care system emphasizes expensive acute care over prevention.

We could literally save thousands of lives that are now being stunted or lost — if we could reduce the ravages of: cigarette smoking, which will prematurely kill 37 million Americans now living; of alcoholism, obesity, and accidents. But we lack a health care system with economic incentives as strong to prevent as they now are to cure.

Clearly we must act.

Clearly our health care system has become an urgent national problem. One evidence of that is the deep concern of top corporate executives about health care costs for their employees. Major national employers like Ford, General Motors and IBM are worried — deeply worried — about health care costs. They are asking what they, and we, can do to guarantee quality health care for all — at reasonable cost.

Let me suggest some answers.

President Carter, as you know, has pressed forward on the problem of costs. He has sent to the Congress legislation that would control the precipitous rise in hospital costs — the most inflationary sector in the health industry. That proposal — a limit on increases in total hospital revenues — is merely a stop-gap solution; a necessary transition to more long-term reforms.

For the long term, we must learn to organize health resources more effectively; distribute health care benefits more fairly; emphasize prevention and establish an effective system of national health insurance.

Another important step we can take is to give major national impetus to the movement that Dr. Sidney Garfield and the Kaiser family launched forty years ago: prepaid Health Maintenance Organizations, for which the national model is the Kaiser-Permanente Health Plan.

Forty years ago, Dr. Sidney Garfield was asked by Edgar Kaiser to provide health care services to five thousand workers and their families on the building site of the Grand Coulee Dam in eastern Washington.

Dr. Garfield's idea, which he had developed earlier in Southern California, was simple: a group of doctors, paid in advance for their services, would provide continuing medical service.

That idea has grown into the Kaiser-Permanente Medical Care Program, which today serves more than three and one-quarter million members with highest-quality, efficient, reasonably priced medical care.

Under this plan, families enjoy a high level of care. But they pay less, because the system is more efficient; because it emphasizes early intervention and prevention.

Today, I want to voice a national commitment: We intend to give impetus to this idea nationwide. We intend to help make it possible for every American citizen to have the option of joining a health maintenance organization.

Why do we in government consider this so important?

A Health Maintenance Organization provides a comprehensive range of medical benefits, including physicians' services and hospitalization, to its enrolled members and their families for a prearranged, prepaid fee. Unlike physicians in the fee-for-service system — who only get paid if they furnish more care, and who get paid more if they furnish more expensive care — the HMO has an incentive not to engage in wasteful hospitalization; not to run repetitive or unnecessary tests, not to refer patients to an unnecessary specialist. The results are impressive:

HMOs can reduce hospitalization by 30 to 60 percent below other insurance plans.

Because hospital expenses represent almost 40 percent of all medical costs in the United States, simply eliminating excess hospitalization could save the government and patients billions of dollars.

The quality of medical care in HMOs is excellent: doctors have strong incentives to give good care. HMOs emphasize preventive care — periodic examinations, medical education, good nutrition, well-baby care.

HMOs encourage access to health care; promote continuous, coherent care, not sporadic, episodic care. And because the consumer knows the cost of services in advance and all at once, competition is possible. This is the way the whole system should be moving, instead of simply reimbursing people for the cost of episodic visits to treat ailments, when they reach the acute and more expensive stage.

Earlier today, at a ceremony granting Federal recognition to the Kaiser Health Plans, I outlined some steps we are taking within government to encourage the development of HMOs: steps to eliminate red tape and other obstacles.

Let me announce now a major action with far-reaching potential. I am today writing to the chief executive officers of the five hundred largest corporations in America to urge them to offer HMO membership to their employees whenever possible and to take the lead in developing HMOs for their employees.

I am also inviting each of the 500 largest corporations to send representatives to a conference in Washington on February 7 to explain the advantages of HMOs and discuss how we can work with them to make available HMOs for the employees of every large employer in this nation and to establish a network of compatible HMOs so that benefits will be easily portable. They will be joined by health industry experts, government officials and labor representatives.

This confrence will give them an opportunity to advise me as to any problems they encounter in trying to develop an HMO; and to let me know how they think we in Washington can encourage their efforts — with information, technical assistance or other resources.

To each profit-squeezed, cost-conscious executive of a major company in this nation, I would put the following question: Why not provide the same high-quality health care that your employees are now receiving for 10 percent, 20 percent, 30, or even 40 percent less than you are now paying?

So the modest idea that occurred to Sidney Garfield in the Southern California desert a generation ago became a national monument to his vision.

And so another achievement fostered by the Kaiser family enters American history, along with the Grand Coulee Dam and the liberty ships of World War II. And this achievement may be the most memorable of all.

The health care plan that Sidney Garfield and Edgar Kaiser launched forty years ago is now an idea that enriches life for millions of Americans. It is, in 1977, an idea whose time has come: an idea worthy of serving millions more.

We are going to do our part to encourage that idea.

Let us hope that, as we do so, we can match the sweeping vision, and the earthy practicality, of leaders like Sidney Garfield, whom we honor today — not just for the idea he gave us, but for the pioneering spirit that made that idea possible.

Thank you.

45

RETREAT FROM NATIONAL HEALTH

LEONARD ROBINS

It is now evident that the Carter administration is searching for a way out of the commitment made by candidate Carter to fight for a strong national health insurance program. The current tactic is to delay the introduction of national health insurance legislation until late in 1978 with the explicit wish that it not be considered during the current Congressional session. More fundamentally, the administration seems willing to delay implementation of national health insurance until sometime in the 1980s and to accept any small, halfway measures as a sign of gradual progress. If these views prevail, the net result may well be to abandon the last great unfinished piece of welfare legislation envisioned in Roosevelt's New Deal.

Carter's people do not, of course, use these terms to describe the retreat. Instead, emphasis is being given to the argument that medical-care costs must be controlled before national health insurance is introduced, lest we suffer once again the fraud and cost explosion that followed the introduction of Medicare and Medicaid. But that is a curious argument to hear from avowed supporters of national health insurance. It ignores one of the most compelling arguments for the comprehensive approach favored by the Committee for National Health Insurance (founded by Walter Reuther and now headed by the current president of the United Automobile Workers, Douglas Fraser), and embodied in the Kennedy/Corman bill—which is that basic changes in the organization and public financing of medical care are the prerequisites for controlling the costs of medical care. As Dr. George Silver pointed out in an earlier article in *The Nation* ("The System Is the Sickness," September 10, 1977) ". . . the official reasoning seems to run in a circle of this sort: costs cannot be brought under control until the system is reorganized, but steps toward a national system that will provide for this reorganization cannot be taken until costs are under control."

Moreover, the administration's own plan to take a step toward control of medical-care costs by attempting to place a 9 percent ceiling on hospital cost increases shows the failure of this strategy. The proposal has made absolutely no headway in Congress, and has been criticized on all sides as an attempt to deal with an isolated sympton, rather than the causes of increased medical-care costs.

The Carter retreat on national health insurance should come as no surprise. As President he has never been strongly committed to national health insurance, and when he was campaigning for the office his support of legislation in this area was similar to his support of the Humphrey-Hawkins bill—late, grudging and forthcoming only during the heat of the crucial Pennsylvania primary, when it seemed necessary to demonstrate a commitment to major social reform. Later, this commitment was reinforced by the pressure on Carter from his strongest union supporters, the UAW and its then President Leonard Woodcock.

We know the outcome of Humphrey-Hawkins. Enormous pressure by a united liberal-labor-black coalition met strong resistance in the White House, and a resulting compromise ensued in which President Carter endorsed a watered-down version of the original legislation. There is a real question whether this should be considered a victory for supporters of Humphrey-Hawkins. In any case, the proponents deserve great credit for their perseverance and for using campaign promises and the Democratic Party's platform as bargaining tools to obtain at least some action from the new administration. (See "The Promise of Humphrey-Hawkins" by Dorothy R. Steffens, *The Nation*, January 21.)

A similar compromise on national health insurance could in no way be construed as even a partial victory for those committed to a major reorganization of our medical-care system. The lesson to be learned from the failures of Medicare and Medicaid (partial changes in the means of financing, deliberately designed not to affect the medical-care delivery ssytem) is that whatever the benefits of incremental reform in other areas of social policy, piecemeal change in our way of financing medical care is not only inadequate, it is typically

---

Leonard Robins teaches courses in health planning and policy in the School of Urban Sciences, University of Illinois, Chicago Circle.

THE NATION. Leonard Robins. 2/11/78.

dysfunctional. Yet there is a real danger that that is exactly what we are about to get.

Despite many avowals to the contrary, it is a good bet that the next piecemeal change in our medical-care financing system will be the enactment of catastrophe insurance—that is, protection against unexpected and devastating medical expenses. Its political attractiveness is obvious: it would both relieve some of the worst fears of the American people and would initially cost the U.S. Treasury only a few billion dollars. It would, unfortunately, itself be a catastrophe.

Catastrophe insurance is not merely insufficient, it is wrong in both theory and practice. First, it continues the illusion that better health can be attained primarily by an increased use of medical technology and drugs rather than through changes in the physical and social environment and personal life styles. Second, it reinforces the American practice of discouraging preventive medicine by continuing the pattern of requiring individuals to pay fully for initial medical expenses. Finally, while it may seem that crisis medicine is a finite quantity, in contrast, for example, to the unneeded and hence unnecessarily dangerous tonsillectomies encouraged by our fee-for-service system of paying physicians and hospitals, the fact is, as the renal dialysis program and the case of Karen Ann Quinlan demonstrate, that physicians can always find more procedures to perform in the name of a one-in-a-million chance. The availability of catastrophe insurance would further stimulate the increasing prevalence of high-cost/low-benefit medicine.

In short, the financial relief for the few made possible by catastrophe insurance would be purchased at the expense of major cost increases for us all and the reinforcement of the worst aspects of our medical-care system. Only those who take the sardonic view that increasing the faults of our medical-care system is beneficial because it will increase the outcry for major change should be encouraged by the possibility of its enactment.

Any attempt to renew the drive for a strong and comprehensive program of national health insurance (Kennedy/Corman) will probably have to accomplish three major tasks—two dealing with the subject directly and one dealing with broad social policy.

The first, paradoxically, is to develop an acceptable fallback position. It is most improbable that a comprehensive national health insurance program can be passed in the next two or three years, even if the present administration swings over to a position of enthusiastic support. However, something is likely to be done in this period, because politicians will want to run for office claiming that they acted on behalf of the people's health. What we need, therefore, are policies and proposals that pave the way for an effective, comprehensive national health insurance system, rather than counterproductive measures that would delude people into thinking that the main problems of a medical-care system had been solved. The key strategy here is to resist an add-on program for everybody (catastrophe insurance) and to get behind a comprehensive program of medical-care financing and organizational reform for a selected population. Dr. Silver's previously mentioned article suggested that a comprehensive national health insurance program should begin with children, and there are strong reasons for agreeing with him. Pediatric care differs qualitatively from medical care for adults in its emphasis on prevention and ambulatory care rather than on acute care and hospitalization. Moreover, changing demographic patterns suggest that we may soon be having a surplus of pediatricians. For these and other reasons, it seems likely that the public would most strongly support, and the providers would be least likely to resist, changes in the financing and delivery of medical care for children.

It will be tragic if all the groups in favor of improved medical care at lower cost should fall back to a position that leads away from their ultimate goal—national health insurance. Unfortunately, the current distrust between proponents of Kiddiecare and of Kennedy/Corman (charges of political naiveté and sellout are common) have hampered each, and thereby made resistance to catastrophe insurance more difficult. What is needed is an integration of the two approaches that recognizes both the probable need to begin with the children and the logical progress from Kiddiecare to a comprehensive national health insurance system for all.

More fundamentally important for the success of national health insurance, however, is the development of a powerful, grass-roots social movement intensely committed to restructuring the medical-care system. Comparing today's debate over national health insurance with the struggle in the early 1960s over Medicare, one is struck by the absence of passion in the current controversy. A clear majority is, and has been for some time, in favor of national health insurance, just as a clear majority was in favor of Medicare. Up to now, however, no group has assumed a role similar to that played by the National Council of Senior Citizens in the Medicare struggle. Until a similar group emerges to symbolize and dramatize the failings of today's medical-care system, the organized interests committed to the status quo may continue to resist change, withstanding the "objective forces" that make it increasingly necessary.

The problem in developing such a movement is that the main failing of our medical-care system—built-in incentives for ever rising medical-care costs—is effectively hidden by the variety of parties responsible for payment: individuals, private insurers, state and local governments and the national government. This variety prevents the public from grasping the true costs of medical care and weakens the sense of urgency for overall change. Yet despite the difficulties, the building of a committed constituency for national health insurance is essential.

Notwithstanding these problems, it would be an error to focus only on the tactical mistakes or the general weakness of the movement for national health insurance. It was wise to emphasize the importance of forcing the Democratic Party and President Carter to go on record in support of that insurance. Moreover, the view that health care is a right continues to gain acceptance, and the organized supporters of national health insurance now have more political weight than do its opponents. The American Medical Association, in particular, is much less influential since it lost the fight against Medicare.

The main reason why the campaign for national health insurance does not pick up speed is unlikely to be found in an analysis of the specific questions of health policy and politics. Instead, this failure is probably part of the current disbelief in governmental intervention as an effective approach to any social problems, part of a general concern with, to use Nathan Glazer's phrase, "the limits of social policy." Ultimately,

therefore, the main task of those favoring comprehensive reform in our system of medical-care financing and organization will be to challenge and change the current "neo-conservative" mood of the country.

This mood is particularly harmful to the cause of national health insurance. While an effective health insurance program should, at most, increase health-care costs only very marginally at the start, and is essential to cost control in the long run, it would mean a massive shift in expenditures from private and state and local budgets to the national budget. Thus, it has the appearance of being a truly vast new undertaking. In a period of economic trouble, when the Carter administration is preoccupied with holding down *federal* expenditures and balancing the *federal* budget, it is easy to argue that the time is especially not right for this new social program.

But at the heart of the problem are not economic facts but social values. If the will, belief and commitment to national health insurance were present, the obvious superficiality of focusing on federal expenditures for health, rather than on total health expenditures, could be easily exposed. How the current mood of social-policy conservatism, widespread in the American people and present to a disappointing degree within the Carter administration, is to be overcome is beyond the scope of this article. But at least the proponents of national health insurance will be more effective if they recognize the influence of the social-policy climate on their struggle.

Under present circumstances, therefore, we must expect that issues like national health insurance will be unresolved for quite some time. Without in any way minimizing the importance of electoral politics, it must be recognized that victories at the polls are not enough. Resisting social change is easy; promoting change requires more than assigning Democrats to the seats of power.

46

Black/White Income Differences, 1967-1974

Saul Hoffman
Survey Research Center
The University of Michigan

Despite a decade of government programs which have attempted to improve the economic status of black workers, the median income of black families is still only about 60 percent as large as that of white families. Not all of this difference is necessarily due to discrimination; some differences between blacks and whites, like education, are, from an employer's standpoint, legitimate sources of wage differences. Still, economists have estimated that even if blacks had all the characteristics of white workers — the same average amount of education, the same representation in unions, the same percentage living in higher-wage urban areas, and so on — their wages would be about 20 percent lower than whites' wages.

Age and the Earnings Gap

Since the mid-1960s, many economists have attempted to explain the nature and causes of black/white earnings differences. One finding of this research was that discrimination seemed to affect some subgroups more severly than others. One of the more puzzling—and troubling—findings was that the earnings gap between blacks and whites was greater for older workers than for younger workers. That is, the earnings of black workers, expressed as a percentage of the income of white workers of the same age, tended to fall steadily with age. This finding was clearly evident in Census data from 1960 and 1970 and in many other studies as well. The table presents the Census figures; it shows the ratio of weekly earnings of black workers to the weekly earnings of white workers for high school graduates according to their age in 1960 or 1970. In 1960, the youngest group of blacks earned about 71 percent as much as young white workers, while blacks over age 50 earned less than 60 percent as much as whites of the same age. By 1970, the earnings gap had narrowed in each age group, but it was still largest for the oldest workers and smallest for the youngest ones.

Age	Ratio of Black Earnings to White Earnings*	
	1960	**1970**
22-25	.714	.806
26-30	.714	.791
31-35	.682	.749
36-40	.690	.750
41-50	.648	.698
51-60	.590	.690

*for high school graduates

Dual Labor Markets?

This finding was troubling because it suggested that black workers encountered increasing discrimination as they grew older. One economist who studied the question concluded that "the whole notion of a career with steady advancement is rele- vant only for white males."* A number of other economists had already suggested something like that, on the basis of their studies of the economic problems of low-income blacks in urban ghettos in Boston and Chicago. They advanced what was called the "dual labor market model" or the "job competition model;" in general they argued that the major problems of low-income workers was not so much that they lacked skills as that they were unable to gain access to those good jobs for which they were, in fact, qualified.

Labor market discrimination against black workers was a key element in this explanation. Proponents of the dual labor market theory argued that one manifestation of discrimination was to deny black workers access to many good jobs and to relegate them to dead-end jobs in what was called the secondary labor market. Good jobs were those which provided stable employment, good wages, and, more importantly, an opportunity to learn new skills and eventually obtain better jobs. Blue-collar jobs in unionized employment or within the more capital-intensive industries and white-collar jobs within large organizations were usually thought to be examples of good jobs.

In contrast, there were the "bad jobs" — dishwashing, casual labor, and some nonunionized blue-collar work — which provided neither high wages, stable employment, nor any real opportunity to learn job skills. If black workers tended to get stuck in these dead-end jobs in disproportionate numbers or if they were denied promotions, then as they grew older their earnings would increase less rapidly than the earnings of otherwise similar white workers, just as the Census figures showed.

The Census results and the explanation given to them also had serious implications for public policy. Throughout the 1960s, government policy was largely based on the assumption that by improving the quality of education available to blacks, black/white earnings differences could be eliminated. But if the labor market itself was a vehicle for discrimination, then the education strategy could be only partially successful at best.

An Alternative View

To be sure, not all observers subscribed to the dual labor market theory; the basic empirical finding that discrimination appeared to increase over the life-cycle was challenged by several economists. They noted that the Census findings and all other similar studies were based on information about *different* individuals of *different* ages rather than the *same* individual as he aged. In particular, they speculated that the larger earnings gap of older workers might be due either to large differences between blacks and whites in the quality of education — especially for older, southern blacks — or to the lingering effects of the more severe labor market discrimination which older blacks faced when they first looked for jobs. These economists argued that the Census findings reflected primarily "vintage effects" — the differences between older and younger workers— rather than any inherent tendency toward increasing life-cycle discrimination, and this argument has come to be known as the "vintage hypothesis."

*Robert E. Hall, "Wages, Income, and Hours of Work in the U.S. Labor Force," in *Income Maintenance and Labor Supply*, ed. Glen Cain and Harold Watts (Chicago: Rand-McNally, 1973), p. 393.

This article appeared in ECONOMIC OUTLOOK USA (4:2, Spring 1977, pp. 28-29), a quarterly publication of the Survey Research Center, The University of Michigan, P.O. Box 1248, Ann Arbor, MI 48106.

EXPERIENCE-EARNINGS PROFILE FOR BLACKS AND WHITES

Workers 20-29 in 1967

Real Hourly Earnings ($)

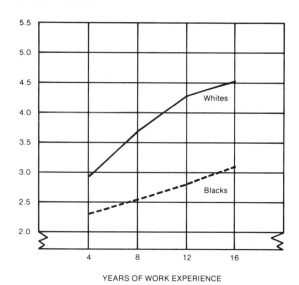

YEARS OF WORK EXPERIENCE

Workers 30-39 in 1967

Real Hourly Earnings ($)

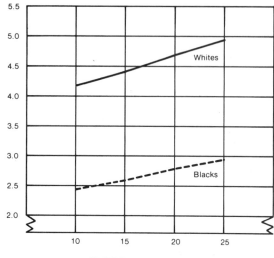

YEARS OF WORK EXPERIENCE

Findings from a Panel Study

Recent research at the Survey Research Center has looked carefully at this question of "life-cycle discrimination." The research was undertaken as part of the Panel Study of Income Dynamics, a large study of the economic behavior and status of American families. The Panel Study is unique in that it has followed a representative national sample of American families year after year, for nine consecutive years, in order to try to understand some of the changes that occur in families over such an extended period of time. Because the study has obtained information on an individual's earnings each year, it is possible to compare the growth in earnings for black and white workers since 1967.

The analysis of "life-cycle discrimination" using the Panel Study data suggests that elements of both the dual labor market theory and the vintage explanation are correct. The chart summarizes the findings for two groups of workers, those who were between ages 20 and 29 in 1967 and those between ages 30 and 39 in 1967. It displays the relationship between average hourly earnings and years of work experience — what economists call an experience-earnings profile.

For the younger workers, black/white earnings differences did tend to increase with each additional year of work experience. Consider, for example, what happened from 1967 to 1974 to the earnings of workers who had been working for six years as of 1967. The average earnings in 1967 of the white workers in this group were about $3.30 per hour, while for the black workers earnings were about $2.40 per hour. Over the next eight years, however, the earnings of the white workers grew almost twice as rapidly as those of the blacks. By 1974, the average earnings of the white workers had risen by almost a dollar an hour (in real terms, adjusted for inflation) while the earnings of the blacks grew by only about 45¢. As a result, average black earnings were then only about two-thirds as large as average white earnings, compared to almost three-fourths as large in 1967. The differential growth in earnings from 1967 to 1974 was less dramatic for workers who had more years of work experience in 1967, but throughout this age group white earnings grew more rapidly than black earnings.

Unemployment also affected these workers differently. While it was, of course, a serious problem for many groups of workers during the past few years, unemployment hit black workers most severely. Almost two-thirds of the young black workers in the study were unemployed at least once from 1967 to 1974, and, as high as this figure is, it does not even include teenage blacks who have the highest unemployment rates of all. In contrast, about half of the young whites suffered some unemployment during the period.

For the workers who were aged 30-39 in 1967, the story is quite different. The earnings growth for both blacks and whites was almost identical, about one-and-a-quarter percent per year in real terms. This finding may, in part, reflect the effects of affirmative action programs. There is no indication at all that black and white workers are participating in different labor markets, as the dual labor market theory suggests. Still, as the chart shows, it would certainly not be correct to conclude that black/white earnings differences are no longer a matter for concern. Although for these workers the earnings gap did not increase from 1967 to 1974, the difference in earnings remained large throughout; for workers in this age group, blacks earned only about 60 percent as much as whites.

Conclusion

The results for the two groups of workers are, then, mixed. The equal growth rate of earnings for the older black and white workers is certainly encouraging and tends to support the vintage hypothesis. But the lower earnings growth and the higher unemployment incidence which existed for the younger black workers are troubling and consistent with the dual labor market theory. This finding suggests that black workers may indeed encounter special problems at about the time they first enter the labor market. And the income deficit suffered by blacks at all age levels seems certainly larger than that supportable by real productive differences which might continue to exist between the races.

47

Young Blacks Out of Work: Time Bomb For U.S.

Angry at society, poorly educated and lacking job skills, their numbers are reaching explosive proportions. Massive public and private efforts have failed so far to solve one of the nation's most perplexing problems.

Drifting further and further out of the American mainstream is a growing army of the unemployed whose intractable joblessness baffles the experts.

A minority within a minority, these are black youths and adults being left behind not only by the white majority but by an expanding black middle class.

Poorly educated, untrained for available jobs, often unmotivated to seek any type of gainful work, they cluster in big-city slums to form a subculture that leans heavily on welfare, crime, drugs and alcohol.

Some had jobs but lost them in the recent recession or when urban employers started moving out to the suburbs. Others, however, are well into their 20s and 30s without ever having held a job successfully.

Authorities have tried many ways of solving the problem. But antidiscrimination laws, taxpayer-financed education and job-training programs have failed to reach what has turned into a seemingly impenetrable core of the unemployed and unemployable.

Result: Reaching and helping this alienated segment of society has become a pressing domestic problem, a source of explosive friction between the races and a major challenge to local leaders, Congress and the White House.

Although many individual blacks have made enormous strides, the civil-rights era has proved something less than an economic boon for blacks as a whole. The wide disparity between the median incomes of black and white families has narrowed only slightly since the 1950s.

Unemployment among blacks has consistently held at about double the rate for whites, until this year when the gap began to widen even more. In October, 15 per cent of the black labor force was jobless, compared with 6.1 per cent of the white. For black teen-agers, the rate was a towering 40 per cent, against 14.8 per cent for white teen-agers.

It is this chronically high rate of joblessness among black youth, who should be benefiting most from a rainbow of new opportunities opening up in recent years, that is most discouraging to black leaders, economists and government officials. The proportion of young blacks working or looking for work has been dropping steadily through periods of prosperity as well as recession.

Accounting for only one tenth of the black labor force, but one quarter of the unemployed, the black population from ages 16 to 20 is "the most serious part of the over-all problem of black unemployment," says Bernard E. Anderson, associate professor of industry at the University of Pennsylvania's Wharton School of Finance.

Soaring expectations that marked the black-rights movement of the 1950s and 1960s have given way in many areas to intense frustration and anger. Unable for whatever reason to earn a living, many fall into a lifetime routine of handouts and public charity. Others strike out at society in general through such activities as robbing, prostitution, looting and random arson. A significant portion withdraw to their own shadow world of drugs and liquor. Comments a State employment counselor in Atlanta, whose clientele is about 90 per cent blacks: "The people who come through here have a hopeless 'what's the use' attitude. It's usually their last resort."

YOUNG BLACKS ARE DROPPING OUT

Young black men and women—born since the Supreme Court struck down racial segregation in 1954, afforded better educational opportunities than previous generations, the focus of special aid for a decade—would seem to hold the best hope of breaking the race's cycle of poverty.

But instead of expanding, the job market for young blacks appears to be contracting. The official unemployment rate for black teen-agers climbed from 35.4 per cent in 1972 to 39.3 per cent in 1976. Monthly rates this year have ranged as high as 45.4 per cent.

Official statistics take into account only those actively seeking work. They do not include "discouraged" people who say they want to work but are not looking for a job. Counting these potential workers, the National Urban League estimates that black teen-age unemployment has soared well above 50 per cent. In a few areas, such as Oakland, Calif., authorities say it is as high as 70 per cent.

WHO ARE THE UNEMPLOYED?

Out of total unemployment of	6,221,000

Whites
4,774,000

Blacks
1,348,000

Other races **99,000**

AMONG YOUTH—

White teen-agers
1,131,000

Black teen-agers
328,000

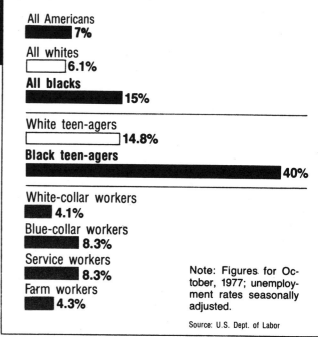

UNEMPLOYMENT RATE

All Americans
7%

All whites
6.1%

All blacks
15%

White teen-agers
14.8%

Black teen-agers
40%

White-collar workers
4.1%

Blue-collar workers
8.3%

Service workers
8.3%

Farm workers
4.3%

Note: Figures for October, 1977; unemployment rates seasonally adjusted.

Source: U.S. Dept. of Labor

Latest figures show that only about a quarter of the nation's black teen-agers have jobs, down from 38 per cent two decades ago. "There is nothing now on the horizon to change these trends," warns a study for the Joint Economic Committee of Congress.

Much of the black unemployment problem is concentrated in the central cities—areas where business is often in decline and job opportunities are dwindling.

The discouraging pattern is repeated in city after city: Blacks moved in from the rural South and other regions after World War II. Whites and middle-class blacks fled to the suburbs. Plants, factories and shops soon followed, causing a loss of jobs and tax revenue. Local services including public education began to slip, prompting more businesses and affluent residents to pull up stakes. It is a cycle of deterioration that continues today in many American cities.

Stranded in urban slums have been those least able to cope with a demanding and competitive society—the young, the old and the disabled. For them, broken families, poverty, isolation and despair have become the norm.

Adding to the problem: While white birth rates have declined sharply in recent years, the rate among low-income blacks has remained high. Black children born in record numbers in the 1950s and 1960s are now reaching maturity, making job prospects for this age group bleaker than ever. The young black population will continue to expand at least into the mid-1980s, according to official projections.

Meanwhile, blacks are being squeezed by a changing job market that increasingly puts a high premium on good education, motivation, skill and experience.

Although the educational gap between blacks and whites measured by years of schooling has narrowed substantially, the difference in the quality of their education has not.

Black leaders frequently blame the urban public schools for turning out graduates who are ill prepared for work. "The young people can't fill out a work application because they can't read," complains a National Urban League official in Los Angeles. Some trace the present difficulty to the late 1960s when educational standards were lowered in many urban black communities to meet militant demands for courses stressing racial pride.

Now there is a shift back to fundamentals. But it comes too late for many thousands of youngsters who have emerged from school as functional illiterates.

Even those graduating from high school with job skills may find that they have been trained in a field that is already vastly overcrowded or one that is becoming obsolete. In Brooklyn, youngsters at one vocational center are learning to operate printing presses of a type that haven't seen commercial use in decades. In Dade County, Fla., schools are training cash-register operators despite a surplus of these workers in the area.

Employers say many young black job seekers not only are unskilled but frequently show little understanding of what work is all about. Many have never been taught the importance of getting to work on time, taking orders from a superior, grooming themselves or getting along with others.

"When you've grown up in a family with no father present, an unemployed mother, and maybe a brother who's in jail, the world of work is something you naturally don't know much about," says a black leader in Philadelphia.

IN THE GHETTO: DWINDLING HOPES

For a closer look at the problem, visit a typical slum neighborhood in New York City's South Bronx.

Here are areas of extreme poverty, long since deserted by those on their way up the economic ladder and now ruled by street-wise hoodlums and hostile youth gangs. Many of the streets are barren of commercial activity, pocked with fire-

YOUNG BLACKS OUT OF WORK
[continued from preceding page]

gutted buildings and heavy with a feeling of hopelessness. Loitering teen-agers and young adults eye passers-by suspiciously. Out of school, nothing to do, resentment building, they simply wait for something to happen.

Youngsters in areas such as the South Bronx often wind up in trouble with the law, which gives them a police record that makes them that much less employable. Drug addiction takes a heavy toll. Teen-age pregnancy is common.

Many turn to an array of social-welfare programs—from disability benefits to Aid to Families With Dependent Children—that can be more lucrative than a low-paying job.

A Labor Department official explains: "More people are seeking alternatives to work." In the 1960s, welfare claims by mothers with children grew rapidly. "Now," he says, "we have a 'disability explosion' among males, particularly nonwhites, that has gone almost totally unnoticed."

Previously, many aimless youngsters were drafted into the armed forces, where some learned skills and discipline. Now most ghetto youths shun voluntary enlistment. Says Andrew Young, U.S. Ambassador to the United Nations: "When we did away with the draft, we closed the door of opportunity, in a sense, to a large segment of our society."

Complicating the problem for blacks is the fact that they are running into increasing job competition from white women, who are joining the labor force in large numbers, and illegal immigrants, who are often preferred by employers because they "work hard and scared."

Industries that formerly hired masses of low-skilled people have automated or relocated abroad where labor is cheaper. Even the small shops and "mom and pop" stores that once provided early work experience for young people have all but disappeared from the hostile inner-city environment.

Other potential employers generally are uninterested in hiring and training young people. Many have minimum-age requirements that exclude persons below age 22 or so.

Last year, 1,500 employers in New York City were asked to join in a subsidized on-the-job training program. "We got absolutely no positive response," notes a city official.

Some businessmen say they would be willing to hire young applicants and train them, but not at the required minimum wage. Whether the wage floor, soon to rise to $2.65 an hour, inhibits employment is hotly debated by economists. After examining the issue, the Joint Economic Committee concludes: "The weight of academic research is that unemployment for some population groups is directly related" to the statutory minimum wage. Still, Congress defeated a recent effort to enact a lower minimum wage for youth, although it cut some of the red tape for small businesses that want to hire a few students at reduced wages. Among those opposing

a youth wage differential was organized labor, which fears it would mean fewer jobs for adults.

JOBS THAT GO UNWANTED

What puzzles many ordinary citizens is that even when jobs are scarce, there are sometimes few takers for menial and hard-labor positions that are available to the uneducated and unskilled.

In many urban areas, there are shortages of domestics, yard workers, janitors and kitchen helpers. But young blacks, instilled with racial pride, frequently say they want no part of what they derisively call "dead end" or "jive" jobs.

Recent stress on the importance of meaningful jobs, says black economist Walter E. Williams, of Temple University, "is unfortunate because it creates false and unrealistic labor-market expectations among our youth."

Comments the University of Pennsylvania's Professor Anderson: "The difference between many white kids and inner-city black kids is that a white kid can take a menial job knowing he'll eventually move on to something better. A black kid sees his father and his mother—all the people he knows—doing that kind of work. For him it's not just a way station; that's his destination. So why hurry to get there? That job will be around when he's 25 or 30."

Even better jobs in the suburbs often fail to attract inner-city applicants. One reason: In many localities, public transit is expensive and spasmodic beyond the city limits.

A suburban Philadelphia firm once tried to stimulate its hiring of inner-city blacks by providing free bus service to and from the plant. The experiment failed. Those who took jobs soon quit, citing the inconveniences of rising early and being confined on a bus for hours a day. "It was a new experience for them," notes Andrew Freeman, former executive director of the Philadelphia Urban League.

Why do some cling to the slums even though job opportunities and living conditions might be better elsewhere?

Representative Shirley Chisholm (Dem.), of New York, observes: "People want to live where they feel comfortable, where they know their neighbors and have a sense of identity. So it's not easy when you offer them something— maybe out West where they have all this fresh air and can get the kids out of the ghetto. They won't jump and go, even though it might be a better situation for them."

GOVERNMENT: EMPLOYER OF LAST RESORT

Indications are that the unemployed of all ages overwhelmingly want to work if given the opportunity. In Detroit, a rumor that General Motors or Chrysler is hiring will bring thousands of job seekers of both races to the plant gates. Last summer, hordes of New York youngsters, many of them black, swarmed an office that was taking applications for Government-subsidized summer jobs.

Although experts agree that ideally some way should be found for private industry to absorb more of the nation's unskilled and semiskilled millions, the Government increasingly is stepping in as the employer of last resort.

Included in the Comprehensive Employment and Training Act (CETA), which Congress expanded this year, are programs to create public-service jobs and help disadvantaged persons to compete in the job market. Funded at 12.8 billion dollars, CETA programs are expected to serve 5.6 million, including 1.8 million minority youth, by next year.

POPULAR VIEW:
NO SPECIAL TREATMENT

Most Americans oppose granting preferential treatment to minorities and women in getting jobs or entering college, according to a recent Gallup Poll.

The survey found that, despite claims of past and present discrimination, 81 per cent of those questioned felt that ability as measured by test scores should be the main consideration in hiring and admitting people to schools. Only 11 per cent favored preferential treatment, and 8 per cent had no opinion.

and other work programs have found that few participants successfully make the transition to "real jobs" in the private sector when their training or subsidized job is over.

Another problem: Evidence of substantial misuse of CETA funds has surfaced in city after city. Instead of providing jobs for the hard-core unemployed as Congress intended, some local administrators have been found to be favoring less-needy people, including relatives of officials, and using program money to help meet regular city payrolls.

In New York, for example, a study found that relatively few of the 20,000 workers hired under the newly expanded public-service-employment program had been picked from low-skilled minorities. Many were middle-level workers previously laid off by the city during its financial crisis.

As big and expensive as federal job programs have grown in recent years, they are minuscule in comparison with the problem they address. For instance, after funds to create jobs for youth were spread around the country, New York received authority to hire only 6,000 people. The city has half a million teen-agers potentially eligible.

THE SEARCH FOR BETTER SOLUTIONS

What's the answer?

Manpower experts and black leaders are divided on many of the causes as well as the solutions to black unemployment. But many agree with Professor Anderson's observation that "no amount of economic growth" is going to solve all the problems of depressed inner-city areas.

Most foresee an expanding role for the Government in creating jobs for people who cannot compete in the labor force. To be effective, they add, such programs must be better targeted to reach the truly needy. Already before Congress are several bills to aid the chronically unemployed, including President Carter's proposal to create some 1.4 million jobs for welfare recipients. At the same time, labor specialists doubt that the Government is financially able or administratively capable of providing all the jobs needed.

In addition to a robust and growing economy, any long-term solution, they say, should include these elements:

• Greater public and private effort to improve conditions in the urban communities so that business and industry will want to return. City services need to be restored, slums cleaned up, and crime and graft brought under control. Some cities may have to offer tax breaks or other incentives to lure employers back.

• Greater access to jobs in the suburbs and beyond for inner-city residents.

• More emphasis on education, career counseling and job training. Studies indicate a need for programs that allow young people to continue their education while they work, rather than having to choose between the two.

• Continued vigilance in eliminating racial discrimination as a factor in private employment.

• More stress by the black community on self-help and the rewards of the work ethic. One encouraging trend: Successful blacks are increasingly eager to work with the disadvantaged and serve as positive role models for ghetto youth.

Calvin Pressley, of the New York City Opportunities Industrialization Center, a black-run organization that prepares black youngsters for jobs in private industry, puts it like this: "The only way we're going to affect this large market of unemployed and untrained is to provide them with quality training for quality jobs. The key is opportunity. That's what most people are looking for. Very few are looking for a handout."

Also enacted largely as a response to persistent joblessness among minorities was the Youth Employment and Demonstration Projects Act of 1977.

Budgeted at 1 billion dollars, this statute sets up a number of experimental and demonstration programs to train and prepare disadvantaged young people for entry into the labor force. More than half of the 443,000 initial participants are expected to be minority-race members. Authorized under the Act are a Young Adult Conservation Corps and several urban-training efforts to supplement existing CETA programs. In addition, Congress extended the Job Corps training program and a summer work-experience program for youth.

But as federal manpower programs expand, so does criticism of their long-range effectiveness.

The summer youth program, for instance, has been widely cited for waste and for failing to give participants useful work to do in return for their pay. Opponents charge that youngsters are assigned tasks without supervision and later return to the street no better off than they were before.

Backers claim that many of the summer-jobs program's early deficiencies have been overcome. Still, studies of this

USN&WR

Often, few takers can be found for the hard or menial jobs available in many areas despite high unemployment generally.

This article was written by Associate Editor Don Bacon, aided by the magazine's bureaus in New York, Chicago, Detroit, Atlanta, San Francisco, Los Angeles and Houston.

Myth, Reality, Equity and The Social Security System

James N. Morgan
Survey Research Center
The University of Michigan

The Social Security system has been much in the news recently. A number of plausible statements are repeatedly made about it:

1. It's going broke because payments are exceeding receipts, and the Trust Fund is heading for zero, leaving trillions of dollars in unfunded liability.
2. We must stick with the "pay as you go" system, and dare not pay for any of the benefits out of general tax revenues, or we will violate the insurance principle that makes benefits a matter of right rather than charity.
3. Social Security taxes are regressive, taking a larger share of income from those earning less than $15,000 than from those earning more.
4. The Social Security system discourages saving and hence the investment we need for economic progress.

Actually, the first two of these are absolutely false, the third is true but irrelevant and misleading, and the fourth is of doubtful truth and (in any case) relevant more for problems of general economic management than for an analysis of social insurance policy. Misunderstandings are apparently so serious and so pervasive that it is necessary to start a discussion of the realities involved by looking at the basic economic facts on which a social insurance system rests.

The Importance of Interest

In a society without any social security system, individuals by themselves or through their employer can save during an average of forty years of working life and buy a lifetime annuity on an expected lifespan at 65 of about 15 years.[1]

That forty years accumulation of savings will earn interest in a properly-functioning market economy. The productivity of real capital, made possible by the willingness of the savers to forego current consumption, produces a yield of 2 to 3 percent (annually) in constant-value dollars. In the world as we know it there is also inflation, and market interest rates tend ordinarily to be higher than the true interest rate by the rate of inflation. To be sure, savers cannot always recover the full amount added by inflation, and short-run inflations can occur without compensatingly high interest rates, but for simplicity we will assume that the real annual interest rate is about 3 percent.

Compounding of interest over such long periods as the average working life makes an impressive — even startling — difference in the amounts which one can reasonably expect to receive in retirement. With a 3 percent annual rate, forty years of saving $1,000 a year will accumulate $35,401 in interest in addition to the $40,000 principal. Further, additional interest earned while this sum is being used up as periodic retirement benefit payments will add another $19,303, so that nearly *58 percent* of total retirement benefits are *interest*. Given that inflation has been and is likely to remain with us, the assumption of (at least) a 6 percent market interest rate is more realistic, and at that rate our $40,000 in savings will provide a total of $238,950 in retirement benefits, more than 82 percent of it being interest! (See the table.)

The Trust Fund Issue

The question now arises, where is the interest paid or accumulated in the Social Security system? Nowhere. The so-called "trust fund" is a small balancing account, no real (that is, fully funded) trust account having ever been created, for good and sufficient reasons.

Recall that Social Security began in the depths of the Great Depression. At such a time, with arguments as to whether there were 10 or 20 million unemployed, it's easy to visualize the problem of taxing payrolls for the billions of dollars necessary to fund the system fully — not to mention the difficulties of trying to invest such amounts. There were really only two alternatives: buying government bonds or common stock. In the former case the interest would have come out of taxes anyway, and in the latter case the government would have ended up owning much of American industry. We have a word not much honored in this society for government ownership, and while socialism probably seemed more attractive in the thirties than at any other time, it is unlikely to have been favored by a majority even then.

Beyond these philosophical considerations are the fiscal consequences of fully funding Social Security from its beginning. Those people or firms who might have sold bonds or stock to the trust fund would almost certainly not have spent the proceeds, given the economic conditions of the times. The result of such removal of spending from consumption without its being offset by additional investment would have been a completely unacceptable deepening of the Depression.

Furthermore, there were many older people either on (state or county) welfare or eligible for it, but too proud or unknowledgable to get it, so the first great act of Federal revenue sharing was to make some of them eligible for Social Security benefits without having "earned" them by a lifetime of saving via payroll taxes.

Intergenerational Considerations

Thus began the great fictional explanation of the system: claiming that Social Security was financed on a "pay as you go" basis (though in any real sense it was not), with each generation taking care of a previous one in return for a similar promise of being cared for themselves. We would have been

PERCENT OF TOTAL RETIREMENT BENEFITS FROM INTEREST RATHER THAN FROM ORIGINAL CONTRIBUTIONS, AT VARIOUS INTEREST RATES

Years of Contribution	Years of Retirement	Interest Rate			
		3%	4%	5%	6%
35	20	57	68	76	82
40	15	58	69	77	83
45	15	61	72	81	86
40*	18	59	70	78	84

[1] It's true that men don't average 15 years, but an annuity that continues part of its payments to the surviving spouse after one spouse dies costs enough more to make 15 a reasonable assumption.

*Early retirement assumption (contribution ages 22-62, benefits ages 62-80)

Reprinted from ECONOMIC OUTLOOK USA, Autumn, 1977, by special permission. Copyright 1977 by The University of Michigan. A more complete discussion of this topic is available from the author at the Survey Research Center, P.O. Box 1248, Ann Arbor, MI 48106.

more accurate and honest, and we might have avoided much of the current nonsense, had we explained that each generation pays its own way, except those first few who couldn't afford it, and that each generation's saving earned them the *right* to interest as well as principal return later on. The consumption foregone by each generation in its paying of Social Security taxes makes possible additional capital accumulation which, in turn, enables a higher future living standard for themselves and succeeding generations — a higher living standard which they should continue to share in during retirement. Of course, the organization of the economy may be such that the savings provided are not transformed into productive investment — but this is not the fault of those doing the saving, and they should not be penalized for the failures of the economy's managers.

Benefits to which each generation is entitled can be ascertained. Actuaries can make calculations of the benefits resulting from whatever levels of payroll taxes are democratically agreed upon, assuming *market* interest rates earned on the cumulative amounts paid in. That done, the inflation-adjustment of benefits would be justified as payable out of the higher-because-of-inflation interest rates "paid" on the funds which have been accumulated (in theory). Additional desired benefits, such as payment for disability or survivors, can be priced into current payroll taxes since they involve an expected value of total benefits times a known probability in a given year (of becoming disabled or dying, for example). There might still be some desire to increase benefits to those who had not earned them in the full economic (insurance plus annuity) sense, but such intergenerational transfers would then be open and above-board.[2]

If we then start with the moral imperative that people who contributed to a social insurance system deserve a return that includes interest accumulation, we have a way of keeping the system basically a contributory one, without arguing about where the current benefit payments are "coming from." There will still be a kind of redistribution within each generation, between the lucky and the unlucky. That kind of insurance redistribution, in the form of disability benefits, survivor benefits, and the implicit subsidy to those who live a long time from those who die early, is generally regarded as equitable and deserves the term "social insurance."

Rationalizing the Current System

Suppose we agree to rationalize the system (in both the American and British senses of that term) so that it is equitable, each generation paying its own way and earning interest on its accumulated "savings": what then?

For the generation which has contributed during all or most of its working life to Social Security, there must be the general understanding that such savings have facilitated some of the increase in living standards which are now enjoyed by all of society. To be sure, that saving may have seemed to have been done by others, who in turn thought and think they own its fruits (interest and dividends); and those currently working undoubtedly feel that they are "entitled" to the higher real wages which they are now receiving. But equity demands that those who have been paying into the Social Security system now have the right, upon retirement, to some of that higher "earned" income, namely the amounts necessary to pay them back with (realistic) interest.

Some are currently rewriting history and arguing that Social Security has discouraged and is discouraging saving rather than providing it, but this confuses total saving with Social Security saving. It is true that having such a system implies a need for national levels of investment sufficient to provide the productivity (and thus increased output) from which the implied interest on savings generated by payroll taxes can be taken. Indeed, economists should have been working out the implications of the system for optimal goals for aggregate investment, rather than concentrating entirely on its implications for short run fiscal policy. The differences between cash payments (of working generations) and cash benefits (mostly of other generations) do affect fiscal and monetary balance, but so do many other things like wars and shifting international trade balances. That some such effects occur is no excuse now for fiscal-policy tinkering with the equity of the Social Security system.

What does this imply for the future? For one thing, that the so-called trust fund, always a fiction, has outlived whatever usefulness it may have had and should be abolished (or at least renamed) in favor of reasonable actuarial calculations. Payroll taxes should be set on the basis of desired benefits assuming a 3 percent real return on people's contributions. And, for the already retired, benefits should be adjusted on the basis of crediting market interest rates to their (imaginary) reserves — and this as a matter of right, not as an "adjustment" to rising price levels or a "gift" from those currently working.

To avoid such an honest solution by simply raising payroll taxes on current workers will surely create a cumulative and massive problem for the future. When those generations get to retirement age they can appropriately ask why, since they paid much higher payroll taxes, they don't get proportionately higher retirement benefits. We could postpone the showdown a while by raising payroll taxes again, but the problem would recur with the next generation.

Where should the money "come from," other than payroll taxes? That question should probably be decided on the basis of the current equity and incentive effects of the whole tax structure, rather than on some complex estimate of which current incomes might have benefited most from the postponed consumption of the earlier generations as they paid their Social Security taxes. And it really would only confuse the issue to pretend that some of the Social Security benefits "come out of" current Social Security taxes, and the rest out of general revenue. They *all* come out of general revenue, which includes contributions from payroll taxes.

There are some noninsurance redistributions within the system, of course, largely produced by the floors under benefits, and the fact that not everyone has dependents who may survive to receive benefits. The system in that sense is more "unfair" to those who never marry or never have children than it is (for example) to women in general. Further, considering both benefits and taxes it is not regressive, but progressive, for a substantial proportion of lower-income beneficiaries. High income people pay a smaller proportion of their income in

---

[2]One might wonder how it has happened that, in the absence of interest earned on a fully funded trust account, payroll taxes contributed by about forty age groups of workers have balanced the benefit payments to about 15 age groups of retirees. The answers: larger and larger working generations, failure of some to retire at age 65, and adjustment of benefits to compensate for inflation but not real economic growth. An example will illustrate the more realistic long run equilibrium conditions. If we had a stable population all of whom lived exactly 80 years and retired at 65, for every 80,000 people there would be about 40,000 working and 15,000 retired. Assuming that workers all earn $10,000 per year and pay $1,000 into Social Security, and that the retired all receive the annuity that 3 percent true interest would provide, namely $6,314 per year, then the aggregate contributions to the system would be $40 million and the aggregate benefit payments over $94 million. The large difference reflects the contribution of compound interest, which in turn should reflect the additional economic growth made possible by rational investment of the funds withdrawn from consumption during each worker's lifetime.

payroll taxes because of the covered-earnings ceiling, but there is also a ceiling on benefits.

Finally, let us put to rest that size-of-generations bugaboo. While relatively larger cohorts of retirees will require larger proportions of the national income, it is in substantial part their savings (including their Social Security savings) which have made possible the larger gross product from which their retirement benefits will legitimately be drawn. It is not the changing sizes of the generations that will cause us trouble, but our head-in-the-sand refusal to make the Social Security system a true social insurance system with honest actuarial calculations.

Summary

The system is not going broke, the balance in the trust fund is irrelevant, the differing sizes of generations means nothing in terms of the intergenerational equity of the system, and most of all seeking "pay as you go" balance by raising payroll taxes simply sets us up for big problems in the future. It might clear the air to remove what little noninsurance redistribution still exists within the system, given the potential improvement in our noncontributory income maintenance programs. Then the system, which is after all *predominantly* a social insurance scheme, could be defended strictly on that ground.

A Tax Credit for College Tuition?

YES—"Middle America desperately needs help"

Interview With Senator William V. Roth, Jr.

Republican, Of Delaware

Q Senator Roth, why do you favor a tax credit for college-tuition expenses?

A It's the easiest, simplest method of helping the big group that now gets no educational aid. Middle America is finding it increasingly difficult to send their children to college. This approach will help the greatest number for the least money.

Q How would a tax credit work?

A You would total up your federal income-tax bill and then subtract $250 if you spent that much on college tuition.

Q What would that cost the government?

A My proposal will cost roughly 1.2 billion dollars the first year. The cost would be around 2.4 billion dollars annually if the credit is increased to $500.

Q Will that upset the budget?

A No. As a matter of fact, my proposal costs exactly the same as the one the President has proposed to finance loans and grants to college students.

Q Who would get help under your plan?

A Like all tax credits, it would be available regardless of income, but something like 75 percent of the benefits will go to those making $30,000 or less. Even people who earn more than that are finding it difficult to send children to college.

Q The President says any help should go to those most in need. Don't you agree with that?

A The vast majority of federally backed loans and grants for education are now going to those making $12,000 or less. I've been a supporter of those programs because it's important to give those at the lower end of the economic scale the opportunity to go to college. But now middle America desperately needs help.

In the old days we had what we called upward mobility— where the average person could, by working a little harder, buy a better home, take a good vacation and send the children to college. Today, many of these people feel they are being pressed downward by mounting taxes and inflation, and they're getting angry. They say, "We're paying the bills, but the government has forgotten us."

Q But isn't there an element of waste in giving aid to families earning more than $30,000?

A There is waste in the present programs. These existing HEW [Health, Education and Welfare Department] programs waste hundreds of millions of dollars in administrative costs. In my tax-credit proposal, there is practically no administrative cost, and the money will all go to the people we're trying to benefit.

Middle America is entitled to have some benefits, too. The

NO—"Why should we give every man, woman and child 250 bucks?"

Interview With Representative Fortney H. "Pete" Stark

Democrat, Of California

Q Representative Stark, why do you oppose giving families a tax credit for college-tuition expenses?

A It's unfair and inequitable. It distributes too little to the people who need it, and may distribute a lot to people who don't need it or who, under the American tradition of paying your own way, shouldn't have it. It's also cumbersome, hard to administer and complicates the tax form.

Q Wouldn't the tax credit help some people who can't qualify for federal loans and grants now but need help?

A Sure, but the Senate version of the President's bill to help on tuition costs proposes making some grants available to families with incomes as high as $25,000, and loans without limit on family income. I think that's the direction in which we should move.

We can't take care of all the people who say they want help. We don't have that much money, without cutting the military budget in half. If we did that, you'd hear screams from the same people who are asking for the college aid that would far drown out the request for that.

Q Wouldn't a tax credit for middle-income families be simpler and more direct?

A Absolutely not. Doing things through the tax code has gotten to be terribly complicated. Anybody who believes you could claim a tax credit just by filling out one line on your tax return has never filled out his own return.

Tax credits are very cumbersome. The people who itemize their deductions and fill out complex tax forms have to fill out several lines to justify any kind of a tax credit, not just check a box.

Besides, we ought not give money away through the tax code. We should authorize it and appropriate it so we know exactly who's getting it and how much it's costing us. Once you bury something like this in the tax code, you'll never get it out.

The education committees in the House and Senate are the proper ones to be making these decisions, not the tax-writing committees. They understand education. They've studied it. They've been doing it for years.

Q Compared with loans or grants, a tax credit would give a family more discretion in using the money it earns, wouldn't it?

A You're absolutely right. It gives the family this much discretion: It allows a family whose children are out working their way through a community college, where the family is still deducting for that child, to take the 250 bucks and put it in their pocket and not help the child at all. That's too much discretion.

I'd want to see some strings attached to college aid. There's a need concept that's got to be maintained, which

Interview With Senator Roth (continued)

fact is, increasing costs are making it more difficult for middle-income students to go to college. At the same time, the enrollment in the upper and lower-income brackets has remained fairly stable.

Q Why not simply broaden the availability of assistance under existing programs?

A A tax credit involves a different approach. This is money families have earned and should keep rather than give to the government. The problem is people in Washington think all earnings belong to the government. In fact, the opposite is true.

All I am saying is: Let those who earn it keep more of their own money to spend on college expenses. They're not asking for a handout.

Q Given the great expense of college these days, would a credit of $250 really help much?

A One could always wish for more. I think $250 is a significant help. Most parents who write me look upon it as a step in the right direction, and over 7 million students would benefit.

Q Won't the expense of your proposal mean that there will be less money available for subsidized loans and grants to students?

A No, absolutely not. I think college loans and grants—the amount of money made available—will continue to rise in the future.

Q Is it possible that colleges will simply increase tuition charges by $250 to skim off the credit?

A It would not have that effect any more than would the President's proposal or any other federal-aid program. For every increase in college costs, there's a drop in enrollment. So you've got a restraint on college administrators to be competitive costwise.

Q If a credit is allowed for college expenses, why not allow it for sending children to private elementary and high schools?

A There is a proposal pending for tax credits for those expenses—which I also support.

Q Should taxpayers who already pay for public schools also subsidize those who send their children to private schools?

A People who use the private schools share the tax burden of public schools. This is just a matter of balancing things out. In the past, people had the choice of public or private schools, but taxes—not only at the federal but also at state and local levels—are so unrealistically high it is becoming increasingly difficult for families to exercise that option.

Q Would the tax credit make it even more complicated than now for people to figure out their income-tax bills?

A It will add one line to the IRS form. The most significant aspect of the tax-credit approach is simplicity.

First of all, you don't require people to fill out detailed forms and applications. You don't require them to disclose all their personal financial background. All you say is they can subtract $250 from their tax bill—very simple, compared with what they would be required to do under the grant-and-loan proposal.

Second, you don't require an army of bureaucrats investigating, reviewing and deciding who to help and not help—as you do under any plan with income restrictions.   □

Interview With Representative Stark (continued)

the tuition credit ignores. Why should we vote to give every man, woman and child in this country 250 bucks, whether they need it or not?

Q Which would be more helpful to a family with an income of, say, $20,000 a year—the present system of loans and grants, or a new tax credit?

A In many cases, the credit would offer less help. For one thing, loans go up to $2,500 a year, and a total of $7,500 for three years in college. Grants come to $1,600—and they would be increased under the President's plan.

What's more, a credit comes too late—six months after you spend the money for tuition. If you're short of cash, you need help in September and January when the bills come due, not in March or April when your income-tax refund arrives.

Q What about using a tax credit to help families pay to send children to private elementary and high schools?

A That would destroy the public-school system and help millionaire families as much as those who really need the help. It's true that parents who send their kids to private schools end up paying twice, but this is a voluntary decision on their part.

If we enact the tuition tax credit, parents with kids in public schools will pay twice involuntarily—once for public schools and once to subsidize private ones. That to me is patently unfair. Besides, there's a question whether a credit for those who send children to parochial schools would be constitutional.

Q Haven't there been problems with the loans and grants for college education that you prefer—defaults, for example?

A Not many. These are workable programs. They started with the veterans' benefits from World War II, which many of us went to college under. After that came loans and grants for other youngsters on the basis of need. Defaulted loans—mostly related with shoddy proprietary schools—have provided the only touches of scandal. Aside from that, the only complaint we've ever had is that there hasn't been enough money.

Q But many families complain about the forms and the bureaucracy of the grant program. Doesn't that discourage people who need help?

A The families that are complaining about the bureaucracy and the forms are exactly the families who want a handout. And they're mostly high-income families.

My point is: We don't give money away in the government. We provide assistance to those who need it, and we're charged with making sure that we do it in an orderly fashion that we can account for. And so, if you want to get government assistance, you necessarily must have the government supervising that.

I think people want to make sure that their money is spent honestly, and they don't want people ripping it off. So those who want the money have to subscribe to minimum limits.

Q Do you think a tax credit might be cheaper than expanding the system of loans and grants?

A Absolutely not!

The tax-credit scheme would be far more expensive. But more important, it's a question of who gets the money.   □

WHAT IS PARITY?

"We're not going to plant anything until we get that parity, and we mean it, damn it!" said Wayne Eakins, a striking farmer, at a December rally in Washington D.C. The major demand of the AAM strike (see accompanying article) is for price supports at 100% of parity.

The **parity price** of a farm product is an estimate of what the product's price would be if, ever since 1910-14, farm prices had been going up as fast as the price of goods and services that farmers buy. Since the 1920's, when the concept was invented, parity prices have been rallying points for farmers organizing for higher agricultural prices. From 1933 to 1973 the federal government used parity prices in its formula for determining farm subsidies.

The **parity index**, used in calculating parity prices, shows how much the cost of goods and services that farmers buy has increased since 1910-14. The parity index was 689 last December, meaning that the prices farmers pay were 6.89 times as high as in 1910-14.

In 1933, one of the first New Deal laws set up an Agricultural Adjustment Administration (AAA). The AAA paid farmers not to grow crops, and bought products from farmers at support prices that were fixed percentages of parity prices.

The AAA calculated parity prices by multiplying the parity index by the prices of products during 1910-14. This method is now called "old" parity. For example, the old parity price of wheat for December is the parity index, 6.89, times the average price of wheat in 1910-14, 88.4¢ a bushel — which equals $6.09 a bushel. Since wheat actually sold for $2.47 a bushel in December, or 41% of old parity, a farmer can buy only 41% as much with one bushel of wheat today as in 1910-14.

In the 1930's, the AAA supported farm prices at 52% to 75% of parity, the percentage varying from product

to product. During World War II the support prices were raised to 90% to 95% of parity. In the war years this did not cost anything, because market prices were well above parity; but after the war, farm interests in Washington were able to keep support prices at 90% to 95% of parity until the Nixon administration.

Imbalances among different crops began to appear after World War II. Some crops, like cotton, had gone up in price much faster than others, like wheat, since 1910-14. This meant that the difference between market price and parity price was relatively greater for wheat than for cotton, so wheat farmers were getting relatively bigger subsidies than cotton farmers.

In 1948, to equalize subsidies among different crops, Congress invented "new" parity. This is based on an imaginary 1910-14 price for each product, called the "adjusted base price." The adjusted base price of a product is the average price over the last ten years, divided by an average of how much all farm product prices have increased since 1910-14. The "new" parity price is the adjusted base price multiplied by the parity index.

For example, the adjusted base

price of wheat, as of last December, was 73.3¢ per bushel. This is less than the actual 1910-14 price (88.4¢) because wheat prices have gone up more slowly than the average of all farm prices. The new parity price is the parity index (6.89) times the adjusted base price, or $5.05 per bushel. This method was used by the Agriculture Department in calculating support prices from 1948 to 1973.

In 1973 the Nixon Administration got rid of price supports tied to parity and substituted a system of "target" prices set at the discretion of the Secretary of Agriculture. The Secretary was not too discreet (remember Earl Butz?) — one of the big Nixon scandals was the dairy industry's effort to buy a high target price for milk with contributions to Nixon's re-election campaign.

The current target price for wheat is $3 a bushel, higher than the market price of $2.47, but still less than what some striking farmers say it costs to grow wheat (around $3.50). That's what the strike is about.

Sources: USDA, *Agricultural Prices*, 12-30-77; Schapsmeier, *Encyclopedia of American Agricultural History*, 1975; Rasmussen and Baker, *The Department of Agriculture*, 1972; USDA, *Agricultural Outlook*, 11-77; Wilcox and Cochrane, *Economics of American Agriculture* (2d ed).

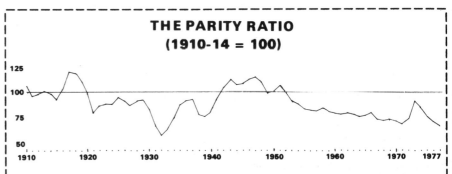

THE PARITY RATIO
(1910-14 = 100)

The parity ratio is the average market price for farm products divided by the average parity price (see text). The 1977 parity ratio of 67 means that it takes 100 pounds of farm products to buy what 67 pounds could buy in 1910-1914. Except for a brief upsurge in 1973-74 the parity ratio has been falling since the Korean War. The parity ratio is not a perfect measure of how well off farmers are. Today farmers buy many things that they produced for themselves back in 1910-1914, but on the other hand, farm productivity has increased sharply since that time.

Dollars & Sense magazine, 324 Somerville Ave., Somerville, MA 02143 (monthly, $7.50/yr.).

**They feel they have been betrayed
by the system they believe in**

Farmers on the March

CATHERINE LERZA

The striking farmers of the American Agriculture Movement are angry. More than that, they are disillusioned by the workings of the political system in which they believe so wholeheartedly.

A story comes to mind: One night last winter, Ag Movement farmers occupied a Department of Agriculture building in protest against the Carter Administration's failure to negotiate with them. Sometime in the wee hours of the night, a burly Texas farmer began to weep. A friend put his arm around the farmer's shoulders, and the man sobbed, "You know why I'm crying? I'm crying because the only way I can get into my Department of Agriculture is to break in. And now I can't even go to the bathroom without a guard with me. I can't believe things have come to this."

Hours after the mid-April defeat of the striker-supported Emergency Agriculture bill in the House of Representatives, thousands of farmers and their families marched, spontaneously and without a permit, down Pennsylvania Avenue from Capitol Hill. Converging in front of the White House, farmers demanded that Jimmy Carter come out to talk. "We're the backbone of this country," a farmer called out. "You ought to be proud to come talk to us."

Carter never put in an appearance. He was eating dinner with the prime minister of Romania. His no-show was interpreted as a slap in the face. The President was too busy entertaining a foreign head of state — a Communist, no less — to come out and face his people. Farm people — just like Carter himself.

"He's not President Carter to me anymore. He's just Carter now," a farm woman mumbled. In fact, the latest Ag Movement button reads "Impeach Carter." The crowd took up an "Impeach Carter" chant after a half hour of fruitless waiting in front of the White House. The

---

Catherine Lerza is a free-lance writer and organizer who works on agricultural issues in Washington, D.C.

scene took me back to similar gatherings, held for different reasons, in front of the Nixon White House. The anger, the frustration, and the hurt were the same.

The big difference is that striking farmers can severely affect the economy. As students, my contemporaries in the late 1960s had no clout, except as social irritants. Farmers have power — and they plan to use it.

"Naw, I ain't gonna plant more than half my land," farmer after farmer told me. "Consumers will be hurting. We wanted to do it different, but we got no choice now."

On the way down Pennsylvania Avenue, I talked at length to a middle-aged Michigan corn farmer who said he had followed USDA/land grant college advice about farming all his life. "They said I had to get big to be efficient. So I got bigger. I did what they said. Now I can't get no loan. The bank says I shouldn't even bother to plant. And you know what's behind all this?" he asked. "You heard of the Trilateral Commission?" He explained that "one worlders" in the Trilateral Commission wanted to see American agriculture controlled by foreign interests — especially Arab money. "And Carter's one of 'em," the farmer told me.

"That Bob Dole. Now he's a real friend to us," a Kansas farmer said. Senator Dole was the author of the "flexible parity proposal" enthusiastically supported by Movement farmers, a one-year emergency plan that would have given farmers higher target payments — reaching 100 per cent of parity levels — increasing in proportion to the amount of land held out of production. Before the House voted on the Emergency Agriculture bill, members of Dole's staff distributed literature to the hundreds of farmers who surrounded the Capitol Building hoping to get into the House galleries to watch the big vote. The Dole press release told farmers that the President was "sacrificing" family farmers "in the name of inflation." As the farmer's friend, Dole picked up as many political points as Carter lost.

When Ag Movement farmers came to Washington,

---

they had four demands: that no agricultural products be sold for less than 100 per cent of parity; that an agricultural producer board make and review Federal agriculture policy; that restrictions be placed on agricultural imports, and that all Federal policy announcements relating to agriculture (embargoes, loan levels, and the like) be made far enough in advance to permit farmers to plan their operations around them.

In essence, farmers wanted protection from the uncertainties of the free market, without giving up the freedom of that free market. The Carter Administration said the Movement demands were impossible and that provisions of the 1977 omnibus farm bill would take care of everything. Congress, after a couple of months under siege by Movement farmers, pulled together emergency one-year proposals that addressed short-term economic problems. These proposals were attacked by the Administration as inflationary and by many members of Congress, notably Senator Edmund Muskie of Maine, as "budget busters." The Movement supported an amalgam of House/Senate proposals which was approved by the Senate, only to be soundly defeated in the House.

After the defeat, the chairmen of the Congressional Agriculture Committees, Senator Herman Talmadge of Georgia and Representative Tom Foley of Washington, pledged to go back to the drawing board to develop long-range schemes to improve and protect farm income. But farmers are now bitter and disappointed. They see Congressional rejection, along with Carter's veto threat and an eleventh-hour USDA attempt to make concessions considered inadequate by the Movement, as a signal to plant only 50 per cent of their acreage. They also plan to work for the defeat of "enemy" members of Congress.

"You know, I think that if the Administration had made its proposals last December, the Movement might have gone along with them," a Congressional aide told me. "But it was too little, too late. The farmers were too angry about the way Carter treated them at first."

By the time I left the White House rally, I was angry too — angry at the Administration, Congress, and the striking farmers. All have demonstrated the kind of shortsightedness in policymaking that will create continued instability in the U.S. agricultural economy and allow the continued exploitation of boom-and-bust agricultural cycles by big banks, big grain dealers, big food processors and retailers, and a handful of big farmers.

The President and Secretary of Agriculture Bob Bergland ducked the issue as long as possible and chose to play down the real economic desperation of Movement farmers. In doing so, they may have destroyed any possibility of exerting leadership in agriculture policy. Members of Congress, for the most part, went one of two ways in their response to the farm strike — they climbed on the Ag Movement bandwagon in this election year, or they went along with the Administration.

But it is the farmers who ought to know better than to accept short-term solutions to a long-term problem. Most of them refuse to look at any issues but those which directly affect farm prices, so they have focused almost totally on 100 per cent of parity. "This is an economic problem," a Minnesota farmer told me somewhat testily when I suggested that other issues might be involved in the farm crisis. "Just give us fair prices — we'll do the rest," he said. But what farmers really ought to fear is what appears to be the future structure of American agriculture. Will we have family-owned and operated farms, or will we have agricultural production controlled by outside investment capital? It may not be the "one worlder" Trilateralists whom farmers ought to blame for their troubles, but a more subtle conspiracy of Government and private interests working to push agriculture into an industrial mold — agribusiness. Even attainment of 100 per cent of parity would not be enough to stop, or even control, these forces.

Parity had made headlines, but the real issue is not the overall size of Federal agriculture payment programs, but who benefits from them. And underlying that issue is an even deeper one: Were Federal farm programs set up to do what the public — farmers and consumers alike — thinks they are doing?

Family farms are a mainstay of political rhetoric, embodying everything good about America — independence, self-reliance, and competition. But behind the rhetoric, Federal farm policy since World War II has been based on the assumption that there is a "farm labor problem" — too many people working the land. As Richard Nixon's Secretary of Agriculture, Earl Butz, succinctly put it, farmers ought to get big or get out.

The Presidents and Secretaries of Agriculture of the past three decades have praised family farmers as the most efficient units of production in the world and bastions of competitive free enterprise, but Federal farm policy has inexorably reduced the number of these farmers to praise: In 1945 there were 5.8 million farms in the United States, while today there are only 2.3 million. Federal policy has helped create farming units so large and so dependent on expensive methods of production that few people can afford to own them. This has meant that fewer farmers (or corporations) own larger pieces of land, and that the nation's agricultural system is moving toward what agricultural economists carefully call a "two-tiered" system of production: one person owns the land and someone else farms it. A less careful name for this is tenant farming. Finally, Federal policy has resulted in middle-income farmers ($2,500 to $40,000 gross income per year) earning an ever-larger portion of their annual income away from the farm in order to stay on the land.

Since 1973, cash receipts from farming have increased, but increasing production costs (mainly in the price of fuel and petroleum-based agri-chemicals) have eaten up any net gains in farm income. Net yearly income per farm is down an average of about $4,000 since 1973, the USDA estimates. In order to boost their declining income, more and more farmers and their families have begun to take jobs off the farm. A farm wife told me that she and some 800 farmers in her northern Michigan county now hold off-farm jobs. "That's 800 jobs that could go to some-

60 per cent of all Federal farm payments, with more than one-third of total payments going to the $100,000-a-year farmers.

In 1977, big farms received about $2,340 each in Federal payments. Middle-sized farms, on the other hand, received about $500 each. This estimate (by the Library of Congress Research Service) is not quite accurate, but even these aggregate figures demonstrate real discrimination against small and moderate-sized family farms. And they give the lie to eloquent rhetoric about Federal concern for the family farm system of agriculture.

Susan Sechler, an agricultural analyst formerly with the Agribusiness Accountability Project and now with the USDA, likens Federal payment programs to a safety net. But, as she pointed out last fall in a *New York Times* article, most of our farmers are now slipping through the holes in the net.

Is access to credit the answer for farmers? After the defeat of the Emergency Agriculture bill, House Agriculture Chairman Tom Foley said he would act immediately on an agricultural credit bill in an attempt to placate farmers. But farmers themselves, although they need production loans every year, say refinancing is not the answer: Farmers already owe too much.

Agricultural economists estimate that farmers bear $8 worth of debts for every dollar of annual income — the worst debt service ratio farmers have ever faced. Cynthia Guyer, director of the agriculture project of the Conference on Alternative State and Local Public Policy, puts it simply: "Farmers don't need credit — they need income." They need an income that is stable, that does not fluctuate between boom prices like those that accompanied the Russian wheat deal and the price disasters of the past year.

For instance, a simple and non-inflationary way to increase farm income is to reduce production costs. This can be done by helping farmers move away from highly mechanized, energy-intensive farm methods that rely on petroleum-based fertilizers and pesticides and big machinery toward systems that conserve (or even produce) energy. Organic, or quasi-organic, farming methods that use natural fertilizers (such as manure), crop rotation, and green manure crops to improve soil fertility use less energy than do conventional farming methods. A 1976 study by researchers at Washington University in St. Louis showed that commercial organic grain farmers in the Middle West produced yields nearly equal to their conventional counterparts, and that organic farmers had far lower production costs. Thus, the overall cash flow income picture was much better for organic farmers.

Costs can be cut through the introduction of energy-conserving farm technology — solar-heated barns, generation of methane gas from manure, wind-powered irrigation systems, and the use of smaller, family-farm-sized machinery. Such technology is not in the pipe-dream stage, but is already working on farms all over the country. The Small Farm Energy Project in Nebraska, funded by the Federal Community Services Administration, is having great success in its on-the-farm demonstration program helping twenty-five Nebraska farmers cut down

body else, city people," she said. "We don't want to be working off the farm, but it's the only way we can stay on."

USDA figures show that the largest segments of off-farm income occur in the largest farms (where farmers often earn income as bank vice presidents or board members) and in the smallest (which the USDA now considers "rural residences" rather than farms). The 1.2 million farmers in the middle — the family farms of American mythology — by not making much from farm operations ($2,000 to $10,000 per year) and not much from off-farm jobs ($6,000 to $10,000 per year) wind up with an average net annual income of about $12,000. Ironically, most of these $12,000-per-year farmers own farm land and equipment worth well over $200,000.

Who, then, are the wealthy farmers about whom those of us who live in the city hear so much? There are only about 450,000 American farmers who have more than $40,000 per year in gross income, and only about 150,000 gross $100,000 or more. About 5.6 per cent of all American farms accounted for 59.6 per cent of all agricultural production in 1976. If current trends do not change, 10 per cent of all farms will sell 92 per cent of all farm output by 1986, economists estimate. The farmers in the $40,000-per-year-plus bracket receive more than their energy use, install such renewable energy systems as solar collectors on their farms, and use the best possible energy conservation techniques. The project is working — farmers are reducing energy use and production costs — using systems that farmers build and install themselves at the lowest possible costs.

Another way to increase farm income is direct marketing. If farmers could market some of their production directly to consumers — a real possibility for vegetable, fruit, dairy, and poultry producers — they could charge higher prices for their products than they are able to charge wholesalers or processors. Consumers, on the other hand, would pay less. Direct marketing systems could revitalize regional agricultural systems, cut transportation, processing, and storage costs, and permit farmers to stay on the farm without outside, off-farm income. Some states, notably West Virginia and Georgia, have tried to keep small farmers on the land through state-operated and supported marketing systems. "It's better than welfare," West Virginia's Commissioner of Agriculture observes.

Federal payment programs could be restructured so that they do not encourage farmers to increase their acreage. Under the present system, farmers receive Federal payments on a per-bushel basis — the more they produce, the more payment money they receive. This means that those who need the program most end up with the smallest share of the payments. The USDA could limit the number of bushels for which a farmer can receive direct payments (target prices) or loans. A payment cap that reflected the desire to shore up family farm operations could accomplish what political rhetoric cannot — protecting the family farm as an economic and social unit through the removal of a major incentive for unlimited farm expansion.

Payment programs cannot be operated without placing some demands on farmers. For instance, participation in payment programs should be tied into participation in soil erosion control programs. Farmers complain that they cannot take good care of their soil because they are forced into continuous, all-out production, but it is not clear they would adopt sound soil conservation methods if left to their own devices, even if the pressures were reduced. The health of the nation's soil is too important to rest on the whims of the free market or on an individual farmer's inclinations.

A Federal grain reserve system should be a key element of any stable food/agriculture policy. Many farmers distrust reserves because the Federal Government might choose to dump grain on the market when prices are high. However, reserves are also a way of preventing severe fluctuations in grain prices and could, if carefully administered, provide the nation — and the world — with a food safety valve.

Consumers should be assured that the prices they pay in the supermarket bear some relationship to farm prices. As Ag Movement farmers are fond of pointing out, in 1973, when a loaf of bread cost less than it does today, the value of the wheat in that bread was twice what it is now. Similar statistics apply to the value of sugar in soft drinks and other consumer items. The Federal Government could do farmers and consumers a great service by letting the public know how much of the retail cost of staple items goes to the farmer, how much to processors and other middlemen, and how much to the retailer.

The American Agriculture Movement has told the public that farmers are the economic victims of a cheap food policy. And it is true: The average return on investment in a farm operation is three per cent, compared to the 10 per cent return on investment for most food processors and retailers, and an average of 20 per cent for the petroleum and minerals industries. One economist told me that farmers earn, on the average, about $3 an hour, if their income is figured on the basis of a 3 per cent return on investment. If per-hour-wages are computed using a 10 per cent return-on-investment figure, farmers wind up with a negative income.

As striking farmers have told the public and the President many times, no other industry would continue to operate if its return on investment were so low. That's why a strike seems more logical to some farmers than does continuing to accept falling income and rising debts. The question is whether this historic farm strike will herald the beginning of a new, progressive agriculture policy or become just an opportunity for a few politicians to make a name for themselves — at the expense of American farmers and consumers.

A new agriculture policy should do more than shore up the present system. It should involve overhauling USDA programs, redirecting services of the state cooperative extension services which operate out of America's land grant colleges, and redirecting agricultural research to serve the needs of small and medium-sized farmers who want to *stay* small or medium-sized.

A few members of Congress have proposed a Family Farm Development Act which would do just that. One of the authors of the bill is Representative Rick Nolan of Minnesota, a wholehearted supporter of the American Agriculture Movement. While he supported the Emergency Agriculture bill out of loyalty to the Movement and his rural constituents, he also sees the need for long-range policy changes. "There's more than one way to cook a chicken," Nolan has said, and his staff continues to work both with Movement farmers and in support of the Family Farm Development Act.

In any case, neither the President nor Congress can afford to ignore the farm strike. Farmers have just begun to comprehend the scope of their economic power, as well as the ways of legislative politics in Washington and in their home districts. They will use both with increasing sophistication during this election year.

During that march down Pennsylvania Avenue, I asked a farmer what he planned to do next. He answered me quickly, "Well, I'll go home and plant a little. But I'll be back." Then he smiled and pointed to a yellow button he wore on his blue-and-red Ag Movement tractor cap. It said, "We have only just begun to fight."

Farmers gain little, consumers lose more

The farm strike has wrung some concessions from the Administration to no one's great astonishment. But these gains will cost money, and can only be seen as another in a series of setbacks for the nonfarm public.

The "tractorcades" are gone now, the lobbyists have disbanded, and while the picket signs haven't been destroyed at least they've been put in storage. The strike by the American Agriculture group is winding down for the moment, and if it can be termed a qualified success, that's because its greatest support came from Washington, not Winnebago.

This is not particularly surprising; Washington makes almost an annual ride to the farmers' rescue. Nor is it noteworthy that farmers are less than satisfied with President Carter's concessions. What is news is that the prospect of even higher food prices and more federal aid is causing a roar of dismay from consumers and taxpayers that threatens to drown out the farmers' voice in the enactment of future farm legislation.

On the surface, the farm picture looks fairly bright. Prices received by farmers for all raw commodities had risen about 20% by April from the seasonal low of last September, when record harvests of corn and soybeans were in progress. And much of the price rise in recent months stemmed from higher-than-expected prices for meat animals — particularly cattle and hogs. Reflecting this strength, broiler prices have also risen (chart, page 10).

Crop prices also advanced in March and April. The largest gainer has been soybeans, as the Brazilian drought drove up demand for — and thus the price of — U.S. beans. Grain prices are rising, too, in response to both strong export demand and farmers' increasing participation in the wheat and feedgrain set-aside programs and their heavy entries of grain in the price-support program.

Most of this year's rise in farm product prices was caused by bad weather. Excessive rains in California damaged fresh vegetable crops and hampered harvesting operations, while the winter storms in the Midwest and Northeast cut into livestock supplies and disrupted the flow of farm commodities and food products to many markets.

After seven consecutive months of increase, prices received by farmers for their raw products in April were 9% higher than a year earlier. But this upsurge was partly offset by a 6% rise during the past year to a new high in prices paid by farmers for goods and services used in production. This put the April ratio of the index of prices received to the index of prices paid at 96 (1967=100), a bit better than the 94 of a year earlier but one-third below the August 1973 high of 144.

The official parity ratio paints a less favorable picture of farm economics. This measure was only 71 in April, versus 106 in August of 1973. In theory, 100% of parity seeks to re-establish the purchasing power that farmers enjoyed in the prosperous 1910-14 period. Critics of parity claim it's an outmoded concept and fails to take into account productivity increases brought about by the vast technological advances made since those base-period years. For example, in 1977 corn production averaged almost 91 bushels an acre; in 1910-14 the average was only about 26 bushels.

But regardless of its failings, the concept of 100% of parity is still the touchstone for farm groups like American Agriculture. Setting a deadline of December 14, 1977 for a nationwide farm strike if 100% of parity weren't achieved by that date, American Agriculture representatives lobbied in many state capitals and in Washington, D.C. and picketed food stores across the nation. But except for some scattered violence and minor disruptions, the strike fizzled out. The movement was unable to enlist enough farmers to participate in its cause to stop the distribution of foodstuffs to market.

Most of the farmers actually "on strike" were grain farmers from the West, South and

Farm prices – on the upswing

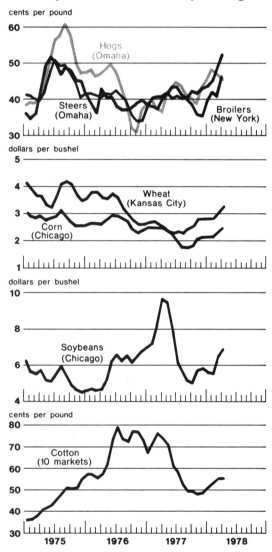

cents per pound

Hogs (Omaha)

Steers (Omaha)

Broilers (New York)

dollars per bushel

Wheat (Kansas City)

Corn (Chicago)

dollars per bushel

Soybeans (Chicago)

cents per pound

Cotton (10 markets)

1975   1976   1977   1978

Midwest. But although these were the producers with the biggest gripe over low prices last winter, they had the least impact on prices in the winter months and the least at stake in striking at that time.

When spring arrived, the American Agriculture strike leaders switched their strategy, calling on farmers to reduce crop plantings by as much as 50%. In fact, they precipitated an emergency farm bill in Congress that, among other provisions, would have boosted price supports in proportion to the amount of wheat, feedgrains and cotton taken out of production. For example, if a producer left acreage equal to 50% of his wheat plantings idle, he would get a target support of $5.04 per bushel, or 100% of parity for his wheat.

The emergency farm bill was passed by a small margin in the Senate, only to be decisively defeated in the House. If it had passed, the bill could have cost anywhere from $2.1 billion to as much as $13 billion, depending upon weather and farmer participation. Even if the bill had passed the House, President Carter had indicated he would veto it.

Tactical shift

In an attempt to head off passage of the bill, the Administration took actions to "sweeten" the current farm program. These included, among other things, expanding and liberalizing the farmer-owned reserve program for grains, purchasing wheat in the market to build an emergency reserve of 220 million bushels, and encouraging lower wheat and feedgrain production by offering farmers more incentives to participate in set-aside programs. The Administration also increased loans for soybeans to make them more competitive with other crops, and encouraged passage of an economic emergency loan program to make it easier for farmers and ranchers to get credit and repay debts.

Despite defeat of the emergency farm bill, which represented a severe blow to the hopes of the American Agriculture movement, farm legislation in this session of Congress is still a possibility. Congress has already approved a bill to pump $4 billion in emergency credit into the farm economy, and the President reportedly is prepared to back legislation giving him discretionary power to raise grain and cotton support target prices in years when set-aside acreage reduction programs are in effect. Although willing to raise the 1978 wheat target price from its current level of $3 per bushel to $3.40, the President opposes support increases for this year's crops of feedgrains and cotton. Even without new legislation, the

1978 target price for wheat will rise to $3.05 per bushel if the harvest does not exceed 1.8 billion bushels.

Despite the efforts of the American Agriculture movement and the vagaries of weather, most farmers apparently are planning to plant about as much this spring as they did last year. Thus, another bumper harvest is likely, barring unfavorable growing conditions or widespread compliance with the Administration's programs to reduce output via set-aside programs to bolster the prices of key crops.

Better days ahead

Even without a new farm bill, the outlook for farm income has improved considerably in recent weeks. Earlier this year, the Department of Agriculture had predicted that farmers' realized net income — which peaked at nearly $30 billion in 1973 — would in 1978 remain close to the 1977 estimate of $20.4 billion. But according to Secretary of Agriculture Bob Bergland, farmers' realized net income in 1978 could hit $24 billion, the third highest ever (chart at right). He attributed the upward revision to the fact that wheat, feedgrain and livestock prices have substantially strengthened in recent months due to the Administration's latest actions and because farmers are participating in the grain reserve and set-aside programs.

Although failing in its attempt to secure 100% of parity for farm products, the American Agriculture movement did attract considerable attention and achieve some of its goals. But its chief weakness was that it was mainly confined to grain producers. The goal of 100% of parity for grains was not widely supported; livestock producers in particular feared the higher costs. For example, if corn prices were at 100% of parity, corn would become too expensive to feed to cattle, hogs and chickens. Also, producers of other non-grain commodities felt that the legislation calling for high support prices for grains wouldn't do much for them.

If the American Agriculture movement's strike was not a complete success, it was at least a partial victory in terms of the conces-

Farm income
Better times ahead?

billions of dollars

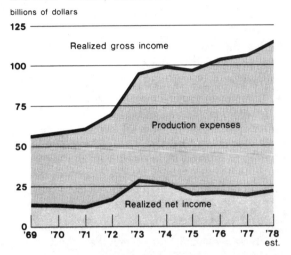

sions it won from the Administration. But these same concessions, while not as far-reaching or as expensive as the emergency farm bill would have been, must be considered another in a series of setbacks for consumers and taxpayers.

As the April 11 issue of *Milling & Baking News* pointed out: "The principal worry with efforts to spur increased acreage withdrawals . . . is the vulnerable posture this creates for the American consumers, as well as for foreign lands depending on America as a food source. There is an inherent geometric price threat where cropland has been artificially reduced by Treasury payments."

The key word is "geometric." For every acre of cropland a farmer takes out of production, the nonfarm public pays twice — through higher prices at the supermarket and a heavier tax load.

The farmer's problems are not new. But neither are they confined to the farm. The great majority of American households has to contend with rising inflation and debt burdens that seem heavier every year. And as the protests get louder, the government might be forced to put the farmer in the same category as the businessman when deciding who pays for lunch.

A PRIMER ON AGRICULTURAL POLICY

*By Marvin Duncan and
C. Edward Harshbarger*

Agricultural policy is attracting a growing body of followers. As Senator Herman E. Talmadge, Chairman of the Senate Agricultural Committee, puts it, "Times have changed in the development of agricultural policy. It used to be that only farmers and the government were concerned over farm programs and little national attention was paid when we passed a farm bill. Today, agriculture touches everyone in America, and its importance is widely recognized. Our people have been reminded that milk does not come from plastic containers and that bread does not originate at the bakery."[1]

However, the rationale for an agricultural policy is confusing to many people. Further, the expressed goals for policy are unclear and frequently conflicting and the terminology is often unfamiliar. Thus, to promote greater understanding of agricultural policy and its various goals, this article examines agriculture's role in the general economy and the unique characteristics of agricultural production. Moreover, because common understanding of policy issues and terminology is helpful, a glossary of frequently used terms is included to assist interested persons in discussing the issues. A future article will examine the evolution of U.S. farm policy and discuss policy goals.

THE ROLE OF AGRICULTURE IN AN INDUSTRIAL SOCIETY

Over the years, agriculture has become increasingly integrated into many different facets of the U.S. economy as both a supplier and user of goods and services. When those industries that supply inputs to farmers as well as those that process and market farm products are included in the picture, agriculture and its backward and forward linkages account for about one-sixth of GNP, about one-fifth of total employment, and about one-fourth of export earnings.[2] Because of this interdependence, agricultural policy must now be viewed in terms of this nation's goals for economic growth, employment, and price stability, and not necessarily in terms of what is beneficial solely to farmers.

What Does Agriculture Produce?

In 1976, the U.S. Department of Agriculture (USDA) estimated that total output from the agricultural complex amounted to $300 billion. Of this amount, cash receipts from farm marketings totaled about $100 billion, while the remainder represented the cost of marketing: the added costs of processing, packaging, transporting, and merchandising the products between the farmer and the consumer. Clearly, a $300-billion industry is capable of providing a large number of jobs and generating a substantial amount of income within the general economy. Furthermore, any new developments in an industry of this size are bound to have a significant rippling effect on other economic sectors.

During the past few years, rapidly rising food prices have caused great concern among

---

[1] *Farmland News*, June 30, 1977, p. 5.

[2] *A New U.S. Farm Policy for Changing World Food Needs*, Committee for Economic Development, New York, N.Y., October 1974, p. 29.

Reprinted from Federal Reserve Bank of Kansas City *Monthly Review*, September–October, 1977.

policymakers and consumers alike. As a result, the public has learned more about food production and the costs of marketing. In 1975, consumers spent about $185 billion for food, and the figure for 1976 was probably around $200 billion.[3] Since the farm value of these outlays was about $55 billion, the bulk of consumer expenditures for food went toward defraying the costs of marketing—at least $100 billion on the food items produced domestically. Labor costs are the largest component of the marketing bill, accounting for about one-half of the total. Thus, in 1975 and again in 1976, approximately $50 billion was paid to an estimated 6 million workers in the food processing and distribution system.

The sharp rise in agricultural exports has also added stimulus to the economy. A study by USDA indicated that the $22 billion in foreign sales in fiscal 1975 probably generated an additional $21 billion in business activity in transportation, manufacturing, food processing, and construction.[4] Thus, the multiplier effect was almost 2. These shipments and the attendant increase in business activity were responsible for about 1.2 million jobs. From this evidence, it should be clear that agricultural producers make many valuable contributions to the economy providing food and opportunities for additional employment as well.

What Does Agriculture Consume?

Agriculture has undergone dramatic change during the past 40 years as farms have become fewer but larger. One manifestation of the technological revolution has been the substitution of capital items for labor, with the result that the ratio of purchased inputs to total inputs has risen sharply. Thus, modern farmers now depend heavily on other businesses to supply them with the goods and services needed to produce food efficiently. Because of this increased dependence on outside suppliers, coupled with sharply higher prices since 1970, production costs in agriculture have sky-rocketed. In 1976, these costs were about $81 billion as compared with $44 billion in 1970. While this sharp expansion in production costs has impaired the net cash flow position of many farm operations in recent years, a considerable amount of additional business activity has been generated in the economy by these expenditures.

According to USDA, farmers spent $7 billion for capital items in 1971.[5] More recently, however, capital expenditures in agriculture have been exceeding $12 billion annually. It was estimated that the $7 billion spent for new capital items in 1971 produced an additional $8 billion worth of business activity—the multiplier effect was more than 2. To maintain this level of economic activity, nearly 650,000 workers were needed to produce and deliver farm capital items in 1971.

Capital spending in farming is only the beginning. Farmers also spend substantial sums for fertilizer, feed, seed, fuel, labor, and interest. All of these outlays also have a multiplier effect in the economy. In 1976, about 72 per cent—or $58.7 billion—of the production costs in agriculture were of nonfarm origin. Assuming a multiplier effect of 2.0, these outlays produced perhaps an additional $60 billion in business activity in the economy. Obviously, many jobs were associated with this additional business. Hence, in our modern economy, agriculture is no longer a self-sufficient industry offering a unique way of life to farm people. Rather, agriculture is an integral part of the economic system that accounts for a significant amount of economic activity in the United States.

---

[3] *Agricultural Outlook*, U.S. Department of Agriculture, Economic Research Service, AO-19, March 1977, p. 9.

[4] *Agricultural Outlook*, U.S. Department of Agriculture, Economic Research Service, AO-4, September 1975, pp. 15-17.

[5] *Agricultural Outlook*, U.S. Department of Agriculture, Economic Research Service, AO-7, January-February 1976, pp. 17-19.

WHAT IS DIFFERENT ABOUT AGRICULTURE?

A special agricultural policy in this country is—in large part—premised on the assumption that agricultural producers face business management problems that are unique to their industry. Common wisdom among members of Congress and agricultural producers has generally supported this view. The result has been the enactment of a series of farm bills by congress over the past few decades.

Increasingly, however, questions are being asked and judgments—both private and public—rendered as to the uniqueness of agriculture and, hence, the need for a special agriculture policy apart from a national policy on food. Increasingly, questions are raised about who the recipients of agricultural policy benefits are, about the implications of such policy on the structure of agriculture, and about how well past and present agricultural policy has served producers and consumers. Although answers to these questions lie outside the scope of this article, it is helpful to have some understanding of the characteristics of agricultural production that tend to make it unique.

Many Producers

The agricultural industry in the United States has historically been characterized as having many small producers—none of whom supply enough of the market to affect the price of the product. The wide dispersion of production decisionmaking has made it very difficult for farmers and ranchers to make group decisions on production or marketing. While this has generally been conceded by policymakers in the past, is it still true?

The U.S. farm population has been declining both absolutely and as a proportion of the total population, to 8.86 million persons and 4.2 per cent of the U.S. population in 1976. Nonetheless, there are still 2.8 million farms in the United States and most of them are operated by full or part owners (87 per cent). Despite the fact that 36 per cent of all farms in 1975 had annual sales of more than $20,000, and despite the growing importance of these commercial farms, U.S. farmers have not been very successful in coordinating planting and marketing decisions for their own benefit. For example, wheat acreage in the United States was reduced by only 7 per cent for the 1977-78 crop year and production hardly at all, although there was widespread agreement among wheat farmers last summer that another 2-billion-bushel wheat crop would add to the surplus and severely depress wheat prices. Thus, although the productive capacity of U.S. agriculture is being concentrated in progressively fewer hands, there are still too many producer decisionmakers to permit successful organization and control of production.

Inelastic Demand

Food products generally face an inelastic demand by consumers, as is fairly typical for a basic commodity with few good substitutes. That is, for a given percentage change in the price of a farm product offered for sale, the quantity demanded changes by a smaller percentage in the opposite direction. A small shortfall in production below an equilibrium level tends to cause agricultural product prices to soar—an event welcomed by farmers and ranchers but dreaded by consumers. Conversely, a relatively small increase in output tends to cause agricultural product prices to plummet.

Total demand for agricultural products tends to grow about as fast as the population in a prosperous and adequately fed country such as the United States. Thus, during recent years, there has been an increased dependence on export markets to dispose of the abundant U.S. agricultural production. While this development has produced valuable foreign exchange earnings and has firmed domestic product prices, it has also added to the instability in the agricultural picture because the long-term prospects for exports depend in large part on worldwide weather conditions and the policies of foreign governments.

Since farmers and ranchers have typically made next year's production plans based on this year's prices, there is a tendency for farm prices to fluctuate widely. High prices one production period will likely result in higher production and sharply lower prices the following period—followed by tendencies toward reduced production and higher prices in a future period. The generally inelastic demand for agricultural products has magnified the price instability resulting from this type of production planning. Thus, one of the goals of farm policy is to lend greater price stability to farm product markets.

Resources Fixed in Use

Resources devoted to agricultural production are quite specialized and frequently are substantially less valuable in other productive uses. For example, rangeland used in the production of beef may have no other equally valuable use. Similarly, very expensive and highly specialized farm equipment—such as that used in producing sugar beets—may have relatively little use or value in the production of most other crops.

Thus, resources devoted to a type of agricultural production tend to be locked into that use in the short run, even though such a use may be unprofitable. In the short run, the losses resulting from shifts to other types of production may exceed the losses from continuation of previous production patterns.

Biological Production Processes

Biological production processes are not amenable to quick and substantial shifts. It is typically not possible to stop a biological production process once it has started (a cow bred or a crop planted), without losing a substantial part of the variable costs of production. Consequently, production decisions and actions tend to be relatively irreversible.

The time required to produce a crop is determined by the maturity date of the crop and the time required to produce cattle of slaughter weight will depend on growth rates and feeding practices. In the case of cattle, for example, about 38 months (over 3 years) are required to increase beef production—that is from the time a heifer calf is born until that animal's first offspring can be sold as a 1,000-pound slaughter animal.

Once a biological production process has been started, variability in final production levels is determined by factors over which the producer has limited control. Animal and plant diseases can sharply reduce output. Weather conditions also have marked effects on production levels. For example, harsh weather during the winter and spring of 1976-77 limited the U.S. December-May pig crop to a 2 per cent increase, despite a 5 per cent increase in the number of sows farrowing (female pigs giving birth). Lack of adequate moisture and excessive heat during the growing season can sharply reduce production levels from crops.

Farmers are right when they contend that certain aspects of agricultural production are unique. Despite the fact that farmers and farm businesses are becoming more like their city counterparts over time, some significant differences remain. The differences discussed here will continue to make it hard for farmers to adjust to rapidly changing market conditions.

A GLOSSARY OF TERMS

The casual observer is frequently confused and frustrated by the use of specialized terms to describe various aspects of agricultural policy and programs. Further, the terms are often used incorrectly. A few of the more commonly used terms are described here to serve as a basis for better understanding of policy discussions.[6]

---

6 Definitions are based on current farm legislation. Legislation presently under consideration in Congress may change the more technical aspects of the definitions—not only for future years but in some instances for 1977 as well.

Parity Price

The parity price for an agricultural commodity is that price (in current dollars) that will give the commodity the same purchasing power—in terms of goods and services bought by farmers and certain production costs—as the commodity had during the 1910-14 base period.[7] Although the actual calculations required to derive parity prices are rather complicated, the basic concept of parity is fairly straightforward. To use a simple example, if—in the base period—50 bushels of wheat could have been sold and the proceeds used to purchase a ton of fertilizer, then the parity price of wheat at any given moment in time is that price which would enable a farmer to purchase a ton of fertilizer with the proceeds from 50 bushels of wheat. As a practical matter, however, parity prices are predicated on the average change in prices of all goods and services rather than on individual items.

In the past, parity prices have been considered by many to represent "fair" product prices and have been used as a factor in determining Government price support levels and marketing order prices. However, when parity price standards are used as a measure to assure a specified net farm income, 100 per cent of parity prices may yield a farmer a higher real net income now than would have been true in 1910. This is true because the parity formula does not take into account increases in farm efficiency as measured by an average index of productivity. Thus, as

productivity increases, returns to resources used in production equivalent to 1910-14 can be obtained with lower parity levels.

Acreage Allotments

During the 1920's, the U.S. Government—at the urging of farmers—developed programs for farmers that included reducing the acreage of certain major crops in order to limit production, and thus to raise farm prices. For example, a plan was proposed under which individual acreage allotments would be assigned to individual farmers based on their previous acreage, production, and sales records. Such a proposal, with some modifications, was first enacted into law with the Agricultural Adjustment Act of 1933. Acreage allotments in some form have been around ever since.

The chief objective of acreage allotments was to establish and maintain levels of production of certain agricultural commodities that the market could absorb at prices considered fair to producers. The Secretary of Agriculture—after determining the acreage necessary to supply domestic requirements, projected export sales, and normal carryover of a crop—announced a national acreage allotment for each crop covered by such legislation. Crops covered in 1977 are corn, grain sorghum, barley, wheat, cotton, peanuts, rice, and some kinds of tobacco. If the national allotment for a crop was changed, that change was allocated among states and ultimately among farms on a proportional basis. In recent years, producers of most crops with allotments have been able to grow more than their allotted acreage without incurring any penalty. Farm legislation currently being considered by Congress would do away with historic allotments for growers of wheat, feed grains, rice, and cotton, but not for growers of tobacco and peanuts. Future benefits of farm programs would be distributed on the basis of what a farmer had planted, not on the basis of allotments that currently reflect production patterns of the 1950's.

---

[7] Actually, the parity price for a commodity is calculated using an "adjusted base price," which is derived by dividing the average price received by farmers for the commodity in the previous 10 calendar years by the average Index of Prices Received by Farmers (1910 – 14 = 100) for the same 10-year period. (Both the numerator and denominator are adjusted to allow for unredeemed government loans and other supplemental payments from price support operations). This "adjusted base price" is then multiplied by the most recent Index of Prices Paid by Farmers including Interest, Taxes, and Wage Rates (1910 – 14 = 100) to yield the current parity price for the commodity.

Commodity Credit Corporation

The Commodity Credit Corporation (CCC) is a U.S. agency under a permanent Federal charter, having been formed in 1933 under Delaware law as a corporation wholly owned by the Government. Its board of directors is composed of seven top USDA officials. The CCC has an authorized capital stock of $100 million and authority to borrow up to $14.5 billion.

A major function of the CCC is to support prices of agricultural commodities through loans, purchases, payments, and other operations. The CCC assumes ownership of defaulted nonrecourse[8] commodity loans, and thus acquires ownership of commodities used for domestic and international food aid programs. It also purchases some commodities for use in these programs, and provides nonsubsidized intermediate-term (up to 3 years) credit to foreign buyers of U.S. agricultural products. CCC operating losses are borne by the U.S. taxpayers.

Loan Rate

The loan rate is the level at which the Government will support a commodity's price. The terms "support price," "price support," and "loan rate" are used interchangeably. Loans to farmers are granted by the CCC using the commodity as collateral. For example, wheat produced during 1977 is valued at $2.25 per bushel at the farm for CCC loan purposes (Table 1).

If the price of the commodity rises above the loan rate during the term of the CCC loan, the farmer may sell the commodity, repay the CCC loan with interest, and capture the price advantage of timely marketing. If the price of the commodity does not rise above the loan rate, the farmer can default on the nonrecourse loan and turn the commodity over to the CCC

---

[8] In nonrecourse loans, the property used as collateral for the loan may be turned over to the lender as full settlement of the loan.

Table 1
LOAN RATES AND TARGET PRICES FOR 1977

	Loan Rate	Target Price
	In Dollars Per Bushel	
Wheat	2.25	2.90†
Corn	2.00†	2.00†
Sorghum ‡	1.70	1.62
Barley ‡	1.50	1.39
Oats ‡	1.00	*
Rye	1.50	*
Soybeans	3.50	*
	In Cents Per Pound	
Upland cotton	42.58	47.80

*These crops are not covered by present target price legislation.
†As proposed in the Agricultural Act of 1977.
‡Loan rates and target prices (where applicable) for these crops may also be increased for 1977 since they are typically set by the secretary of agriculture at a level that is fair and reasonable in relation to corn loan and target price levels.
SOURCE: U.S. Department of Agriculture.

as full settlement of the loan. Thus, despite market price fluctuations, the loan rate becomes the floor or lowest price for the commodity that the farmer needs to accept.

Target Prices

Target prices are "fair" price levels set by Congressional action for wheat, feed grains, cotton, and rice. Provision is made for escalation in target price levels in future years based on increases in certain production costs. If the average price for one of these commodities during the first 5 months of the market year falls below the target price level, cooperating farmers receive a "deficiency payment" from the Government, providing the target price is above the CCC loan rate. Deficiency payments are transfer payments to cooperating farmers.

This payment is calculated as the difference between the target price and the higher of the average market price or the loan rate. If the 1977 market price for wheat were $2.24 per bushel, the loan rate $2.25, and the target price $2.90, a farmer would receive a deficiency payment of 65 cents per bushel of wheat ($2.90 − $2.25 = 65¢). The quantity of wheat on which this deficiency payment could be collected would be calculated by multiplying the smaller of the farm's allotment acres or planted acres times its normal yield per acre.[9] Under current farm legislation no farmer can collect more than $20,000 per year in payments under the deficiency payment and disaster payment programs, except in the case of rice farmers where the limitation is $55,000. However, legislation presently under consideration in Congress will likely raise the payment limitation levels—perhaps retroactively to cover the 1977 crop year.

Marketing Orders

Authorized by the Agricultural Marketing Agreement Act of 1937, marketing orders are agreements between producers and Federal or state governments that either fix the wholesale price of farm products or support prices indirectly by controlling the supply of commodities reaching the consumer. Orders are now in effect for milk and for a variety of fruits and vegetables.

Marketing orders are established through a process including producer petitions, public hearings, and a referendum vote by producers. They are frequently used to bring stability to markets that are inherently chaotic because of the weak bargaining position of producers and the special characteristics of the commodities. Products that are very perishable, require a lot

---

[9] This method of calculation is provided for 1977 in legislation currently being considered by Congress. Previously the farm's allotment acres were used in the calculation of the deficiency payment. In future years only planted acres will be used in the calculation.

of processing, and vary widely in quality and yield are potential candidates for marketing orders. Thus, marketing orders are designed to establish and maintain orderly market conditions and to assure reasonable profits to producers while providing adequate supplies at more stable prices to consumers. With milk, the orders establish minimum wholesale prices within a geographic market area called a milkshed; while for fruit and vegetables, the prices are influenced indirectly by the establishment of grade, size, and quality standards which effectively limit the quantities reaching the consumer. Once an order is established, all producers are bound by the regulations and all sales in the specified market must adhere to the pricing policy of the order. Marketing orders also have the practical effect of limiting competition in a market and excluding foreign products from a domestic market.

Federal Crop Insurance Corporation

This organization provides all-risk insurance to farmers eligible for coverage. Approximately 25 different crops are insured in different parts of the country, primarily in the commercial producing areas. In 1975, the program was available in about one-half of the 3,000 or so counties in the continental United States.

By law, the crops cannot be insured for more than production costs. However, farmers may designate the extent to which they want protection, and the premiums are set accordingly. The program is designed so that indemnity payments amount to 90 per cent of the premiums (the remainder is held in reserve for unexpected costs), so farmers are essentially paying the full cost of the benefits. Congressional appropriations cover the administrative costs of the program. Since the insurance can be cancelled or denied to various areas or individual producers with a high loss history, many farmers must either rely on private insurance firms for protection or bear the risks themselves.

Disaster Payments

Disaster payments represent a form of free insurance—provided by the Agricultural Act of 1973 and the 1975 Rice Act—to eligible wheat, feed grain, cotton, and rice producers. A continuation of these benefits is expected under farm legislation currently being considered by Congress. Basically, payments are made if farmers are prevented from planting their crops or if yields fall below specified levels because of natural hazards. Thus far, expenditures under these provisions have been running between $280 million and $550 million a year.

The disaster payments mechanism has several weaknesses, although the new legislation may correct most of them, at least for wheat and feed grains. For example, under the old program, if farmers exceeded their acreage allotments, it was possible to sustain a severe loss and not be eligible for disaster payments because total output still exceeded the trigger point which was tied directly to production from allotted acreage only. Obviously, those producers without allotments received no benefit at all. In addition, payments to eligible producers were not prorated in any way to reflect the timing of the loss, the productivity of the farm, and the costs of production. Hence, the key to benefitting from this program was to establish eligibility.

The new legislation being considered would provide for two kinds of disaster benefit calculations for wheat and feed grain producers. If a disaster *prevented planting* of the usual crop or any other nonconserving crop, a farmer could receive a payment equal to one-third of the target price on the smaller of 75 per cent of the projected (normal) production from the intended planting *or* 75 per cent of the production from last year's planted acreage of the crop. On the other hand, if production of a *planted crop* were reduced below 60 per cent of its projected (normal) yield by disaster, a farmer could receive a payment equal to half the target price on the difference between actual production and 60 per cent of the projected production on the acreage planted for harvest.

CONCLUSION

Agricultural policy formulation has long been hampered by the assumption that the problems affecting agricultural producers were transitory. This has led to a policymaking environment in which programs of short duration were developed to meet the needs at hand. Further, there have been sharp and frequent shifts in policy directions as policymakers responded to what they perceived to be basic changes in the policy environment. Nonetheless, it should be clear after more than 45 years of public debate and legislation that agriculture is faced with fundamental and continuing adjustment problems of a long-term nature.

Because of the growing complexities of agricultural production and its interrelatedness with the general well-being of Americans, a compelling case can be made for taking the long view in policy formulation. Producers and consumers both need to know the "rules of the game" well into the future, as do foreign customers. It is demonstrably true that producers and consumers will not be satisfied with a public policy of no government intervention in agriculture. Consequently, formulating a policy that addresses the sometimes conflicting goals of all interested parties in a balanced and objective manner is an important, but unfinished, public policy task.

Economic penalties of propping the dollar

MARCH 13

Foreign exchange traders were obviously disappointed today over the details of the American-German accord on rescuing the dollar, which did little more than increase the marks available to the U. S. to $4 billion. As a result, the dollar dropped like a stone. Clearly, pressure is building in this country for more active U. S. intervention to stabilize the value of its currency. And the interventionists are advocating that the U. S. float a major foreign-currency loan to accumulate a vast pool of foreign exchange to defend the dollar.

But to Rudiger Dornbusch of the Massachusetts Institute of Technology, a rising star among international econ-

Dornbusch: Support for the dollar would slow U. S. economic growth.

omists, such efforts to prop up the dollar would be a grave mistake because dollar stabilization will cost the U. S. economy dearly in markedly slower economic growth.

Testifying last week before the House Banking Committee, Dornbusch argued that U. S. economic policy should have two overriding objectives: moving the economy toward full employment and preventing the inflation rate from accelerating. Just as the evidence of the past few years shows that slowing economic growth is a very poor way of dealing with inflation, it would be no better to prop up the dollar to prevent a relatively small increase in the U. S. price level, he says. To attack inflation directly, Dornbusch advocates abandoning the proposed personal income tax cut and, in its stead, forgoing Social Security increases, reducing excise taxes, and cutting taxes for business to spur capital investment.

But artificially stabilizing the dollar ultimately boils down to reducing the U. S. money supply, raising interest rates, and slowing down the U. S. economy, especially investment, says Dornbusch. For example, if the U. S. uses marks to sop up extra U. S. dollars to prevent their value from declining, this simply reduces the total U. S. money supply, as sellers draw down their checking accounts to pay for the marks. Similarly, directly raising U. S. interest rates to attract foreign capital, and thereby support the dollar, has much the same adverse effect. Investment is reduced, Dornbusch notes, impairing the economy's ability to cope with future inflation as well as immediately slowing real output.

As the dollar has declined over the past year, the U. S. has gained an increasing competitive advantage over Germany and Japan, even after adjustment for inflation, Dornbusch finds. And he views foreign pressures on the U. S. to stabilize its currency as nothing more than a U. S.-financed program "to keep foreign employment high." Moreover, he argues that a bond issue to raise foreign exchange for the Federal Reserve to intervene in exchange markets will enable some foreign central banks to get out of dollars with no risk that their dollars will fetch lower prices as they are offered for sale.

Elaborating on his testimony, Dornbusch brands as "blackmail" those foreign efforts, including Germany's, to force the U. S. to stabilize the dollar under the threat that otherwise the dollar will be dumped. But he believes that it would be foolhardy for foreigners to put all their eggs into marks or Swiss francs, and the odds therefore are heavily against any further mass move out of the dollar. "The Arabs, for example, could get whipsawed by an appreciating dollar," he says. Moreover, no more than 50% of the Organization of Petroleum Exporting Countries' surplus money is held in dollar-denominated assets, he notes. So, to some degree, OPEC has been indexed against the decline in the dollar.

Dornbusch therefore maintains that the U. S. should continue its target for domestic economic expansion, keeping interest rates low to provide for increased investment in productive capacity. "If that means some further dollar depreciation, then so be it," he says.

Reflections on the U.S. Balance of Payments

Henry C. Wallich

As we look, from the year-end watershed, upon what happened in 1977 and what is likely to happen in 1978, we can derive some satisfaction from progress made and progress that we have reason to believe lies ahead. In international comparison, the United States economy did well in 1977 and seems likely to hold its own in 1978. Nevertheless we face serious challenges. At home, while growth has been reasonably satisfactory, unemployment and inflation continue at excessive levels. Important adjustments in fields like energy remain to be made. Internationally, we confront a very large current account deficit and have witnessed a substantial decline in the dollar. These are matters to keep in mind as we count such blessings as we have.

What governs exchange rates?

We operate under an exchange rate regime in which it has been accepted that underlying economic and financial factors are to govern the level and movement of exchange rates. In the long run, I believe that this is not just a prescription for exchange market policy, but an imperative of economic life. Unrealistic exchange rates cannot long be sustained in a world in which the flows of goods, services, and particularly capital are gratifyingly free and are becoming increasingly large.

In the short run, to be sure, exchange rates can be influenced by factors other than these fundamentals. Uncertainties, erroneous perceptions, and destabilizing speculation are likely to bring about departures from time to time. In recent months, exchange markets seem to have passed through such a period. In particular, I believe that erroneous perceptions have played a role in the recent turbulence of the market.

One erroneous perception seems to have been an apparently widespread belief that the United States is practicing so-called "benign neglect" with respect to the value of its currency. Many market participants seem to have derived this conclusion from the fact that U.S. exchange market intervention, although rising of late, has been conducted on a relatively moderate scale. In my view, any thought that the United States is unconcerned about the value of its currency, and perhaps even would like to see it decline in order to gain a trade advantage, is altogether wrong. The United States has many reasons to want its currency to be as strong as the fundamentals would justify.

Effects of exchange rate depreciation

First, we have learned that exchange rate depreciation contributes significantly to inflation. This has been the lesson of the devaluation of 1971 and subsequent exchange rate movements. Prior to that, it had been widely thought that the small size of our foreign sector meant that the dollar rate had almost no influence on the domestic price level. Experience has shown that depreciation influences prices beyond the export and import sectors. Domestic prices are influenced also through the mechanism of competition. A depreciation of the dollar reduces competition for a wide range of domestically sold goods. Moreover, since 1971, the foreign sector of the U.S. economy has increased from 6 percent of GNP to 10 percent. The American economy has become more open. Thus the immediate impact of exchange rates on domestic prices has also increased.

Second, the price of oil is an important factor that may be influenced by the exchange rate of the dollar. Some OPEC spokesmen have said that their decisions about price will be influenced by what happens to the dollar. Although it seems clear to me that this is not a valid argument and that the OPEC would damage their own interests by raising the price, one must recognize that the price of oil is of enormous significance.

Third, the usefulness of the dollar as a reserve, trade, and investment currency, both to the United States and to the world, depends on the dollar remaining an attractive asset. The United States draws advantages from this international role of the dollar. It facilitates, for instance, the smooth financing of a large current account deficit. But we must bear in mind that a currency in which the assets of official and private parties are denominated will always tend to be compared with whatever the strongest major currencies are at the

HENRY C. WALLICH is a Member of the Board of Governors of the Federal Reserve System. This article is his address at the joint luncheon of the American Economic Association and American Finance Association in New York City, December 28, 1977.

time. Investors will compare the returns from holding dollar-denominated assets with the returns available on assets denominated in other currencies, making allowance for differential interest rates and exchange rate movements. If a widespread feeling should gain ground among investors that dollar assets are unattractive, an effort to get out of these assets into other currencies could produce great instability.

Finally, the value of the dollar influences business conditions abroad. When the value of an asset that is so widely held becomes uncertain, the plans of businesses and households may be upset, leading possibly to a reduction in investment and perhaps even consumption abroad. When the dollar declines sharply, profits in export industries and import-competing industries abroad shrink, and so does investment. The world's recovery from recession, which is proceeding at a painfully slow pace, could be further slowed, unless countries abroad are able to take advantage of such added slack to engage in additional stimulation.

Does intervention help?

U.S. interest in a strong dollar is undeniable. It would be a mistake, however, to say that this interest should be measured by the scale of U.S. intervention in the exchange market. That intervention has been adequate to the degree of disorder in the market. As disorder has mounted in recent weeks, so has the scale of our intervention. But exchange market intervention should not and indeed cannot influence basic trends. These trends rest upon fundamentals.

The evidence that intervention cannot dominate exchange market trends is all around us. In the course of the year 1977, net intervention purchases of dollars by major central banks have amounted to more than $30 billion. It is probable that this intervention has had an impact on the value of the dollar, but it has not prevented a 5 percent depreciation of the dollar against the weighted average of major currencies during 1977. The reason for this could be a perception that fundamentals did not justify a higher value for the dollar. It is only when fundamentals are appropriate and the market has moved out of line with them that intervention can be expected to have a lasting effect. But the reason could also lie, as already noted, in market psychology, which has often shown itself capable of exaggerating exchange rate movements. Fundamentals do not necessarily assert themselves instantaneously or with complete precision.

Current account deficit

It is necessary, therefore, to examine the fundamentals of the dollar. The large current account deficit of the United States is the principal factor now being looked at by the market. This deficit was not fully anticipated and hence has led to a change in the market's evaluation of the dollar's prospects. But it is necessary to look through the size of the deficit to the circumstances that produce it and that are likely to condition its duration. One important component of the deficit is the volume of oil imports, now at a rate of 9.5 million barrels a day, worth about $45 billion at an annual rate. Of course, this amount is not a proper measure of the "oil deficit." That measure is not even correctly taken by the excess of U.S. oil imports over exports to the OPEC countries, since we also have large invisible net receipts from the OPEC countries for which data are not readily available. Moreover, a bilateral deficit can in some degree be covered by bilateral surpluses with other countries. For instance, the modest surplus that the United States has in its trade with some European countries, which in turn are selling to the OPEC countries, is an indirect way of covering a part of the oil deficit.

Nevertheless, unrestrained U.S. consumption of oil and a consequent mounting of our oil imports is rightly regarded as a heavy burden on our trade account. The energy legislation now in the Congress, preceded by the measures announced by the President, should bring a reduction in the upward trend of our oil imports. Conservation of energy and development of additional and substitute energy sources is widely recognized to be necessary for reasons of national security that go beyond considerations of the balance of payments.

A second important component of the current account deficit is of a cyclical character. The United States has moved well ahead of the rest of the world in recovering from the 1974-75 recession and moving into new high ground. We can reasonably expect that eventually the rest of the world will follow. No one, I am sure, wants the United States to reduce its current account deficit by slowing down its economy. The underlying character of the deficit must be assessed, therefore, by making a cyclical adjustment. What, in other words, would be the magnitude of the deficit if the world as a whole were at reasonably full employment?

The methodology of a cyclical adjustment involves estimating first what economic activity and prices, both at home and abroad, would have been if there had been full employment during the period in question. Then trade flows can be estimated. An econometric model that relates U.S. trade flows to such income and price estimates suggests that the U.S. trade deficit of about $30 billion might be $10 to $20 billion lower if there were full employment in major industrialized countries. Since the surplus of about $12 billion on services would not be much changed by a return to high employment, the U.S. current account deficit of about $18 billion would be very substantially reduced under those conditions.

Not too much weight should be attached to calculations like these, particularly since we do not know how long it might take the world to return to high rates of employment. And, in assessing such very tentative calculations, it should also be borne in mind that some deficit for the United States is not inappropriate so long as the OPEC countries maintain a sizable surplus. The deficits corresponding to that surplus must be shared around the world. While the United States, under ordinary conditions, and, given its wealth and economic structure, ought to be a capital exporter, a sharing in the non-OPEC world's aggregate deficit does not seem inappropriate so long as some other countries may have difficulty financing large deficits.

Competitiveness

Computation of a cyclically adjusted U.S. trade deficit, nevertheless, does not resolve the question whether the United States has not in some fundamental sense lost competitiveness. An analysis of the fundamentals, therefore, must focus also on competitiveness.

There is a fair amount of evidence on this point. Some of it comes from the analysis of market shares of exports. The United States' share of exports of Group of Ten countries (a measure that minimizes the impact of recent unusual developments in petroleum and other commodity markets) declined in 1976 and again slightly in the first half of this year. But those declines followed three years of increases in the U.S. share of exports in the wake of two years during which exchange rates had been substantially realigned. Thus the U.S. share, which measured 20.0 percent during the first half of this year, is essentially unchanged since 1971 when it measured 20.1 percent. And it should be noted that many countries that have traditionally been large customers of ours have not expanded particularly rapidly during this period.

Another source of concern about

competitiveness apparently is ready to be laid to rest. Research dating from the 1950s to the mid-1960s seemed to indicate that the elasticity of demand for U.S. exports with respect to foreign income was substantially below the elasticity for the exports of others with respect to our own income. More recent work by the Federal Reserve staff indicates that there is no statistically significant difference between those elasticities. In other words, so long as the United States and the rest of the world grow at approximately the same rate, these studies suggest that U.S. exports and imports should grow at roughly equal rates.

Finally, some evidence on competitiveness comes from the calculations of "real" exchange rates. These are exchange rates adjusted for international differences in rates of inflation. The real exchange rate of the dollar will remain unchanged with respect to any other currency or group of currencies so long as the movement in the nominal exchange rate is equal to the differential movement of prices.

Like all index numbers, calculations of real exchange rates raise questions as to the kind of index used, and the starting level. For some countries, for instance Japan, different indexes yield very different results. For the United States, however, the four customarily used indexes—consumer prices, wholesale prices, export unit values, and unit labor costs—all yield approximately the same result. If a comparison is made between the dollar's value at the beginning of the float of exchange rates in March 1973, as well as the average of rates during the period from March 1973 to the present, the real exchange rate of the dollar on a trade-weighted basis has depreciated and competitiveness has increased.

The real exchange rate of the Deutschemark (D-mark), computed similarly, shows little change over the same period. For the yen, as

noted, meaningful results are more difficult to obtain.

It must be remembered that an absence of major changes in real exchange rates is not necessarily evidence of equilibrium. When real rather than monetary shocks cause changes in the balance of payments, real exchange rates ought to change. But when examination of structural factors in the world economy suggests that no major adjustment is needed, movements in the real rate can be regarded as indicative of changes in competitiveness, particularly when the various indexes tend to produce roughly similar results.

One further element of competitiveness of the dollar remains to be considered. It relates to the capital rather than the current account. How competitive is the dollar as a capital asset? This depends both on interest rates and on expected exchange rate movements. Together they produce the total expected return on dollar assets in terms of foreign currencies. The dollar solidified its role as the world's leading reserve and investment currency during the postwar period when interest rates were low in the United States and high almost everywhere else. Meanwhile, this relationship has been reversed with respect to the strongest currencies. U.S. interest rates today are significantly higher than those of Switzerland, Germany, and even Japan.

During periods of market turbulence, when exchange rates and related capital values change rapidly and substantially, interest rate considerations are likely to fade into the background. But, when markets settle down, interest rates are bound to carry weight. Today, interest rate differentials among three important investment currencies—the dollar, the D-mark, and the Swiss franc—reflect very closely differential rates of inflation experienced in the three respective countries. Real interest rates in these countries, in other words, are approximately equal.

In this fundamental sense, the dollar does not seem to have lost competitiveness as an asset. If that can be accepted, one would conclude that the financing of the U.S. current account deficit, which in 1977 was accomplished almost entirely through movements of official capital resulting from intervention, can also be accomplished by private capital, at an unchanged exchange rate.

Elements of dollar strength

Let me summarize the elements of strength of the dollar as I see them. First, there is a large cyclical component of the deficit. We do not know how long it will take other countries to return to high employment, but at any rate there is light at the end of the tunnel.

Second, there is the modest improvement in U.S. competitiveness since 1973, as measured in terms of the "real" exchange rate. It reflects the moderately good, though far from excellent, inflation performance of the United States. The main contribution to future strength of the dollar will have to come from a continuation and improvement in this performance.

Third, there are several other indicators of effective competitiveness of U.S. goods, especially market shares and demand elasticities. This competitiveness should begin to show through as world trade recovers.

Fourth, there are substantial interest rate differentials with respect to competing currencies. As markets settle down, these should increasingly assert themselves.

Not yet in this picture is concrete evidence that oil imports will be held down. Even strong legislation, such as I expect to be enacted, will not reduce U.S. oil imports in the immediate future. But this legislation, once in place, should provide assurance to the markets that dollar strength will not be sapped by spiraling oil imports and that, indeed, the longer-run prospect is for reduced U.S. dependence on imported oil in the future.

56

Is the dollar skidding on an oil slick?

The belief that the dollar's decline is caused by oil imports is as fallacious as it is popular. The real villain is overexpansionary money growth, not high-priced energy.

Guilt can be a civilizing force. Sometimes it is used to keep society from straggling off the path of progress. But sometimes it is manufactured to no good purpose. For example, a great guilt-inducing apparatus seems to have been set up recently to persuade the U.S. public that its outsize appetite for foreign oil is the main cause of the dollar's downswing in world currency markets.

The dollar's exchange rate and the country's hunger for imported oil are both hot topics today, and rightly so. Each is well worth discussing separately. In particular, the huge volume of U.S. oil imports should be weighed carefully in terms of economic efficiency, national security and international impact. The need to examine such aspects of the problem is not at issue here. What is in question is the current practice of linking up the U.S. energy deficit with the dollar's decline. Connecting up these two highly charged subjects produces only a shower of sparks, a smoky aroma of sin and not much else.

Yet the connection is being made again and again. Usually the first stage of the operation is to point out that the U.S. oil-import bill may come to about $42 billion this year. Next, it's noted that, without those oil imports, the United States would be running a healthy trade surplus (chart, page 8). Then it's suggested that the United States, by overindulging in oil, is wrecking its balance of payments, weakening the dollar and thereby undermining something called "world monetary stability." Conclusion: The United States owes it to itself and to the world to cut back hard on its oil intake —so as to right its trade balance and strengthen the dollar.

In this way, guilt on an international scale is laid on American shoulders. But the burden is not worth bearing. Insofar as it's accepted, it contributes unnecessarily to the current U.S. fit of self-doubt. Incidentally, it also obscures the true reason for the dollar's fall — and may even accelerate its decline on those days when the latest monthly U.S. trade deficit is announced.

One quick antidote for this exchange-rate *angst* is to realize that it's an egregious error to focus on a single sector of the trade account — and to carry it down through the balance of payments to the exchange rate. A country's oil-import bill, in and of itself, does not necessarily affect its currency's value. For proof, see Germany and Japan, whose oil-import bills have soared since 1972 — but whose currencies are stronger now than they were then.

But American guilt feelings are seldom easily dispelled. So perhaps the best remedy is to see exactly why there is no inexorable connection between U.S. oil imports and the dollar's exchange rate. The key to this understanding is the overall balance of payments.

Some readers will feel that they'd rather live with guilt than suffer through an explanation of the overall balance. But the guilt merchants are not about to give up. At the next twitch of the dollar's exchange rate, they will be back with their fiery sermons against U.S. oil profligacy — and it may be better to be armed against them.

Offshore accounting

In this battle of ideas, the overall balance is the vital intersection of knowledge. Anyone who commands that intersection can throw off the attackers. To seize that intersection, two steps are required. The first step involves seeing the balance of payments as a kind of table or grid of information, summing up U.S. transactions with the outside world. The second step is to grasp how monetary pressures work through this grid to affect exchange rates.

The basic format of the balance of payments can be outlined by harking back to Robinson Crusoe on his island. Crusoe raises crops and sheep; he has no oil for his lamps. He imports oil from the nearby OPEC islands. In exchange, he gives the OPEC islanders an IOU, which he will redeem next year by sending them two sheep. So Crusoe's balance of payments consists of his trade account, which is in deficit — an oil-import deficit — and a capital account, which is in surplus since he exported an IOU.

Crusoe's accounts, like any country's balance of payments, are divided in two. One section covers transactions in so-called real resources, his oil imports. The other section covers financial transactions, his IOU.

Like Crusoe, a modern country conducts trade in merchandise goods, including oil. The results are summed up in its trade balance.

But such a country also exchanges services of various kinds with other countries, and these services are classed as real resources, too. The results of these exchanges, along with the trade balance, are included in the country's current account. It sums up the "real" side of the country's balance of payments.

As in Crusoe's books, the financial side of a country's transactions — except for official dealings by central banks and the like — are shown in its capital accounts. Such financial flows into and out of the country, like Crusoe's IOU, are matched against the real flows in the current account. When real flows are totted up against the financial ones, the result is the overall balance.

For 1977, it looks as though the U.S. overall balance will show a deficit in the neighborhood of $20 billion. But this overall deficit does not in any way correspond to the results of U.S. dealings with the OPEC countries.

If anything, the massive U.S. payments for OPEC oil since 1973 have been substantially offset by OPEC purchases of U.S. assets — stocks, bonds, bank deposits, real estate — in a way that resembles Crusoe's use of an IOU. In other words, U.S. imports of oil from the OPEC countries have been largely self-financing.

To be sure, conventional balance-of-payments accounting treats OPEC investments in the United States somewhat differently from the way they are treated in the framework sketched above. But this simplified approach is probably more helpful in understanding the distinction between the oil deficit and the overall balance of payments.

Money factor

To understand why the U.S. overall balance is in deficit — and how this affects the dollar's exchange rate — a second element must now be added to the picture. This element is money.

Each sector of the balance-of-payments grid responds to what can be described as monetary pressures. Such pressures are generated by differences between the country's supply of and demand for money.

To the uninitiated, it may seem faintly comical to talk of the demand for money. Most people probably feel that their demand for money is almost infinite. They want as much as they can get. But in this case, what's meant by demand for money is less exciting. It's the total amount of money — usually defined as cash and checking-account deposits — required to fulfill all the functions of money in the daily conduct of a country's affairs. As a rule, this collective demand grows gradually as national income gradually increases. Against this slowly growing demand is set the growth of the country's money supply, which is more variable.

This is where the balance-of-payments table comes in, because the payments grid is affected by changes in monetary pressure caused by the variations in money-supply growth. When the money supply grows faster than the demand for it, an excess of money develops — and it can then be said that mone-

tary pressure inside the country is on the rise.

As the pressure rises, some of the excess money tends to spill out of the country through the balance-of-payments grid. Specifically, part of the excess may be spent to buy more foreign goods and services — so that an outflow of money shows up in the "real" side of the payments balance. Or some of the excess may be spent on foreign investments — so that the outflow appears in the financial side of the grid. But regardless of whether these outflows occur in one or another sector, or in both, their ultimate cause is a building up of monetary pressure.

Since the overall balance sums up the net result of all the changes throughout the grid, it reflects the net impact of the rise in pressure. In short, the balance swings down, toward or into deficit, by an amount that corresponds to the pressure's rise.

Slow change

The main point here is that the change in money pressure is what makes the overall balance swing. To illustrate: Assume that monetary pressure inside Country A is the same as it is everywhere else in a world of fixed exchange rates. Now, suppose that Country A's oil-import bill suddenly rises by several billion dollars a year. Residents of Country A who consume the oil must pay for it out of their money holdings. As a result, the value of these holdings sinks temporarily below its usual level.

In the short run, there is nothing much country A's oil consumers can do about this situation, since their patterns of consumption, investment and borrowing cannot be altered at once. Thus, with everything else unchanged, the sudden rise in the oil-import bill causes the country's overall balance to swing downward momentarily.

But this state of affairs does not last long. Since the money balances held by Country A's residents are now below the accustomed level, they set about rebuilding them. In the short run, they do this mainly by borrowing more and lending less. Country A's credit conditions tighten, its interest rates rise. This

Oil imports
A rising role in U.S. trade

billions of dollars (customs basis)

* First-half data at annual rate.
Source: Department of Commerce.

makes it both attractive and necessary for its businessmen to borrow abroad — and for foreign banks to step up their lending to them. The outflow of oil payments is offset by the inflow of capital. Consequently, the big rise in the country's oil-import bill has only a short-lived impact on the overall balance, which swings back up, reflecting the fact that monetary pressures have not changed.

But now, suppose that the growth of Country A's money supply had been accelerated by several billion, just as the oil-import bill rose by the same amount. In that event, the outflow of money for oil payments would have generated no money shortage in Country A. There would have been no reason for the inflow of capital to increase. The overall balance would have swung down and stayed down — not because of the oil-bill increase, but because of the rise in Country A's domestic money pressure.

Spillover
In these examples, it was assumed that in the world outside Country A money pressures were all the same and never-changing. In real life, the opposite is true. But in any case, what determines Country A's overall balance is the difference between monetary pressure inside that country and in the world outside. And for the currency markets, too, this factor is crucial.

If monetary pressure in Country A is higher than in the rest of the world, more of Country A's money tends to spill out in the form of a deficit in the overall balance. The money flows into the foreign-exchange markets, adding to the amount of Country A's currency already there. This tends to drive down the currency's exchange rate — provided that exchange rate is flexible.

Insofar as the exchange rate drops, it tends to stem further outflows of money from Country A. It does this in many ways. For example, the rate's fall cuts the external buying power of Country A's currency, reducing the incentive for the country's residents to buy foreign goods. It also cuts the foreign-currency prices of Country A's exports, stimulating their sales. This, coupled with the residents' own attempts

to spend more at home, pushes up Country A's domestic prices. All these changes combine to reduce the monetary pressure inside Country A and to shrink the deficit in its overall balance of payments.

Continuing pressure
But none of this occurs if the central bank of Country A or those of other countries intervene in the exchange markets, buying up Country A's currency to keep its exchange rate from falling. In that case, Country A's overall balance remains in deficit, reflecting the continuing monetary pressure inside Country A. So long as the exchange rate is held unchanged, the outflows of Country A's money eventually swell the money supplies of other countries. A resulting general rise in inflation tends to equalize the monetary pressures everywhere.

Perhaps these simplified examples suggest a comparison between Country A and the United States. After all, since early this year, monetary policy has been a good deal more stimulative in the United States than in other low-inflation countries. And as a result, excess dollars have spilled into the currency markets.

During the year's first half, the dollar would have weakened on the exchanges had it not been for large official purchases of dollars in these markets. The U.S. overall deficit came to about $11 billion in the first half, and only some $4 billion of that was financed by OPEC purchases of U.S. assets. The rest reflected official intervention to shore up the dollar. What's more, incomplete data indicate that, in the third quarter, the overall deficit may have run in excess of $7 billion — and more than $6 billion of that was financed by official intervention.

If anyone feels guilty about buying gas for his car or heating oil for his home, he may have a good guilty reason — but not one that's connected with the dollar's exchange rate. A cutback on oil imports would improve the U.S. current account. Over the long run, it would do nothing for the overall deficit or the dollar. For their weakness, the only cure is slower money growth.

57

The international economic order that has prevailed since World War II is crumbling

The Sinking Dollar and The Gathering Storm

SIDNEY LENS

Imagine the turmoil if Pennsylvania were to stop selling goods to New Yorkers because it already had too many New York dollars, and no way to get rid of them. Factories would close, workers would lose jobs, banks would call in loans. The crisis would pervade the whole economy.

No such thing happens, of course, because under the single sovereignty of the *United* States, all of us — including Pennsylvanians — must accept the dollar as legal tender; the law says so. And we must pay our debts, or the courts will declare us bankrupt and seize our property. There is a certain discipline in our *internal* economic order that promotes stability and encourages growth.

That kind of discipline, however, does not exist in the *international* economic order. There is no true *United* Nations, with a body of laws and the power to enforce them. What has held the world economy together for most of the past century — to the extent that it *has been* held together — was first a *Pax Britannica* that lasted until World War I, and then a *Pax Americana* that has dominated the years since World War II. For decades the pound sterling, backed by gold and a strong British economy, was so stable that all nations accepted it as the world medium of exchange, and the British navy was so awesome that other nations rarely challenged British policies on free trade or on division of the world's colonial riches.

From 1945 to 1971, all of the "free world" nations similarly accepted the stable U.S. dollar, worth one-thirty-fifth of an ounce of gold, as the yardstick by which value was gauged. The American economy flourished as none ever had before, and it was buttressed by the most for-

Sidney Lens is a contributing editor of The Progressive.

midable military machine ever known. Virtually every nation outside the communist bloc found it expedient to follow the economic lead of the United States.

But the dollar, like the pound of the 1930s, has foundered. In terms of gold, it is worth only one-fifth of what it was only six years ago; in terms of domestic purchasing power, it is worth half of what it was in 1965. Charles Schultze, chairman of President Carter's Council of Economic Advisers, says the fall of the proud dollar is a problem "but not a catastrophe." It seems obvious, however, that what is at stake is the "free world" economy and its political alliances, and that we may soon confront the sort of international disorder that wracked the planet in the 1930s, when neither Britain nor the United States was able to impose discipline on Germany, Japan, and Italy.

The symptoms of the crisis are, in some respects, bizarre. In the last dozen years the United States has exacted from its allies a sort of reverse lend-lease. It rang up ever-increasing balance-of-payments deficits to pay — in part — for such military adventures as the Vietnam war and for the worldwide network of U.S. military bases. In settlement of those deficits, central banks of foreign nations were flooded with dollars which — until mid-1971 — were redeemable for gold. But since 1971, when the dollar was divorced from gold, these gluts of U.S. currency can only be redeemed for American goods. And there is no way America's trading partners can absorb enough U.S. imports to use up their accumulated dollars.

In fact, U.S. capitalism has found an ingenious method of milking its allies: It runs up a trade deficit every year by importing far more than it exports — last year $27 billion more — and it hands its allies pieces of paper called dollars, which are really just IOUs backed by nothing. Thus,

Germany, Japan, and other industrial nations are awash in dollars of tenuous value. Central banks are holding more than 125 billion such dollars, which are, for all practical purposes, no longer exchangeable for valuables (such as food or machinery) but actually constitute a huge American debt. Many experts believe the United States will never pay this debt, just as Britain and France never paid their World War I debts to the United States.

America's allies — particularly Germany and Japan — find themselves in a peculiar dilemma: While they don't *want* dollars, they must accept them, because otherwise their foreign trade would drastically decrease and their economies collapse. And these allies have a vital stake in keeping the dollar strong; when it declines, they must raise prices for their exports and lose vital markets in the United States.

An example: If a Volkswagen cost 16,000 marks when one dollar was worth four marks, an American could buy the German automobile for $4,000. But if the dollar slumped to one for two marks (its present value), the same car would have to cost $8,000 in the United States, and would be driven from the market by the Ford Pinto or the General Motors Chevette. Since the American market plays a decisive role in international trade, Germany needs a strong dollar to keep its own economy from faltering.

The oil-producing nations also have an interest in keeping the dollar strong; they are paid for petroleum in that currency. When the dollar falls in value from one for four marks to one for two marks, the $14 they get for a barrel of oil buys only half as much German steel. This is so serious a problem for OPEC members that there have been discussions, especially in Kuwait, of tying the price of oil not to the dollar but to a "package" of currencies, including the mark and the yen. If this were done, Americans would pay substantially more for their energy, with devastating consequences to the U.S. economy and that of the whole "free world."

Compounding this instability is the mounting debt load carried by the less developed countries (LDCs). As of 1972, the non-oil-producing LDCs owed $83 billion to private banks and international lending agencies; by 1976, that total was $179 billion, and by the end of this year it will be $235 billion. A substantial portion of these loans can not be repaid because the countries involved simply do not have the money. Of every four dollars now owed, one goes to liquidate previous loans; by 1980, that portion is likely to be two out of every four.

The probelm is not that LDCs will go bankrupt and that the Pentagon will send in the Marines to auction off, say, the government house in Zaire or the pyramids of Egypt. There is no danger that the International Monetary Fund (IMF) or the multinational banks (which increased their loans to LDCs to $80 billion as of the end of 1976 — fifteen times what they were nine years earlier) will let any "friendly" LDCs go under. If a country can't pay, the banks and IMF simply ply it with more loans — to pay off previous ones.

There are two difficulties, however, with this sleight-of-hand exercise: One is that as a condition of the loan, the recipient nation must agree to keep its doors open to multinational corporations' investments and trade even if that runs counter to the nation's interests. The LDCs would, of course, be better off if they could establish native industries owned by themselves and plan orderly development based on the needs of their own people rather than on the needs of foreign companies headquartered in New York or Amsterdam. Those foreign companies care little about the internal market (except for a small middle-class market); they concentrate, instead, on exports that further pauperize the host countries.

LDCs which rely on foreign loans invariably forfeit their autonomy. From 1950 to 1970, for example, U.S. firms added $1.7 billion to their holdings in four Andean countries — Chile, Peru, Bolivia, and Venezuela — primarily to increase production of such export commodities as copper, tin, and oil. But in the same period, these multinationals repatriated $11.2 billion to the United States, leaving a net loss to those countries of $9.5 billion. When the repatriation of profits, interest payments on $61 billion in foreign debt, shipping costs, and trade deficits are added up, Latin America suffered a drain of $7.1 billion in 1976. The $22 billion in U.S. investments thus intensified the continent's crisis.

The second difficulty for harried LDCs is that they must agree to "austerity" as the price for being temporarily bailed out. The financiers, private and public, demand that the LDC loan recipient reduce spending on such "frills" as schools, roads, hospitals, and health clinics; that they cut or eliminate subsidies for bread or rice; that they "hold the line" on wages — in sum that they lower living standards and increase unemployment if they want more loans.

In 1976, when President Anwar Sadat tried to implement the IMF demand that Egypt abolish subsidies for food and fuel, riots erupted and almost 800 people died. Last year, Peru — which could not meet $700 million in payments due on a $5 billion loan — was offered a $105 million credit by the IMF. The condition, as usual, was "austerity" — budget cuts, a wage freeze, price increases on necessities. When the Peruvian government tried to carry out this mandate, it encountered demonstrations and a general strike.

In this untenable situation, the non-oil-producing LDCs have no choice but to insist either that the loans be canceled or that there be an international agreement to raise the price of the raw materials they sell to advanced countries — or both. The industrial nations, with the United States in the vanguard, have, of course, been resisting these pressures. If they continue to do so, there is increasing likelihood of more revolutions in the Third World (and secessions from the *Pax Americana*), or of outright repudiation of the debts.

These alternatives pose serious difficulties for the international financiers. As of 1976, American banks alone held $50 billion in LDC paper, and the thirteen largest U.S. banks earned profits of $886 million — about half of

'The basic reality is that the Pax Americana has run its course....'

their total profits — on their two-thirds share of this business. Suppose that $5 billion or $10 billion or $20 billion of that loan portfolio should default: American bankers would have to write off those loans, and to maintain their liquidity they would have to call in their loans to U.S. corporations, thereby causing a serious industrial cutback — and unemployment — at home. On the other hand, if the LDCs are allowed to raise prices on bauxite, sugar, and other commodities, the cost of producing aluminum, cereals, and other products will also increase. There does not seem to be a comfortable solution.

A few nations are benefiting from the present crisis — the OPEC members, especially Saudi Arabia and Iran. Oil prices have more than quadrupled in five years, and these countries are accumulating wealth at a rate that would put Nineteenth Century American robber barons to shame. It is generally agreed that the twelve OPEC members will have $250 billion in foreign reserves by 1980.

But what can they do with the money? Some is invested in the economic infrastructure and industrial plant of their nations. Some goes for conspicuous consumption of luxury goods. Quite a bit is spent for arms purchases from the United States — purchases that the Carter Administration can not or will not terminate for fear of suffering a retaliatory increase in petroleum prices.

But billions of dollars are left unspent each year, and the only place to put them — since they obviously can not be invested in the Soviet bloc and since the OPEC states do not have the industrial wherewithal to invest in developing countries — is in the West.

That provokes other problems and other sources of world friction. The United States wants to receive petrodollars from OPEC states to absorb part of the U.S. balance-of-payments deficit. But it certainly does not want those funds used to buy out General Motors or Exxon or the Chase Manhattan Bank. Nor does it want too many oil dollars placed in bank accounts to be withdrawn at will; a sudden withdrawal would cause a run on those banks.

So far, the oil countries have been persuaded to put a major share of their surplus funds in special *nonmarketable* U.S. Treasury bills. This allows petrodollars to be recycled with the least impact while easing, to some extent, the U.S. balance-of-payments problem. The difficulty is that the added funds ultimately find their way into private banking channels and, through those big banks, into the world economy as loans, including loans to LDCs. It is a vicious circle, and nobody knows how to break out of it.

What we do know is that the international economic order fashioned under the *Pax Americana* grows more fragile day by day, and that the political stability it has sustained for two decades is also crumbling. We have what

Michael Hudson, a perceptive writer who used to work for Chase Manhattan and Continental Oil, calls a "global fracture": Instead of a reasonably disciplined global system, it threatens to fragment into regional or even national entities. The commitment to free trade is being abandoned, and the new cry is for protectionism. The foundation of the postwar international money system — the dollar — is "floating," mostly floating downward, with severe consequences for world trade.

The United States is not totally helpless in this state of affairs: It still can exert important levers of power — its military forces, its great industrial potential, its enormous purchasing capacity, and, not least, its position as the world's leading exporter of grain. As a CIA report put it in August 1974, "The U.S. now provides nearly three-fourths of the world's net grain exports, and its role is almost certain to grow over the next several decades." Despite this immense power, however, American leverage is declining; it no longer suffices to enforce the discipline of a *Pax Americana*.

In these circumstances, the nations of the world are bound to seek realignment. The Common Market nations of Western Europe, for instance, would like to make a deal with the Arab countries that would reduce their dependence on the United States. And it is quite possible that Japan may once again try to establish an Asian community of nations encompassing China and separate from Washington's "free world."

At the same time, the United States is striving for a new world banking system that would transfer the dollar "overhang" (along with the LDC debt and the British debt) from one central bank to another — but never allow the debt to come back to the debtor for redemption. In this way, the debts would become "world assets": In effect, they would be canceled and everyone would start over again at square one. Obviously those who hold dollars, sterling, or LDC paper are not overly enthusiastic about this approach.

All of the banking measures and political maneuvers are clearly only stopgaps. The basic reality is that the *Pax Americana* has run its course but that no alternative has emerged to exert the kind of discipline needed if the international economic order is to remain at even keel.

Unless the nations of the world choose to resolve their problems in a futile war that will destroy them all, the logic points inexorably to the formation of a genuine international political compact — one that encompasses *international planning* to husband dwindling world resources and divide income and wealth equitably among people and nations. Without a world plan in which the motivation for economic development is human need rather than corporate profit, the present crisis will endure.

58

Hold That Line

When Saudi Arabia and Iran agree to a price freeze," Indonesian oil minister Muhammad Sadli lamented last month, "you really can't do anything about it." Sadli couldn't have been more right. The Saudis and Iranians wanted to freeze world oil prices—and despite the bitter opposition of half their fellow members, that's just what the Organization of Petroleum Exporting Countries wound up doing last week. Meeting amid awesome security in the posh Venezuelan seaside resort of Caraballeda outside Caracas, the cartel's thirteen members deliberated for only a day and a half, and their "agreement not to disagree," as OPEC secretary-general Ali Muhammad Jaidah put it, was really a face-saving gesture designed to preserve the appearance of unity. But its import was a reprieve for the whole world economy: it meant that, for the time being at least, the price of oil would stay where it is.

For the most part, the opposition of Saudi Arabia and Iran to a price increase reflected their pragmatic conclusion that, with the world currently awash in oil, they couldn't have made it stick. What's more, the Saudis and once-hawkish Iranians were worried that a stiff hike would be a major setback for the still-shaky world economy. "They are scared of sparking another recession," said Washington energy-consultant Charles Ebinger. Nonetheless, for political reasons, radical members such as Libya,

Iraq and Algeria wanted to raise prices anyway—by as much as 23 per cent.

The arguments went on behind a tight security cordon. Taking no chances following the terrorist attack led by the notorious "Carlos" on OPEC dele-

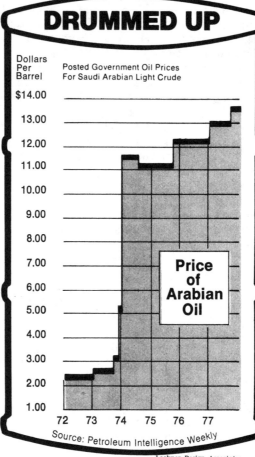

DRUMMED UP

Dollars Per Barrel

Posted Government Oil Prices For Saudi Arabian Light Crude

$14.00
13.00
12.00
11.00
10.00
9.00
8.00
7.00
6.00
5.00
4.00
3.00
2.00
1.00

Price of Arabian Oil

72 73 74 75 76 77

Source: Petroleum Intelligence Weekly

Leckner Design Associates

gates at their 1975 gathering in Vienna, the Venezuelan Government turned the meeting site into an armed camp. Combat soldiers carrying automatic rifles guarded the entrances to the Melia Caribe Hotel, where the conference was held, while gunship helicopters patrolled the highways and nearby mountains.

Last Ditch: The price hawks were determined to wrest some sort of compromise from the Saudis and Iranians and in a last-ditch effort to get them to agree, President Carlos Andrés Pérez of Venezuela called for a 5 to 8 per cent price hike— with the proceeds earmarked for the poorest of the Third World's lesser-developed countries. But the effort was a futile one; with Saudi Arabia, Iran and their Persian Gulf allies accounting for

roughly 65 per cent of the cartel's production, the question of which side would prevail was never in doubt.

In the short run, the de facto decision to hold the line on prices will hurt the cartel. Because of inflation and the recent decline of the dollar—the currency in which OPEC members are paid—petroleum prices will probably fall in real terms next year. Executive director John H. Lichtblau of the Petroleum Industry Research Foundation predicts a drop of 8 per cent in the first half of 1978.

Moderation: That pleases the Saudis no more than the radicals. But even so, "The current market situation demonstrates that a freeze is needed," said Saudi oil minister Ahmad Zaki Yamani. Despite a bout of tourist's stomach, Yamani attended all the meetings in Caraballeda and lobbied vigorously for moderation. Sluggish world economic growth this year, a relatively mild autumn and the introduction to world supply lines of crude from the North Sea, the North Slope and Mexico have combined to leave the West with far more oil than it needs. In an effort to maintain prices, Saudi Arabia, Kuwait, Venezuela and Nigeria have all found themselves forced to cut back production drastically. The Saudis, for example, who were pumping close to 11 million barrels a day from their fields last spring, are now producing just under 8 million barrels a day.

In all, says the U.S. Department of Energy, OPEC is currently withholding nearly a fifth of its capacity. Still, it is producing more than it can sell. As a result, notes Ebinger, "a lot of OPEC countries have been shaving prices a few cents a barrel in an effort to market their oil." Libya, for example, has been selling its Es Sider crude, which has a posted price of $14 a barrel, for as little as $13.67. Nigeria's Bonny light crude, posted at $14.63, is going for $14.05.

Future Prices: To be sure, the oil glut is only temporary. As soon as the world shakes off the lingering effects of the last recession, oil demand will revive, and the huge petroleum surpluses will disappear. "What the price of oil will be after 1982, only God knows," Iranian Prime Minister Jamshid Amouzegar said earlier this year. But until the market firms up again, the cartel will be vulnerable to fragmentation—a risk the cautious Saudis would prefer to avoid. "The current oil surplus affects the existence of OPEC," Yamani told reporters last week. In order "to preserve the unity of OPEC," he added, his country was

"obliged" to follow the course it did.

For oil consumers, such prudence amounted to an especially welcome Christmas present. Jimmy Carter, at home in Plains for the holidays, pronounced it "Great!" — a sentiment echoed widely in Europe. "We are greatly relieved," said a spokesman for the Common Market. "Every percentage point increase in the price of oil would have meant an additional $500 million on our balance-of-payments deficit."

The big question was how long the de facto price freeze would last. President Carter offered the hope that "it continues all during 1978." That seemed unlikely, but no one could say for sure since the answer depended on a host of variables, among them such unpredictable factors as the progress of Egyptian President Anwar Sadat's peace overtures to Israel.

Special Meeting? Qatar's oil minister, Abdul Aziz bin Khalifa al Thani, suggested that nothing is likely to change until OPEC's next scheduled meeting six

months from now. But there is nothing to prevent members from calling a special meeting before then—and some are already laying the groundwork. "I am very optimistic," said Libyan oil minister Ezzedin al Mabrouk, who was pushing for a 10 per cent increase and at one point reportedly threatened to walk out when it became clear that the Saudis and Iranians wouldn't bend. "I think we are going to have a meeting in the next three months in order to review prices again."

But while, in parliamentary terms, all OPEC members are equal, some are clearly more equal than others—and Saudi Arabia, the undisputed *primus inter pares* of the group, is not reluctant to remind its fellow exporters of that fact. "We will take the responsibility of fixing prices" for OPEC, Yamani said bluntly at the conclusion of last week's meeting. In the end, the price freeze will last just as long as the Saudis want it to.

—ALLAN J. MAYER with RON MOREAU in Caraballeda and WILLIAM J. COOK in Washington